Introduction to the administration of justice

Introduction to the administration of justice

Second Edition

Charles A. Foster
Chemeketa Community College

Diane Machunze
Chemeketa Community College

Robert Blanchard
Riverside City College
American Justice Institute

JOHN WILEY & SONS
New York   Chichester   Brisbane   Toronto

Library of Congress Cataloging in Publication Data:

Foster, Charles A   1940-
    Introduction to the administration of justice.

    Edition of 1975 by R. E. Blanchard.
    Includes index.
    1. Criminal justice, Administration of—United
States. I. Machunze, Diane, 1947-   joint author.
II. Blanchard, Robert E., 1938-   Introduction to
the administration of justice. III. Title.
KF9223.B54 1979   345'.73'05   78-13498
ISBN 0-471-04079-7

Printed in the United States of America

10 9 8 7 6 5 4 3 2 1

Preface

There are several introductory texts on the market that deal with the criminal justice system. Many of them, however, provide material in a very rigid, descriptive manner. This text goes beyond the descriptive process (which is essential) and includes issues that are confronted within the criminal justice system—some that have been resolved and some that have not even been discussed. This textbook provides the reader with an appreciation of not only how the system is supposed to work, but some of the realities and dysfunctions of the system. We hope that this book will then be a springboard for further research or further inquiry by the reader in hopes of obtaining solutions—or at least to reduce the amount of dysfunctional characteristics that we find in our system of justice.

Some of the new additions in this book have been in the area of developing professional standards, particularly for law enforcement, correctional personnel, and the more critical appraisal of the judicial segment of criminal justice. Historically, judges and lawyers have been treated somewhat benevolently. More recently, however, it is becoming more and more apparent that a good deal of the inequities that are generated from our system of justice are brought about by the current judicial structure and its practitioners.

Each chapter of the text not only lists the objectives, but it also provides a number of discussion issues, many of which are controversial. We believe that new ideas and eventual change will occur through controversy. One thing is apparent: the criminal justice system is not perfect, and only through continued study and research will the degree of imperfection come into focus, hopefully leading to meaningful change.

We have organized the text in a logical, sequential manner. Beginning with an overview of the criminal justice system, we then explore the nature and scope of criminality and the function and interrelationships of the major criminal justice components. We have not attempted to demonstrate any hierarchical arrangement that is frequently observed, because reality dictates that one component is not subservient to another.

This textbook differs significantly from others in that it is simple and direct in its presentation. We believe that learning is the result of seeking answers to the appropriate questions. Learning is therefore the responsibility of the teacher-student relationship, and not those of us who have arranged the printed words.

We thank the many individuals who contributed to this book: Dan Scannell, Santa Rosa, Junior College; Thomas Goldrick, Rockland Community College; Pamela Mayhall, Pima Community College; and Calvin H. Zimmer, Prince Georges Community College for their thoughtful and helpful reviews. We also thank Barb Melton for her assistance in helping to research data pertinent to topical areas in the text. Finally, our gratitude is extended to Grace Hauth for her splendid typing. All of this, however, would not be forthcoming without the editing help of Charlotte Shelby and the guiding hands of Bob Pirtle of Wiley.

Chuck Foster
Diane Machunze

Contents

Introduction to the administration of justice

PART 1
Introduction

Overview of the criminal justice system

The study of this chapter will enable you to:

1. **Understand and outline our system of criminal justice.**
2. **Demonstrate how each subsystem relates organizationally to the other subsystems.**
3. **Discuss some of the alleged inequities within the criminal justice system.**
4. **Be encouraged to explore possible solutions for the problem areas cited.**

he criminal justice system has been charged with finding justice and serving society, yet the criminal justice system is a reflection of the inequalities prevailing throughout our society.[1] Why?

This book is concerned with a system in our society that may be compared to a tunnel through a mountain. The tunnel through it joins a series of connecting rooms: the institutions of the American criminal justice system.

In this first chapter we will use the word institution in two different ways: first, as a general term describing a long-established organization made up of people with many inherited ideas and procedures dedicated to, or established for, the purpose of public service. The second (and specific) definition is that of penal institutions—buildings where people are locked up to serve out sentences imposed by courts.

The criminal justice system is merely one of the many institutional systems that make up our environment. Our world is a mass of systems; educational systems, religious systems, governmental systems, economic systems, and many others.

Any criminal justice system is an apparatus society uses to enforce the standards of conduct necessary to protect individuals and the community. It operates by apprehending, prosecuting, convicting, and sentencing those members of the community who violate the basic rules of group existence. The action taken against lawbreakers is designed to serve three purposes beyond the immediately punitive one. It removes dangerous people from the community; it deters others from criminal behavior; and it gives society an opportunity to attempt to transform lawbreakers into law-abiding citizens.[2]

This system is composed of several components which handle separate tasks. These components are identified as

    1. Police (FBI, sheriff, state trooper, and others)

[1]Ken Jackson, "Ex-Con Coalition Offers Blueprint," *Fortune News*, June 1974, p. 2.

[2]The President's Commission on Law Enforcement and Administration of Justice, *The Challenge of Crime in a Free Society* (Washington, D.C.: U.S. Government Printing Office, 1967), p. 7.

2. Courts
   (a) Prosecutor
   (b) Defender
   (c) Judge
3. Corrections
   (a) Probation
   (b) Confinement (county jail, city jail, state penitentiary, federal penitentiary, community-based corrections)
   (c) Parole

Note that probation is a corrections process that is also an alternative sentence available to a judge in a court. Depending on the area of operation of a probation program, its administration might be the responsibility of a court or of a corrections program.

Although these components are separately organized, none are independent of each other. The courts cannot function unless the police first arrest the suspect. There would be no need for corrections unless the courts sentenced individuals to those correctional institutions. The activity or direction of each organized part of the criminal justice system has a direct effect on the activity of the other parts.

Many people are aware of the existence of the various institutions that comprise the criminal justice system, but most individuals remain naive or confused about the functions of each part. Most of us can easily identify some of the inhabitants of these institutions, such as the uniformed police officers directing traffic, the black-robed judges scurrying down the hall to the courtroom, or the correctional guards who occupy the watch towers of many of our state and federal penitentiaries. However, for the most part, law-abiding citizens who never enter the criminal justice system know relatively little about the inner workings of the system and the compromises and frictions between the components of the system.

Public attitudes and myths

Part of the confusion the public has concerning our institutions in the criminal justice system has been brought about by television, movies, and novels. These media have created a mythology about the criminal justice process that is difficult to dispel. Much of the fiction about police, for example, has glorified the role of detectives, creating the impression that they are the most important menbers of police departments. This is certainly not so: most police work is done by patrolmen. Patrolmen usher many more lawbreakers to the criminal justice tunnel entrance than do detectives. Other mythology: fictional lawyers, such as Perry Mason, have glorified defense attorneys and have spread a lot of false information regarding courtroom procedures and the adversary encounters we call criminal trials. The trend has been to portray defense attorneys as heroes, and prosecutors as unrelenting, unscrupulous characters who will resort to any means to convict a defendant, guilty or not. Judges have been diversely portrayed, ranging from weak, ignorant, corrupt, or even comic characters to white-haired, godlike figures who dispense justice with divine authority. Corrections as a whole has been badly defamed in fiction. Probation and parole officers are generally ignored, but popular literature— from *I was a Fugitive from a Georgia Chain Gang* in the 1930s to *Cool Hand Luke* of the late 1960s—abounds with sadistic wardens and prison guards.

More realistic fiction about police is now being written, however. Joseph Wambaugh's *The Choir Boys* and *The Black Marble* are examples of this new trend.

One of the purposes of this book is to help dispel some of the myths that cloud the operation of our criminal justice system and prevent reform or constructive change by obscuring the strengths and weaknesses of its institutions. With this end in mind, let us "walk" an individual through the system from beginning to end and show what he experiences as he passes through the connecting institutions. Then we will describe and explain why the individual institutions occasionally seem to be in conflict with each other.

The institutional order followed presumes that the accused person is an adult or a juvenile being processed as an adult, a procedure possible in some states. We will learn later that the institutional order for juveniles being processed as juveniles is somewhat different.

The chronology of the system

An individual enters the criminal justice system when he or she is suspected of having been involved in a criminal act, either as a suspect, victim, or witness. A crime is an act that is in violation of a law prescribed by a city, county, state, or federal jurisdiction. A crime may also occur if a person fails to perform some act which he or she is required to do by law. The failure to perform such a duty is called an omission. An example of an omission would be the failure to perform the duties required by law when a driver becomes involved in an accident. Another example of an omitted act would include a person's failure to file his income tax as required by federal and state law.

Police

After a crime is committed, the first component of the criminal justice system—the police—becomes involved in the process. When a crime is committed, the police are summoned to the scene of the occurence. When the police officer arrives, he or she may find a witness who observed the crime and can identify the person who committed it. The police officer may then arrest the identified person at once and charge him with the crime. The police officer might however choose to await additional investigation before arresting the suspect. But if the police officer has personally observed the violation of the law, he may immediately make the arrest and book the violator into jail, charging him or her with the crime that has been committed. (See Figure 1-1).

It is important to note here that although a person may commit a crime, he may not automatically become involved in the criminal justice process. A person becomes involved only if he or she is arrested for the crime. We shall discover in Chapter 2 that many crimes are committed, but that only a portion of those crimes are solved through the arrest of an individual. Thousands of persons commit crimes for which they are not punished by law. Part of this inequity stems from the inability of the police to arrest all law violators. However, part of the responsibility must also be attributed to the public who for a variety of reasons may not report a crime even though they are the victims of that crime.

Crimes fall into two broad categories: felonies and misdemeanors, rated according to their seriousness as judged by the penalties attached to them by law. A felony is generally defined as an offense that is punishable by death or by imprisonment in a state (or federal) prison. Felonies punishable by death are traditionally referred to as capital offenses. The general definition of a misdemeanor is that it is any offense that is not a felony. Misdemeanors, therefore, are minor crimes with minor penalties attached.

As a matter of law in most jurisdictions, anyone (either an officer or a private citizen) can make an arrest without a warrant for a felony or a misdemeanor attempted or committed in his presence, or for a felony committed outside of his presence on receipt of reliable information that a felony has been committed. We will not discuss the subject of citizens' arrest powers here because such arrests are exceptions rather than the rule. Almost all arrests are made by professional law enforcement officers who presumably have the training and experience necessary to make legal arrests.

Whenever an officer interferes with a citizen's individual personal freedom by detaining him even briefly or by arresting him, it is a serious matter; the officer must have a reason for doing so *before* he stops the individual. But an innocent citizen stopped and questioned and even frisked on the street by an officer and then released should not presume that the officer has done something illegal, something that has violated the citizen's civil rights. The officer may have a valid reason for being suspicious that the citizen is unaware of; if so, he can legally perform a sufficient investigation to confirm or eliminate the suspicion because police have *investigative* as well as *arrest* powers. After stopping a suspicious person, the officer, if he has reason to believe the person stopped might perform an act of violence, may frisk him by patting him down in order to feel for a weapon and may detail him to ask questions. Of course, this type of action on the street is an intrusion on the right to privacy, but generally courts have held that the right to privacy must yield when police are drawn into a lawful "threshold" inquiry because they have reason to suspect unlawful conduct. (For a further discussion see Chapter 10.)

The citizen has been stopped, questioned, perhaps frisked, and then released. If this is all that happens, he does not enter the criminal justice system. He has lingered briefly at the entrance, but he has not entered.

Arrest Alternately, the officer may arrest the citizen. Arrest is a procedure defined by our laws and is basically uniform in all the 50 states as well as in the federal government's criminal procedures. There is nothing new about it. Our law of arrest, based on the British common law, has not varied significantly in over 300 years.

Arrest is defined as follows: "The apprehending or restraining of one's person in order to be forthcoming to answer an alleged or suspected crime."[3]

Police should, whenever possible, obtain an arrest warrant prior to arresting a person. Arrest warrants are written documents obtained from an impartial judicial officer who demands a sworn statement of incriminating actions or circumstances called probable cause. But in most cases time will not permit this. Legal arrests without warrants can therefore be made in emergency situations requiring immediate police action.

A police officer making a arrest for a felony or misdemeanor, with or without a warrant, must warn the suspect of his constitutional rights—the so-called Miranda Warning as follows:

1. You have a constitutional right to remain silent and say absolutely nothing. If you do make a statement, you may stop at any time.

2. Anything you say can and will be used against you in a court of law.

3. You can have a lawyer here to help you while we ask you questions.

4. If you don't have a lawyer, one will be appointed for you if you want one now.[4]

Although the Miranda ruling is explicit in what is required to be said to a suspect, recent controversy has developed regarding when and in what circumstances the Miranda Warning must be read to an individual (see Chapter 10).

After arresting a person, the police officer will book him at the police department. The arrested person is photographed, fingerprinted, and asked questions relating to his background and identity. These administrative procedures do not violate a person's constitutional rights if he has been legally arrested. Also, if the person has been legally arrested, and if the police suspect intoxication by alcohol or narcotics, they may obtain blood

[3]*Blackstone Commentaries*, 289, p. 1679 (1897 ed.).

[4]*Miranda v. Arizona, 384 U.S. 436 (1966).*

samples from him without violating his Fifth Amendment rights against self-incrimination, provided that proper medical procedures are followed. There are some states, however, that have an implied consent policy with regard to obtaining blood or breath samples in cases of suspected intoxication while driving. The implied consent law makes it legal for a police officer or medical officer to obtain these samples without the suspect's permission. If the suspect is conscious and refuses to give his consent to have these samples taken, he will lose his right to operate a motor vehicle. But, the police cannot introduce these samples into a court of law if they are illegally obtained (see Chapter 10).

After a brief period of detention the police may release the person without filing formal charges. A victim may decline to press charges or a witness may decide not to testify. Release after brief police detention is the first of the legal exits in the criminal justice system.

Courts   If retained in custody, the person should be taken before a judicial officer without undue delay. This step, called an initial appearance in some jurisdictions, a first appearance in others, is the arrested person's first contact with the institution of the courts. The judicial officer—magistrate, justice of the peace, or commissioner—formally notifies the arrested person of the charges against him and advises him of his constitutional rights. If this judicial officer finds the charge or the arrest defective in some way, he may release the arrested person. This is an other legal escape hatch. If the charges are not dismissed, the judicial officer will generally set bond for his reappearance at a later date for a preliminary hearing. In petty offenses a summary trial may be held against the arrested person at this stage without further processing and his case disposed of, by release if found not guilty, and probably by the payment of a fine if found guilty. If found guilty, the person pays his fine and is released. If he is indigent (without money), he may have to serve a short sentence in jail instead of the fine.

As stated in the Miranda Warning, an accused person is entitled to have a lawyer present at any time he is questioned by the police about any crime he allegedly committed. If indigent, the judicial officer may appoint a private attorney to represent him. In jurisdictions that support a public defender's office, indigent defendants are represented by the public defender. If the defendant has funds, he must retain his own attorney. Many communities also have legal aid societies to provide legal assistance to indigents in addition to the public defender's office.

Bail bond   After any judicial officer sets a bond, the accused must post it in cash, property of equivalent value, or he must hire a professional bondsman to post the bond for him, at a fee amounting to 10 percent or more of the bond. This fee, dependent on the restrictions imposed by state laws and the bondsman's opinion of the degree of risk he is assuming, is not returnable to the defendant. If the accused person has no money for bond or bondsman, he may have to wait in jail during the period of time he is working his way through the system.

Posting a bail bond is the method traditionally used in our criminal court system to ensure the defendant's appearance in a designated court *instanter* (when summoned) or at a designated time on a designated date. If the defendant does not appear, the bond may be forfeited—impounded—by the court and an additional charge of bond default may be filed against the defendant. In later chapters, we will discuss the criticism of the practice of requiring money or property bonds for release of person awaiting judicial action, which obviously discriminates against the poor. We will also at that time discuss the current trends in bail reform.

Release or jail It is becoming a common practice that judges, especially in the federal courts, release defendants on personal recognizance, or own recognizance, to await further judicial action, rather than requiring them to remain in jail because of lack of funds. Release on recognizance generally is granted when the defendant has no prior criminal record, or a minor one, and the judge believes that he will not flee the jurisdiction to avoid trial. So, if the defendant makes bond in any form, he has found an exit from the system, a temporary one to be sure, since the bond acts as a string to bring him back when he is wanted.

However, if the defendant does not have the money for bond and has a background that causes the judge to believe he will probably flee if released on recognizance, the judge will send him to jail to await the disposition of his case. When this occurs, the defendant, generally through his attorney, may file an appeal to reduce what he considers to be an excessively high bond: he may be successful in having the bond reduced to an amount that he can afford.

Usually, between the time of arrest and court appearance for trial on a serious charge, the accused will ask for and be granted a preliminary hearing or examining trial. The defendant will request this to find out in advance as much as he can about the evidence gathered against him and to attempt to legally suppress (prohibit the use of) as much of the evidence as possible. This is the first critical adversary encounter between the prosecutor and the defense counsel. The procedure often determines whether a trial will be held at all. If the defendant is successful in obtaining a judicial ruling suppressing most of the evidence against him, the charges may be dropped and the defendant freed, or the charges may be reduced. So it may possibly create an escape hatch. But even if it does not, it tests the evidence and gives the defendant a much better idea of the strength of the case against him.

In felony cases the accused will be brought before the trial court for his first formal appearance, called an *arraignment*, by the issuance of a document called an *information* or one called an *indictment*. Both are formal, written accusations of crime. An information is prepared by a prosecutor on the basis of information submitted by police or citizens. An indictment is prepared by a grand jury.

Grand jury A grand jury is defined as follows:

A jury of inquiry who are summoned and returned by the sheriff (or U.S. Marshal in federal procedure) to each session of the criminal courts, and whose duty is to receive complaints and accusations in criminal cases, hear the evidence adduced on the part of the state (or federal government), and find bills of indictment in cases where they are satisfied a trial ought to be had. They are first sworn by the court. They vary in size in various jurisdictions.

A grand jury meets in secret session, hearing witnesses and examining evidence, and the defendant has no right to appear before it without the grand jury's permission. If the grand jury decides there is sufficient evidence to warrant a trial, it issues a "true bill" resulting in the defendant being indicted. If the grand jury decides that the evidence is insufficient, it issues a "no bill," which results in the charges against the defendant being dropped. Thus, a "no bill" can be another escape hatch for the defendant. Some states have no grand jury systems; others seldom use it. Grand juries practically never hear misdemeanors, only felonies. Even in jurisdictions where grand juries are widely used, misdemeanors are almost always brought into court by the use of informations.

Arraignment After the issuance of an information or indictment, the defendant is arraigned. He makes a formal appearance in his trial court to hear the charge against him read and to enter a plea. A possible temporary escape hatch may open here if his defense counsel can find something technically wrong with the formal charge, information or indictment, as presented. If nothing is found wrong with the charge, then he must make a choice; he must decide whether to plead guilty or not guilty to the charge.

If the defendant enters a plea of guilty and "throws himself on the mercy of the court," the judge sentences him then and there, or at a later date, to a term of probation or institutional confinement. A plea of guilty immediately ushers the defendant into the third stage of the system: corrections.

Plea of not guilty If the defendant enters a plea of not guilty and demands a trial, in rare instances it is possible for him to be tried before a judge without a jury, but this is the exception rather than the rule in felony cases. If we have a jury trial, a *petit* (trial) jury, usually consisting of 12 persons, must be selected from a larger group of citizenry, called a panel of veniremen, assembled in the courtroom. In picking the jury, the prosecutor and the defense counsel are given the opportunity to question the panel generally, individually, or both generally and individually, in order to come

[5]Henry Campbell Black, *Black's Law Dictionary*, 4th ed. (St. Paul., Minn.: West Publishing Co., 1968).

up with 12 people acceptable to both. Each side has a designated number of "strikes"—rights to bar certain individuals of the panel from serving on the trial jury. In some jurisdictions 2 or 3 extra alternate jurors are chosen, in addition to the basic 12. These alternates sit in the jury box during the trial and listen to the proceedings, but they do not become jurors, entering into deliberations and voting on the verdict, unless they replace one or more of the regular jurors who die, become disabled, or are excused during the course of the trial.

In the United States, court trials are conducted as adversary proceedings. A trial can be compared to a boxing match between a professional and an amateur who is allowed to hire the services of a professional to fight for him. The prosecution has the district attorney or one of his assistants as its champion. The defendant, generally a nonattorney, must hire an attorney, accept one when appointed by the court, or seek the aid of the public defender. While the attorneys carry on their legal battle, the judge acts as an impartial referee, carefully watching, ready to intervene if he observes any illegalities or encroachments on the rights of the defendant. The philosophy behind the adversary proceeding is that the contest between the two trained legal champions, fought in the presence of an impartial referee, will cause justice to prevail: the guilt or innocence of the defendant will be established beyond a reasonable doubt, and the jury will return a just verdict based on this proven guilt or innocence.

At the conclusion of the trial, if the jury does find the defendant not guilty, he is freed. He has found a legal exit. If the jury cannot come to a unanimous verdict as to guilt or innocence and deadlocks, the judge may declare a mistrial. Then the defendant will have to be tried again on the same charge, probably before a different jury, or the prosecutor may decide his case is not strong enough to win and will request that the charge be dropped. Thus, a mistrial may or may not be a legal exit for the defendant.

Corrections

If the jury finds the defendant guilty, the judge or the jury, depending on the laws of the state, will set the penalty and the defendant will be relegated to corrections. On being sentenced to corrections the defendant faces two possibilities: probation or institutionalization. Here we use the specialized definition of institution, as a prison or reformatory where the convicted person is confined.

If the sentence is probation, the defendant leaves the courtroom in the custody of a probation officer. The probation officer has already made an investigation of the defendant's background and has probably expressed the opinion in open court that he considers the defendant to be "probation material," someone who can still make a contribution to society without being sentenced to confinement.

The probation officer generally has more people in his (or her) caseload than can be adequately supervised. His attitudes may be stern or sympathetic: his background may be in sociology or social work, or he may be a retired law enforcement officer with or without any academic background. He will state the rules regulating his client's conduct during the prescribed period of probation, the types of place where the probationer can and cannot work or live, and the types of person with whom he cannot associate. The probation officer's supervision extends to seeing that the probationer adheres to any special requirements imposed by the court, such as financial restitution to a party injured by the probationer. A reporting schedule is arranged; the probationer will be required to contact the probation officer in person or in writing at stated intervals. The probation officer may make surprise visits to the probationer's residence or his place of employment to verify that he lives where he says he does, works where he says he does, is not associating with criminals, and is complying with all special requirements.

If the probationer completes his sentence successfully, the probation officer meets with him for a final interview. If the probationer does not live up to the standard of conduct imposed, the probation officer will have the defendant brought back before the judge and, in most instances, the judge will revoke the person's probation and send him to an institution.

Let us return briefly to the termination of a trial in which the defendant has been found guilty and the court has not sentenced the defendant to probation but to a term in a penal institution. The defendant will be transported to an institution without delay to begin serving his sentence, unless he files an appeal of some sort, which may or may not become an escape hatch.

The subject of penal institutions will be covered in detail in later chapters. Even the most lenient and comfortable of them are unhappy places for the inmates, some of whom break rules, which causes them to lose time off for good behavior and serve their entire terms in prison. Others may commit additional crimes in prison and receive additional prison sentences. Most inmates, however, obtain an earlier release than their sentences specify because of good behavior. These inmates serve a supervised period of parole or conditional release outside the institution prior to the full expiration of their sentences.

During this period they are supervised in much the same way as are probationers. In fact, federal probationers and conditional releasees are supervised by the same federal probation officers. Supervision practices vary throughout the different state jurisdictions: some states use the same staffs for both probationers and parolees and others use separate agencies.

When the person completes his period of parole successfully, he is in the same situation as the probationer who has successfully completed his probation. Both have "paid their debts to society" for breaking the law, and both have emerged at the opposite end of the criminal justice system.

Friction within the system

This route we have described through the justice system seems easy enough to follow with all exits clearly marked, but problems arise along the way because of frictions between the institutions involved. In many cases their institutional roles and goals seem to oppose each other. The adversary system of the courtroom, although certainly not perfect, seems to be the best method yet devised to ensure a fair trial, but unfortunately the adversary system within the criminal justice process as a whole is not confined to the courtroom. It pervades the entire criminal justice system, often causing the individual institutions—police, courts, and corrections—to become adversaries rather than colleagues in the overall quest for justice. Why? Mainly because of "people" problems. Let us examine some of them.

First, the police. Police departments tend to be closely knit, paramilitary organizations with strong group ties. Generally, policemen think of themselves as policemen rather than as individuals who happen to be employed by police departments.

The police institution is situated alongside the courts institution. Courts are dominated by lawyers in all component parts: judge, prosecutor, and defender. In their education and training, lawyers are taught to think of themselves as individuals more than are the police. We mentioned earlier that in court lawyers are professional adversaries. Both the prosecutor and the defender think of themselves that way. The judge himself, although not an adversary in the trial setting, is an attorney appointed or elected to his post from their ranks. Judges maintain their individuality and generally resist being organized into a tightly knit system, You might say that lawyers and judges tend to be soloists who resist playing together as an orchestra.

Here we have the police institution with its tendency toward group thinking connected as a feeder device to the courts, an institution made up generally of self-assertive individuals. These two institutions are expected to cooperate very closely in the operation of the criminal justice system, but because of their basic compositional differences it is easy to see why they do not always do so.

A police officer arrests an individual for a crime, and his investigation convinces him that the individual is guilty. When he presents his case to an assistant district attorney, he may be put off by the prosecutor's seemingly skeptical attitude. The prosecutor is "testing" the strength of the case, but his searching, sometimes brusque, questions on such points as probable cause, legality of search, or use of physical force may offend the officer and put him on the defensive. The officer may receive the impression that the prosecutor thinks he is lying or that he did something wrong. The officer may have had to make his arrest in a tense, dangerous situation amid uproar and confusion; and now, in the quiet of the office, this lawyer seems to be trying to hindsight him by asking all sorts of questions about why he did this and why he did not do that, concentrating on legal details rather than on the important fact that the arrested person is guilty of a crime and deserves punishment.

Then, after the assistant district attorney authorizes or accepts prosecution, the case finally goes to trial. The officer takes the stand and testifies as a witness for the prosecution, and the defense attorney, on cross-examination, harasses him with all sorts of questions—some intentionally insulting—intended to shake his credibility and composure. The officer may feel that he is being unfairly attacked by the defense counsel and that the prosecutor and judge are doing nothing to help him. In fact, the prosecutor and the judge may ask the officer some rather searching and unexpected questions themselves if the defense counsel during his cross-examination uncovers some investigative error on the part of the officer. Perspiring under the limelight of the witness stand, the officer concludes that all three members of the court's institution—prosecutor, defense counsel, and judge—are all after *him* instead of the defendant.

What the officer should learn early in his career is that he must know the rules of criminal procedure better than the prosecutor and the judge. He must learn them; they must be ready for his use at all times. In the midst of an altercation on the street he cannot call for a short recess to research a legal point in his office or library. He must make quick, sure legal decisions on short notice. When the officer does learn the procedures well and gains confidence in following them, he can sit solidly in the witness box and ride out the barrage of questions without losing his composure.

Then the trial is over. The jury goes out to deliberate its verdict. Three things can happen as a result of their deliberations, and two of them are bad as far as the police and prosecution are concerned:

1. The defendant is found guilty.
2. The defendant is found not guilty.
3. The jury deadlocks and a mistrial results.

If the jury finds the defendant guilty, the police officer and prosecutor congratulate each other on their victory. But if the probation officer makes a report recommending probation, both may become irritated at the probation officer for being "weak-kneed" or "soft on criminals." Institutional friction. If the judge accepts the recommendation and puts the defendant on probation, then the prosecutor and the officer are irritated at the judge as well as the probation officer. More institutional friction. On the other hand, if the judge does not accept the probation officer's recommendation, this irritates the probation officer, the representative of corrections. He has made his investigation and believes the defendant to be probation material, or he would not have so recommended. In the estimation of the probation officer, the judge has no heart; he is a "hanging judge." Still more institutional friction.

If the jury finds the defendant not guilty, the officer and prosecutor are downcast, and the defense counsel and the defendant are flushed with victory. The defendant, carried away with emotion, may hug his champion, the defense counsel, and shake hands with the members of the jury, congratulating them on their fairness and their intelligence in seeing through the false charges of the prosecution. To the chagrin of the officer, the defendant (whom the officer is sure is guilty) swaggers from the courtroom scot-free. To the chagrin of the prosecutor, defense counsel may favor him with a superior smile and say something like, "Better luck next time, Charlie."

After a mistrial or a not guilty verdict comes a period of meditation and reflection for both the officer and the prosecutor. Rationalization enters the process.

The policeman goes back to the police station and explains to his fellow officers that the prosecutor or the judge lost the case; he wants to make it clear that losing the case was not his fault. His fellow officers, who have been through the same experience, may not be impressed by his explanations, and may ridicule him about his "defeat." The officer may learn something constructive from his experience and do a better job next time, or he may become permanently bitter toward the institution of the courts.

The prosecutor's rationalized meditation on the cause of the verdict or nonverdict will generally result in a different opinion than the officer's. He may feel that the case was lost because of faulty investigation or the hostile attitude of the judge.

Another potential source of friction between police and prosecutor is plea bargaining prior to trial. The prosecutor has a heavy caseload. Acting on the facts set forth in a police investigative report, he has charged a defendant with first degree murder. Looking over the reports of later investigation, he can see that the trial will be lengthy and complicated and perhaps difficult to prove beyond a reasonable doubt. Defense counsel comes to him with a proposition. The defendant will enter a plea to murder in the second degree, a lesser charge, if the prosecutor will not contest it and will not recommend the maximum sentence. To avoid a lengthy trial with a dubious outcome, the prosecutor will agree. This decision may irritate the police officer who has spent a lot of time on the case and who believes that such a deal allows the defendant to "get off too light."

Both the prosecution and the police appear united in the belief that, as a general rule, people convicted of crimes are not locked up often enough or given long enough sentences when they are. This vindictive attitude irritates the inhabitants of the corrections institution who generally think of themselves as social workers rather than as avengers of wrongs. A majority of corrections people stress the undeniable fact that there is no uniformity in the sentencing for comparable crimes, and they allege that prejudice, discrimination, racial bias, and poverty are often the deciding factors in determining who gets the longest prison sentences. They charge that the police and courts are mainly interested in "warehousing" lawbreakers rather than in rehabilitating them. They charge further that the police and courts are primarily interested in punishment and not in eliminating the causes of crime.

Over the years corrections has experimented with four major philosophies of handling convicted persons: restraint, reform, rehabilitation, and reintegration. None has proven especially successful. The philosophies will be described in detail later.

The criminal justice process described until now assumed that the offender was an adult, or a juvenile being tried as an adult, a procedure possible in some jurisdictions. In cases involving juveniles being processed as juveniles, the same institutions are involved—police, courts, and corrections—but the juvenile may make contact with them in a different order than does the adult.

Juveniles in the criminal justice system

An important point to keep in mind is that in the United States, since the turn of the century, the basic attitude of the criminal justice system has been that juveniles are children to be helped rather than punished whenever possible. This philosophy has been one of the main sources of institutional friction within the criminal justice system as far as the processing of juveniles is concerned.

Most cases involving juveniles come to the attention of the police first. A patrolman apprehends a juvenile for an offense and turns him over to the juvenile unit of his department or to a juvenile probation officer at a detention or intake center. If he is turned over to the police department juvenile unit, that unit may hold an informal hearing and release the juvenile to his parents, dismissing or adjusting the charges without further processing. If they do not release the juvenile to his parents or guardian, the police will take him to a juvenile detention center where he will be interviewed by an intake officer who will determine whether or not to request court action. This interview is generally called an intake hearing. As a result of his interview, the intake officer may make "nonadjudicatory disposition" of the case by referring the juvenile to a welfare or social service agency for counseling, medical care, or some other form of aid. If the intake officer believes the case warrants it, he will refer the matter to the juvenile court for adjudication. A point to remember is that juveniles are not "tried" in juvenile court; their cases are "adjudicated" there.

Generally, the intake officer will refer cases to the court for adjudication when one of the following conditions is present:

1. The juvenile is dangerous to others.

2. The juvenile is dangerous to himself.

3. The juvenile should be protected from some part of society; he is in danger from others.

The court may release the juvenile at the adjudicatory hearing or may go through full adjudication, a legal process very like a trial in which the juvenile is represented by legal counsel. As a result of adjudication, the court may place the juvenile on probation or sentence him to a term of confinement in a juvenile institution. As in the case of adults, juvenile probation may be revoked if the client does not follow the general or specific terms of probation and, as a result, the client may be sent to serve time in a juvenile institution. Also, the juvenile may be afforded early release from confinement on parole in a manner similar to the procedure followed by adults.

Many of the same "people" problems arise in the institutions of the juvenile criminal justice system as in the adult system. An additional source of friction may appear within the police institution, between the juvenile unit and the line units of the police department. Regular patrolmen and detectives may develop the feeling that the members of their own department in the juvenile unit are too soft on juveniles who commit crimes.

The use of community auxiliary agencies is growing in the field of juvenile criminal justice. More and more delinquent juveniles are being referred, or diverted, to these community agencies—some of them volunteer—for supervision, foster care, and counseling, in order to keep them from being processed by the criminal justice system and acquiring a criminal record.

Many of these agencies, such as Alcoholics Anonymous and drug treatment facilities, are also available to adult offenders. The quality of the services offered by the auxiliary agencies varies from community to community, and institutional friction frequently develops among these agencies themselves and between the auxiliary agencies and the institutions of the criminal justice system. So it goes, adversary relationships arise from conflicts of roles and goals, and valuable time is wasted—time that could be more profitably spent in achieving our goal of universal justice by unified action of our institutions.

The unjust system

The criminal justice system "deliberately sacrifices much in efficiency and even in effectiveness in order to preserve local autonomy and to protect the individual."[6]

But few benefits are provided by the state or federal government for the victim of a criminal act. It is ironic that we strive so hard to preserve a defendant's rights, to secure the medical treatment and legal protection that he requires, while the victim receives little or no compensation from

[6]*The Challenge of Crime in a Free Society*, p. 7.

the state for the injury he may have received as a result of the crime. (However, a few states have recently started victims' compensation programs. See Chapter 2.)

If the victim wants to file a complaint against the individual who committed a crime, he must testify in a court of law. This may require that the victim be absent from his job for a period of time to testify at the trial. The victim may be paid a minimal fee ($5–$10 per day) for appearing on behalf of the state, regardless of what his daily wage may be or whether he risks losing it. In essence, then, the victim may be operating at a financial loss in order to help the criminal justice system seek justice.

The victim may also be subjected to intense cross-examination by the defense attorney. In many states, the victim of a rape may be questioned quite thoroughly and harshly about her past sexual experience. Some states have begun to pass laws making it illegal for defense attorneys to question a victim's sexual history unless it is specifically linked to that of the defendant.

Figure 1–2 makes a valid comparison between the victim's involvement in the criminal process and the defendant's rights in the justice system. It is not surprising that many victims and witnesses become bitter about our system of justice and question the system as an instrument of preserving society and the rights of all individuals.

Recently, one victim of the system became so outraged at our justice process during her divorce that she wrote a book describing her experiences.[7] Based on three years of research and her experiences in court as a juror, witness, plaintiff, defendant, and observer, Strick contends that the adversary system of justice encourages and rewards the worst qualities in human beings—that our adversary system of justice inevitably results in a conflict between winning and trying to reach the truth. It is because of this conflict, however, that many of the participants are invited, even encouraged, to fight and lie. The author does point out that this behavior might be alleviated if lawyers were not paid by their clients (thus not obligated), but salaried by an agency independent of the federal government. According to Strick, the salaries of the lawyers would be determined by their diligence in getting at the truth and by their display of humanity.

Although the author of *Injustice for All* has alluded to the injustices of the adult criminal justice system in her book, many people feel that inequities occur in our juvenile justice system as well, inequities that benefit the perpetrator. Victims, as well as bystanders and police, often marvel at the number of times a juvenile is repeatedly arrested and returned home without "prescribed punishment." Although the philosophy of the juvenile court is treatment rather than punishment, individuals and police have urged state legislators to take a new look at juvenile crimes and juvenile court procedures. At the same time, court personnel and state legislators are trying to resolve the conflict within the limits of the law. They are also

[7]Anne Strick, *Injustice for All: How Our Adversary System of Law Victimizes Us and Subverts True Justice* (New York: G.P. Putman, 1977).

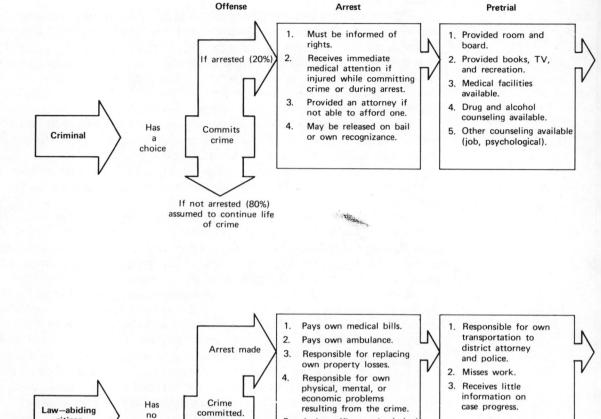

Figure 1-2 The criminal injustice system. *Source:* Courtesy Harl Haas, District Attorney's Office, Multnomah County, Portland, Oregon, 1976.

1. Provided with state—appointed attorney.
2. Can plea bargain.
3. Can change venue.
4. Can delay trial.
5. Can invoke Fifth Amendment.
6. Can move to suppress evidence.
7. May be acquitted by reason of insanity.
8. In only 3% of all committed crimes is an offender convicted.
9. Can appeal.

1. A presentence study is conducted to aid judge in sentencing.
2. Alternatives to incarceration are numerous.

1. Provided room and board.
2. Access to medical and psychological treatment.
3. Opportunity to improve education.
4. Opportunity to develop job skills.
5. Can participate in work release and other minimum security programs.
6. Numerous rehabilitation programs.
7. Eligible for early parole.
8. Good time credit available.

1. Many transitional programs available.
2. Personal loans available.
3. Large percentage continue life of crime.

1. Provides own transportation and parking costs.
2. Pays own babysitting or other costs.
3. Must recount criminal incident.
4. Subject to cross—examination.
5. The "victim's attorney" represents the state (general public) not the individual victim.
6. Victim has no right to appeal verdict.
7. No victim waiting room.
8. Paid $5 a day for their time in court.
9. Treated like a piece of evidence.

1. Has no voice in court decisions, pleas, presentence or sentencing.
2. Usually are not notified or present at time of sentencing

1. Often unsatisfied with results of criminal justice system.
2. May fear retaliation.
3. Continues life with fears, damages, injuries, traumas.
4. Is expected to continue to support a system that treated them with less respect than for the offender.

trying to preserve the philosophical idea that a juvenile is still a child and not an adult and should be treated and protected as such. (See Chapters 2, 3, and 5 for further discussion of juveniles.)

In spite of the alleged inequities in our criminal justice system, the system does seek to implement justice and to benefit the individual, the victim, and society. We may see that the scale with which it serves all three might be lopsided at times, but nevertheless it does try to accomplish the goal within the boundaries of the laws prescribed by the state legislatures and Congress. In the following chapters we will point out how the system works and why it works in this manner.

Summary

This chapter has explained how the American system of criminal justice is organized. An adult offender entering the system progresses through various institutions in the criminal justice process in the following order: police, courts (judge, prosecutor, and defender), and corrections (probation, institutionalization, and parole).

Each of the institutions has one or more legal exits if the traveler can find them. Most of these exits are in the institution of the courts and require professional legal guidance to find. After reaching corrections, the only exit remaining is the other end of the system.

"People" problems arise between the institutions because each follows inherited codes and procedures that often conflict. This institutional conflict hampers the functioning of the overall system.

Juveniles charged with delinquent acts contact the same institutions, but in different order than do the adults, generally making contact with a probation officer (a member of the corrections institution) prior to going to court. Also, juvenile cases are "adjudicated" rather than "tried." The underlying philosophy is that they should be helped when possible rather than punished.

At the conclusion of the chapter we examined some of the alleged inequities in our system of justice and examined the victim's view of criminal justice.

TOPICS FOR DISCUSSION

1. Discuss the organizational structure of the criminal justice system.

2. Discuss the various responsibilities each subsystem is charged with.

3. Discuss the various conflicts that arise between each subsystem and explain why they occur.

4. Explain the differences between the benefits provided to defendants and victims in our system of justice.

5. Explain the juvenile justice system and how it differs from the adult justice process.

2

Survey of the crime problem

The study of this chapter will enable you to:

1. **Differentiate between the legal definition of crime and the social implications of crime.**
2. **Understand the difference between white-collar crime, victimless crime, and visible crime.**
3. **Grapple with the immensity of the crime problem.**
4. **Understand the various factors that contribute to the volume and type of crime discussed in the Uniform Crime Reports.**
5. **Realize the need to search beyond the face value of crime statistics.**

Is crime deviant behavior or does it reflect the statutory law?

Who benefits and who is victimized by the legal concept of law?

Within the past fifteen years the problem of crime has become one of the major concerns of the American people. Their awareness of the acceleration of the crime rate has created a campaign for resources to combat this rapid growth in crime. These resources (funds, manpower, equipment) have been given to law enforcement agencies, courts, and correctional systems in an attempt to prevent crime, arrest violators, determine the guilt or innocence of those accused, and to rehabilitate offenders. However, in spite of additional resources, the components of the criminal justice system have been relatively ineffective in resolving the crime problem in our country. We will examine this problem later in the chapter.

What is crime?

Before surveying the crime problem, it will be helpful to define the term crime. The legal definition of crime is an intentional act or omission in violation of law without justification, to which a penalty is attached.

Act or omission

We see then that crime can be not only an overt act, such as murder, robbery, or assault; but that failing to act can also constitute a crime. For example, failure to file an income tax return, refusal to assist a police officer upon demand, or failure to stop after a traffic accident and identify oneself and render aid to the injured are all omissions that constitute crimes.

Intent, or *mens rea*

The legal definition of crime also states that this act or omission is committed intentionally. Intent, or *mens rea*, must be present for an act or omission to constitute a crime.

Mens rea, or *guilty mind, means that the individual engaged in willful wrongdoing and that he intended the wrong to occur. To demonstrate* mens rea *it must be proven that the person intended to behave in a manner which violated the law.*[1]

No crime without law

Notice that in the legal definition of crime the acts or omissions must be in violation of the law. In other words, no actions, omissions, or deeds are illegal unless there is a written law proscribing (forbidding) such acts as being in violation of law.

Often many citizens become enraged when the police fail to arrest an individual for various kinds of behavior, even though the police explain that the individual is not violating the law, and they have no grounds to make an arrest. No citizen can be arrested unless he has violated a specified law. We must also realize that no agency within the criminal justice system can take action unless given specific authority to do so by the law.

Without justification

What acts or omissions in violation of law are justifiable? "The courts have ruled that there are certain justifications for violating the law and extenuating circumstances. Examples of these justifications which have been used for defense are ignorance of the law, insanity, mistaken facts, drunkenness, duress, entrapment, and consent of the victim."[2] Although ignorance of the law, mistaken facts, drunkenness, entrapment, and consent of the victim are sometimes used as excuses for violating the law, they are by no means acceptable defenses in all cases.

No crime without punishment

In addition to the maxim, "no crime without law," we see that there is no crime or criminal act without punishment. The definition of crime states that these acts or omissions against the law must have a penalty. Many professionals believe that we must have laws with punishments to coerce most people to respect the law and to follow the rules and regulations of society; that punishment acts to control or compel people to act in a given fashion so not to infringe upon the rights of others. An example of this coercion might be applied to our driving habits. We are compelled to observe traffic laws not only because it is safer for us to do so, but also because if we fail to comply we might receive a traffic ticket.

The need for laws, regulations, regulators

Whether human beings live in a primitive setting or in a highly complex society, they are interdependent and must cooperate for their mutual

[1]Harold Vetter and Clifford Simonsen, *Criminal Justice in America, The System, The Process, The People* (Philadelphia, Pa.: W. B. Saunders, 1976), p. 29.

[2]Sue Titus Reid, *Crime and Criminology* (New York, Holt, Rinehart & Winston, 1976).

benefit and survival. They must engage in a variety of social, economic, political, and occupational relationships. This interaction must be covered by rules of conduct. Studies of primitive tribes, both ancient and contemporary, have shown that even in the absence of written rules, the conduct of the individual member is regulated for the welfare of the group. Anarchy, or the total absence of rules, cannot be tolerated if the group is to maintain its stability and that of subsequent generations.

Each society, therefore, is engaged in the process known as social control, by which society or the group prescribes (directs) or proscribes (forbids) certain behavior on the part of its members to insure the success and survival of the group with a minimum of friction. Broom and Selznick comment:

The individual gains much from his involvement in social organization, but he always pays a price. That price is the acceptance of restraints, of limitations on the freedom to do as he pleases. [3]

Berger and Berger explain:

Social order is maintained by enforced compliance with the social norms and rules that are thought to insure the effective operation of the particular society. . . . There are a variety of devices of social control, varying from physical force to mild psychological pressure, that are supposed to protect and enforce these norms and rules. [4]

Although the rules of required behavior have developed from cultural customs through the system of common law, the United States relies upon various written laws created by cities, counties, states, and the federal government. These written laws spell out the obligations placed upon our citizens as well as specify which conduct is unacceptable.

The law, however, is not a dead collection of rules; it is a living instrument. New laws are passed based upon new and changing needs, other laws are amended or repealed, and decisions from higher courts constantly refine the law. Although new laws are often placed on the books with relative ease as an answer to a given problem, we have experienced difficulties and reluctance on the part of lawmakers to modify or eliminate existing laws in response to our changing society. The term institutional lag is the label used to describe this delay in governmental response.

This highly refined system of law is administered by our criminal justice personnel, the three main components of which are police, courts, and corrections. Without professional personnel assigned to the system, the law would have little value.

When the law is broken or peace is threatened, we rely on police agencies to take appropriate action to maintain social order. In order to maintain social order they must adhere to prescribed ethical conduct for

[3]Leonard Broom and Philip Selznick, *Sociology* (New York: Harper & Row, 1968), p. 20.

[4]Peter L. Berger and Brigitte Berger, *Sociology: A Biographical Approach* (New York: Basic Books, 1972), p. 277.

the profession and guard the constitutional rights and privileges guaranteed to all persons, even if they are in violation of societal norms.

A growing field, which is also concerned with providing protection, is that of private and industrial security. A primary reason for the growth in this field stems from the inability of police and other governmental agencies to adequately provide protection for private property and commercial businesses.

Law enforcement duties include investigation and arrest, but adjudication must always and without exception be the province of the courtroom presided over by a judge. The judge should carefully rule on the law and insure that justice is rendered to both society and the defendant, a challenge that is placing increasingly high demands on the judiciary.

Correctional officials face a particularly difficult challenge. They are responsible not only for the security of their institutions, but for the rehabilitation of the convicted offenders, who must be returned to society with the expectation that they will not again commit criminal acts.

The quality of justice depends strongly on the quality of the personnel administering the system of justice. The people who have dedicated themselves to such a career are devoting their energies on a full-time basis to what is the responsibility of all of us. Given this great responsibility, American society must attract and train and retain and support the best men and women in the criminal justice system.

Classifications of crimes

Crimes are classified according to the seriousness of the offense. Generally, the more serious the offense the greater the penalty. The classification of crime is broken into two main categories known as felonies and misdemeanors. (In some states, infractions are considered crimes.) A felony is a serious crime for which a defendant can be imprisoned in a state (or federal) prison. A felony may be punishable by death, in which case it is referred to as a capital offense. A misdemeanor is any other crime, which may result in imprisonment in the county or city jail. A few states, such as Michigan, are exceptions to this rule in that a few serious misdemeanors may result in a short term in the state prison.

Crimes can be violations of local, city, or county ordinances, the state penal code, or, in the case of federal offenses, violations of the United States Penal Code. Some criminal acts may violate state as well as federal laws. For example, the robbery of a bank or theft of merchandise in an interstate shipment can be prosecuted either under the state law where the offense occurred or by the federal government. In such cases local police and the Federal Bureau of Investigation have what is called overlapping jurisdiction.

Although legal definitions of crime are specific, sociological definitions are much broader and encompass any act harmful to society. This includes many problems not traditionally viewed as criminal. Those who subscribe to the broad sociological definitions of crime charge that air pollution, water pollution, the failure to educate, or the denial of equal opportunities in housing and employment are, in fact, so harmful that they can be included in the category of crime. It is difficult to deny that the severe smog in some of our cities is, indeed, more harmful and dangerous to the lives of millions of Americans than is, for example, a simple assault.

We have transferred some harmful activities from the category of "sociological crime" into the category covered by the legal definition. For example, many cities have begun to provide criminal penalties for industrial pollution. However, enforcement and punishment have often failed to act as a significant deterrent. For example, one oil company that was cited for unlawful air pollution for the fifth time in one year received a fine of $250!

Arguments can be made that those situations and conditions truly harmful to human life should receive greater attention from the agencies of criminal justice. However, law enforcement agencies tend to focus their enforcement capabilities toward visible crime, crimes that directly affect the public and which are more readily identifiable by police agencies as law violations. These visible crimes are reported yearly in the Uniform Crime Reports. Not only do law enforcement agencies direct most of their resources toward combating visible crimes, but the courts also spend the majority of their time prosecuting individuals who are alleged to have committed these visible crimes.

White-collar crime

Since most of the components of the criminal justice system are engaged in combating visible crime, a large majority of crimes go undetected that do not fit into this category of law violations. These crimes are often referred to as white-collar crimes.

White-collar crime may be defined as those offenses committed by persons acting in their occupational roles. The offenders in this case are middle- and upper-class businessmen and members of the professions who have, in the course of their everyday occupational activities, violated the basic trust placed in them or acted in an unethical manner. In many cases these people are the ideal members of the community: physicians, accountants, and lawyers dedicated to their work, but overcome by the conflict because to survive in our competitive society they must adhere to the dictates and values of the organization.[5]

Although most agencies of the criminal justice system recognize the seriousness of white-collar crime it continues to exist, perhaps because of

[5]Bruce Cohen, *Crime in America* (Itasca, Ill.: F. E. Peacock, 1977), p. 367.

the inability of law enforcement agencies to detect these crimes. According to Edwin Sutherland, the problem is compounded further because:

1. The criminal courts are very lenient toward persons accused of white-collar crimes.
2. No effective method of dealing with offending corporations under criminal law has yet been devised.
3. Efforts to make criminal law more effective in cases involving corporations have been blocked by business interests.
4. Action in the civil courts and regulations by boards and commissioners are widely relied upon to protect society against white-collar crimes.[6]

Generally speaking, white-collar crime can be divided into seven basic categories:

1. Fraud
2. Misrepresentation
3. Restraint of trade
4. Rebates
5. Violation of trust
6. Misrepresentation by silence
7. Bribery

Fraud may be described as any action involving deception, such as filing a misleading financial statement which might be used to encourage stockholders to buy stock in a company with an unstable financial background. In November 1977 one of America's largest investment corporations was charged with fraud, prosecuted, and fined for encouraging stockholders to buy stock in such a company.

Misrepresentation, another form of deception, may be used to advance sales of particular products. Consumers may be led to buy a product based solely on the merits of what is promised in the advertisements of such a commodity. Misrepresentation is charged if such allegations as promised are unfounded.

Restraint of trade violations imply the responsibility of federal agents to make sure that large corporations do not violate federal trade regulations. Another form of white-collar crime involves the process of *rebates*. Rebates are usually given in the form of cash to a company, a kickback for buying products from a producer.

Many financial institutions, law firms, and banks are given a great deal of responsibility in handling trust accounts and arranging monetary exchanges. Any falsification of records involving these transactions could *violate a basic trust*.

[6]Edwin H. Sutherland, "Crime and Business," the Annals of the American Academy of Political and Social Science, Vol. 217, September 1941.

Just as there may be a case of overt misrepresentation, there may also be misrepresentation by silence. If a shipment of cattle is diseased and the seller says nothing, this is just as serious as claiming that the cattle are perfectly healthy.

Bribery, in the case of white-collar crime, may include the payment to public officials and others in order to rescind a zoning policy dealing with urban boundaries. It may also involve payment in order to secure permission to use substandard building materials in construction projects.[7]

The President's Commission on Law Enforcement and the Administration of Justice, *Task Force Report; Crime and Its Impact* (1967) estimated that each working day employees made off with a little over $8 million worth of their employer's cash or merchandise. This loss of $8 million represents a total annual loss of over $2 billion. It is interesting to note however that in 1965 the FBI Crime Index reported that $815 million was lost in the commission of crimes against persons. Losses in the form of crimes against property in that same year amounted to approximately $3,932,000. As an example of the contrast between white-collar crime and the Index crimes as reported by the FBI, it has been estimated that one chain store lost nearly $100,000 a year due to burglaries and robberies, and at the same time lost more than $600,000 due to embezzlement. It is virtually impossible to assess the amount of loss in dollars attributable to white-collar crime. But in May 1978 the Associated Press reported a loss of $44 billion a year. The total loss in dollars of white-collar crime is significantly higher than the annual loss due to either property crimes or crimes against persons as noted in the Index of Crimes as reported by the FBI annually.

Victimless crime

Another category of crime, known as victimless crime, has caused considerable debate among law enforcement agencies and the community. Victimless crimes are those acts or forms of conduct currently prohibited by law, in which no one suffers injury. Such acts included in this category are prostitution, abortion, noncommercial gambling, homosexuality, and other forms of private sexual behavior.

Debates concerning victimless crime revolve around several issues. One issue is whether the law should regulate moral behavior. Other controversies focus on the inconsistent enforcement of these laws by law enforcement agencies. Further problems are related to the methods used to arrest and prosecute persons who engage in these acts. In addition to these concerns, many professionals question the wisdom of pursuing the prosecution of these crimes when our courts are already tremendously backlogged.

[7]Bruce Cohen, *Crime in America*, p. 36.

Historically, the law in the United States has regulated certain kinds of moral conduct. In 1918 a federal law was passed prohibiting the sale of alcohol, in an attempt to regulate the use of alcohol by the American people. Although the statute remained on the books for many years it was continually abused until 1933 when the Prohibition Act was finally repealed.

Today a similar moral question has been raised over the use of marijuana. Many states are currently questioning the validity of severe punishments for those individuals possessing small amounts of marijuana for their own use. The state of Alaska, perhaps the most permissive in its law regarding the use of marijuana, has reexamined this issue. Currently, residents of Alaska are permitted to grow, manufacture, or possess any amount of marijuana in their own home for their own use. Other states (e.g., Oregon) have reduced the penalty for possession of less than one ounce of marijuana to an infraction: the fine for this infraction to be not more than $100. Marijuana, like alcohol, has created another phenomenon—a lack of respect for the law.

When the law attempts to regulate moral behavior, it is useful only if it is consistent with reinforcing the norms of society. As we learned, trying to prohibit the consumption of alcohol was not totally consistent with the mores of all the people. And the law was repeatedly disregarded by many during Prohibition. Many times law enforcement agencies failed to arrest local bootleggers, and the people themselves did not regard the bootlegger as a criminal. The result was that when the law was applied unequally and inconsistently, it created a further disregard for the law.

Inconsistent enforcement of the law has been a continuing controversy regarding the crimes of homosexuality and prostitution. Sodomy is considered a crime in many states, but enforcement of the law is primarily directed at homosexuals, although sodomy is an act in which many heterosexual couples engage. This results in unequal enforcement of the law. Prostitution is also illegal except in Nevada. Although prostitution involves two individuals, rarely is the second party arrested or convicted. Most law enforcement agencies and the courts arrest and prosecute only the female participant in the act of prostitution.

Further controversy involving victimless crimes revolves around the techniques used by police to enforce these laws. Each individual in the United States is constitutionally guaranteed the right of privacy. In order to detect crimes between consenting individuals (generally committed in private), police must use legally questionable techniques to arrest individuals violating these laws. Such methods might include entrapment, illegal wire-tapping, and electrical devices used to videotape or to view private interchanges.

The attempt to suppress vice leads to corruption and demoralization of the police force. Bribery is not uncommon, especially among gamblers and others connected with organized crime who can afford to pay for police protection. On occasion the police may become corrupt by joining in the illegal activities. Or they become frustrated in attempts to catch violators and thereby begin to chisel at procedural rights. Further, by placing police in charge of enforcing laws regulating victimless crimes they are diverted from more serious violations of the law. [8]

Aside from the difficulties of legally enforcing these particular crimes, we must also weigh the merits of enforcing these laws and adding to the burden of our already overcrowded courts. In 1973 it was estimated that in the state of New York it took from 14 to 16 months to try a defendant after arrest! By continuing to arrest individuals participating in these victimless crimes, this burden will not diminish.

Overview of the crime problem nationwide

In 1927 an attempt was made to standardize crime reporting techniques used by law enforcement agencies throughout the United States. The International Association of Chiefs of Police were the first group to propose criteria for the uniform collection of crime statistics. This function was later taken over by the Federal Bureau of Investigation in 1930. Each year since, the FBI has annually published crime statistics in the publication known as the *Uniform Crime Reports.*

These statistics are gathered voluntarily from law enforcement agencies throughout the United States. In 1976 these statistics accounted for

Table 2-1
Arrests for drug abuse violations, 1977. FBI chart.

	Total	Heroin or cocaine	Marijuana	Synthetic narcotics	Other
		(Percent distribution)			
Northeastern States	100.0	18.3	72.5	3.8	5.4
Sale/manufacture	20.1	6.5	10.9	1.2	1.5
Possession	79.9	11.8	61.6	2.6	3.9
North Central States	100.0	8.2	71.7	3.4	16.7
Sale/manufacture	22.0	3.2	11.1	1.1	6.6
Possession	78.0	5.0	60.6	2.3	10.1
Southern States	100.0	6.2	80.9	3.8	9.1
Sale/manufacture	18.2	2.0	11.1	1.4	3.7
Possession	81.8	4.2	69.8	2.4	5.4
Western States	100.0	22.4	57.6	.7	19.3
Sale/manufacture	14.6	5.4	6.5	.2	2.5
Possession	85.4	17.0	51.1	.5	16.8
Total	100.0	13.2	71.2	2.8	12.8
Sale/manufacture	18.2	4.0	9.7	.9	3.6
Possession	81.8	9.2	61.5	1.9	9.2

Source: (Tables 2-1 to 2-11; Figures 2-1 to 2-4, 2-7) *Crime in the United States, 1977, Uniform Crime Reports* (Washington, D.C.: U.S. Government Printing Office, 1978).

[8] Reid, *Crime and Criminology*, p. 45.

approximately 98 percent of the total national population. Approximately 99 percent of the population living in metropolitan areas, 96 percent of the population in other cities, and 92 percent of the rural population were included in the 1977 crime statistics.

In an effort to measure the extent of crime in the United States seven types of offenses, known as the index crimes, have been selected:

1. Murder and nonnegligent manslaughter
2. Forcible rape
3. Robbery
4. Aggravated assault
5. Burglary
6. Larceny
7. Auto theft

Figure 2–1 shows that these seven index crimes have increased 25 percent between 1973 and 1977.

Breaking the offenses down into violent categories (murder, forcible rape, robbery, and aggravated assault) versus crimes against property (burglary, larceny, and auto theft), we note that crimes of violence have increased 2 percent collectively while property crimes have decreased 4 percent in the 1976 to 1977 time period.

Expressed in numbers, there were 10,935,800 Index Crimes reported in 1977, which represents an decrease of 3 percent over reported crimes in 1976.

It must be recognized, however, that the majority of the reported crimes are crimes against property (91 percent) compared with crimes of violence (9 percent).

Table 2–2 shows not only crime increases and decreases but also crime rates. To understand the difference, let us first examine the Crime Index. The Crime Index is simply the number of reported index crimes from the seven categories per 100,000 population. If we can imagine a city with

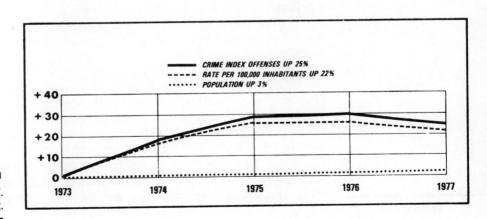

Figure 2-1

Crime Index total, 1977. FBI chart.

exactly a 100,000 population that has 10 reported index crimes occurring in a given period, then the Crime Index in that city for that period will be 10. This means that the risk of becoming a victim of one of the index crimes is 10 per 100,000 people.

It is this risk factor expressed in Table 2–2 by the expression, "rate" (sometimes also referred to as crime rate). In other words, the crime increase lists only the rise in crime, although the crime rate takes into account any change in population.

The Crime Index for the United States (the number of index crimes per 100,000 population) was 5,055.1 in 1977, a −3.3 percent decrease from the previous year.

Note that under the heading, Estimated Crime in 1977 in Table 2–2, we find not only the total number (10,935,800) but also the Crime Index for the United States (5,055.1). Numerically, this represents a decrease from 1976 of 3.3 percent but, taking the population into consideration, a −.4 percent decrease in the crime rate is indicated. The table also shows the breakdown of crime into violent crimes and property crimes. Note that, rounded off to the nearest whole figure, there have been increases and decreases in the incidence of crime from 1976 to 1977 as follows: murder, up 1.8 percent; rape, up 11.1 percent; robbery, declined 3.7 percent; aggravated assault, up 6.4 percent; burglary, down 1.2 percent; larceny, down 5.8 percent; and auto theft, up 1.1 percent.

Table 2–3 explains the crime picture by region by listing the Crime Index (described in the table as rate per 100,000 inhabitants). The Western states have the highest Crime Index with 6,574.7 and the Southern states the lowest with a 4,618.1 Crime Index. Similar comparisons can be made from this chart in the violent and property categories as well as for each of the index crimes.

Table 2-4 gives breakdowns of crimes similar to these categories listed in the regional table except that the information provided here is based on area analysis (metropolitan areas, rural areas, and cities and towns outside the metropolitan areas). The Crime Index is a very high 5,813.6 in the metropolitan areas, lower in other cities with 4,198.0, and the lowest in rural areas with a 2,012.5 Crime Index.

Figure 2–2 may be of particular interest to those who are students of the urban problems of decaying cities and the flight to the suburbs and surrounding rural areas.

Although crime in the large cities still remains a major problem, trends in the arrest rate by their area appears to be shifting. Crime in the cities with over a 250,000 population through the 1973–1977 period seems to have remained fairly static. However, both the suburban and rural areas are showing an increase in the arrest rate, and there has been a significant upward trend since 1973.

One may speculate that crime control and prevention efforts in the large cities have become increasing factors of deterrence for the criminal. Adding to this changing picture may be that much wealth is moving to the

Table 2-2

National crime, rate, and percent change, 1977. FBI chart.

Crime Index offenses	Estimated crime 1977		Percent change over 1976		Percent change over 1973		Percent change over 1968	
	Number	Rate per 100,000 inhabitants	Number	Rate per 100,000 inhabitants	Number	Rate per 100,000 inhabitants	Number	Rate per 100,000 inhabitants
Total	10,935,800	5,055.1	−3.3	−4.0	+25.4	+21.7	+62.7	+50.0
Violent	1,009,500	466.6	+2.3	+1.5	+15.3	+11.8	+69.7	+56.4
Property	9,926,300	4,588.4	−3.8	−4.5	+26.6	+22.8	+62.1	+49.4
Murder	19,120	8.8	+1.8	------	−2.6	−6.4	+38.6	+27.5
Forcible rape	63,020	29.1	+11.1	+10.2	+22.6	+18.8	+99.0	+83.0
Robbery	404,850	187.1	−3.7	−4.4	+5.4	+2.2	+54.0	+42.0
Aggravated assault	522,510	241.5	+6.4	+5.6	+24.2	+20.4	+82.2	+67.9
Burglary	3,052,200	1,410.9	−1.2	−2.0	+19.0	+15.4	+64.2	+51.3
Larceny-theft	5,905,700	2,729.9	−5.8	−6.6	+35.8	+31.8	+69.6	+56.3
Motor vehicle theft	968,400	447.6	+1.1	+.3	+4.3	+1.1	+23.6	+13.9

suburbs, that the suburbanites have not yet learned through experience to be security conscious, and that growing freeway networks also assist the criminal in his travels.

Figure 2–3, referred to as the FBI Crime Clock, lists the frequency of occurrence of various crimes. The Crime Clock is a popular teaching tool in many police academy training programs. Its weakness is that it does not reflect any changes in population.

Police departments clear crimes when they arrest and charge the offender; when the offender is identified, but some circumstances beyond

Table 2-3

Crime rate by region, 1977. FBI chart.

Crime index offenses	(Rate per 100,000 inhabitants)			
	Northeastern States	North Central States	Southern States	Western States
Total	4,957.1	4,635.6	4,618.1	6,574.7
Violent	510.3	373.5	451.8	575.8
Property	4,446.9	4,262.1	4,166.3	5,996.9
Murder	6.9	7.2	11.3	9.3
Forcible rape	22.7	24.7	29.4	43.2
Robbery	261.2	162.7	140.3	213.7
Aggravated assault	219.5	178.8	270.8	309.7
Burglary	1,403.6	1,153.7	1,336.1	1,932.7
Larceny-theft	2,417.0	2,707.7	2,524.7	3,520.8
Motor vehicle theft	626.3	400.7	305.6	545.4

Table 2-4

Crime rate by area, 1977.
FBI chart.

Crime index offenses	(Rate per 100,000 inhabitants)			
	Total United States	Metropolitan areas	Rural	Other cities
Total	5,055.1	5,813.6	2,012.5	4,198.0
Violent	466.6	558.9	172.7	267.4
Property	4,588.4	5,254.7	1,839.8	3,930.6
Murder	8.8	9.7	7.8	5.0
Forcible rape	29.1	34.6	14.1	14.2
Robbery	187.1	243.7	20.9	47.9
Aggravated assault	241.5	271.0	130.0	200.2
Burglary	1,410.9	1,609.3	767.2	997.0
Larceny-theft	2,7829.9	3,092.9	954.4	2,718.3
Motor vehicle theft	447.6	552.5	118.1	215.4

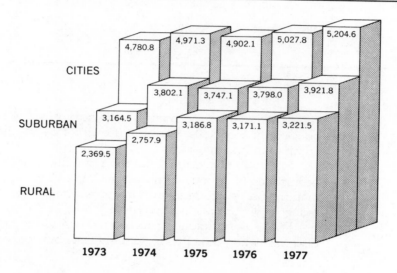

Figure 2-2

Arrest rate by area,
1973-1977. FBI chart.

police control prevent prosecution; or when the police establish the fact that the reported crime did, in fact, not occur ("unfounded").

American law enforcement cleared 21 percent of the reported index crimes. Figure 2–4 illustrates the various degrees of success in clearing (solving by arrest) the index offenses. It is of interest to note that police have a much greater success rate in clearing crimes against the person than in clearing crimes against property. This may be because police are able to devote greater time and manpower to crimes of violence, and also that such offenses are witnessed more frequently by others than are thefts and other property offenses.

Of the people arrested in 1976 for Crime Index offenses, 83 percent were prosecuted, and of those, 66 percent were convicted of the original charge and 7 percent were convicted of a lesser charge. See Figures 2–5 and 2–6.

Tables 2–5 to 2–11 outline some of the distinguishing features of the

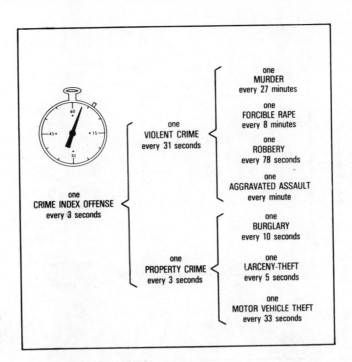

Figure 2-3

Crime clock, 1977. FBI chart.

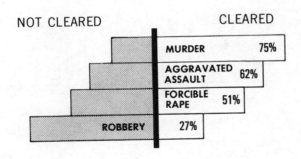

Figure 2-4

Crimes cleared by arrest, 1977. FBI chart.

Figure 2-5

Serious crimes in the
United States and
percentage of suspects
imprisoned for these
crimes. Source: Adapted
from National
Commission on the
Causes and Prevention of
Violence, *Final Report*
(Washington, D.C.: U.S.
Government Printing
Office, December 1969),
p. xviii.

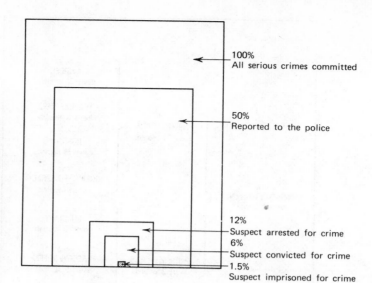

100%
All serious crimes committed

50%
Reported to the police

12%
Suspect arrested for crime

6%
Suspect convicted for crime

1.5%
Suspect imprisoned for crime

Figure 2-6

Percentage of persons
arrested on felony
charges who are
convicted and sent to jail
or prison.

Jurisdiction	Percentage of arrestees convicted	Percentage of convicted felons sent to jail or prison
Washington, D.C.	33	18
Chicago	26	15
Baltimore	44	28
Detroit	58	20
Los Angeles County	46	28
San Diego County	34	14
Average	40	20

Source: J. Eisenstein and H. Jacob, *Felony Justice: An Organizational Analysis of Criminal Courts* (Little, Brown, 1977).

Table 2-5

Murder and nonnegligent
manslaughter

Most frequent month	December
Most frequent weapon	Firearm
Most frequent victim:	
Age group	20-24
Sex	Male
Most frequent offender:	
Age group	18-22
Sex	Male

Table 2-6
Aggravated assault

Most frequent month	July
Most frequent weapon	Blunt objects and hands, fists, feet
Most frequent offender:	
Age group	18-22
Sex	Male

Table 2-7
Forcible rape

Most frequent month	August
Most frequent offender:	
Age group	18-22

Table 2-8
Robbery

Most frequent month	December
Most frequent weapon	Firearm
Most frequent offender:	
Age group	16-20
Sex	Male

Table 2-9
Burglary

Most frequent month	August
Most frequent offender:	
Age group	15-19
Sex	Male

Table 2-10
Motor vehicle theft

Most frequent month	August
Most frequent offender:	
Age group	15-19
Sex	Male

Table 2-11
Larceny-theft

Most frequent month	August
Most frequent offender:	
Age group	15-19
Sex	Male

seven offenses included in the Crime Index. The summer months appear t be the most frequent time when these crimes occur with the exception c murder and nonnegligent manslaughter and robbery. The age bracket c the most frequent offender also points out that crimes against propert (burglary, motor vehicle theft, and larceny) are being committed by younger offender than those crimes against persons.

Figure 2–7 identifies the ages of individuals arrested for Index Crime in the United States, and makes a comparison between those arrested in certain age bracket with their age distribution representative of their totc in the national population. We see that the most arrests are of persons i the age grouping of 15 to 30.

This is indicative of the trend of the last decade—that the age of th offender is dropping.

Interpreting statistics with caution

The analyses that we have presented in this section are based on the *Crime in the United States, 1977: FBI Uniform Crime Reports*, published b the U.S. Department of Justice. Although the data have great value i

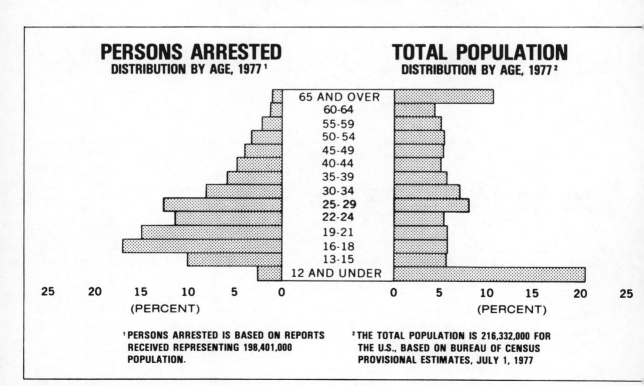

Figure 2-7   Persons arrested; distribution by age, 1977. FBI chart.

understanding America's crime problem, they should nevertheless be seen in perspective.

First, not all crime is reported to the police and is, therefore, not counted in the FBI statistics. Second, police departments are not required to report their crime statistics to the FBI. Even the law enforcement agencies that do submit the proper forms to the FBI may be reporting less than accurately.

Incidents can be classified by police in a variety of ways. For example, when a police department has to approach its city council for an increased budget, it may be tempted to count certain incidents in categories more likely to make the city council sympathetic to the needs of police. Furthermore, whether the police have a suspect in custody or not may influence the way they classify an offense. For example, a purse snatch may be classified as a theft or as a robbery depending upon the degree of force used by the perpetrator. If no suspect is known, some officers will classify the incident as a theft while, if a suspect is known or in custody, they may classify the crime as a robbery, thereby clearing a more serious crime.

Crime increase or decrease must also be viewed with care. A decrease in crime statistically may simply mean that the citizens have a lowered confidence level in police and simply do not report crimes. On the other hand, a rising crime rate may be a sign of increased quality in community relations, the arrival of a new chief of police, or other factors that suddenly bring the public to report more crimes as a manifestation of a new-found faith and trust in law enforcement.

We must also caution against seeing the FBI statistics as reflecting all types of crime. Press releases often refer to the seven Index Crimes as "serious crime," but it must be recognized that although some of those crimes are indeed serious (murder, rape, and others), included in the Index Crimes are the offenses of larceny over $50 and auto theft, and excluded are arson, the sale of heroin, and other acts that are dangerous or have greater potential harm than, for example, the theft of an automobile.

Former Attorney General Ramsey Clark maintains that "crime has many faces," and speaks of:

White-collar crime (which) converts billions of dollars annually in tax evasion, price fixing, embezzlement, swindling, and consumer fraud. Organized crime reaps hundreds of millions in gambling, loansharking, drug traffic, extortion, and prostitution, corrupting officials and resorting to force, including murder when necessary, to accomplish its purposes. . . . Corruption in public office—bribes, payoffs, fixes, conflicts of interest—occurs in every branch of government, legislative, executive, judicial, administrative, and at every level, federal, state, and local. [9]

Ramsey Clark's message is clear: There is much serious crime that never finds its way into the FBI's Crime Index.

[9]Ramsey Clark, *Crime in America* (New York: Simon and Schuster, 1970), pp. 35, 36.

Crime factors

Crime is a social problem and the concern of the entire community. The law enforcement effort is limited to factors within its control.

Uniform Crime Reports gives a nationwide view of crime based on police statistics contributed by local law enforcement agencies. The factors which cause crime are many and vary from place to place throughout the country. Some of the conditions which affect the volume and type of crime that occurs from place to place are briefly outlined as follows:

Density and size of the community population and the metropolitan area of which it is a part.

Composition of the population with reference particularly to age, sex, and race.

Economic status and mores of the population.

Stability of population, including commuters, seasonal, and other transient types.

Climate, including seasonal weather conditions.

Educational, recreational, and religious characteristics.

Effective strength of the police force.

Standards of appointments to the local police force.

Policies of the prosecuting officials.

Attitudes and policies of the courts and corrections.

Relationships and attitudes of law enforcement and the community.

Administrative and investigative efficiency of law enforcement, including degree of adherence of crime reporting standards.

Organization and cooperation of adjoining and overlapping police jurisdictions.

Source: Clarence M. Kelley, *Crime in the United States, 1976, Uniform Crime Reports*, (Washington, D.C.: U.S. Government Printing Office, 1976).

The study of crime and crime trends can be approached in a variety of ways depending on the information desired. Some criminologists have made in-depth studies of variables in crime, such as age, sex, race, ecological factors, and seasonal variations.

Crime is complex. Just as the reasons for crime are complex, so are the solutions. Let us beware of those who have simplistic explanations. Let us be wary of those whose vocabulary regarding offenders is limited to "laziness," "no character," and "anyone can make it." Let us also be wary of those who see as solutions simply more police, more armamentarium,

50-year prison sentences for everyone, and bigger and better jails and prisons.

Let us listen to those in our society who see the need for improving the quality of life by improving education, housing, clothing, food, and medical care—the necessities of life.

Victimology

In the past, society has paid a great deal of attention to the defendant in the criminal justice process, but it has only been recently that the victim has received any assistance from the federal government and the communities themselves. We saw in Chapter 1 that the defendant is guaranteed certain rights in the justice system; however, the victim at times is guaranteed no privileges and no immunities, in a court of law where the defendant in such time may claim these privileges. The victim of the crime may suffer a great monetary loss. This loss may come in the form of money lost due to hospitalization, loss of value of property taken, loss of earnings, and any other related costs. New York, Hawaii, Maryland, Massachusetts, New Jersey, Illinois, Wisconsin, and California are some states that have recently instituted compensation programs for victims of crimes. These programs are set up in order to compensate the victim for criminal injury due to a bodily injury or death suffered as the consequence of a criminal act.

The payment to victims varies from state to state implementing this program (see Table 2-12). The victim's receipt of monetary compensation will also vary according to the amount of injury. Rhode Island, Hawaii, and Alaska require no specified loss before the victim can file a claim. Other states have specified amounts before a victim can file for compensation.

Although monetary payment to the innocent victim of a criminal act may be a panacea, it leaves many unresolved questions. For instance, if an individual is a victim of an aggravated assault, and as the result of his injury misses four weeks of work and incurs large hospital bills which are paid by his insurance, should the defendant pay for the hospital bill in addition to the victim's estimated loss of earnings? Another problem might arise if a person falls victim to an assailant and is critically injured, but the assailant is never identified or arrested. Is the victim in this case entitled to compensation? If the victim of criminal acts dies, will his family receive payment? If so, will the payment be for wrongful death, or for a period covering the victim's estimated net earning power?

Questions like this continue to arise with victim compensation programs. We must find a solution to these problems so that this program is equitable to all parties involved. Monetary payment to an innocent victim of a criminal act might be an incentive for citizens to become involved in

Table 2-12
Victim compensation analysis by state.

Provisions	Alaska	Calif.	Del.	Hawaii	Ill.	Ky.	La.	Md.
Administration	Department of Health & Social Services	State Board of Control	Violent Crimes Compensation Board	Department of Social Services	Court of Claims	Crime Victims Compensation Board	Department of Employment Security	Department of Public Safety and Correction Institutions
Financial means test	Yes	Yes	No	No	No	Yes	Yes	Yes
Minimum loss	No	$100 or 20% of net monthly income	$25	No	$200	$100 or 2 continuous weeks salary	$100 or 2 continuous weeks salary	$100 or 2 continuou weeks salary
Maximum award	$25,000	$10,000	$10,000	$10,000	$10,000	$15,000	$50,000	$45,000
Restitution programs	No	Perpetrator fined commensurate with offense	Additional 10% fine paid to special fund	No	No	Criminal reimburses fund	Courts levy fine against criminal— paid to special fund	Additiona $5 levied c all fines fo criminal offenses
List of crimes covered	Yes	No	Yes	Yes	Yes	No	Yes	No
Residency requirements	None	Must be a resident of state	Must be a resident of state	Crime must occur within the state	Crime must occur within the state	Must be a resident of state	Crime must occur within the state	Crime mu occur within the state
Limitations on applications	Apply within two years— Report crime within five days	Apply within one year	Apply within one year	Apply within 18 months	Report as soon as possible— $200 deducted— must cooperate	Apply within 90 days— Report within 48 hours— Cooperate	Apply within one year— Report within 72 hours— Cooperate	Apply witl 180 days— Report within 48 hours— Cooperate
Attorney's fees	Paid out of award	Not to exceed 10% of award or $500	Not to exceed $1000 or 15% of award— paid in addition to award	Not to exceed 15% of award— paid out of award	Paid on appeal only and determined by court	Set by board	Set by board	Set by board— paid in addition to award
Requirements of law enforcement	Hospitals and police officials must inform possible claimants	Hospitals and police officials must inform possible claimants	No	No	No	Police must inform possible claimants	No	No

Source: *North Dakota Law Review* SB: 7-49 1976.

Mass.	Minn.	N.J.	N.Y.	N.D.	R.I.	Tenn.	Wash.	Wisc.
Court System	Department of Public Safety	Department of Law and Public Safety	Crime Victims Compensation Board	Workmen's Compensation Bureau	Workmen's Compensation Bureau (Special Court)	Circuit Courts	Department of Labor and Industry	Department of Industry, Labor and Human Relations
No	No	No	Yes	No	No	Yes	No	Yes
$100 or 2 continuous weeks salary	$100	$100 or 2 continuous weeks salary	$100 or 2 continuous weeks salary	$100	No	$100 or 2 continuous weeks salary		$200
$10,000	$10,000	$10,000	$15,000	$25,000	$25,000	$15,000	System comparable to Workmen's Compensation laws	$10,000
No	Criminal reimburses victim	No	No	No	No	$20 additional fine on all crimes plus 20% of all fines levied	Perpetrator owes debt to fund	No
No	No	Yes	No	No	Yes	No	Yes	Yes
Crime must occur within the state	Crime must occur within the state	None	Crime must occur within the state	Crime must occur within the state	Crime must occur within the state	Crime must occur within the state	Must be a resident of state	Crime must occur within the state
Apply within one year—90 days for death—Report within 48 hours—$5 fee for applying	Apply within one year—Report within 5 days—Cooperate	Apply within one year—Report within 3 months	Apply within 90 days—Report within 48 hours	Apply within one year—Report within 72 hours—Cooperate	Apply within 2 years	Apply within one year—Report within 48 hours—$5 fee	Apply within 180 days of injury—120 days of death—Report within 72 hours	Apply within 2 years—Report within 5 days
Set by court—not to exceed 15% of award—Paid out of award	Set by board	$40 per hour—paid in addition to award	Set by board—paid out of award	Set by board—paid in addition of award	Paid from fund by order of special court	Not to exceed 15% of award—paid in addition to award	No provision within Act	Not to exceed 20% of award—paid out of award
No	Police must inform victims of right to apply	No	No	No	No	No	No	Law Enforcement Agencies must supply forms

the criminal justice system. By becoming involved, citizens may be the necessary catalyst in reducing our ever-present crime problem.

Summary

In this chapter we have seen that crimes can be viewed in a strictly legal sense or in a broader, sociological view. In a complex society such as ours, we must have laws ("social contracts"), enforced by police, subject to adjudication by the courts, and sanctions against the offenders by the correctional system.

In analyzing our crime problem we looked at the impact of white-collar crime and the enforcement of victimless crimes. This chapter has discussed crime statistics, particularly statistics issued by the FBI, and their values as well as their shortcomings.

New programs involving compensation to innocent victims of crimes were also discussed. Finally, it was suggested that America's crime problem is too complicated to be solved by more police, more severe sentences, and bigger and better jails. We must look to the causes of crimes, to the basic quality of life, in order to understand the behavior of our fellow citizens.

TOPICS FOR DISCUSSION

1. How is disrespect for the law created?

2. What can be said about the reliability of the Uniform Crime Statistics?

3. Define the legal concept of crime.

4. Critically examine our effectiveness in dealing with white-collar crime and its cost to society.

5. What are the current trends in crime throughout the United States?

6. Justify and criticize victim compensation programs. Analyze some of the inherent weakness in this concept.

3

Explanations of criminal behavior

The study of this chapter will enable you to:

1. **Explain the administrative and legislative theories of crime causation.**
2. **Understand the biophysical theory of crime causation.**
3. **Define the theory of socioeconomic determinism as an explanation of criminal behavior.**
4. **Understand the contemporary theories of crime causation.**
5. **Realize that the study of criminal behavior is presently an ongoing problem with no definite solutions.**

Since the early 1800s we have consistently sought the causes of criminal behavior. As yet we have failed to sufficiently understand the process by which any one individual becomes a criminal—why?

All societies, however backward, have considered specific forms of human conduct undesirable. Some actions are more severely forbidden than others, but the acts most frowned upon are those identified as "criminal." People caught engaging in criminal acts are treated with public contempt, they may be temporarily or permanently removed from the rest of society, and they are generally punished for their transgression. The punishers have been mobs, priests, kings, public executioners or prosecutors, and the like, depending upon the structure of the society, but there has been no society that has not devised some method of attempting to force its members to observe its taboos.

In modern times, people have sought to understand what causes a person to violate the laws of his society. The assumption seems to be that people should want to observe the law as a matter of course, and if they do not, there must be a reason—something has gone wrong. However, to this day, no general cause of crime has been found, although the search has been based on many different attitudes. Much information has been gathered in recent years on crimes and criminals, but the cause of criminal behavior has eluded us.

In the pages that follow you will read about some of the major theories of the causes of crime. Your familiarity with these ideas will prevent you from being misled into the belief that there is some simple solution to the "crime problem."

Historically, crime has been attributed to environmental conditions, such as slums, poverty, poor family life; to some defect, such as mental illness, physical disability, or biochemical deficiency in the person who commits the crime; to the interpersonal influences of bad companions, gang activities, or unhappy school experiences; or finally, to social structural factors, such as inability to get good jobs, alienation from the norms of the society, prejudice, and other social forces that prevent a person from obtaining his goals through legitimate means.

Curiously, several basic approaches to the explanation of crime have developed or evolved parallel to each other. There has not been any clear evolutionary development of a single theory of crime similar to the way theory has developed in other fields. In physics or biology, for example, there is often a breakthrough in research that confirms some basic propositions of a major theory out of which new research and knowledge grow. Unfortunately, in the field of criminology, we are unable to point to similar achievements.

Crime is as old as man himself, so attempts to explain it go back to the time when man first began to recognize the transgressions of his brother. Modern explanations of crime are generally traced to the mid-eighteenth century when the first efforts at a scientific explanation were attempted. But many of them can be traced back farther to a few central ideas that are centuries old. These same ideas resurface sometimes with a new element that captures the imagination of the public and creates the notion that a new theory of crime is born. The purpose of this chapter is to describe some of the more prominent theories that have cropped up during the last century or so, and to organize them in such a way that you will be able to see their common threads.

Administrative and legislative theories

One of the oldest explanations for crime finds the reason in the law itself. Without criminal law there would be no crime, and obviously no criminals. Crime is therefore a matter of social definition as manifested in the criminal statutes of that society. This theory emphasizes the process by which certain behavior comes to be labeled criminal rather than what causes crime. Let us begin with the position expounded by one of the best known of the classical criminologists—Cesare Bonesana, Marchese de Beccaria (1738–94)—an Italian social philosopher whose influence extends into the twentieth century.[1]

Beccaria and his British contemporary, Jeremy Bentham (1748–1832), were disturbed that the jurists of their day were permitted both to define which behavior was "criminal" and to assign whatever penalty they felt appropriate. Beccaria felt that this was often done in a capricious and unjust manner, without the benefit of legislative control. He believed that the people of the society rather than an individual jurist should define what was criminal, and that legislatures, representative of the people, should be the source of criminal law and its penalties, not the judges.

The major reforms proposed by Beccaria and Bentham concentrated

[1]Cesare Beccaria, *On Crimes and Punishment*, English trans. (Indianapolis: Bobbs-Merrill, 1963).

on what would constitute an appropriate penalty system. It is only at this point that we gain some insight into how they explained crime. The penalty system they proposed was built upon a hedonistic principle that assumes that people weigh alternative behaviors in terms of the relative pleasure or pain they will produce. If the pain outweighs the anticipated pleasure, a person will be afraid to perform the act. They further believed that the most effective deterrent to criminal conduct was swift and sure punishment with penalties severe enough to outweigh any possible gain from the act. These penalties would be written into the criminal law so that they would be known in advance and could be taken into consideration when a criminal act was contemplated, Beccaria and Bentham believed that the amount of crime a society experiences is determined by the effectiveness of its social control mechanisms—such as the threat of pain—in deterring crime.

Emile Durkheim (1858–1917), a French sociologist, said that crime can be found in every society and suggested that it might be necessary for the well-being of society. A society without crime would be inconceivable and undesirable, according to Durkheim, since there would always be a minority of people who would try to innovate, thus testing the limits of society's moral conscience in an effort to change the rules. In his view, most crimes were committed by people residing on the moral fringe of a society.

Not only did Durkheim consider crime a normal condition in a healthy society, but also that crimes were relative in nature. What might be criminal in one society might not be in another; what was criminal was a matter of where a particular society decided to draw the line. Criminal behavior was not in itself sick or unnatural, he said. Criminals were really innovators who were ahead of their time in a sense. They were labeled criminals for behavior that the next generation might very well accept as legal or normal behavior.

An American sociologist of this century, Thorsten Sellin, agreed with Durkheim that crime is a relative thing; but Sellin went further to point out that much crime is a result of cultural conflict within a society caused by a minority's attempt to impose universal rules of behavior on all members of society.[2] Crimes increase when there is doubt in many minds that the behavior forbidden by the criminal law is really criminal. American society—made up of many cultures and ethnic groups—is especially susceptible to culture conflict and, therefore, can expect a higher crime rate than other societies.

The contemporary theory closest to the views of these men is offered by Richard Quinney.[3] He maintains that crime is primarily a matter of social belief as expressed in the criminal code, so without criminal law

[2]Thorsten Sellin, *Culture Conflict and Crime* (New York: Social Science Research Council, 1938).

[3]Richard Quinney, *The Social Reality of Crime* (Boston: Little, Brown, 1970).

there would be no crime. Quinney sees crime as a reflection of the moral and social concerns of the people who make the laws of a society or those people who have substantial influence over legislators or the legislative process. The kinds of behavior that come to be defined as crime and the emphasis of enforcement are heavily weighted against the politically powerless. Conduct engaged in by influential people, which may be more socially costly or threatening, escapes similar treatment in the criminal code. This occurs because they (the politically powerful) control the process that both defines and enforces the criminal code. They are able to get legal restraints effectively applied against those whose crimes arouse their indignation; they can prevent their own misconduct from being labeled criminal; or, failing this, they can effectively defend themselves against the application of criminal charges.

Perhaps the best documentation of Quinney's position came about 30 years ago in research conducted by Edwin Sutherland on white-collar crime.[4] Sutherland made the point that many crimes were committed by persons of respectability and high social status in the course of their occupations. He contended that such crimes are widespread, but that an index of their frequency is not found in police reports. He maintained that prosecution for this kind of crime frequently was avoided because of (1) the political or financial power of the parties concerned, (2) the apparent triviality of the crimes, or (3) the difficulty of securing evidence sufficient for prosecution, particularly in the case of crimes by corporations.[5]

In summary, these theorists have maintained that crime is a normal product of the conflict between the definers of crime and those whose conduct is defined as crime. Crime is not caused by any personality or biological defects, nor is it the product of overpowering social forces working upon an individual, forcing him to embark upon a criminal career. Crime is inevitable so long as there are strong differences of opinion among segments of a society about human conduct and acceptable means for reaching one's goals. These theorists believe that the volume of crime in any given society is proportionate to the amount of effort put forth by those in control of the society to deter or suppress it.

Biophysical theories

In direct contrast to the theories just described, other opinions hold that man is not a self-determining creature who is able to choose between alternatives, but rather that he is a being whose behavior is determined or "caused" by certain biological or physiological conditions. This position was first put forth as a scientific approach by Cesare Lombroso in the last

[4]Edwin Sutherland, *White-Collar Crime* (New York: Dryden Press, 1949).
[5]Edwin Sutherland, "White-Collar Criminality," *Am. Soc. Rev.*, 5 (February 1940).

half of the nineteenth century.[6] He maintained that there were three major classes of criminals: born criminals, insane criminals, and criminaloids. He considered born criminals to be throwbacks to a lower, more primitive evolutionary form of man, and believed that about one-third of all offenders were born criminals. According to Lombroso, insane criminals included such persons as idiots, imbeciles, or psychiatric cases; criminaloids were a large catchall class of those not having any of the physical characteristics of the born criminal, but whose mental or emotional makeup caused them, under certain circumstances, to indulge in vicious and criminal behavior.

Lombroso's theory was later proved incorrect, but he is generally recognized as the first person to attempt a purely scientific explanation of crime. He consistently emphasized the need for a direct study of the individual criminal, using precise measurements and statistical methods. His major contribution to the study of crime may well have been his persistent emphasis on a scientific approach to the subject.

Interest in the biological or genetic approach to crime did not die with Lombroso. Several other outstanding attempts have been made to find a biological basis for criminal behavior. In America, perhaps the most noted studies have been those by Ernest Hooton, William Sheldon, and Eleanor Glueck.

In 1939, Ernest Hooton stirred a great deal of controversy with the publication of *Crime and the Man*, in which he argued on behalf of his belief in physical determinism.[7] Hooton had made 107 anthropometric measurements (anthropometry is the science of measuring the human body and its parts) of 14,477 convicts and compared these measurements with a control group consisting of 3203 noncriminals. He concluded that the criminals appeared to be distinctly physically inferior to the noncriminals. In addition, he stated that there was a relationship between specific types of body build and particular offenses, such as murder, assault, robbery, and sex offenses.

Other scientists, like William Sheldon and the Gluecks, have reached different conclusions. Unlike Hooton, they have maintained that delinquents are actually physically superior to the normal population, if superiority is defined as the athletic type of body build—muscular, tightly knit, and physically solid. William Sheldon developed an elaborate scheme by which he classified individuals according to body build and temperament.[8] His research on 16 delinquent youths identified among the 200 residents of the Hayden Goodwill Inn in South Boston (a private treatment institution) indicated that they were, without exception, boys with an

[6]Cesare Lombroso, *Crime, Its Causes and Remedies* (Boston: Little, Brown, 1911).

[7]Ernest A. Hooton, *The American Criminal: An Anthropological Study* (Cambridge: Harvard University Press, 1939).

[8]William H. Sheldon, *Varieties of Delinquent Youth: An Introduction to Constitutional Psychiatry* (New York: Harper & Bros., 1949).

endomorphic-mesomorph body build; that is, a body build generally associated with the stereotype of an athlete.

Using Sheldon's classification of body types, the Gluecks reported: (1) the boys who were mesomorph (muscular) in constitution were found to be members of delinquent groups in much higher proportion than in nondelinquent groups; (2) delinquent groups have a much smaller proportion of ectomorphs (lean, thin body build); and (3) ectomorphs and endomorphs (round, plump body build) and balanced types are decidedly subordinate among the delinquents.[9]

The work of H. J. Eysenck probably represents the most recent theory based on biological factors.[10] He has developed a complex theory of the biological basis for personality, one portion of which attempts to explain criminal behavior. He maintains that criminals are people with unstable, extroverted personalities. Instability is seen as a biological condition in which a person is highly sensitive to stimuli around him and is, therefore, very emotional in nature. Extroverts show a strong tendency to cortical fatigue, a condition that retards the development of the inhibitions that usually control behavior. The criminal is a person who has unusual difficulty in learning from his experiences, so he continues to behave in ways that others disapprove of, in spite of the penalties that he receives as a consequence of his behavior.

Eysenck probably offers the best general biological theory currently under study today, but there is considerable research being carried out that examines the possible link between specific physiological or genetic factors and specific types of crimes. It now seems clear that such things as blood-sugar level, imbalances in body hormones secreted by the ductless glands, brain tumors, and the like are closely associated with highly aggressive violent behavior.

The much-publicized XYY chromosome and its relationship to crime is another example of a genetic factor currently being investigated as a possible explanation of crime. Studies concerning chromosomal deviation have been based on the finding that there are males, and only males, who have an extra male chromosome, called the Y gonosome; that is, they display an XYY combination rather than the usual XY. Although it is true that there have been varied and conflicting results from the various studies looking into this deviation, there are some suggestive conclusions that seem consistent throughout. Among criminals, it has been found that the chance of possessing an extra Y gonosome is up to 60 times greater than for the general population. On the whole, the XYY physique is taller and thinner than members of control groups. There is a tendency toward a higher frequency of aggressive and disturbed behavior. Higher rates of violent crime are found among men with an extra Y gonosome, and they begin their criminal activity at a relatively early age. Although it is clear

[9]Sheldon and Eleanor Glueck, *Physique and Delinquency* (New York: Harper & Bros., 1956).

[10]H. J. Eysenck, *Crime and Personality* (New York: Houghton Mifflin, 1964).

that a greater proportion of criminals than noncriminals exhibit the XYY syndrome, the link between this syndrome and criminal behavior is not yet clearly demonstrated nor understood.[11]

Socioeconomic determinism

At the beginning of the twentieth century, the emphasis shifted toward blaming all major social problems on the economic system of society. This theory, often referred to as economic determinism, cites the economic inequalities within society as a major cause of crime. William Bonger, a Dutch criminologist, strongly supported this view.[12] He maintained that the capitalistic economic system was particularly effective in creating crime because it placed such an extraordinary emphasis upon the acquisition of wealth.

There does seem to be one clear relationship between economic concerns and crime: the more value a society places upon property, the more criminal laws it develops to protect that property. The number of laws in the United States that deal with property far outnumber the laws that deal with crimes against the person. It is also true that crimes committed against property are more than 10 times greater in number than the crimes of murder, assault, and rape. The great volume of crimes committed involving property or money would seem to support the contention that much crime in America has an economic base.

The economic determinists have had difficulty in demonstrating exactly how economic variables influence crime. Studies of the statistical relationship between crime rates and business cycles have indicated that crimes against property tend to increase during times of prosperity rather than depression, as one might predict. If crime is indeed a product of economic need, it should be most frequent when economic conditions are at their worst.

The fact that official crime statistics show that disproportionately large numbers of the poor are found guilty of crime has been offered as evidence that poverty causes crime. However, critics of the economic determinists contend that the statistics indicate only that the crimes of the poor are more socially visible than the crimes of middle-class and upper-class people (white-collar crimes), and that the poor are less able to defend themselves against criminal prosecution as successfully as those with more money and education.

Some theorists have suggested that prosperity that is unequally shared aggravates the feelings of economic deprivation among the poor by increasing the social distance between the "haves" and the "have-

[11]M. Amir and Y. Berman, "Chromosomal Deviation and Crime," *Federal Probation* (September 1969).

[12]William Bonger, *Criminality and Economic Conditions* (Boston: Little, Brown, 1916).

Myth and reality

One of those "sociological myths" that doesn't seem to want to go away is that poverty causes crime—and that we won't reduce crime unless we first reduce poverty.

To the simplistic, the theory seems valid. Most people in prison are from a background of poverty—ergo, poverty must be the main cause of crime. Right? Wrong.

Because if that theory were literally true, crime would be decreasing in this country—instead of increasing, since poverty has been going down for 40 years or more. Unfortunately, for the theory's sake, as well as for the country's sake, exactly the opposite phenomenon has taken place.

The greatest decline in poverty has directly coincided with the greatest rise in crime in this nation's modern history!

The figures tell the story:

	Percent living below poverty line	Violent crime rate	Property crime rate
1950	27	167	1745
1975	12	434	3910
Percent Change	−55%	+160%	+124%

In short, in the period when poverty in this country declined by 55 percent, violent crime rose by 160 percent and property crime rose by 124 percent.

Thus, the argument that poverty causes crime is a statistical fraud.

Source: Warren T. Brookes, "The Myth That Poverty Causes Crime," *Boston Herald American*, 1976.

nots." Robert Merton, in a discussion of the sources of crime, noted that motivation for most crime can be traced to the frustration felt by members of society who have been taught to want social prestige and economic affluence, but who have been deprived of a legitimate means of attaining these goals. The criminal social structure provides an alternative "ladder to success" for people who have been denied full participation in the legitimate economic and social system of the society. Crime is committed as a means of satisfying a desire for those material things that are held out for all to see—rich and poor alike—since substantial differences exist in the economic means available to acquire them. Crime is seen as a response to overstimulation of economic needs rather than to actual poverty or economic destitution.

Donald Taft agrees with Merton and argues that the American emphasis upon competition and materialism has been the major source of criminal motivation in the society.[13] The inconsistency between what is promised and what can be achieved legitimately by "have-nots" creates feelings of economic discrimination that encourage economically deprived people to use criminal means to obtain the things they want and are unable to obtain through legitimate means.

In the 1950s a new direction was taken in the attempt to relate economic variables to crime. The emphasis turned away from pure economic need to the *social* implications of being poor in an affluent society. Since delinquency was thought to be most prevalent in poverty-stricken neighborhoods, some theorists tried to explain the relationship between poverty and delinquency. Albert Cohen contended that delinquency was the lower-class boy's path to success since he could not compete in the school system, where the rewards were closely tied to middle-class standards of performance. The lower-class boy suffered from what Cohen called "status frustration."[14]

Cohen maintained that being unable to succeed in the schools forced the lower-class boys to seek recognition on the street. Lower-class boys, he thought, grouped together in defense against their rejection in school, and street gangs emerged that had a subculture (sometimes called a contraculture) that was built upon rejection of the major values of the middle-class system. Since the middle class valued neatness, property, education, and postponement of immediate gratification in favor of long-term goals, the lower-class boy adopted a value system that was pleasure-oriented, "now"-oriented, and malicious and destructive in nature. Boys turned to delinquency as a means to social success rather than to economic success, but they did so as a result of the socioeconomic conditions related to being lower class.

Cohen's writings stimulated much research and discussion regarding the relationship between social class and crime or delinquency. Some alternative ideas have since been advanced in response to Cohen's explanation. Walter B. Miller, an anthropologist, agreed with Cohen that the lower-class boy who finds himself unable to cope with the middle-class bias in the public schools ultimately drops out of school. However, Miller does not think that this is what leads to delinquency. He believes that the lower class has developed certain responses to poverty, which he calls "focal concerns," which eventually lead the lower-class child into conflict with the legal authorities. He views delinquency as the product of well-established cultural traditions of lower-class life, rather than the result of a conflict with middle-class values.

Richard Cloward and Lloyd Ohlin agree with Merton on those socioeconomic factors among the poor that contribute to delinquency.

[13]Donald Taft, *Criminology*, 3rd ed. (New York: Macmillan, 1956).

[14]Albert K. Cohen, *Delinquent Boys: The Culture of the Gang* (Glencoe, Ill.: Free Press, 1955).

Return to basics needed

In my opinion one of the causes for the growing crime rate has been the decline of one of the basic tenets that this country was founded on—individual responsibility. Our forefathers believed that a person was responsible for his or her own actions. If a person did wrong, that individual should pay the price.

In recent years some sociologists and other social scientists have held that individuals are not responsible for their actions. Instead, individuals are supposedly products of their environment, the society, or various other forces. The result has been the decline of individual responsibility and at the same time a rise in crime.

Attempts to ignore facts of life have not negated those facts. They have not gone away. Human beings are responsible for their actions. A return to this basic view will help in deterring and punishing criminals.

Source: Congressman John Ashbrook, "Return to Basics Needed to Fight Crime," *Human Events*, September 20, 1975.

Whereas Cohen emphasized the issue of alienation of the lower-class boy from the middle-class oriented school system, Cloward and Ohlin feel that his legitimate avenues to success are blocked and that he must accept illegitimate alternatives. They see the delinquent boy using crime as an alternate route to success; he finds many opportunities for gain through criminal activity in his neighborhood. They note, however, that the opportunities for gainful criminal behavior are also unequally distributed in society. There are lower-class neighborhoods too poor to make robbery worthwhile; therefore, gainful criminal opportunity is limited. Here a different kind of response is found—a conflict response. Violence and alienation are characteristic of this response, but unlike gainful criminal activity, it seldom leads to social success. It merely illustrates that the boy is striking out at a society that he holds responsible for his frustration.[15]

Crime as learned behavior

An approach held at the beginning of the twentieth century was that criminal behavior is learned, often from others engaged in similar escapades. Gabriel Tarde, a French jurist and social psychologist, said that criminal behavior is learned from others through "imitation or suggestion"

[15]Richard Cloward and Lloyd Ohlin, *Delinquency and Opportunity* (Glencoe, Ill.: Free Press, 1961).

just as one learns to play a sport or an apprentice learns a skill.[16] Tarde saw street gangs as the training ground for most delinquency, since it was on the street that boys shared with each other the specific details about crime.

Although Tarde's ideas were not accepted by many people at the time, his basic idea was restated in a more sophisticated form by Edwin Sutherland in what later came to be known as the theory of differential association. In a classic work on professional theft, Sutherland developed the idea that crime and criminal values are transmitted from one person to another. His book, *The Professional Thief*, describes young thieves learning both techniques and justifications for theft from professional thieves.[17] Criminal behavior occurs, he said, when the person believes that there are more reasons for violating the law than observing it. According to this theory, criminal behavior is socially acquired by contact with others who are disposed to crime, and this influence is most evident in delinquent gangs.

Frederic Thrasher, in his study of more than a thousand gangs in Chicago, concluded that street gangs make chronic truants and delinquents out of street boys and mold them into finished criminals. It is through the gang that a young prospective criminal makes his first contact with older professionals, such as "fences" who buy stolen property. Also, the intense loyalty generated within the gang membership encourages the delinquent's participation in the gang's criminal enterprises and provides him with moral support when he gets into trouble with the law.[18]

Environmental influences

Criminality has been traced by some theorists to social environmental conditions, such as slums, overcrowding, lack of recreational facilities, or family and community disorganization. A group of sociologists at the University of Chicago conducted numerous studies from the 1920s through the 1940s, which examined the relationship between man's social environment and the incidence of broad social problems, such as divorce, unemployment, suicide, and crime. Their research indicated a correlation between crime rates and the distance one lived from the central city. They noted that cities evolved over time and, in this process of evolution, the central city deteriorated and became a socially and physically unhealthy place to live. Statistical studies based upon court and police data showed that crime rates were highest in the slum areas of the city and steadily declined as one moved out to the commuter zone or suburbs.

[16]Gabriel Tarde, *Penal Philosophy*, trans. Rapelje Howell (Boston: Little, Brown, 1912).

[17]Edwin Sutherland. *The Professional Thief* (Chicago: University of Chicago Press, 1937).

[18]Frederick M. Thrasher, *The Gang* (Chicago: University of Chicago Press, 1927).

Who's Killing Whom?

Dr. Donald Lunde, who teaches psychiatry and law, told 400 persons at the National Homicide Symposium that studies should be conducted to identify persons most likely to murder so that potentially homicidal persons can be identified and helped.

In his studies, Lunde has found that males have been three times as likely to kill or be killed as females, that black males have nine times the risk of white males, and that black females have five times the risk of white females.

Persons have been most likely to be murder victims or murderers at the ages of 15 through 30, and more Southerners have resorted to murder than residents of New England, he said.

"In the South Atlantic states, for whites and blacks, there have been 13.4 murders per 100,000 persons," Lunde said. "But in the New England states, the rate is 3.6 murders per 100,000—the lowest of any area. This represents different cultural attitudes about the use of force."

Lunde also said persons who have owned guns represent high risks, as well as persons who have made previous threats to kill someone.

Source: *Capital Journal*, Salem, Oregon, October 27, 1977.

These Chicago sociologists maintained that all major social problems, including crime and delinquency, were closely associated with the ecology of one's residence. Clifford Shaw and Henry McKay sought to identify the specific conditions characteristic of the high-crime areas. They were able to show that high-crime-rate neighborhoods were deteriorated, transient, dirty, and crowded. But they were not able to clearly show how or why these conditions produced crime or why many people who grew up under these slum conditions did not resort to crime, and why others who grew up in good neighborhoods did resort to crime.

Walter Reckless and Simon Dinitz thought there might be some kind of internal personality factor that "insulated" some slum children against delinquency in spite of their exposure to delinquency-generating environmental conditions.[19] They wanted to explain why some children, and not others, succumbed to delinquency and crime in the slum neighborhood. Their research on the self-concept (the kind of person one believes himself to be) of both delinquent and nondelinquent boys indicated that children with good self-concepts were much less likely to get involved with the police or court than children whose perceptions of themselves were

---

[19]Walter C. Reckless, Simon Dinitz, and Barbara Kay, "The Self Component in Potential Delinquency and Potential Nondelinquency." *American Soc. Rev.*, 22 (October 1957).

poor. Amos suggested that the poor self-concept of a delinquent may develop from his lack of a father image.[20] The delinquent may have rejected his father as a model for his image or he may have been reared in a fatherless home. In either case, the lack of a family masculine image with which to identify could cause him, according to Amos, to rely on the delinquent group for a masculine image. The development of a positive (good) self-concept appeared to be closely linked to strong, two-parent family relationships characterized by warmth, cohesiveness, and positive rewards for conformity.

In a similar vein, other theorists point to the widespread family disorganization among slum residents as the real cause of their high crime and delinquency rates. These theorists point to volumes of statistical data that show that the majority of persistent offenders come from homes that are broken, either in reality or psychologically, as evidence that the family is the real source of criminal behavior. Everything from discipline to type of toilet training used by families has been examined in an effort to isolate the specific characteristics of family life that are responsible for crime.

The most recent theory using environmental factors tries to relate crime to a combination of external environmental factors and internal personal factors. Its central idea is that crime occurs when there is a breakdown in the controls on behavior. Containment theory, as proposed by Walter Reckless, is based on the assumption that there exists in man an outer and an inner control system or "buffers."[21] Outer containment consists of the "holding" power or capability of society, groups, organizations, and communities to keep persons within the desired norms of society. Inner containment is defined by Reckless as the ability on the part of the individual to respect and follow the norms of society. The main force behind inner containment is a favorable self-image or concept that results from successful socialization, primarily within the family. He also recognizes three other components of inner containment: goal orientation, frustration tolerance, and retention of norms and standards.

Reckless believes that if an individual possessing a high degree of inner containment finds himself in highly containing groups or organizations, the likelihood of his becoming involved in delinquency or crime is almost nonexistent. However, the chances of criminal and delinquent involvement are maximized when both inner and outer containment are either absent or weak. They are not able to effectively operate as "buffers" against deviancy and thus restrain the person from crime.

The major difficulty confronting those who take the environmental approach is tracing crime to any identifiable set of environment factors. Although it seems true that crime is most prevalent where social environmental conditions are poorest, how these conditions cause human beings to commit crime is still not clearly understood.

[20]W. E. Amos, "A Study of Self-Concept: Delinquent Boy's Accuracy in Selected Self-Evaluation," *Genetic Psychology Monographs* 67 (1967).

[21]Walter C. Reckless, *The Crime Problem* (New York: Appleton-Century-Crofts, 1967).

Psychoanalysis and crime

There have been many theories suggested to explain crime in terms of its relationship to the individual's psychological makeup. Specifically, they hold that early childhood experiences leave an indelible imprint upon the child's unconscious mind which, in turn, affects later behavior. The criminal is seen as an individual who is mentally ill, driven by unconscious motivation over which he has little or no control.

Psychoanalytic theory, conceived by Sigmund Freud (1856–1939), assumes that all human behavior is motivated and, hence, goal-oriented in character. However, neither the motives nor the purposes of any given act can be understood by observing the overt act itself. Behavior can be understood only in terms of the subjective meanings and significances that the person himself attaches to his action.

Freud believed that the structure of the personality consisted of three basic components: id, ego, and superego. The id represents the pleasure principle and is primarily aimed at avoiding pain and obtaining pleasure. The id is the basic source of motivation for human behavior. The superego is the internal representative of the traditional values and ideas of society as interpreted to the child by his parents: it functions as the conscience of the person. It is the moral arm of the personality, representing the ideal rather than the real, and it strives for perfection rather than for pleasure. The ego is said to obey the reality principle, and its chief function is mediating between the id and superego.

Freud had little to say concerning crime, but some of those who adhere to his psychoanalytical principles have written at great length about crime and its cause. Psychoanalytic theories of crime tend to fall into three major categories or groups. The first group sees criminality as a form of neurosis. A neurotic individual may be characterized as suffering from guilt and anxiety brought about because of the overactivity of the superego with its relentless demand for perfection. Generally, it is believed that the criminal neurotic suffers from a compulsive need for punishment to alleviate his unconscious guilt, so he commits crime in order to gain this punishment.

The second group describes the criminal as an antisocial person who has either a poorly developed superego or no superego at all. He is unable to cope properly with the restrictions of his society. He also lacks adequate internal controls, thus allowing the id to go unchecked. His sole basis for judging any act, then, is one of pleasure and pain.

The third group sees criminality as a product of faulty family relationships. Criminal activity is carried out to gratify needs that would usually be met and fulfilled within the family—such needs as security, recognition, acceptance, status, and self-esteem. Instead, the criminal directs his activity into illegal channels of delinquency and crime as a means of securing substitute satisfactions for his faulty family situation.

Abrahamsen, a noted psychoanalyst, believed that an instability of three factors leads a man to crime: criminalistic tendencies, mental resistance, and situation.[22] By criminalistic tendencies are meant the individual's subconscious desires, phobias, compulsions, and obsessions that wait for the right moment to emerge from the subconscious mind and to be acted out. He emphasizes the theory of unconscious guilt as in the neurotic, and feels that only by penetrating into the deepest layers of the human mind are we able to trace the motives that link the criminal to the past; motives of which he himself has been unaware.

Through socialization, repression, and inhibition, a person develops mental resistance that, in turn, prevents criminalistic tendencies from becoming criminal behavior. Furthermore, the more the person leans toward crime (low resistance), the weaker the precipitating events would have to be to bring it out; the less the criminal leanings, the greater the precipitating events needed to call it forth. These precipitating events Abrahamsen calls the situation. We must consider all three aspects simultaneously in order to explain crime and the individual's interaction with it.

It seems plausible that some people commit crimes because they are emotionally or psychologically unstable or defective. Occasionally, one reads in the newspapers about some bizarre killing or sex crime committed by a person who is clearly mentally deranged. However, many studies of the personalities of criminals have shown that most of them are psychologically normal. Furthermore, psychiatrists have often given conflicting diagnoses of criminals who have pled insanity as a defense against criminal culpability.

At the present time there is no generally accepted psychological explanation for crime. The vast majority of persons defined as mentally ill are not criminals, and the majority of criminals are not mentally ill. Whatever relationships may exist between crime and mental illness must involve factors other than the mental state of the criminal. Otherwise, all criminals would be mentally ill and vice versa.

The future of criminology

This brief review of a wide variety of explanations for crime may have confused you. As we said at the beginning of this chapter, no specific causes of crime have been found, although the search has been conducted from many different points of view. The study of crime and criminals goes on at a faster pace than ever before, but there is little evidence that we are any nearer to the understanding of crime than we were one hunded years ago. One possible reason for this lack of progress may be found in the kinds of assumptions that have been made by those who have proposed explanations for crime. Almost all of the theories that we have

[22]David Abrahamsen, *Crime and the Human Mind* (New York: Columbia University Press, 1969).

examined have assumed that man naturally conforms to social order. In other words, they all assume that man is basically good (noncriminal) by nature. If he commits a crime, it must be because something must have gone wrong with him. His wrongdoing has been variously blamed on his mental state, his biological condition, his social environment, or his associations with others.

Perhaps the time has come for us to challenge this assumption. What kind of theory of crime would we develop if we assumed that man was essentially *nonconforming*, and that he conformed only under certain conditions that could be personal or social in nature? The whole focus of our research would have to shift from an attempt to understand crime to an attempt to understand why there is not more crime. What keeps the majority of people from committing crime? If we knew the answer to this, we might know more about "deterrence" and "crime control"—concepts that we hear much about but so little understand.

The idea that crime is normal behavior has been suggested by a number of theorists over the years. As Merton and others have suggested, the central issue to the motivation of crime is the inability on occasion to find legitimate means to legitimate ends. They see most crime as the result of someone resorting to these illegitimate means to achieve otherwise legitimate objectives. One might assume that most of us would resort to the most efficient means available to us, legal or not, were it not for certain restraints put upon us by ourselves or others. Criminologists of the future may emphasize more research on the social-control process that keeps people within the boundaries society has set for the conduct of its members, rather than looking for causes of behavior that the law happens to define as crime.

Another assumption that has dominated criminological theory is "determinism." Determinism may be defined here as the belief that every human act and decision is the inevitable consequence of antecedents (prior events or conditions), such as traumatic (damaging) events or physical, psychological, or environmental conditions, which are independent of the human will. Until recently, most theories of crime have assumed that a particular criminal act could be explained by tracing it back to these guilty antecedents, which might be an unhappy home life, slums, alienation from school, or physical or mental defects, to name a few. Every person is a product of his antecedents; every criminal, a victim of them, forced to commit crimes by factors beyond his control. This theory held that the events or conditions that preceded the criminal act made the act itself inevitable; in the same sense that dropping a stone from a window made it inevitable the stone would fall to the ground.

Many contemporary theorists are challenging a deterministic view of human behavior. They assert that man is a determiner of his own future; that an individual knows that his action is legally considered a crime and is aware of the consequences if he is caught. He makes the choice of his own free will to take the risk involved in committing the crime to achieve his goals more effectively or efficiently than he can by legal means. This view seems to fit the world as we know it better than the complex theories that try to link criminal behavior with many complicated "causal" factors. The theory agrees that crimes may be committed on impulse, but even then they are committed with full awareness that society will punish the doer—if he is found out.

In the past, the most influential theory of criminal behavior was the "medical" model, that is, the belief that the criminal was a sick person who needed treatment in the same way as did the person with an organic illness. According to this theory, the sickness produced the criminality, and since it made no sense to punish a sick person, subscribers to this theory placed great emphasis on treatment and rehabilitation rather than on punishment. To illustrate this trend, we might point to the sharp decline in the use of punishment as a tool of social control during the past century, and the rise of counseling, therapy, and physical treatments ranging from brain surgery (lobotomies) to tranquilizers (chemotherapy).

In recent years, however, more emphasis has been placed upon considering the criminal to be a normal human being, completely responsible for his actions. Even after the conviction of a crime, a person is often allowed to continue as a free member of society, on probation. This is called reality therapy and puts the responsibility for correction on the individual himself rather than upon society. This change may indicate that we are now beginning to abandon the medical model in favor of a personal responsibility (existential) model of human behavior. This would challenge still another assumption of the past which perhaps has slowed our progress toward the control of crime.

Television as a determinant

Perhaps one of the newest theories will evolve around determining the effects of television violence. The Zamora case is a good example of this trend. The defense that had been planned for the accused youth in this case will unquestionably trigger further research on criminal behavior that may be caused by viewing repeated and suggestive acts of violence on television and movies.

On June 8, 1977, Ronald Zamora, a 15-year-old Miami youth, was arrested by Miami police after he confessed to killing his 82-year-old neighbor. The neighbor, Mrs. Elina Haggart, was shot to death by Zamora and another juvenile accomplice when she discovered the two boys burglarizing her home.

In October 1977 the Zamora case was tried before a Miami jury. During the course of the trial, Zamora's attorney, Ellis Rubin, repeatedly tried to introduce evidence that linked television violence to the cause of his client's behavior on June 4th. Zamora's parents testified that Ronald watched television six hours a day and refused to eat unless the television was on. They stated that he lived in a fantasy world of television.

Rubin attempted to prove in the trial that Ronald Zamora was "innocent because he was suffering from and acted under the influence of prolonged, intense, involuntary, subliminal television intoxication." Part of the evidence gathered in this case were studies linking television violence with aggression. Nelson Faeber Jr., one of Rubin's legal aides, said that approximately 2300 studies had been made on television violence and its effects on aggression, and they had collected a large number of those in an attempt to use them as evidence in Zamora's trial. However, trial judge Paul Baker would allow as evidence only those study results that linked specific television shows to specific acts of violence.[23] Defense Attorney Rubin conceded that there were no such specific studies. Zamora was later convicted of first degree murder.

The Zamora case is not the first in which television has been accused of having lethal influence. A month before the Zamora case was tried, a defendent accused of murder in Hartfield City, Indiana, indicated that he and his accomplice had watched "Helter Skelter" (a dramatization of the Manson murders) before killing four brothers in a trailer camp. "Helter Skelter" had been one of Zamora's favorite television shows, in addition to "Kojak," "Baretta," and "Starsky and Hutch."

Margaret Hanrratty, a psychologist in Florida, indicated that 18,000 television murders would be seen by the average youngster before he reaches the age of 18. (Hanrratty was to have testified in the Zamora case, but after Judge Baker interviewed her, he refused to allow her to testify.) Other psychologists studying the effects of television violence hace conflicting points of view. Some believe that television violence produces a vicarious release of aggression; others maintain that television teaches children that violence is a successful way to handle problems, thereby encouraging a child to act aggressively in coping with his own problems. Furthermore, as stated by the University of Minnesota's Institute of Child Development in 1970, "Television can and does transmit physically violent acts to children, but does little to convey the meaning or the consequences of such acts."

Summary

For centuries, theories have been proposed to explain a specific cause of crime, theories based on economical factors or individual defects, such as mental illness or physical disability. Society as a whole is often blamed because of prejudices that will not allow attainment of legitimate goals. The studies have provided a great deal of information, but they have not given a cause for crime.

The theories have covered many different areas. Some of them are (1) administrative and legislative, (2) biophysical, (3) socioeconomic deter-

[23]"The Zamora Case: T.V. Gets a Reprieve," *Science News*, October 15, 1977, p. 247.

minism, (4) crime as learned behavior, (5) environmental influences, and (6) psychoanalysis.

The study of crime and criminals goes on at a faster pace than ever before, but there is little evidence that we are nearer to understanding crime than before. The theories to date assume that man is a conforming creature; theories that assume a nonconformity may tell us more about crime.

Another assumption that has dominated criminology is determinism, which is now being challenged, as well as is the medical model.

We can make no definitive statements about the kind of theories of criminal behavior that will be developed in the future. There is evidence that some old assumptions are being challenged, and a new theory focused on social control is emerging. It seems probable there will be less interest in attempts to explain crime as a personal "sickness" or as a result of broad social environmental conditions. The new theories will probably resemble closely the administrative and legislative theories described in this chapter, but they will also contain significant ideas from the other theories reviewed, especially the theories dealing with the social control of legitimate means of attaining social objectives.

TOPICS FOR DISCUSSION

1. Discuss the major reforms suggested by Beccaria and Bentham.

2. Discuss the differences and similarities between the sociological viewpoint of crime and the psychoanalytic viewpoint of crime.

3. Discuss the past trends in explanations of criminal behavior and describe the implications these trends have had on the correctional field.

PART 2
The Police

4

The Police: an historical perspective

The study of this chapter will enable you to:

1. **Learn the history of police science in America.**
2. **Understand the distinctions between various levels of law enforcement.**
3. **Know the methods of selecting law enforcement administrators.**
4. **Examine some of the significant developments of police service.**
5. **Develop your awareness of the objectives of law enforcement.**

The development of a police system in the United States has evolved over a long period of time, more as the result of external pressure for change than pressure from within. Today there are more than 40,000 police agencies in the United States, the majority consisting of ten men or less. This large number of individual police departments is the result of local citizens' fears of a centralized police bureaucracy and the desire for local control. The rapid proliferation of police agencies during the early 1900s, without adequate planning and coordination, has contributed to the problems facing many departments today. Only in the last twenty-five years have realistic efforts been made to develop minimum standards and a professional approach to police work. And because the worthwhile goals that many police departments are striving for today have not been adopted by law enforcement as a whole, the enlightened minority of police must continue to press for change if true professionalization is to come.

Background of the police system

The first formal police departments began in Europe. One of the earliest police units, known as the Bow Street Runners or "Thief Takers," was formed by Henry Fielding, a London magistrate, who saw the need for such a group as early as 1725. It was not until 1750, however, that this small group of men were formed to fight crime in London. Although the Bow Street Runners had some successes, their reputation was often marred by a willingness to cooperate with criminals to collect the rewards offered by citizens for the recovery of property; a practice that led to frequent instances of corruption.

Around the beginning of the nineteenth century, largely as a result of the Industrial Revolution, many people began to move to the cities of Europe. During this period unemployment was high, housing was virtually impossible to find, and slums became a common sight. Crime began to rise. Riots and demonstrations became almost a daily occurrence. Policing was generally viewed as a community effort; citizens were required to take turns serving as watchmen. This system, known as the watch and ward, had been effective in the towns and villages but was inefficient in the cities. Merchants hired guards, and various types of private groups designed to meet specific crime situations were formed. Bands of thieves roamed the streets virtually at will, robbing the unprotected. When the people lost faith in their governments and spoke out, greater restrictions on free expression were imposed by the governments, which worsened the problem.

Despite increasing public concern, it was not until 1829 that Sir Robert Peel, the Home Secretary, after revising the criminal code to meet the needs of a reformed police service, introduced into Parliament, "An Act for Improving the Police In and Near the Metropolis." Known as The Metropolitan Police Act, this is seen by many as the beginning of modern law enforcement. The Act provided for a carefully selected police force, and was formed despite public opposition. The first 1000 policemen were selected from a list of 12,000, and during the first three years of operation there were 5000 dismissals and 6000 forced resignations; a tribute to the standards set for the fledgling department. In less than a decade the London police force had become an accepted and admired department, and Robert Peel's name was immortalized. Even today the London policemen are referred to as Bobbies, in honor of Peel.

Origins of police in the United States

The development of a police system in the United States has been similar to that of England and other European countries in many ways, although the size of the United States and its division into sovereign states have resulted in some marked regional differences. As the settlers arrived in the United States, each group brought many of the traditions of their homeland, with England having the most significant impact on American policing. The night watch, constable, and sheriff forms of policing were all English contributions to our system.

On the East Coast the night-watch system, which required male citizens over the age of sixteen to serve without pay, was the most prevalent form of policing until the early 1800s. The families migrating inland and to the South and the West generally adopted the sheriff form of policing, in which an individual was either hired or elected to perform police functions, frequently in addition to another job.

These early systems provided adequate safety for citizens: people usually knew each other personally. The common bonds existing in each community provided strong social control. Survival frequently meant depending upon one's neighbor. However, as the cities began to grow and fill with strangers, more crime problems began to develop. The night watch ultimately proved ineffective; in time people who were unable or unwilling to perform their watch were permitted to hire others to take thei place. Those who hired out as substitutes were frequently unfit for an work, much less as watchmen: inefficiency, laziness, and corruption be came more common. Where other forms of policing, such as the sheriff an constable systems, had been adopted, abuses of power became so fre quent that by the end of the nineteenth century there was growing unres in virtually every American city.

Development of police systems in the United States

The growth of American cities was accompanied by an increasing crim rate, and it was soon realized that a night watch was not only inefficien but outdated. Immigrants arrived daily in great numbers, many withou adequate funds or jobs to sustain them. The growth of slums was inevita ble and, in them, crime was rampant. In attempting to control the masse of the slums, those in power frequently passed laws designed to suppres the minorities—most of them recently arrived from Ireland, England, an other European countries—to "keep them in their place."

To cope with a growing crime rate, Philadelphia established a pai day and night watch in 1833 with a grant of money from Stephen Girarc The day watch consisted of 24 men; the night watch, 120; all under th command of a captain. Promotion within the department was based o merit: this is believed to be the first police promotion system based upo capability rather than on political favor.

Five years after Philadelphia established its force, Boston establishe a day watch that was separate from the night watch. The lack of coord nation between the day and night watches created numerous problems; was not until 1850 that they were combined.

In 1844 New York City established a police department of 800 mer headed by a chief of police. The New York department closely resemble the London department and became the model for other emerging polic agencies throughout the United States.

By the middle of the nineteenth century all of the larger cities ha established some form of paid police department. In the West, San Fran cisco founded a small police force in 1850 that grew to some 400 men b 1878. In 1851 Los Angeles formed a voluntary force of 100 men, an Chicago established a police force patterned on the New York department

Despite the growth of formal police departments in American cities counties and many towns continued to use a sheriff as the chief law en forcement officer. During these early years sheriffs were usually politician and political hacks, many of whom had little interest in law enforcemen Today most states still have elected country sheriffs, although the quality c candidates has improved greatly, and most sheriff's departments ar staffed by professional law enforcement officers. Unlike municipal departments, the sheriff is elected (in a few areas, appointed) to serve a county and is responsible to a board of governors or supervisors. In many jurisdictions, especially in rural areas, the sheriff's department is the largest law enforcement agency and may be called in to assist small towns during disorders or to aid in the investigation of a major crime. Usually, the sheriff provides basic police services to unincorporated areas of the county and to incorporated cities that contract for these services.

Critical periods of development in American policing

Perhaps the most crucial factor prohibiting the development of professional policing in the United States has been a lack of adequate concern by the people, which might have led to better planning and support. Throughout the nation's history police have played a major role, yet in most cities they are not held in high esteem, despite the lip service that is paid to professionalization. Some of the fault lies with the police service itself, which until recently has not attempted to achieve the high standards and qualifications of those professions they wish to emulate.

The early years   The concept of organized policing in the United Stated did not really take shape until the turn of the nineteenth century, when most of the larger cities in the United States saw the need for some form of organized force to handle the growing crime problems. James Richardson believes that,

. . . The children of the foreign born suspended between two cultures and often learning the ways of the city more quickly than their parents, provided the raw material for the "dangerous classes."[1]

The rapid growth of slums and high unemployment contributed to the crime problem. In Chicago the great fire of 1871 not only leveled the city, but it brought new criminals in its aftermath, thereby adding to the problems of the Chicago police. In the West law enforcement was more often than not carried out by Vigilantes, whose system of justice left much to be desired. Nathaniel Pitt Langford in *Vigilante Days and Ways: The Pioneers of the Rockies* describes the activities of Vigilantes in the West.[2] Their tracking and hanging of robbers and thieves are in sharp contrast to present standards. The law was tempered with little mercy in those days.

During the early years corruption in policing was not uncommon, and

[1]James F. Richardson, *The New York Police: Colonial Times to 1901* (New York: Oxford University Press, 1970), p. 51.

[2]Nathaniel Pitt Langford, *Vigilante Days and Ways: The Pioneers of the Rockies* (New York: AMS Press, reprint, 1973).

it ranged from paying a city official to obtain a job to the acceptance of bribes by policemen. Frequently, a new political administration meant an entirely new police department because police jobs were political appointments. As Richardson pointed out, "Many local and subsequently state political leaders looked upon the police department primarily as a source of patronage and a tool for swaying elections."[3]

In 1894 the New York State legislature formed the Lexow Commission to investigate the New York City Police Department. The Commission produced a report that highlighted many of the problems facing municipal police departments at that time. Unfortunately, its impact was relatively weak and few changes were made to improve the New York City department. During those years, gross lack of discipline, dishonesty, drunkenness, and extortion were the rule rather than the exception on city police departments, and during the latter part of the nineteenth century—frequently called the Spoils Era—American police morality was at its lowest.

By the end of the nineteenth century the spotlight of reform was on the police, and many departments began to change. Probably the most significant innovation in municipal policing was the adoption of the civil-service concept.

Civil service was designed to remove politics from policing, by requiring police appointees to pass objective tests—the theory being that a written examination would reduce favoritism and insure impartiality. Most major police departments today have adopted the civil service system, although its requirements vary from area to area. Some departments require only a written examination, while others require a combination written-oral examination. The use of psychological examinations has also become popular in recent years.

Although the civil service system did have beneficial effects on police selection, little was done to change the nature and working conditions of police during the early years, and little or no emphasis was placed upon education and training. Indeed, the best policeman was often viewed as the one who was the toughest, and brawn took precedence over brains.

The turn of the century

By 1900 the police had become a generally accepted part of the community, and departments were beginning to place greater emphasis upon selection by merit. Political influence, although still present, was lessening.

An event that had great impact on policing took place in 1919, when Congress ratified the Eighteenth Amendment (Prohibition) to curb the sale of liquor in the United States. Between 1920 and 1933 (when the Amendment was repealed), the police were burdened with the responsibility of enforcing a law that was almost universally unpopular. The police reac-

[3]Richardson, *The New York Police*, p. 54.

tion generally was to ignore violations of Prohibition or to become involved themselves in the bootlegging activities brought about by the laws. Graft and corruption were common during this period, and many believe that Prohibition served more to hurt policing than it did to help the public.

The National Commission on Law Observance and Enforcement, known as the Wickersham Commission, was charged with investigating police abuses and procedures. Its 1931 report raised serious questions about law enforcement in the United States. Unfortunately, few of the Commission's recommendations were followed in the years following the report's publication.

Curiously, the depression years (1932–40), which hurt the public, had a beneficial effect on the vocation of police work. The large number of unemployed persons created a vast pool of manpower from which police agencies could draw. Different types of individuals entered police service, some of whom were college graduates who could not find other jobs. This influx raised the general educational level of law enforcement agencies, and is viewed by many as the beginning of a new era in law enforcement.

In some measure, the beneficial changes brought about by the depression were slowed with the outbreak of World War II, which caused a manpower shortage. During the war years policing was generally stagnant, and few changes were made that improved the quality of police work. However, as the war drew to a close, and veterans began to return, many of whom had been policemen, the public once again began to focus upon the law-and-order issue. Organized crime came under greater scrutiny, and pressure was placed upon the police to control a rising crime rate.

An era of change Returning veterans of World War II brought with them many new ideas: perhaps the most significant being the need for training in police work. Prior to 1945 training was sparse and haphazard, and it generally involved an in-service approach. The Federal Bureau of Investigation provided some training for middle-management personnel, but this was limited. By 1950 all of the large police departments had begun to examine their training needs to establish more relevant training programs. The emphasis during these years was on the legal, physical, and procedural—the rulebook aspects of law enforcement. The move toward training based upon human relations was to come later. Nevertheless, it was a beginning; police departments had taken the first step toward providing a professional police service.

During this period the nation was beginning to change. A period of prosperity created new optimism; business began to boom, and each person set out to realize his own dream. But for the minorities, who inhabited the slums of our cities, swelled in numbers by a huge influx of blacks from rural areas, the American dream was hollow.

In the short period between 1950 and 1960 policing began to change once again. Law enforcement now included traffic enforcement. The foot patrolman was rapidly becoming outmoded; a new concept of policing removed patrolmen from the intimacy of the neighborhood, enclosing him in the metal and glass of a patrol car. The white middle class had begun their exodus to the suburbs, leaving the inner city to the minorities and the poor. The public's perception of the police, especially in the slums of the cities, was usually limited by seeing them only in a crisis or emergency situation or in a traffic incident. The personal aspect of police work, which was more common in the smaller towns and villages, virtually disappeared in the larger cities. And with the mass production of television, the public was introduced to a new image of law enforcement, through the eyes of the scriptwriters.

The Korean War had little noticeable impact on policing, at least from an economic standpoint. New veterans returned, many of them entering law enforcement. The military model within police work was firmly established, and selection and training were geared toward the military concept. Most police departments had begin to think about professionalization and, in California, efforts were being made to stress the importance of education in law enforcement.

By 1960 the civil-rights movement had begun to pick up strength throughout the South, and efforts were being made in the northeastern and midwestern cities to inform the populace of the discrimination against black minorities. Soon police departments became objects of racial criticism, both for harshness in their daily contacts with blacks and for their "lily-white" employment policies. The urban disorders of the 1960s brought the hostility into the open, and police departments were faced with a new challenge—riots. The initial police reaction was frequently ineffectual. The establishment of community-relations units and the addition of a few hours of riot control training did little to relieve the tensions between the police and minorities. The report of the National Advisory Commission on Civil Disorders pointed up a significant failure on the part of both the police and the community to deal with the problems of minorities.

Aware of their inadequacies in the field of race relations, the police responded by developing training programs that invited community participation, and they began placing a greater emphasis on the human-relations aspects of police work. These efforts continue today, and their overall impact still is questionable.

Since the mid-1950s the nation has faced an increasingly severe drug problem. The use of narcotics and dangerous drugs by young people has continued to grow, and this phenomenon has added greatly to the police burden. Since the beginning of the 1970s the problem has reached epidemic proportions. The police have responded by making more and more arrests of users—only infrequently do they reach the sources of distribution. The results have been disastrous for thousands of young people caught up in the criminal justice system.

The narcotics and dangerous drug problem has continued to proliferate. In recent years attempts have been made to try new approaches, by affording treatment to addicts and concentrating law enforcement efforts on the pushers and traffickers. The police once again—as they did during Prohibition—have fallen victim to a nationwide problem created by law. In some cities the results have been disastrous, fostering corruption, illegal arrests, and the misuse of police resources.

Demonstrations resulting from the protest against the Vietnam War also contributed to a growing hostility between the police and young people. The tendency of the police to meet this tide of violence with violence has strained the youthful public's trust in law enforcement.

More and more public concern resulted in the appointment of the President's Commission on Law Enforcement and the Administration of Justice in 1965. In 1967 the Commission submitted a report that called for sweeping changes in policing. Few of the recommendations have been carried out, although there are significant signs of a willingness on the part of many police administrators to adopt the recommendations.

In recent years many departments have begun to stress higher education, and a new breed of policeman is now entering the ranks. Most departments have stressed the recruiting of minorities into policing, and some gains are being made. The use of new technology in policing—especially computerized information systems and criminalistics—has also brought change, and the establishment of the Law Enforcement Assistance Administration on a national level has served as a catalyst for introducing these new educational and scientific innovations into police work. Many police departments have begun to move toward professionalization and, in doing so, they have begun to place greater emphasis upon a college education for entrance. This posture is more likely to result in the recruitment of individuals who are prepared to make more complex decisions.

From the public's standpoint, the patrolman of today has come a long way; he is better educated, better trained, and is more aware of society's problems. Despite this, policing is only now on the threshold of a new generation. In many ways the police are at the crossroads, and only the future holds the outcome.

Traditional functions of police in America

The primary functions of the police in America have traditionally been:

1. Prevention of crime.
2. Preservation of order (maintenance of peace).
3. Protection of person and property.
4. Protection of personal liberty.

Prevention of crime

To prevent crime, police engage in patrol activities (visible evidence of police readiness and availability), work with youth, educate the public, and cooperate with other criminal justice agencies. Police authorities have worked to prevent crime in these ways for many years and believe that these activities prevent crime. Research, in the form of saturation, proves that more policemen on the street will reduce some crime in a particular area that is saturated. However, some observers have suggested that even saturation tactics do not actually prevent crime but "move" it to a different area of the city—one that is not saturated with police. But each police rookie soon realizes that most crime is not visible and he will rarely ever actually "see" any crime. Crime is social behavior and criminals do not commit crime—people do. The only real crime prevention is a social climate where the group and each individual decide to respect the dignity of each other to the point that crime is despicable. Until that utopian point is reached and until scientific technology finds a better way, police will continue to patrol the streets in the hope of preventing crime,

Police have been working with youth for many years in many different ways. In recent years, a separate division of the police department or specially designated juvenile officers have been common. Usually a separate youth bureau or juvenile division is established within larger agencies that work exclusively with juveniles and youth. In spite of these ambitious programs, one out of every four male youths in the United States comes to the attention of a juvenile court before his eighteenth birthday. There is a great need for more work to be done in the area of juvenile and youth crime and delinquency.

Police agencies use various means and media to educate the public toward crime prevention. It is impossible to estimate the effectiveness of these programs, but a better informed citizenry is always positive. Some critics of police insist that police crime prevention programs tend to frighten the public, which results in people locking themselves in their homes each night. The idea that a street crowded with people is a safe street becomes inoperable when people remain locked in their homes. Police education programs that result in fewer people on the street enhance the chances of crime occurrence. However, the question arises whether police–public education programs or television sets are responsible for keeping people in their homes at night.

Police agencies cooperate with the prosecutor, the courts, and the correctional agencies in many ways. They provide the prosecution with the information concerning crimes and incidences, give testimony concerning crimes and carry out instructions from the court concerning defendants, and supply correctional agencies with much information concerning offenders.

In general, police agencies attempt to prevent crime in the ways they know best: patrol, working with youth, educating the public, and cooperating with other criminal justice agencies. Other police activities that may assist in preventing crimes include computerized systems that "predict" where and when crime will take place in some cities. Although the evidence is still not conclusive on the effectiveness of these computerized systems in preventing crime, it is becoming apparent that computers have a place in police work. More research and development are needed to place the computer in its proper function in preventing crime.

Preservation of order

Police attempt to preserve order and promote community tranquility using various methods but primarily through the use of crowd control, the handling of family and other domestic disputes, and traffic regulation and control. In general, the police are successful in accomplishing this task.

Public events with large numbers of people involved are controlled by police almost routinely with what often appears to the public to be ease. Actually, good crowd control can be accomplished only by detailed and deliberate planning. New York City police sometimes control 105,000 people entering Central Park from various entrances, seat them on the grass, observe them during a three-hour concert, and supervise their exit with no injuries at all on a hot summer evening. To the trained police observer, who is aware of the difficulties and possible serious ramifications involved in handling a crowd of that magnitude, it is truly a thing of beauty. Granted, a certain amount of consent on the part of the public is necessary to accomplish such a task, but professional police work by experienced men is the key to control. Other similar situations involving large numbers of people are handled every day by police with excellent results.

In answering noise complaints or family or other domestic disputes, the police are arbitrators and frequently settlers. These potentially volatile situations take up a large share of police time and are often very difficult to handle from a police perspective.

The area of preservation of order that is most demanding of police time and effort is the handling of traffic. Included in the handling of traffic are not only vehicles, pedestrians, and parking, but also traffic accident investigations, accident prevention, school safety programs, crossing guards, bicycle licensing and regulations, and various other traffic-related agencies and programs. Imagine the number of traffic and parking signs that must be created, designed, painted, and hung in a city like New York or Chicago.

The migration of city residents to suburbia has resulted in a particular problem. Most of the occupations take place within the cities, and each weekday hundreds of thousands of people must be moved into and out of these cities. The entrance into a city comes usually between 7:30-9:00 A.M. and the exit from 4:00-6:00 P.M. In a city like Detroit nearly 300,000 people are moved in and out five days a week. In cities like New York and Chicago, subways carry large numbers of people, and transit police are hired to police these modes of transportation.

Traffic control is perhaps the largest single and most expensive function of most police agencies. To handle the problem, most large metropolitan police departments formed traffic divisions or bureaus to work exclusively with traffic. Smaller local police units, who cannot afford a separate traffic section, include it with daily duties of all uniform police.

Many large police agencies use meter maids and traffic wardens who work only in traffic situations and earn less than does a patrolman. Several European countries have utilized traffic wardens for a number of years with apparent success. London police officials insist that female traffic wardens find much less antagonism from motorists in giving tickets for traffic violations. Some American police officials argue that only trained policemen should handle traffic because many criminals and potential criminals are apprehended during routine traffic duties. But their critics insist that general police training and patrolmen's salaries are not needed. It is probable that future traffic and its auxiliary functions will be handled by quasi-police agencies, and the personnel involved will be limited in function and will receive lower salaries. A possible future influence on this decision will be the necessary environmental control of petroleum use. Since automobiles cause a large part of the pollution in cities like Los Angeles and New York, it is possible that automobiles will be limited or banned from sections of these cities in the near future. Shortages of gasoline may also restrict individual use of automobiles. It may be centuries before the effects of the automobile on the environment are fully realized. At any rate, traffic in the form of automobiles and trucks has consumed vast amounts of police time and public money in America in the past few decades.

Protection of person and property

Many policemen see the protection of person and property as their primary function during both on-and off-duty time. Traditionally, both the public and the police have agreed that this function is their most important reason for existence. Most police feel that they accomplish this by the following activities:

1. Enforcing the law.
2. Apprehending violators.
3. Recovering stolen property.
4. Investigating crime.
5. Assisting in the prosecution and conviction of those who violate the law.

Protection of personal liberty

Police are designated as the protector of America's personal liberties, and both the public and the police feel that they serve this function. Police supposedly provide this service by instructing the citizenry as to their rights and privileges in reference to the law and by protecting the individual citizens against unwarranted interference by the state.

The new concept of functions of police in America

The new concept of police functions in America, as opposed to their traditional functions, is threefold and of a simple nature. The difficulty involved, generally speaking, is that neither the police nor the public recognize these functions. A massive training and educational program is necessary to point them out to both the police and the public. Once this has been done, police can gain levels of expertise in these areas.

These functions are:

1. Response to citizen complaints.
2. Provision of services to the community.
3. Arrest of suspected criminals.

Response to citizen complaints Police must respond to citizen complaints. According to Ahern:

. . . the policeman finds that his essential role is never to initiate investigation but to respond to complaints. He does not seek incidents out; they confront him. . . . More often than not, he must deal with people who demand that something be done but who are unwilling to resort to criminal sanctions; in other cases an arrest may be totally inappropriate. In these situations, the patrolman has to deal not with crime but with people. That is his stock-in-trade.[4]

Provision of services to the community Traditionally, police have resented being placed in a non-law-enforcement role. In spite of the evidence that indicates that "8 out of 10 calls a patrolman answers will be of a 'social service' variety,"[5] many patrolmen insist they are "cops" and not "social workers." The public call police when they are in great need of help. When a child is struck by a car, when a child is lost or runs away, when a person needs legal advice, and in many other situations where crime is not a concern, the public seek help from the police. Many parents call the police for help when their sons and daughters are found with drugs. They are not asking the police to enforce the law but to provide aid in a family problem. Most police cooperate by answering questions, providing suggestions, giving directions, and rendering a variety of services.

Arrest of suspected criminals A third primary function of the police is the apprehension of suspected criminals. This can be accomplished by the use of warrants that result from complaints and investigations, and in cases where police actually see crime occur.

[4]James F. Ahern, *Police in Trouble: Our Frightening Crisis in Law Enforcement* (New York: Hawthorne Books, 1972), pp. 167-168.

[5]Ibid., p. 168.

Police agencies in America

Crime, or the violation of law, is regarded as a local problem; this attitude has persisted for centuries. If crime is a local problem, a violation of local laws, then the enforcement of these laws must be accomplished at the local level.

Modifications of the local enforcement concept, however, became necessary when certain types of crimes began to flow across community, county, state, and even international boundaries. The result has been the creation of approximately 40,000 separate and distinct policing agencies in the United States. Private police agencies, though they exist in large numbers, are not included in the above figure. The villages, towns, cities, counties, and states all require agencies to enforce their laws. It should be stated that most of these agencies consist of 10 or fewer men, and that the size of one agency may be as high as 30,000. (See Figures 4-1 and 4-2 for additional data.)

In order to gain a clear picture of the many levels, they must be examined separately. All of these agencies are involved in the enforcement of laws that prohibit certain types of behavior which each unit has deemed socially unacceptable. The examination will point out that certain of these agencies also have certain specific purposes.

County police agencies

The counties in America, over 3000 in number, range from those that are entirely rural to those whose entire boundaries are part of a large city. It follows, then, that policing in counties will vary depending upon population density and other characteristics. However, there are certain similarities throughout nearly all county police agencies.

Figure 4-1
Percent distribution of criminal justice system direct expenditure by level of government, fiscal year 1975. *Source:* U.S. Department of Justice, Law Enforcement Assistance Administration and U.S. Bureau of the Census, *Expenditure and Employment Data for the Criminal Justice System: 1975* (Washington D.C.: U.S. Government Printing Office, 1977).

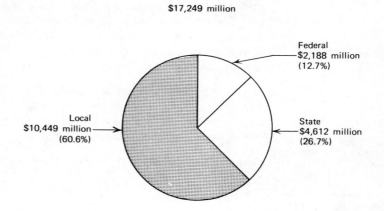

$17,249 million

Federal
$2,188 million
(12.7%)

Local
$10,449 million
(60.6%)

State
$4,612 million
(26.7%)

Figure 4-2

Percent distribution of criminal justice system full-time equivalent employment by level of government, October 1975. *Source:* U.S. Department of Justice, Law Enforcement Assistance Administration and U.S. Bureau of the Census, *Expenditure and Employment Data for the Criminal Justice System: 1975* (Washington, D.C.: U.S. Government Printing Office, 1977).

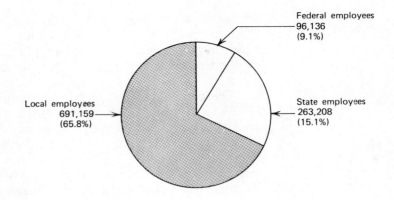

Federal employees
96,136
(9.1%)

Local employees
691,159
(65.8%)

State employees
263,208
(15.1%)

The county sheriff The county sheriff is generally recognized as the highest police officer of the county. However, the qualifications for sheriff in most counties are usually only that he be a citizen, a registered voter, over 21 years of age, and be able to win an election. Experience, education, and special knowledge of law enforcement or a related field are not formal qualifications. Fortunately, most men who hold this office in large agencies are qualified police officials, but the burden of having to run for office every few years cannot help but distract incumbents from many law enforcement duties.

The duties of the county sheriff vary greatly in different areas. In some counties he may be sheriff, coroner, tax collector, supervisor of roads and highways, process server, and play a host of other roles. In most counties the sheriff operates the county jail and, in highly populated areas, this is his major responsibility. As sheriff he also heads the county police, and he is responsible for enforcing the orders of county level courts—a major task in itself. In most cases he serves as supervisor of a staff of deputies who are usually appointed. In more and more cases these deputies may fall under civil service or merit system regulations and are required to pass qualifying examinations.

In some areas the county sheriff derives his income from many sources, usually in the form of a salary plus fees. Other county sheriffs' salaries are fixed by the county board of supervisors and cannot be adjusted during the term of office. Special fees in some counties may be gained from the service of court orders and writs, and from the stipulated amounts he receives for each meal served a prisoner in the county jail. In a few rural counties the sheriff and his family live in the same building that houses the county jail; his wife may serve as jail matron.

In all cases, the county sheriff provides law enforcement services to the unincorporated portion of the county. In the rural counties he will generally provide patrol and general police services to unincorporated territories and sometimes maintain a suboffice on a contract basis in the smaller villages that want a resident police officer. In some counties, generally in the West, an incorporated city that does not wish to establish its own police force may contract with the county sheriff for policing services. In highly populated county areas the police service that the sheriff provides may be extensive, consisting of traffic, patrol, service for juveniles, vice, narcotics, investigative, and other general police activities.

The constable The constable, like the sheriff, is usually elected and serves for a short period of time, usually one to four years. The office of constable is recognized in approximately 20 states, primarily in New England, the South, and the West. Qualifications for the position are minimal—21 years of age, a citizen, and a registered voter or on the tax rolls. The constable may be a minor law enforcement officer, pound-keeper, issuer of election notices, prisoner escort, court bailiff, and tax collector. In some jurisdictions the constable serves under the sheriff and like some sheriffs gains his salary, or part of it, from the collection of fees. In most jurisdictions he serves civil papers issued by justices of the peace.

The marshal The role of the marshal is similar to that of the sheriff on the local level, but is comparatively limited in scope. The marshal is usually an officer of the local municipal court who serves subpoenas and civil papers, warrants of arrest, and sometimes acts as bailiff in lower courts of record and as an escort for prisoners to and from court. He is elected depending on the local jurisdiction. In a few restricted local jurisdictions the marshal's office is incorporated to include the duties of the chief of police as part of his role as town marshal.

Policing the cities

The center of American policing is in the cities—about 4000 cities that employ and enjoy the highest levels of police service in the country. Policing the large metropolitan urban areas has become a highly complex task, and neither the advances of technology nor any advances in the behavioral sciences have had meaningful impact on the difficulty of this task. The vast intricacies and complexities of city life have posed a monumental challenge to urban police agencies. As families and industries migrate to the suburban areas and massive shopping centers are built, the city tax base declines—yet the demands on city police agencies increase.

The largest metropolitan police agency is the New York City Police Department. This department is made up of 305 separate commands and employs more than 37,000 people. One can only speculate on the problems of coordination and control. The annual budget for this agency is approximately $684 million, processes about six and one-half million calls for assistance, and effects nearly 250,000 arrests in the same time period.

State-level policing

Policing on the state level came about either as a result of labor disputes or through the efforts of state legislatures to cope with corruption in the cities. The first state police agency was the Texas Rangers, formed in 1833, to deal primarily with cattle rustling. In subsequent years the Rangers broadened their powers, and today they represent a small force vested with general law enforcement powers.

The two most common assignments of state police agencies are highway patrol and assistance to small local departments in the investigation of crime, usually through the formation of state identification and investigation or intelligence units. Where state police jurisdiction is limited to highways, they usually handle crimes committed on highways as well as general traffic enforcement. Where a state agency has broad police powers, it may be responsible for the policing of towns and operate somewhat like the more traditional department, although on a broader scale, as is the case in Connecticut.

The growth of state police agencies has resulted in the greater use of technology in policing. Computerized records systems and the use of helicopters on patrol are but two examples.

Investigative agencies State bureaus, divisions, and departments of investigation exist in nearly all states. The investigatory agencies found at state level conduct all types of investigation, both civil and criminal, for various state agencies and bureaus, and often for local law enforcement agencies. Many of these units in different states possess great powers and accomplish professional levels of investigation in a vast number of areas that benefit the populace. Examples of this type of agency are the state narcotics commissions.

Identification agencies Central identification agencies exist in most states. Their purpose is primarily to store criminal records and maintain fingerprint files. These state agencies are invaluable to local law enforcement agencies and provide a professional service. In some states these identification agencies are operated by state police, while in others separate state agencies are responsible for the operation.

Criminalistics agencies Criminalistics laboratories exist at state level in most states and serve local, county, and state police agencies in examination, identification, and comparison of physical evidence. These criminalistics units provide professional assistance in crime-scene search in serious cases and lend their equipment and technology in other cases.

Motor vehicle divisions Motor vehicle divisions exist at a state level in all states and compile license, registration, traffic law and offense violations, and serve local agencies heavily in motor vehicle theft and unauthorized use cases. They house a record-keeping center for all types of traffic and motor vehicle information.

Liquor control boards and commissions All states have a board or commission to license sellers, regulate alcoholic beverage sales, and collect revenues from the sales. Their activities include investigation of potential license holders, enforcement of liquor laws, and detection of illegal production. These agencies work closely with the Alcohol and Tobacco Tax Division of the Internal Revenue Service.

Conservation agencies Every state has an agency to protect and help to conserve its natural resources. Many states use state park policemen, forest rangers, or conservation officers to protect their state parks, historic landmarks, and recreation areas. In some, fish and game wardens act to protect wildlife and illegal hunting and fishing activities.

Fire and safety agencies Fire and safety officers and marshals at state levels are responsible for the elimination of fire and safety hazards, investigation of fires, enforcement of fire and safety regulations, and the development of safety and fire prevention programs. These agencies work closely with local fire and safety officials.

Public health regulatory agencies These agencies have the responsibility of enforcing state laws and regulations concerning communicable diseases, licensing of hospitals and nursing homes, food and drug adulteration, and public sanitation.

National guard units and state militias All states have national guard or state militia units, called into action by the chief executive of the state—the governor, who may take this action only in emergency situations to preserve order and protect public safety. This exercise of power by the executive branch of state government is called martial law or martial rule and is invoked only when all other authority and power are ineffective in attempts to protect the state.

Federal-level policing

On the federal level, the growth of law enforcement is directly related to specific national crime problems that emerged during the country's development. The authority for establishing a federal police agency rests with the Congress, and its first act in this area occurred in 1789 when the post of United States Marshal was established. Later that same year Congress created the Revenue Cutter Service to prevent smuggling.

In 1829 the Postal Act was passed, and this included a provision to employ special agents, who were redesignated Postal Inspectors in 1954. The primary role of the Postal Inspectors was to prevent mail fraud and, since its early beginning, the Postal Inspection Service has broadened its scope of responsibility to include any violations involving the mails. As one example of their activity, the Postal Inspectors made over 15,000 arrests in 1969.

Twenty-five agents were hired by the Internal Revenue Service in 1868 to enforce income tax laws, and in 1870 the Department of Justice was formed, largely as a result of problems arising from the Civil War. But it was not until 1908 that President Theodore Roosevelt, recognizing the need for a federal investigative unit in the Department of Justice, authorized formation of the Bureau of Investigation. In 1924 J. Edgar Hoover, a 29-year-old lawyer, was appointed director of the Bureau. Hoover's contributions to American law enforcement are now legend, and during his tenure he did more than change the name of the agency to the Federal Bureau of Investigation. Today the FBI is viewed as one of the most effective law enforcement agencies in the United States, and it has jurisdiction over almost 200 federal crimes. The Bureau continues to be the largest and most prestigious law enforcement agency, employing over 7000 enforcement personnel.

Today there are over 50 federal agencies with some kind of law enforcement responsibility. The U.S. Department of Justice, headed by the Attorney General, incorporates the Federal Bureau of Investigation, the Drug Enforcement Administration, replacing the Bureau of Narcotics and Dangerous Drugs, the Immigration and Naturalization Service, and the Law Enforcement Assistance Administration (LEAA) which, while it does not have enforcement powers, is vested with the responsibility for assisting state and local law enforcement agencies in research, planning, and development.

The Department of the Treasury, in addition to having responsibility for the Secret Service, houses the Customs Department, the Internal Revenue Service, and the Alcohol, Tobacco, and Firearms Division.

Every federal agency has some form of investigative arm or relies upon another agency to carry out its routine investigations. In most cases this involves background investigations on prospective employees and other similar assignments. Most of the criminal work accomplished by federal agencies falls within the domain of the Justice or the Treasury Departments. The work carried out by these agencies is frequently different than that of local police departments and, in large measure, their tasks are not related. For this reason there is little comparison between local, state, and federal law enforcement agencies, at least in terms of their functions. During the past 200 years the development of American policing has been rife with problems, many of them related to the country's history, and many of them unique to policing.

Executive office of the president The National Security Council was established in 1947, and its function is to advise the president with respect to the integration of domestic, foreign, and military policies relating to the national security. Under the direction of the Council is the Central Intelligence Agency (CIA), which has an intelligence-gathering function that is both domestic and foreign. It has come under much public scrutiny in the past ten years because the public is questioning the unstated functions of this agency.

Department of the Treasury The Bureau of Customs was created in 1927. Its principal functions are to collect and assess duties and taxes on imported goods, control carriers and merchandise into and out of the United States, and prevent smuggling and frauds on the revenue process. With the upsurge of the illegal sale and use of narcotics internationally, the Bureau of Customs has become an important and busy law enforcement agency.

The problem of counterfeiting brought the U.S. Secret Service into being in 1865, and since that time it has established itself as one of the more effective investigative agencies in the United States. In 1901, after the assassination of President McKinley, the Secret Service was assigned responsibility for protecting the chief executive and his family. This protective responsibility now extends to the vice-president, presidential candidates, former presidents, their families, and embassies. The United States Secret Service is also charged with the enforcement of laws relating to counterfeiting or forging of United States government notes, securities, bills, and coins. The Secret Service protects the Executive Mansion and grounds, and the Treasury Guard Force protects the main Treasury buildings and the cash, bonds, and other securities in the Treasury vaults.

Department of Defense The Army, Navy, Marine Corps, and Air Force operate within the Department of Defense as do the police agencies of these armed services. Also within the Department of Defense are such intelligence and security agencies as the National Security Agency, the Defense Intelligence Agency, and the Assistant to the Secretary of Defense (Special Operations).

Department of Justice The United States Attorney General is head of the Justice Department, and under his command are the Federal Bureau of Investigation, the Immigration and Naturalization Service, the Drug Enforcement Administration, the United States Marshals, and the Law Enforcement Assistance Administration.

The FBI is responsible for the investigation of all federal laws that have not been assigned to other federal agencies.

The Immigration and Naturalization Service began in 1891 and has been a member of the Justice Department since 1940. Through its Border Patrol it searches out aliens who have entered the United States illegally and investigates violations of immigration and naturalization laws. The Bureau of Narcotics and Dangerous Drugs, now called the Drug Enforcement Administration, was created in 1968, and it functions to prevent, detect, and investigate violations of federal narcotic and marijuana laws. The United States Marshals, founded in 1789, generally perform many of the same services for the federal government that a sheriff performs for a county. The Marshals handle prisoners of the federal district courts, serve orders of the courts, and assist the courts in other matters.

In 1968 the Office of Law Enforcement Assistance (OLEA), later changed to the Law Enforcement Assistance Administration (LEAA), was created to offer federal assistance to state and local governments and to private nonprofit agencies to improve the administration of criminal justice in America. This agency accomplishes its task through financial and technical assistance to state and local law enforcement agencies. The Law Enforcement Education Program (LEEP) is a division of LEAA, which disburses funds in the form of loans and grants to college students presently employed in the criminal justice system and to some other students.

Department of the Interior The Department of the Interior has jurisdiction over 750 million acres of land, including the conservation and development of mineral resources, mine safety, fish and wildlife resources, arid land development through irrigation, and the management of hydroelectric power systems. It is also responsible for the welfare of persons in the territories and island possessions of the United States, plus the nation's scenic and historic areas. Its Bureau of Indian Affairs has guardianship over nearly one-half million native Americans. To perform its duties, the Department of the Interior has established the Division of Inspection, Division of Security, United States Fish and Wildlife Service, Bureau of Commerical Fisheries, and The Bureau of Sports Fisheries and Wildlife. Its National Park Service is well known to all Americans who have visited the many historic sites and national parks.

Department of Agriculture The Department of Agriculture enforces regulatory laws designed to protect the farmer and the consuming public, and it also administers the national forests. The Department concerns itself with animal disease eradication, animal quarantine, meat inspection, and the importation of harmful insects. Its Forest Service administers 150 national forests located in 40 states and Puerto Rico. The Commodity Exchange Authority works to prevent false information concerning crops, markets, and prices, and to protect users of the commodity futures markets.

Department of Health, Education, and Welfare The Department of Health, Education, and Welfare has the responsibility of promoting the general welfare in the fields of health, education, and social security. The Food and Drug Administration, which was created in 1930, has recently been strengthened by Supreme Court decisions, and it works toward promoting purity, standard potency, and truthful labeling in food and drug sales and consumption.

Department of Transportation The Department of Transportation has jurisdiction over the Coast Guard when the country is not at war (in wartime it becomes part of the Navy). The Coast Guard is responsible for the security of seaports and enforces federal laws on the high seas or waters subject to the jurisdiction of the United States. The Federal Aviation Administration enforces safety regulations relating to the manufacture, registration, safety, and operation of private and commerical aircraft. It also inspects air crashes. The Federal Highway Administration supervises a program designed to reduce deaths, injuries, and accidents on U.S. highways.

Independent agencies In the vast number of minor bureaucracies within the federal government, many minor types of law enforcement agencies exist. Most of them are investigative and security branches of larger, regulatory-type agencies, such as the Federal Communications Commission or the Federal Trade Commission.

Government reorganization is continuously taking place. President Carter, in August 1977, directed a comprehensive review of all federal law enforcement missions, tasks, and priorities. The President stated that there is "considerable jurisdictional ambiguity, overlap, and possible duplication among federal organizations performing police or investigative activities."[6]

Summary

The evolution of police systems in the United States has been a long, drawn-out process, with relatively little change in the basic concepts and philosophy of law enforcement. In more recent years police departments have begun to place greater stress on education, training, and technology, and today we are beginning to witness a new era in police service.

With roots in the European model of policing, law enforcement in the United States closely resembles that of England, where Robert Peel pioneered the Metropolitan Police Act in 1829. The rapid growth of our cities combined with the Industrial Revolution resulted in a recognition of the need for organized police departments. By the mid-nineteenth century every major American city had its own police force. During those early years, corruption and political favoritism were the rule rather than the exception, and it was not until the beginning of the twentieth century that Civil Service became widely accepted.

The onset of Prohibition contributed to the deterioration and disrespect of law enforcement by the public and, during this period, graft and corruption were not uncommon. Although the depression years had a negative impact on the country, they are generally viewed as having had a positive impact on policing, because many well-qualified individuals, who could not find employment elsewhere, chose to enter law enforcement.

By the end of World War II, the police service was beginning to question its progress and development and, with the manpower pool created by returning veterans, new ideas and a greater recognition of the need for training took hold. Training programs became a common aspect of most

[6]*LEAA Newsletter*, Vol. 6, No. 12, August 1977, p. 1.

major police departments, and many of the smaller departments created regional training programs, or worked in cooperation with the larger cities. As America entered a period of unequalled growth in the 1950s, police departments began to share in the progress. However, for the minorities, law enforcement was frequently viewed with skepticism and outright hostility. As automobiles became commonplace, the police developed new patrol strategies, which often had the effect of removing them from the streets. By 1960 the civil-rights movement had begun, and the urban riots of the sixties alienated the police and a large segment of the population. This, combined with an increasing drug problem, taxed even the most progressive departments.

Crime in the United States has generally been considered a local problem. This attitude has resulted in the creation of over 40,000 separate police agencies in the United States. These agencies have assumed many different faces under many different names, such as sheriff, marshal, and constable; their primary functions and jurisdictions vary from state to state. Many specialized agencies, such as motor vehicles divisions, liquor control boards, and conservation agencies, are also in operation. The federal government has added to the numerous agencies with many specialized police agencies.

The report of the President's Commission on Law Enforcement and the Administration of Justice in 1968 resulted in a recognition of the need for greater change. Sparked by federal assistance, police departments began to develop new and innovative programs, many of which are still in the embryonic stages. The concept of professionalization has begun to take hold dramatically, and throughout the nation a greater emphasis on training and education, combined with technological advances, are apt to leave a distinct impression on the police of the future.

TOPICS FOR DISCUSSION

1. Discuss some of the primary reasons for the development of police in America.

2. Discuss the relative differences between city, county, state, and federal law enforcement responsibilities.

3. Discuss the advantages and disadvantages of elected law enforcement officials such as sheriffs.

4. Discuss the impact that the automobile and other technologies have had upon police work.

5

The police: functions

The study of this chapter will enable you to:

1. **Understand the fundamental organizational structure of police agencies.**
2. **Discuss the crime control measures utilized by police agencies.**
3. **Understand the discretionary decision-making authority of law enforcement officers.**

You have just completed reading Chapter 4 and you may have resolved some questions about where the police originated, why we have them, and what they do. Before you read this chapter, you should ask yourself how they do whatever they do and what the role of the individual police officer is in our society. You may expand that inquiry to consider some of the unique characteristics of the role of the police in a democratic society. Are all police the same; do all police departments have the same responsibilities? If so, do they all fulfill these responsibilities similarly, or are there some differences in styles and emphases and approaches to their tasks?

The purpose of this chapter is to provide a listing and analysis of the primary functions and specific purposes of the various agencies and levels of law enforcement agencies. Traditionally, these functions and purposes have been listed categorically in various textbooks, in speeches by politicians, and in police training manuals. In recent years, however, Jerome Skolnick, O.W. Wilson, Norval Morris, and many others have provided the criminal justice system with an array of information that indicates that these traditionally accepted functions and purposes do not actually exist in modern democratic America. Perhaps one of the most tragic ramifications of this dilemma is that police may see their function and purpose differently from the way present-day society does.

Characteristics of police organizations

A distinguishing feature of police organizations is their quasi-military structure. The typical military symbols—uniforms, rank hierarchy, insignia, weapons, and equipment—are visible in nearly all police organizations. This creates a tighter organization, but it may detract somewhat from flexibility.

Nature of police organizations

Police agencies usually organize their personnel, equipment, and materials into line, staff, and line and staff functions. The line function is the primary operating function and is accomplished by the patrolmen and investigators when so assigned. The staff function is a supervisory and supportive activity, which may include an investigation, and is usually accomplished by a person holding the rank of lieutenant or higher or provides line personnel with needed services. Other personnel in staff positions are training officers, planners and researchers, fiscal officers, public relations workers, and other ancillary (auxiliary) personnel. All departmental inspectional services, intelligence activities, and criminalistics specialties are also staff positions.

Line and staff functions merge when collaboration is required on particular cases, as when persons in supervisory positions supervise investigations or raids.

Four basic organizational principles are used by many police agencies in their attempt to deliver police service to the public. They include:

1. Chain of command.
2. Unity of command.
3. Span of control.
4. Definition of authority.

Chain of command Chain of command represents the authority by which one gives and another receives orders, and it is the path along which this authority flows. For example, the police chief will tell the deputy chief of a particular method of enforcement procedure he wants carried out on the street. Written orders from the deputy chief will then flow to the commanders who will, in turn, instruct the precinct captains. The precinct captains will see that the chief's wishes are implemented on the street—through the lieutenants to the sergeants to the patrolmen. The chain of command thus allows the chief's orders to be relayed downward quickly. The same process, although in reverse order, is followed when information from patrolmen is relayed to the chief.

Unity of command This concept assures that no patrolman or any other person in the department will have more than one supervisor. This eliminates confusion and insures clarity and coordination. Because police shifts rotate through 24 hours each day, and because time off for personnel is insured by labor laws, police often find themselves with a different person as immediate supervisor on different days.

Span of control This means the number of persons a supervisor can effectively manage, with the determinants of people, distance, and time. The number of people supervised depends on the type of work involved: routine, varied, technical, or complicated. A larger number of people doing routine tasks can be more effectively supervised than if they are doing complicated work.

Distance also affects a supervisor's span of control. If a supervisor's subordinates work within close range of supervision, it is easier than when they are scattered at some distance from him.

The time factor is the third aspect of span of control. Because police departments are open 24 hours a day, the equivalent of 1095 working days a year must be considered. Personnel must be deployed to three different shifts depending on each shift's criminal activity. Some agencies use special task forces during high crime times, often between 6:00 P.M. and 2:00 A.M. A few police agencies are experimenting with 40-hour, four-day weeks for increased effectiveness. Supervisors find it much more difficult to supervise large numbers of personnel during peak periods than during slow periods.

Definition of authority Charts, manuals, and rules and regulations generally define the authority in a step-by-step fashion from the chief to the patrolman and vice versa. These organizational charts are usually posted on personnel bulletin boards and in police locker rooms. The departmental rules and regulations and manuals of procedure outline exactly which positions report to which, and the responsibilities of each position.

Organization of a typical police agency

Organization is the bringing together of people to perform specific tasks and dividing the total workload into individual units for assignment to individual people. Organization by itself will not complete any task. A typical organizational chart for a community of 23,000 is shown in Figure 5-1, and a chart for a large police agency is offered in Figure 5-2.

Most police agencies organize around functions that they must perform in their communities. A complaint comes into the police agency or pressure is applied through various channels, and the police organization initiates an order at the top of the structure that filters down through to operations, verbally or in memorandum form. Depending upon the content of the order, it will be channeled to administration, operations, or services. If the order applies only to one shift, the supervisor of that shift will receive it. He will instruct his shift members on how he wants the order carried out. His men will perform these particular tasks and report the results back to him. The process is then reversed and the results are channeled upward to the originator of the order. Standing orders or policy statements are permanent and are maintained permanently by those concerned, to be used as regular guidelines and procedures.

Line functions

Patrol

The patrol function is the hub of the law enforcement wheel around which all other functions revolve. While most authorities, academic and professional, would readily agree with such a statement, the public has the general impression that the patrol officer's duties are the least important of

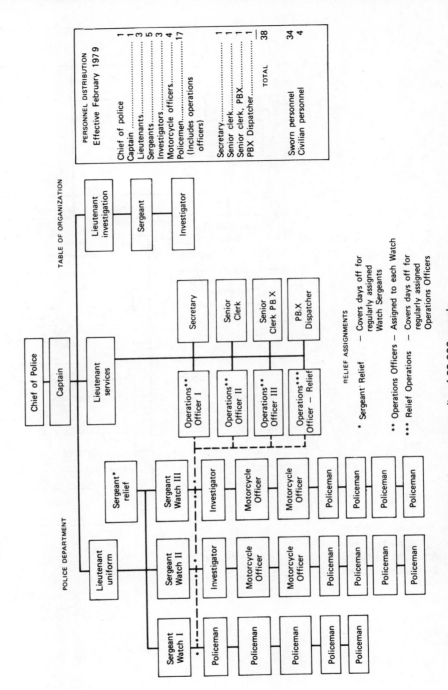

Figure 5-1 Typical organization chart for a community of 23,000 people.

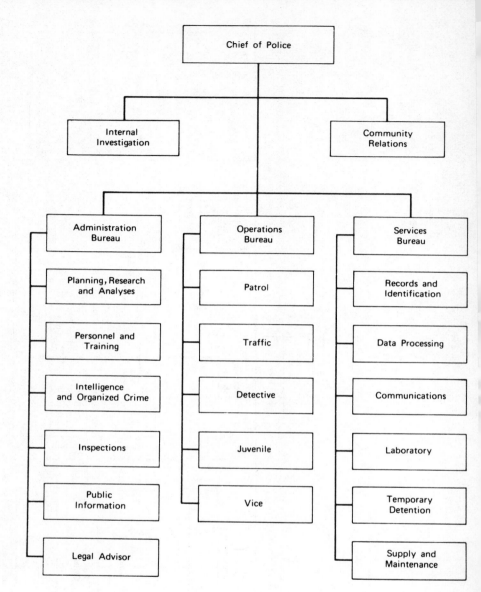

Figure 5-2

One form of a
well-organized municipal
police department.

a police department's responsibilities. Novels, movies, and television programs have elevated the significance of the detective out of proportion at the expense of the uniformed patrol officer. Ironically, the majority of the patrol officers are the most inexperienced members of a police department, yet their function is considered the most important. In the majority of all cases investigated, it is the patrol officer who sets into motion the activities of all other police officers, including the detective. A review of the responsibilities of the patrol officer may help to bring the picture back into its proper prospective.

Under general supervision, more theoretical than real, the patrol officer is responsible for the maintenance of order, the enforcement of laws and ordinances, the prevention and suppression of crime, and the protection of life and property. These goals are achieved by the following activities:

1. Patrolling an assigned area of the community by vehicle, foot, or as otherwise assigned.

2. Responding to emergencies, assigned or observed.

3. Investigating unusual or suspicious conditions.

4. Making arrests, serving subpoenas and warrants, and guarding prisoners.

5. Investigating traffic accidents and directing traffic.

6. Issuing citations to traffic violators.

7. Administering first aid and giving assistance to the injured.

8. Noting and reporting unsafe conditions.

9. Preparing evidence for criminalistics examination or court presentation.

10. Searching for stolen and lost property and lost or missing persons.

11. Providing general information to the public.

12. Writing reports relating to investigations or potential investigations of crime.

13. Analyzing facts, clues, and evidence in the investigation of crime.

14. Operating radio and other communications equipment.

15. Maintaining effective relationships with other law enforcement agencies, employees, and the public.

At some point, each of these responsibilities can become a specialty itself. As the patrol officer develops information, the scope of his investigation may require more detailed inquiry than he has the time or the training for. This is where the remainder of the line, staff, supportive, and investigative service functions come into play. It is here that they lend their particular skills to the patrol officer's investigation in an effort to maintain order, enforce laws and ordinances, prevent and suppress crime, and protect life and property.

Traffic   The traffic officer performs a secondary line function specifically designed to diminish losses from accidents. He accomplishes this by the following activities:

1. Determining facts related to accidents as a basis for accident prevention, and service to involved parties requiring impartial and objective evidence in order to seek civil justice in the settlement of accident losses.

2. Aiding accident victims by administering first aid, seeing to the transportation of those requiring further medical attention, and protecting property inside vehicles.

3. Obtaining the most expedient flow of vehicular and pedestrian traffic consistent with safety.

4. Obtaining compliance with traffic laws and ordinances from motorists and pedestrians.

5. Assisting traffic engineers and traffic safety educational agencies by providing pertinent information relevant to their function.

6. Serving as an inspection, investigation, and reporting force for municipal government in detecting problems and proposing corrective measures.

7. Planning for traffic routing during predictable emergencies and catastrophes.

8. Providing assistance and information to motorists and pedestrians.[1]

The traffic officer may work alone or with another traffic car or motorcycle and may utilize sophisticated radar equipment.

Juvenile   Numerous studies, surveys, and commissions have reflected a need for increased police involvement in dealing with young people. The juvenile officer is in perhaps the best position to work the most effectively with youngsters. It is his responsibility to strive toward the reduction and prevention of delinquency as well as to investigate cases involving juveniles.

In most police departments today, one or more officers are assigned to this secondary line function. These officers generally review all reports involving police contact with young people. Follow-up investigations are initiated in cases where charges are to presented before the juvenile court, or when further contact with the youngster and his parents may seem to be beneficial to that youngster. It is the purpose of juvenile court laws to secure for each youngster the care and guidance necessary for his spiritual, emotional, and physical welfare, preferably in his own home.

Working with that premise, farsighted law enforcement agencies, through the juvenile officer, attempt to cope with a youngster's problems within the community rather than send him to a juvenile detention center where he may receive little if any meaningful help. It is believed that far better results are reached when a youngster's problems are dealt with locally. A juvenile officer may involve himself with family counseling or

[1]George D. Eastman, ed., *Municipal Police Administration*, 6th ed. (Washington, D.C.: International City Mnagers Association, 1969), p. 106.

make referrals to any number of local social service agencies, one of which may be specifically equipped to deal with a particular need.

Alternatives to the juvenile justice system were suggested in 1967 by the Task Force Reports.[2] And federal funds were authorized under the auspices of the California Youth Authority to finance four pilot projects. Since then, their numbers have increased and spread to states other than California. These agencies were designed as an alternative to the juvenile justice system. Counseling and other activities can be arranged for the youngster and his parents. Referrals come from other agencies, the schools and, of course, the police. The service provided is not mandatory, but it does assist the juvenile officer in the social work aspect of the job. This aspect removes the stigma attached to most "establishment" agencies that deal with the problems of young people. The police are obviously in the best position to provide referrals in need of the greatest help.

Vice/narcotics

Major law enforcement agencies have separated the vice and narcotics functions from the general investigative services because of the uniqueness of the problems involved in their investigation. Medium and small police departments, however, must often continue to include these functions as part of general investigative services due to a lack of manpower.

Vice includes prostitution, illegal gambling, use and sale of illegal alcoholic beverages, and the distribution and sale of obscene or pornographic material; and it is almost always tied in some way to organized crime. The investigation of narcotics and vice is best facilitated by a single unit. And since organized crime knows no boundaries, the Omnibus Crime Control and Safe Streets Act of 1968 and the Organized Crime Control Act of 1970 were passed to coordinate investigations at all levels of government: federal, state, and local. The effects of such legislation and cooperation between agencies have yet to be felt, but they will undoubtedly prove beneficial to society.

Officers involved in such activities often take on the appearance and dress of those involved in vice and narcotics. These so-called undercover operations are extremely dangerous. It is not uncommon for an undercover officer to mingle alone and unarmed with extremely dangerous criminals. Because there is no regular pattern to the comings and goings of such criminals, a great deal of time is required for an unknown to become accepted by a group of criminals. This acceptance enables the undercover agent to gather the evidence necessary for a successful prosecution.

Plainclothes

The last of the secondary line functions to be discussed will be that of the plainclothes and general investigative services. Their responsibilities may be basically the same as those of the patrol officer when they operate in

[2] The President's Commission on Law Enforcement and Administration of Justice, *Task Force Report: Juvenile Delinquency and Youth Crime* (Washington, D.C.: U.S. Government Printing Office, 1967), pp. 19–21.

civilian clothing and in unmarked cars. At other times they are used in the investigation of such crimes as commercial and residential burglaries, auto thefts, thefts from autos, and grand theft from persons. They usually work in teams; occasionally with marked patrol units and frequently with vice and narcotics officers. If a uniformed officer feels that his presence may hamper the apprehension of someone in the act of committing a crime, he may request plainclothes units to continue the surveillance or investigation.

Officers assigned to plainclothes and general investigation units are usually seasoned officers who have demonstrated both ability and the desire to perform in such a capacity. The value of using such tactics is related to the kind of illegal activity involved. It is within the capabilities of even the smallest police departments, even if only on a part-time basis.

Information discovered as a result of the arrests made in the Watergate case can be directly attributed to plainclothes officers of the Metropolitan Police Department of Washington, D.C. The Ervin Committee Senate Hearings have disclosed that a lookout equipped with a walkie-talkie had been positioned across the street from the Watergate complex. He most assuredly would have alerted his confederates inside the Democratic National Convention Headquarters had he seen uniformed officers in marked patrol cars.

Staff and supportive functions

Investigative The investigator or detective's responsibility lies in following up and supporting the patrol officer. Investigations are usually classified in two categories: crimes against persons (simple and aggravated assault, murder, rape, and robbery) and crimes against property (buglary, auto theft, grand and petty larceny, and fraud).

The patrol officer generally does not have the time necessary to conduct extensive or drawn-out interviews, laborious file searches, tedious and extensive crime report reviews, or contacts with other law enforcement agencies for assistance. The detective is able to perform these functions. Generally, officers assigned to an investigation unit have had many years of experience and have developed expertise in a particular type of crime, such as murder or robbery, but this is not always the case.

The uniformed patrol officer who is unable to apprehend the perpetrator of a crime at the scene becomes the preliminary investigator. In some departments he simply protects the evidence at the scene until the arrival of other investigators, whose responsibility is to take charge of the case. Since most law enforcement agencies are small, the investigator may be the uniformed officer who responds to the call. It is his job to protect, preserve, and search for evidence that will determine the nature of the crime. From the evidence and the questioning of witnesses, the officer attempts to identify the offender and arrest him.

When it appears that the case is complex or time-consuming, and if the necessary personnel are available, the patrolman will turn over the case to an investigator. From the evidence and identifications developed by the patrolman, the investigator follows up by developing other evidence and identification necessary to lead to arrest and eventual conviction. The rate of clearing cases if the offender is not apprehended at the crime scene or shortly after is very low. Despite the image of investigators in the media, a police agency at any governmental level would be considered highly efficient if cases cleared by its investigators were greater than 12 to 15 percent. The patrolman's response time in relation to the actual time of occurrence is the key for apprehending offenders.

Records

Great strides in the record-keeping function have been made in the last decade, such as adding, automated, and electronic data processing; retrieval and storage capabilities; and computer printout and visual scanning systems. Furthermore, they are updated on an almost daily basis because of the advances in technology.

Record-keeping is important in crime rate determination, uniform classification of crimes, identification, property, persons, and methods of criminal operation. Manpower studies and planning are conducted on the basis of recorded information. Control of property and evidence is also a function of the records unit. Records provide cross-indexing, master name index, traffic and other citations, warrants, and personnel identification information for the entire department. Because of the tremendous cost involved in maintaining modern systems, some agencies have consolidated both records and communication systems in much the same way as private business utilizes computer time-sharing.

A police department's efficiency and effectiveness can often be measured by simply examining its record-keeping system. If it is in a state of disarray and confusion, it is likely that the rest of the department is operating at the same level of inefficiency.

More and more agencies are turning over this key function to civilian personnel trained in administrative duties. The advantages are reduced operating and wage costs as well as the increased manpower utilization that occurs when police officers are reassigned to duties where their training can be put to more effective use.

Communication

To be effective, a police department needs an adequate communication system, particularly important in agencies providing emergency services. For the police there are essentially four areas of communication: the first and most important is between the citizens and their police departments; the second is among the personnel within the department; the third is between the department and other police agencies; and last, since law enforcement does not function alone, but is merely a subsystem within the criminal justice system, communication is necessary between the police and the various other components of the system. To this last area we might add communications with other units of government and the private sector.

Communication takes a variety of forms; doing nothing or leaving a task uncompleted can be kinds of messages, as are body movements and gestures. However, written reports, memorandums, and other paperwork are the bulk of police communication; and, of course, there are the countless spoken words.

The necessity for being precise, concise, and conveying the message quickly in law enforcement communications is primary. Whatever is said must have an exact meaning, because dubious or double meanings can reduce effectiveness and unnecessarily jeopardize the lives and property of others. Any message must be brief and concise, since long and tedious messages consume the important minutes of others and delay the delivery of services to the public. The need for speed of message transmission and reception in police work is well known; codes like the 10-code are designed specifically to reduce the amount of time consumed.

One of the primary communication links between the public and the police is the request for service. Generally, it is done by telephone, but the public will also walk into the station, hail a passing patrol unit, or go to an officer's residence. The public has a wide variety of needs and problems; some are criminal, some are emergencies, and some involve people who do not know where else to turn. Since the police are often the only 24-hour representatives of government, the public turns to them for almost everything.

An interesting observation by a citizen volunteer rider in a patrol car regarding the 30-minute break for a meal by a police officer showed that the officer spent 13 minutes of his break answering inquiries as to when the phone company opened in the morning for paying bills, how one went about shutting off water service, where the good fishing was (from a tourist), and how one might report a neighbor for letting his dog run loose without the neighbor discovering the source of the complaint.

The calls that involve a crime in progress or suspicious circumstances are emergency business in the police department. Part of the new officer's career is spent learning how to report by radio or to write up his responses to these emergencies. During academy training he learns the radio codes and the proper method of report writing that will lead to the determination of just what crime occurred, who did it, and all the other details that will lead to a successful prosecution. From these oral and written communications comes the information needed to function. Many of the calls are for services, and these are also important, requiring the same skill and expertise as investigating and reporting crimes.

Civilians in police work

The use of civilians in jobs normally performed by police officers has increased rapidly in the past 25 years—particularly in larger cities—as police departments have sought to reduce costs and put more men on the beat.

This Urban Institute study describes the experience of 13 police departments in cities of varying size across the country. It should be useful to departments considering whether to hire civilians, to departments already employing civilians but experiencing problems, and to federal, state, and local officials concerned with planning and funding police activities.

The findings are based largely on interviews in 13 cities with 158 people, including police managers, officers in charge of civilian employees, and the civilians themselves. Two types of activities were surveyed: (1) the employment of civilians on jobs in communication, identification, and detention facilities; and (2) the use of civilians in Community Service Officer (CSO) programs. The CSOs are generally 18- to 20-year-olds who assist police officers on the street.

As a whole, police managers and officers were favorably impressed with the use of civilians because they relieved officers for more critical duties, cut costs, and improved service to the public. Many officers felt that civilians performed some tasks better than police, partly because civilians can concentrate on one job since they are not subject to rotation and special assignment as officers are, and partly because officers tend to consider some of the civilianized jobs confining, sedentary, a form of punishment, and not proper police work. Some problems exist, but most are related to police management practices and can be alleviated by improved training and supervison of civilians. Other problems, described as "personality conflicts" by both officers and civilians, result from knowledge and communication which may be overcome with the passage of time.

Officers generally believe the civilians want careers in police work, and a very large proportion (85 percent) recommend that more be hired. Civilians also say that they want to continue police work. Their assessments of benefits and problems closely parallel those of the officers, but they desire improved pay, job security, and training. Also mentioned was the need for more stringent entrance requirements matching the qualifications of civilians for a given job.

The use of civilians reduces overall costs. Salaries average 23 percent less for civilians than for officers and overhead about 10 percent less—though in the larger cities, overhead costs tend to be equal for both.

The degree of a program's success depends on the quality of planning, implementation and management. Even in the few unsuccessful efforts—where civilian jobs were terminated—police managers had no doubt that civilians could have fulfilled job requirements.

Thus, use of civilians in selected roles has been successful. It is likely to be expanded within departments and introduced to others. The variety of jobs for civilians also is likely to increase as its successes and savings are recognized.

Source: *Employing Civilians For Police Work*, U. S. Department of Justice, Law Enforcement Assistance Administration, National Institute of Law Enforcement and Criminal Justice, July 1975.

Because of the mobility of criminals, it is a requisite of today's law enforcement that police agencies contact each other and place information at the other's disposal. Many local agencies are within easy phoning distance or are part of statewide leased line systems. Some share the same radio frequencies. Because of the increased demands on airwaves, agencies are forced to seek alternative means of transmitting and receiving information. Telecommunications have provided the vehicle. A variety of national, regional, state, and local information and message networks have been developed. In Atlanta, Georgia, METROPOL serves the needs of fourteen agencies; in the District of Columbia, WALES serves the Capital and five adjoining counties; SPIN and PIN service the two large metropolitan areas of California respectively. State systems exist almost everywhere; CLETS (California), LETS (Idaho), LIEN (Michigan), FCIC (Florida), as well as many others. Regionally, NESPAC (New England State Police Administrators' Conference), a cooperative network in the six New England states, provides information for local law enforcement.

The exact information capabilities of these and other telecommunication systems vary from system to system. The PIN network in California deals with outstanding criminal and traffic warrants. The system has been expanded to handle parole/probation violators and the names of those who have a tendency to resist arrest. The most complete is New York's NYSIIS. It provides information on vehicle registration, operator's licenses, firearms, criminal histories, fraudulent checks, personal appearance, names, voice prints, fingerprints, warrants, wants, stolen vehicles and parts, and missing persons among others. Information needed "on the street" has always been a critical problem, and what is available varies from jurisdiction to jurisdiction, depending upon the available technology and funds.

National systems are also available. The National Crime Information Center (NCIC), begun in 1967, provides the working officer with information about stolen vehicles, stolen license plates, wanted persons, stolen firearms, stolen property, criminal profiles and histories, and stolen securities. A national telecommunication service, LETS, headquartered in Phoenix, Arizona, allows agencies to send messages to one another. A new project called SEARCH will allow agencies to exchange criminal histories on a national basis.

Despite these technological advances in information transmittal, many of America's smaller departments find these communication services beyond their reach. For example, many of the departments in the Toledo, Ohio, area cannot afford the $100 per month hookup charge for Ohio's LEADS (Law Enforcement Automated Data System).

Communications, in the administrative sense, between members of the same agency is an important aspect for the direction and control of that agency. Paperwork and the spoken word provide the data necessary for decision-making, policy, allocation, budgets, and other tasks. The paperwork of the uniformed patrol officer alone is staggering and a major portion of his working hours is spent in filling out reports. Communication is upward, downward, and horizontal.

Communications outward from the law enforcement subsystem to the rest of the system and private agencies are equally important. Diversion programs and community-based corrections require that the needs and capabilities of each be known. The quality of police work and the way it is communicated, orally and written, determine matters of prosecution and defense and influence the sentencing process. Poor communications make a sham of justice. It takes little imagination to visualize the necessity for precise, concise, and prompt communication in the criminal justice system.

PROMIS

A computer system that can prepare court calendars, issue subpoenas, and warn of possible bail jumpers will be operating in 58 cities by the end of next year.

Known as "PROMIS," an acronym for Prosecution Management Information System, the program is operating in 12 cities and will be in nine more by December.

PROMIS can often tell why people who are arrested often don't go to jail.

"One reason prosecutions often wash out is that victims and witnesses don't turn up on trial day because they haven't even been notified," said William Hamilton, president of the Institute for Law and Social Research of Washington, D.C., and developer of the system.

"And the reason they often aren't notified is because of inadequate administrative procedures.

"PROMIS," he said, "is correcting that."

Financed by LEAA, PROMIS is providing courts and prosecuting attorneys across the nation instant access to arrest and court records that formerly took days to retrieve.

It can determine whether judges in different courts are treating similar cases differently. It can consolidate all a defendant's pending cases. And it can tell what caseloads are being handled by individual prosecutors and judges.

The system can isolate and produce a printout on such items as:
• All felonies in 1975 that involved a gun charge and the defendant was arrested at a specific location.
• All cases in which "Harry Brown" was the arresting police officer and "John Smith" the defense lawyer.
• All cases in which the witness was "John Jones" and the case was dismissed or discontinued for lack of witness cooperation.

Source: *LEAA News Letter*, "Computer Keeps Tabs on Criminals and Caseload," Vol. 6, No. 10, May 1977.

Crime laboratory Criminalistics, the application of biological and physical sciences to the investigation of crime, is conducted in the crime lab. Here, the scientist uses his knowledge to evaluate, measure, compare, and test pieces of evidence collected from the scene of a crime by a police officer or trained criminalist.

The first thing the average person thinks about when a crime lab is mentioned is ballistics (the evaluation of the motion of projectiles shot from firearms, or fingerprints). Actually, the range of the crime lab's capabilities are far greater than one might suspect. Gas chromatography—separating components of complex mixtures; paper chromatography—separating components of complex organic matter; neutron activation analysis—measuring concentrations of trace elements; electrophoresis—studying and separating protein molecules; X-ray crystallography—X-ray analysis of electron distribution and atomic structure; polygraph examination—(lie detection); and voice printing—classifying speech characteristics in much the same way as fingerprints are classified, are some of the capabilities of the crime lab.

Recently, there have been studies that may lead to the identification of microorganisms as being as unique to a particular individual as fingerprints, which can be collected at the scene of a crime within hours after its commission. This new technique is called germ-typing. When available to patrol officers and investigators, it has been used only in cases that invoke emotions or have the public's attention.

Special considerations

Field interviews   This preventive patrol tactic has come under considerable criticism and scrutiny by the community at large, particularly by minority factions of the community. The temporary detaining of a person on the street to determine his identity and the reason for his presence at a particular location and time has been challenged as being violative of Constitutional guarantees. Thus far, the U.S. Supreme Court has ruled otherwise, most notably in their decision in the case of *Terry v. Ohio* (392 U.S. 1 [1968]). The *Terry* decision defined a "stop" as opposed to an arrest and a "frisk" as opposed to a search. Futhermore, the Court specified that a "protective search" for weapons was a lawful police technique.

Critics contend that the majority of the reasons for stopping people, particularly minority group members, are for other than legitimate and lawful purposes. The police contend that their right to stop and question people is fundamental, particularly when it applies to individuals observed in an area where a crime has been committed. Both arguments bear further examination.

In a climate where law enforcement officers may arbitrarily detain a person, it is almost inconceivable that police administrators would not have long ago recognized the potential for indiscretion. Yet relatively few agencies across the country have developed guidelines for their officers in an effort to ensure that such "interviews" are limited and employed under conditions justifying their use. Preventive patrols, of which field interviews are an important element, are effective in the reduction of crime, but just how effective they are has yet to be substantiated.

Beyond the establishment of guidelines of *when* and *where*, police administrators should also concern themselves with *how*. A mature patrol officer will soon learn that the manner in which he conducts himself makes a great difference. It is often the young, inexperienced rookie who, out of eagerness to cure the world of its ills, develops a "badge-heavy" syndrome, which causes animosity among people stopped on the street. A courteous, professionally conducted field interview can achieve good results in obtaining valuable information. But arrogance and rudeness on the part of an officer can act as a catalyst to alienate and incite the person being questioned. Law enforcement must come to grips with those critical issues with which the officer comes into contact almost on a daily basis; the field interview would be a good place to begin.

Preventive patrol: myths and realities

Police patrol strategies have always been based on two unproven but widely accepted hypotheses: first, that visible police presence prevents crime by deterring potential offenders; second, that the public's fear of crime is diminished by such police presence. Thus, routine preventive police patrol was thought both to prevent crime and reassure the public.

The Kansas City, Missouri, Police Department conducted an experiment from October 1, 1972, through September 30, 1973, designed to measure the impact routine patrol had on the incidence of crime and the public's fear of crime. This experiment, made possible by Police Foundation funding, employed a methodology which accurately determined that traditional routine preventive patrol had no significant impact either on the level of crime or the public's feeling of security.

Three controlled levels of routine preventive patrol were used in the experimental areas. One area, termed "reactive," received no preventive patrol. Officers entered the area only in response to citizen calls for assistance. This in effect substantially reduced police visibility in that area. In the second area, called "proactive," police visibility was increased two to three times its usual level. In the third area, termed "control," the normal level of patrol was maintained. Analysis of the data gathered revealed that the three areas experienced no significant differences in the level of crime, citizens' attitudes toward police services, citizens' fear of crime, police response time, or citizens' satisfaction with police response time.

Source: Police Foundation, *The Kansas City Preventive Patrol Experiment, A Technical Report.* 1974, p. iii.

Table 5-1

A universe of assumptions governing patrol modes: marked patrol car.

Supporting Assumptions	Opposing Assumptions
The marked patrol car maximizes police visibility in the community, thereby enhancing the deterrent effect of patrol function.	The marked patrol vehicle places a barrier between the police officer and the citizen and has an adverse effect upon the level of police/citizen interaction, the level of officer rapport with the citizenry, the level of officer information about his beat, and the level of citizen satisfaction with the police. Other modes of patrol, particularly in high-density commercial and residential areas, are significantly more productive.
	The level of patrol visibility has little impact upon the ability of the police to deter crime.
	High patrol visibility detracts from the potential for tactical surprise, thereby lessening the probability of intercepting crimes in progress.
	In high-density commercial and residential areas, foot patrol or a scooter/bicycle variation provides greater visibility than does the marked patrol car.
	High patrol visibility in minority areas creates an image of a "hostile" or "occupying" force.
The marked patrol car provides the greatest amount of patrol officer mobility.	Motor scooters, motorbikes, and bicycles provide greater maneuverability in congested areas.
The marked patrol car maximizes the amount of territory which an officer can effectively patrol.	Vehicular patrol over an extensive area reduces the level of an officer's familiarity with his beat.
	The larger the area patrolled in an automobile, the lower the intensity of coverage in an area.
	It is necessary to weigh the amount of territory covered against the quality of patrol. Particularly in high-density residential and commercial areas, the automobile places a barrier between the police officer and the citizen, thereby inhibiting police/citizen interaction.
The marked patrol car maximizes the safety of the officer while on patrol.	The level of danger associated with officer patrol by foot, motor scooter, and bicycle is grossly exaggerated particularly when officers are equipped with hand-held radios.

Table 5-2
universe of assumptions
governing patrol modes:
foot patrol.

Supporting Assumptions	Opposing Assumptions
In high-density commercial and residential areas, foot patrol provides maximum officer visibility, thereby increasing the deterrent effect of patrol, the level of citizen-felt security, and the level of citizen satisfaction with the police.	Officer visibility has limited if any effect upon the level of effective deterrence. Foot patrol provides less visibility and less sense of presence than vehicular patrol on a given beat. and the diversion of officers from vehicles detracts from the overall level of presence and visibility throughout a jurisdiction. This diminishes the overall level of citizen-felt security and satisfaction with the police.
Maximizes officer/citizen contact and the level of police knowledge about the particular beat.	Increased officer/citizen contact on a foot beat increases the opportunity for officer corruption and thereby detracts from the overall effectiveness of the department. Officer/citizen contact is not important to the effective provision of police services.
Maximizes the order-maintenance function of the police by facilitating reductions in loitering, disturbances, etc.	Has no greater impact on order mainte-nance than does vehicular patrol, but rather confines the capability to the limited area of a foot beat and to the predictable presence of the officer.
Increases the level of citizen-felt security and satisfaction with the police.	Provides less visibility and, therefore, less sense of presence than vehicular patrol on a given beat, and diminishes the overall level of citizen-felt security and statisfaction throughout the jurisdiction.
When coordinated with vehicular patrol on a given beat, provides for the most com-prehensive and effective coverage.	Detracts from the overall coverage which could be achieved by a total commitment to vehicles, and increases the cost of patrol without improving its overall effectiveness.
Results in heightened officer morale and level of job satisfaction due to officers' con-tinued contact with the citizenry and their increased sense of responsibility.	Detracts from officers' morale because they feel it is ineffective and outside the mainstream of police work. Officers prefer automobile patrol because it enhances their ability to respond to "hot" calls and is sub-stantially more comfortable and less tiring.

Table 5-3

A universe of assumptions governing patrol modes: helicopter.

Supporting Assumptions	Opposing Assumptions
For use in urban and suburban areas, the helicopter is an effective vehicle for general patrol activities as it:	The helicopter should be used as a response vehicle and as a crime-specific vehicle, as its general patrol utility appears somewhat limited and its operation is extremely expensive. The helicopter's effectiveness may depend upon the ability to coordinate its activities with those of ground units, and this may be difficult to accomplish.
Permits wide ranging and accurate surveillance of an urban area and is particularly valuable in detecting certain types of offenses.	
Facilitates rapid response to calls for service, and enables surveillance of suspects until such time as apprehension can be effected by ground units. It is also safer than automobiles as a vehicle for high speed chases.	The response time of the helicopter is extremely low only if it is already airborne. If it must respond from the ground, it is very slow.
In general, the surveillance and detection capabilities of the helicopter is considered equivalent to that of two to six ground officers.	While perhaps effective in detecting types of misdemeanors, particularly vandalism, prosecution is jeopardized due to the arresting officer not being the same as the officer observing the violation.
	The noise level effected is extremely high, as is the intensity of surveillance lights. This leads to community dissatisfaction.

Source: (Tables 5-1, 5-2, 5-3) National Institute of Law Enforcement and Criminal Justice Law Enforcement Assistance Administration, U. S. Department of Justice, *National Evaluation Program, Phase I Summary Report, Traditional Preventive Patrol*, June 1976.

Citations (traffic)

Ironically, the only aspect of law enforcement with which the majority of the public ever comes into contact draws almost as much negative criticism as does the field interview. Traffic citations are generally a means of undeserved harassment—or so the recipient of a citation would have one believe. The difficulty is that many people honestly believe that this is the rule rather than the exception.

Again, a lack of appropriate discretion and professional tact on the part of the issuing officer can lend itself to the kind of resentment depicted in the cartoon of the sneering, cynical motorcycle officer, who hides behind a billboard waiting for the unsuspecting motorist.

When warnings are issued instead of citations, authorities generally agree that they lose their effectiveness if issued indiscriminately when a citation was warranted, if officers are allowed the freedom of "excusing" violations because of a driver's good intentions, when accepting frivolous excuses, or if the officer does not wish to be perceived as a "tough cop."

No matter how distasteful a traffic citation may be, there is a direct correlation between the amount of enforcement and the accident rate at any given location. This alone would justify a policy of firm but fair traffic enforcement. If an officer conducts himself professionally, unwarranted criticism will be greatly reduced. Perhaps the cited motorist will examine his driving habits rather than characterize the police officer as rude.

Women's role in law enforcement

The date of appointment of the first policewoman has not been definitely established. Some say the first policewoman was Mrs. Lola Baldwin, appointed in 1905 to work at the Lewis and Clark Centennial Exposition in Portland, Oregon. Others say it was Alice Stebbins Wells or Mrs. Marie Owens of the Los Angeles Police Department who received their appointments in about 1910. Regardless of who and when, policewomen are a twentieth century addition to law enforcement in the United States.

Prior to the 1970s, the primary duties of women were those special assignments best achieved by a woman as protective/preventive agents in the social sense—dealing with the welfare of women and children. They looked for lost children and runaways; investigated and protected women and children in sex offense matters; worked in stores where shoplifting was prevalent; and carried out general duties in the juvenile division. Occasionally, they investigated bad check cases or fraud of the elderly. But the full range of peace officer assignments were generally not available to them.

The years since World War II have seen a rapid dedomestication of American women and an ever-increasing entrance into the ranks of the work force. For law enforcement, the 1970s have been the period in which the American female has demanded full police status and is being placed in the formerly "forbidden" areas—particularly the uniformed patrol division. (See Chapter 16 for a further discussion.)

Special investigative functions

The general investigation of cases in law enforcement is aimed at a specific criminal event committed usually by a single offender or a loosely organized group of offenders. The majority of cases investigated fit this pattern. However, cases of a very special nature occasionally arise in which the criminal activity is not confined to one event or violation; they may be a continuing series of various crimes perpetrated by an organized group. Faced with situations of this nature, agencies have begun to experiment with new investigative techniques and procedures to meet these conditions.

An example of some of the attempts to deal with complex problems, extended investigations, and organized criminal elements is the intraagency task force. In the Kansas City area a metro squad, composed of personnel from seven sheriffs' departments and twenty municipal departments combined with two state police agencies, attacks problems common to all jurisdictions on a priority basis. Special narcotics units like Lane County, Oregon, operate on a permanent basis investigating complex narcotics cases that are prevalent in the area. Other similar organizations, such as the fugitive squad, METROPOL, in the Atlanta, Georgia area, and the Major Case Squad of the greater St. Louis area perform the complex, extended investigations that sometimes involve organized crime.

Presently, most American law enforcement agencies are not structured to handle criminal activities that cross jurisdictional lines and that are multiviolational and interconnected. An addict buys drugs from pushers at a local level. The same addict supports his drug habit as a burglar, car thief, or panderer for prostitutes. The drug pushers may be associated with the people who fence the stolen goods and vehicles or operate prostitution rings. Although each criminal act is isolated, it is interconnected with others and may be directed from above in a loose or formal fashion. The police, however, make initial contacts through isolated or separate incidents: a stolen car, a business burglary, or a complaint from a tourist who lost a wallet in an encounter with a prostitute. Until some pattern emerges—an informer explains the connection or an investigator discovers a connecting thread between the crimes—the follow-up investigation is ineffectual except, perhaps, in solving the individual cases. The criminal organization may be unnoticed and therefore left untouched.

A particular problem area is in the nonvictim crimes—prostitution, gambling, narcotics, payoff to police, and loansharking. Instead of a crime scene in the traditional sense and a complaining party who brings the criminal activity to law enforcement's attention, the police must go out and seek the occurrences and proceed differently. The nonvictim crime is often profitable; enforcement is carried out in an apathetic environment; and prevention is developed only by the police pretending to be the victim. But from these investigations, the interconnected crimes and organized activity can often be discovered because the money from loansharking, narcotics, prostitution, and gambling attracts and often fosters other criminal activities.

Law enforcement agencies require two other functions in the confrontation with organized and interconnected crime. These are intelligence and internal affairs units. The objective of the intelligence unit in an agency is to collect data, collate and store the data, and evaluate and attempt to "read" it, so that information can be made available to the line operations. Other than the broadest outline, little is actually known about intelligence in a police department. Occasionally, the intelligence collection about individuals and their beliefs becomes news and proves embarrassing, but that is about all one knows about the inner workings of a unit. Intelligence officers are selective in choosing those who receive their estimates, facts, and opinions.

Interest in internal affairs, or the police investigation of police, has been renewed as a result of the Knapp Commission Report on the New York City Police Department. Police investigators are assigned the responsibility of investigating allegations of wrongdoing by the police. The types of alleged wrongdoings range from insulting behavior to brutality to the public; and from accepting a free cup of coffee to accepting bribes for allowing crimes to occur. Like all so-called crimes without victims, the victim in police payoffs is actually the public, general morality, or other unmeasurable aspects. The fact that policemen sometimes have to investigate policemen does not inspire confidence in the public. But if internal affairs are conducted correctly, it helps to keep officers from succumbing to temptation and from becoming a law unto themselves.

Criticisms of police organization

American police agency organization has been criticized severely by people both within and outside the police community. Most of the criticisms center around those areas pointed out in the President's Commission Report of 1967. Some of the criticisms are the following: the agencies lack qualified leadership; chiefs and middle-management personnel lack sufficient education and training; many departments are not organized in accordance with well-established principles of modern business management and resist change; many departments lack trained personnel in specialized fields, such as research and planning, law, business administration, and computer analysis; many departments fail to deploy and utilize personnel efficiently; and many departments have not adequately applied technological advances which would benefit law enforcement.

However, an increasing number of police agencies, with financial and technical aid from LEAA and other federal and state sources, have instituted long-range programs of organizational development and are working toward overcoming these organizational weaknesses. They are seeking the advice of nonpolice organizational and management specialists. Good organization has become the goal of practically all large police agencies.

Summary

This chapter has discussed police services, which generally fall into one of two categories: line function or staff and supportive functions. Line functions are led by the patrol unit. Patrol is the center of the law enforcement wheel around which all other functions revolve. Also included in line functions are traffic, juvenile, vice and narcotics, and plainclothes. The staff and supportive functions are investigative, records, crime laboratories, and communications. Communications is of vital importance to the entire criminal justice system. Advances are being made in the area and many experimental programs are underway.

The preventive patrol tactic of field interviews has come under considerable criticism from the community. However, the Supreme Court has ruled in *Terry* v. *Ohio* in favor of this police procedure.

In recent years the role of the policewoman has expanded to include police functions that had been previously closed to them, particularly in the area of uniformed patrol. Another change is the increased citizen involvement in law enforcement. Two major trends are occurring and are likely to expand with the coming years. They are the utilization of reserve and the development of neighborhood crime prevention programs.

Police are working more in the area of special investigations. Cases that cross jurisdictional lines and are multiviolational require special investigation units. Many agencies across the country are trying new programs so as to better deal with this problem.

TOPICS FOR DISCUSSION

1. Discuss the line and staff functions of a police organization.
2. Discuss the basic police methods of reducing crime.
3. Discuss police officer discretion; the forces that mold discretionary decisions.
4. Discuss the trend and directions of police in America.

6

The Police: Styles

The study of this chapter will enable you to:

1. **Present the causes of police role conflict.**
2. **Discuss the different policing styles.**
3. **Demonstrate the source of community perceptions of police.**
4. **Provide an explanation of future police trends.**

In this chapter we shall examine how the police go about their daily business in communities. We shall demonstrate that as organizations and as individuals they differ among themselves in philosophies of policing. By philosophies of policing, we mean their viewpoints and opinions about how they should enforce the laws and preserve the peace. For example, some police departments spend a lot of time on juvenile delinquency programs; others concentrate on patrol and the investigation of crimes, and they deal with juveniles only when they arrest them for specific offenses. Some departments have large, separate traffic divisions; others let the patrol division handle traffic along with its other duties. These differences in emphases indicate differences in policing philosophy. The distinctive pattern of such emphases displayed by a department is that department's policing style.

We shall also look at the individual police officer. Just as departments have styles, so do police officers. For example, in answering a disturbance call involving a fighting husband and wife, one officer may walk in, stop the fight, and ask if either party wishes to file a legal complaint against the other. If neither wishes to do this, as is generally the case, the officer will drop the matter and leave after warning them not to make any further disturbance. Another officer of the same department, however, may sit down and spend considerable time with the couple, listening to their grievances, and trying to help them work things out. Still another officer may help them fill out the forms requesting marriage counseling assistance from a community service organization. He may even fill out the forms himself if they cannot read or write. Each officer handles problems according to his own style, and each style illustrates how that officer makes on-the-spot decisions and how he exercises—note the following phrase, you will see it often in this chapter—*his power of discretion*.

Keep in mind that policing styles and police discretion are complex and controversial subjects. Some veteran police officers and administrators will not even admit that they exist. They are wrong; style and discretion do exist and police display them every day. We shall not attempt to make any rigid rules about whether or not they should be applied. Our purpose is to show that they may benefit or harm a community, depending upon how they are applied.

We shall limit our discussion to community police agencies—generally speaking, these are municipal and county departments—whose broad general jurisdictions put them in close daily contact with the public. Because of their wide range of activities and the broad discretion they give their members in performing these activities, they develop the most diversified and distinctive organizational and individual policing styles.

Conflict in the police role

One of the basic reasons for the American Revolution was that people wanted freedom from an oppressive government. A fear of the potential power of the government to abuse its citizens has long prevailed in the United States. This places the police officer in a difficult role because he represents governmental authority, and he happens to be the representative of government with whom most citizens have the most frequent contact. Furthermore, he is the only governmental official authorized to use force to carry out assignments. This threat of force, although often needed, is frequently resented by citizens. Historically, the police response to this public resentment has been a tendency to isolate themselves from the community and to develop a strong feeling of group solidarity.

What do we mean by role? Role can be generally defined as the expectations held by individuals and groups about *what* an organization or individual employee of that organization is supposed to do and *how* he is supposed to do it. Keep in mind that both organizations and individuals have roles. The police organization has a role in the community, and the police officer has a role in the community and in his organization. Expectations aimed at defining the police organization's role come from the law, the community, and the police organization itself. Expectations aimed at the individual police officer's role come from all of the same sources and also from his fellow employees. These expectations may not be communicated clearly, or they may contradict each other. In both instances, role conflict results.

Most expectations concerning the police role, both as organizations and as individuals, come from the criminal law. Criminal law is both substantive and procedural. Substantive law defines or describes the acts that are prohibited or required. Robbery, murder, and larceny, for example, are prohibited acts; having a driver's license, or obtaining a license to go hunting or sell liquor are required acts. Procedural criminal law describes the correct way to apply the substantive criminal law. Particularly, it describes the procedures that the police must use to enforce the substantive law in a legal fashion, such as warning a suspect of his constitutional rights prior to an interview, bringing him before a magistrate without delay after arrest, and affording him the opportunity to consult with legal counsel.

Conflict caused by substantive criminal law

Two factors create the conflict in the case of substantive criminal law. The first is the shortage of police officers available to enforce laws. Because of this lack, in most communities the police must be selective in the laws they enforce. This is not always a source of conflict, however, because a second source of police role expectations—the community—*does not* want some laws rigidly enforced. But a conflict always arises when there is a difference of opinion between the police and the community over which laws should be selectively enforced. A case in point might be gambling for charitable purposes. A raid on a church bingo game might set off a violent community uproar against the police. The second sensitive area concerns traffic laws. Citizens normally expect a certain tolerance in speeding cases; they expect "warnings," rather than tickets, in such nonmoving violations as faulty headlights and taillights. If the police suddenly begin to rigidly enforce traffic laws, the community, through its political leaders, may demand a return to the old level of tolerance.

In communities where there is a police–community consensus on what laws are to be selectively enforced and what laws are to be enforced tolerantly, the conflict is minimized. Such a consensus is most likely to occur in those rural and suburban communities where a substantial majority of the population have the same socioeconomic and racial/ethnic backgrounds. In these communities the expected standards of community conduct are generally agreed upon and are clearly communicated to the police. The community–police relationship in this type of community tends to become a personal one because the police and citizens know each other rather well.

This close personal relationship between citizens and police rarely exists in large cities. Large cities usually have diverse populations composed of a wide variety of socioeconomic and racial/ethnic groups. Each neighborhood in the city has different expectations concerning the manner in which the police should handle such law violations as gambling, liquor violations, traffic violations, peace disturbances, and juvenile delinquency.

Conflict caused by procedural criminal law

Another source of role conflict for police is procedural criminal law. Ideally, the police should always enforce substantive criminal laws in the manner prescribed by procedural law. Ideally, police should never make illegal arrests, illegal searches of persons and property, or coerce confessions. However, they occasionally do violate procedural laws. The reason for this may arise from community expectations concerning the police role. The community expects the police to deal efficently with the crime problem and may exert pressure, often through political leaders or the news media, to reduce the crime rate. Occasionally, this pressure has led the police to be more concerned with solving crimes and making arrests (enforcing substantive laws) than with doing so in the proper manner (observing procedural criminal law). Here again the legal expectations of the police role and community expectations conflict, and the police organization must adjust to the conflict. The adjustment contributes to the development of a policing style.

Another important source of role conflict is the expectations derived from the police organization itself. Historically, community police agencies have had a tendency to assume that the most important part of their job is dealing with major crimes like murder, rape, robbery, burglary, larceny, and others. This view is given support by the public concern shown to these crimes. At times, however, the policemen's desire to deal efficiently with crime is hampered, in their opinion, by the procedures they must use to solve these criminal cases. Many police officers criticize court decisions that they believe limit their ability to fight crime. Many police departments, especially in the urban areas, have developed a strong orientation toward crime-fighting, and they disregard procedural laws in some cases.

A training officer for an urban police agency once stated that it was important to distinguish between "good" police work and "legal" police work. "Good" police work was the fulfillment of a combination of community and organizational expectations of police performance. He gave as an example of "good" police work a case in which an individual was suspected of selling drugs, but the police had insufficient evidence to arrest him. The training officer said a "good" policeman would stop the individual's car, search it, remove and destroy any drugs found, and then release the individual because of the illegal arrest and search. This is clearly a case in which the policeman would violate procedural criminal laws to do what he perceived his organization and community expected him to do. "Legal" police work would not have allowed stopping the suspect at all.

Adjustment to role conflict: the development of policing styles

Role conflict requires that some degree of adjustment be made in role performance. How do the police respond to these diverse expectations? Numerous individuals have expressed their attitudes on the police role adjustment conflict, some of which will be discussed in this section. In this discussion, the word police will be used mainly to apply to organizations, and only in a lesser degree, to individuals.

Varying theories

In 1931 Hopkins described what he called the police "war theory" of crime control.[1] According to him, considerable public pressure is exerted on police to control crime. This creates a police attitude that favors settling matters with criminals in the streets by the use of excessive physical force if

[1] E. Jerome Hopkins, *Our Lawless Police* (New York: Viking Press, 1931).

necessary. Hopkins found a belief widespread among police that crime was controlled by punishment and that the police job was to administer that punishment. Any police illegalities involving excessive force and violation of procedural rights of suspects were considered acceptable.

From these observations, Hopkins developed his war theory of crime control. His theory was that police believed they were waging a war on crime, and that any methods were justified in winning that war. The basic role conflict discussed by Hopkins is essentially that between the conflicting demands of the substantive and procedural criminal law. The public and the police organization desire that crime be controlled by application of the punitive measures in the substantive law. The police organization and, in some cases, the police officer, desire to punish the offender by legal arrest and confinement in jail. But if procedural criminal law will not permit this because of a lack of evidence, the police may take matters into their own hands and deal out street justice by beating up a suspect with a nightstick or running him out of town.

Westley, in his 1951 research of a Midwestern city, makes observations similar to those of Hopkins.[2] Westley found that some police officers believed it permissible to use violence to gain respect from citizens. Westley also noted that the public regarded the policemen as corrupt and inefficient and that the policemen tended to view the citizens as their enemies. The police believed strongly that the manner in which they wanted to perform their job was in conflict with what was desired by the community.

This is a basic role conflict and the adjustments made by the police were as follows:

1. The police tended to withdraw from the community and isolate themselves by associating only with each other.

2. They disagreed with community desires because of the negative attitude displayed by the public toward the police.

3. They developed the belief that the use of violence to gain respect from citizens was acceptable (e.g., a person who "talks back" should get slapped or punched).

4. They sought to lessen public criticism of police by apprehending as many criminals as possible. In addition, the police organization rewarded its members for catching criminals with citations for bravery and promotions.

5. They accepted the use of violence, and the violation of the procedural rights of suspects in cases where information was required to apprehend criminals, and as punishment for sexual criminals when reluctant witnesses would not testify against them in court.

Banton refers to Westley in his comparative study of American and Scottish Police Departments.[3] In the three American cities studied, two

[2]William A. Westley, "The Police: A Sociological Study of Law, Custom, and Morality" (Ph.D. diss., Chicago, Ill.: University of Chicago Press, 1951; Published Cambridge, Mass.: MIT Press, 1970).

[3]Michael Banton, The Policeman in the Community (New York: Basic Books, 1964).

southern and one northeastern, Banton also found that, because of his job, the officer tended to become separated from the community. This separation created some problems in how police officers made decisions; that is, how they exercised discretion. According to Banton, the exercise of discretion is important to an officer on patrol because much of the time he is a peace officer (peace-keeper), rather than a law officer (law enforcer). The peace-officer role is important in the discusssion of policing styles because it illustrates what laws the department or the community want to be enforced selectively and how the officer acts when he is faced with violations of a law not on the list to be enforced. The role of peace officer forces the policeman to make his own decisions as to how he will handle violations that come to his attention, without leaning on the exact letter of the law as a guideline. This is an especially important role, according to Banton, because the patrolman usually spends much more of his time as a peace-keeper than as a law enforcer.

Another important contributor to understanding how police adjust to role conflict is Skolnick.[4] The adjustment that he describes concerns that between substantive and procedural criminal law. In a 1966 study of two urban police departments, Skolnick found a tendency on the part of police to emphasize the social-order role in preference to the legal-actor role. The police seemed more concerned with using substantive laws to maintain order than in following the guidelines of procedural laws. Above all, says Skolnick, the policeman sees his job as ferreting out crime by being alert and ready to respond vigorously to it, and only later to be concerned with justifications for the arrest or search made.

Skolnick also believes that the emphasis on police managerial efficiency in the United States encourages police to adopt the social-order role, and he believes that this managerial efficiency is often construed as "professionalism." The managerially efficient police administrator advocates statistical production in the form of arrests, traffic tickets issued, and the like.

The more arrests and tickets produced, the more efficient the individual officer and his organization appear on paper, and the more "professional" they seem. Police emphasis on social order through apprehending suspects is given support by this idea of professionalism. Skolnick believes that policemen are too concerned with controlling crime by any means necessary, and not enough with the legal expectations of their role. The police organizations' expectations of the social-order role (which have some community support) are to be efficient in making arrests and to be concerned about how the arrests were made only afterward, when the statistics are in.

[4]Jerome H. Skolnick, *Justice Without Trial* (New York: Wiley, 1967). Skolnick's distinction concerning the order-maintenance and legal-actor role of police is similar to Herbert Packard's crime-control and due-process models. The former emphasizes social control and factual guilt instead of legal guilt and individual justice. Herbert C. Packard, "Two Models on the Criminal Process," *University of Pennsylvania Law Review 113* (November 1964), pp. 1-68.

Wilson has also made an important contribution in understanding the role adjustment of police agencies.[5] In a study of eight community police organizations, Wilson identified three basic policing styles: (1) watchman, (2) legalistic, and (3) service. He said that the differences in styles could be noted when observing how each police organization handled two basic types of situations confronting police: order-maintenance and law-enforcement situations.

Order-maintenance situations are those related to disturbances of the peace or minor conflict between two or more people. Handling these situations is similar to the peace-keeping activities identified by Banton. Examples of peace disturbances might be a noisy drunk, a panhandler, or an apartment dweller's loud radio; examples of minor conflict might be a tavern fight, a family disturbance, or a landlord–tenant dispute. In these situations it is not simply a matter of applying the law; the law must also be interpreted and an attempt made to determine who is wrong and what to do about it. The power of arrest can be used, but frequently it is not. The police officer has broad discretion in handling these situations.

Law-enforcement situations demand a predetermined pattern of police response and much less discretion on the part of the patrolman. In cases of robbery, burglary, or serious assaults, the officer will always make an arrest if possible. Such situations require little interpretation of the law. Although traffic violations are not as serious as robbery and burglary, some of them are serious enough to warrant a predetermined pattern of response. For example, reckless speeding in a school zone will almost automatically result in the issuance of a ticket.

Wilson found more degrees of emphasis given to order-maintenance than to law-enforcement situations. The *watchman* style was frequently used by police involved in order-maintenance functions. This style, he said, tended to overlook, tolerate, or ignore many minor violations of the law, or at most, handle them short of arrest. The organization encouraged the patrolman to follow the path of least resistance. However, although many crimes were ignored as a matter of general practice, the police would occasionally adopt a "get tough" approach when they thought that certain activities were getting out of hand, such as when juvenile fights began developing into large-scale gang fights.

The second style Wilson identified was *legalistic*. The police department using this style encouraged the patrolman to take a law-enforcement view of as many of the situations he encountered as possible. He was then encouraged to view every situation in terms of legal alternatives. The legalistic department desired a single standard of conduct—the law—for the whole community, and generally only one appropriate solution—a legal one—for each situation.

Wilson's third style, *the service*, considers all situations encountered seriously. However, the service style does not formally apply the law as

[5]James Q. Wilson, *Varieties of Police Behavior* (Cambridge, Mass.: Harvard University Press, 1968).

frequently as does the legalistic. Order-maintenance situations are taken seriously, but alternatives other than arrest are often used. Some common alternatives are referral to a social service agency or the development of special police programs (e.g., traffic education, drug education, and others) to cope with order-maintenance problems.

A useful way to compare Wilson's three policing styles would be to contrast their respective responses to an order-maintenance situation involving juveniles drinking beer. The watchman-style police department would ignore the situation, or perhaps confiscate the beer, pour it out, and tell the juveniles to go home. The legalistic-style police department would arrest the juveniles and confiscate the beer for evidence. The service-style police department would probably confiscate the beer for evidence, take the juveniles home to their parents, and then suggest attendance in an educational program on the problems of alcohol, as an alternative to filing juvenile charges.

In a law-enforcement situation such as a "robbery in progress" call, all three organizations would undoubtedly respond in the same way; that is, attempt to arrest the suspect, since there would be little difference among the three styles in police role expectations.

A policing styles model

To help the reader understand more about community policing styles, we shall describe a model that can be used to analyze them. The model is a general one and should not be considered definitive or absolute, but rather as a useful method of examining the distinctive characteristics that represent an organization's adjustments to role conflict.

A basic assumption of this model is that a primary goal of police is to reduce crime and maintain order, in a manner designed to establish a trusting relationship between them and the great majority of citizens. Trust insures community support. The desire for community support reflects a desire to fulfill community expectations of the police role. The concern for reducing crime and maintaining order involves both the law-enforcement and order-maintenance situations described by Wilson, and the law officer and the peace officer roles of Banton. How these activities are carried out determines the style of the police organization.

Police methods   Generally speaking, police methods of reducing crime and maintaining order are directed at two broad causes of crime: (1) the opportunity to engage in crime and (2) the motive for engaging in crime. The word motive will be applied to both the desire and the reasons for the desire to engage in criminal or disorderly behavior.

From the standpoint of the general community, the police methods can be generally classified as either positive or negative in nature. Positive methods are those the general community tends to see as helping to solve crime and disorder problems; negative methods are those the general community tends to see as mere devices used by the police to punish citizens for lapses of behavior. A positive method of response to a rash of juvenile traffic violations would be a police-sponsored training course; a negative method would be to issue more traffic tickets to juveniles.

Some typical methods employed by police organizations to cope with crime and disorder are described in the following pages.

Education The education of the community to protect their own lives and property, and keeping the community informed about such matters as drug problems, the law, and driving problems are standard projects. The contemporary concept of crime prevention often involves educational programs encouraging the citizen to engage in "target hardening" (i.e., increasing protection for home or business). Education can be directed toward both opportunity and motive. Educational programs designed to "harden targets" primarily concern opportunity; programs designed to educate about drugs concern motive. Education is essentially a positive police method.

Apprehension This is essentially a "punishment" method. It implies the "catching" role of the police and includes such activities as criminal investigations (in which the intent is to arrest), undercover work, stakeouts, raids, and the like. It also involves the issuance of traffic tickets, which usually constitutes the most frequent police contact with citizens. Generally, this method is negative as far as the general community is concerned because of its "punishment" connotations.

Deterrence This method generally consists of making the police visible to the public in uniform or marked mobile units. Commonly called patrolling, it is designed to limit both the opportunity and desire to engage in inappropriate behavior. The uniformed, walking beat officer, the marked police car, and the helicopter are the primary means of deterrence. This is both a positive and a negative method because police presence reassures some citizens but frightens or creates anxiety for others.

Saturation This is an extreme form of deterrence that is carried out by "flooding" an area, usually a troublesome one, with police officers. It is directed at both opportunity and motive. Saturation generally includes aggressive patrolling and interrogation practices by police. The aggressiveness of these tactics and their frequent emphasis upon arrests make saturation a negative method.

Mediation This is also called conflict management, crisis intervention, and violence prevention. Essentially, it relies on the ability of specially trained police officers to act as mediators in interpersonal and intergroup conflicts. An example is a family disturbance in which an officer tries to act as mediator between a fighting husband and wife by reducing tensions and identifying some of the reasons for the conflict, to lessen the likelihood of a recurring fight. Since the police are placed in a helping relationship with the citizen, this is a positive method.

Referral or diversion This consists of referring or diverting individual problems to community agencies outside of the criminal justice system. Referral of a fighting husband and wife to a family counseling center may be an alternative after mediation has taken place. Diversion is most common in juvenile and drug cases. Referral and diversion are designed to deal with the motive rather than the opportunity for inappropriate behavior. These are positive methods because their purpose is to help, not punish, people.

Community perceptions of police

Figure 6-1 illustrates police methods concerning opportunity and motive, and their general positive and negative impact on community perceptions of police.

The combination of emphases given these methods constitutes the style of the police organization. To assist in developing a model of policing styles, the term *counselor method* will be applied to a positive method used by police, and the term *enforcer method* will be used to apply to a negative method. Then, generally speaking, the police can be placed in counselor or enforcer roles in the community. Figure 6-2 uses these two basic police roles to create a matrix that identifies styles of community police organizations.

Depending on the degree of emphasis given to the enforcer and counselor roles of police, several styles of community policing can be identified. Emphasis is defined as the tendency and willingness to use certain methods.

Degree of Emphasis	Policing Style
Low counselor and enforcer	Passive
Low counselor, high enforcer	Punitive
High counselor, low enforcer	Personalized
High counselor and enforcer	Integrated

There is a tendency in discussing styles to think of only one style for each police organization, yet one organization can have several styles. These styles may follow shift lines (e.g., days, evenings), specialty (e.g., traffic, investigations), or varying neighborhoods in the community. This is the result of different expectations of performance within the police organization itself; and different expectations create role conflict for which adjustments are necessary.

Passive policing is similar to Wilson's watchman style. Generally, the

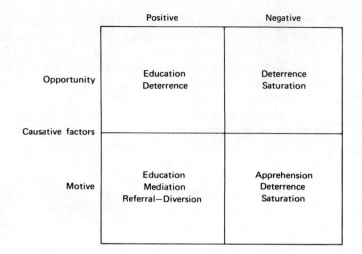

Figure 6-1

Categories of police methods: general community reaction.

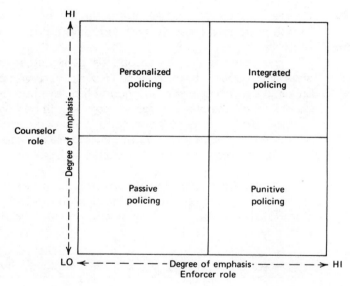

Figure 6-2

The counselor–enforcer model of policing styles.

police ignore many violations and avoid initiating any active programs to deal with crime problems. Passive policing usually occurs because of excessive political influence exerted on the police department to curb formerly aggressive activities. The other extreme, *punitive policing*, occurs when political pressure is put on the police to do something drastic about crime. An urban community that has had a passive police suddenly faced with a rising crime rate may pressure the police to "control" crime. The police response will probably be to engage in aggressive saturation tactics and increase arrests. In practice, punitive policing usually does not last long. The more aggressive the police become, the more the community resists and forces them back into a passive role. The passive-punitive cycle occurs frequently in many cities in which considerable political influence is exerted on the police department.

Personalized policing usually prevails in small communities where police officers and citizens know each other very well. This familiarity results in police decisions based on both the person and the problem, rather than merely on the problem itself. For example, in personalized policing, juvenile delinquents are much more likely to be taken home to their parents for punishment rather than be arrested.

Personalized policing can also exist in large cities that have precinct or neighborhood police stations because the people and the police get to know each other as individuals. This results in police decisions similar to those made in small communities.

The main problem with personalized police decisions is that they often reflect a "helping" role that may not be at all objective. It is one thing for a police officer to refer a person to a family counseling center to help solve a problem; it is another matter for an officer to let a person get away with a law violation because of friendship.

Another problem in personalized policing is that "favorite" groups may develop. In communities with diverse racial populations, middle-class whites may be treated favorably by the police, while the racial minority may be subjected to strict enforcer action. In such instances, personalized policing restricts the helping relationships to selected groups, usually the groups who "run" the community.

Integrated policing represents a balance between the enforcer and counselor roles of police. This balance usually occurs when a community, of whatever size, decides it wants objective, impartial, and effective policing, after the community becomes "fed up" with the other three styles and demands a change. The integrated style uses the enforcer and counselor roles in the combination that is found most effective in achieving the twin goals of controlling crime and maintaining community support. The leadership in an integrated department is likely to use all the police methods described above as community problems call for them. Success will lie in maintaining the correct balance.

Many police organizations are now attempting to change from personalized, passive, or punitive policing to something else by "professionalizing." Two types of professionalism that are now emerging are related to the integrated style. One is Wilson's service model and the other is the model characterized by Skolnick as "efficiency-oriented."

At present, Wilson's service model appears to be prevalent in suburban communities that have no internal social strife. These communities generally have no serious crime problems and are wealthy enough to demand a professional police force.

Skolnick's efficiency-oriented professionalism is prevalent in many large, urban area police departments. This professionalism supports punitive policing by rewarding arrests, the issuance of tickets, and other nega-

tively aggressive tactics. The efficiency-oriented department has not ye
rewarded the police officer for success in the counseling role. Until thes
departments recognize that the enforcer and the counselor roles must b
balanced, and both rewarded, the integrated style will not develop, an
efficient professionalism will not become effective professionalism.

The integrated police style is aimed only at effectiveness. It recognize
the following rules:

1. To be successful in crime control, an organization must develop commu
nity trust and support. The police will never be effective without the activ
support of the community.

2. There are many offenses of the law that can best be handled by positiv
counseling methods.

3. The legal expectations of the police role demand a strong commitment to
strict observance of the procedural rights of citizens.

4. The police role in controlling crime and disorder should not be overl
militant. Citizens of the community should be encouraged by the police t
accept a large part of this responsibility.

5. Historically, the more punitive the police have become in doing their job
the more restrictions have been placed upon them. Alternative roles t
that of the enforcer must be found.

6. The individual police officer must have a strong personal commitment t
professional growth and must constantly educate and train himself to in
sure this growth.

Police officer discretion

As we have said before, discretionary decisions make up the style of the
individual police officer. Several forces mold his discretionary decisions
Some of these are the law, organizational policy, opinions of the othe
officers he works with (his peer group), his personal orientation, the facts o
the situation. Many police organizations have attempted to formulate de
partmental policies to provide guidelines for the exercise of discretion, bu
the police officer faces such a wide variety of tasks and situations that it is
probably impossible to formulate policies to cover them all.

Another vital force exerted on the officer that greatly affects the man
ner in which he makes decisions is what Skolnick calls the "danger-
authority conflict." Police authority brings some unavoidable danger
which creates anxiety for the officers. They become acutely sensitive to
threatening situations and threatening people, and they act aggressively
to protect themselves in situations in which they suspect danger is likely.
The problem is that the police officer may stereotype certain people and
situations as threatening when they are really not, and then make faulty
decisions as a result. Some of these faulty decisions have precipitated
riots and bloodshed in the past.

Another factor that influences discretionary decisions is the fixed idea that, in encounters with citizens, most police expect to be treated with respect and to have their wishes obeyed. When they do not get this response they may exercise their discretion to punish the lack of it. Citizens who "talk back" to police officers may receive traffic tickets for violations that would earn a "polite" citizen only a verbal or written warning.

Many police officers make decisions in peace-keeping, order-maintenance, and law-enforcement situations based on the status of the person involved. Some police treat young people, minority groups, and poor people differently than they do older people, nonminority group members, and people of higher socioeconomic status.

Police officers make decisions daily that do not reflect the expectations of the law or what their organization desires. Police tend to underenforce the law far more frequently than they overenforce it. They are much more likely to make discretionary decisions that are less restrictive than the law than they are to make decisions that interpret the law strictly or abuse the legal rights of citizens.

However used, discretion must be kept in mind by each police officer and police organization. To insure fair decisions by officers, organizations must develop policies insuring a reasonably objective approach to each encounter. Education and training will help in this endeavor. These policies should give police officers guidance as to the performance expected when dealing with specific community groups. As police organizations branch out into counseling activities, it is especially important to create alternatives to arrest that will assist in solving community problems, which is preferable to avoiding the problems or punishing the participants.

The importance of guiding the discretion of police officers cannot be overemphasized. The day-to-day behavior of officers is the practice of justice in society. If this behavior is objective and equitable, justice is more likely to become a reality to the citizens of the United States.

The direction of law enforcement

It is always difficult to forecast with accuracy the trends and directions of any public service when it is in a period of radical change. Several prominent occurrences of the 1960s and 1970s give some strong indication of trends and directions. These trends are civilian involvement; the increasing education, training and knowledge desires of the rank and file; the alternative means of service delivery; and the increasing demands by rank and file to have some say in the direction and control of their chosen profession.

A growing phenomenon is citizen involvement in law enforcement. Two major trends are occurring and are likely to continue and expand with the coming years. First, police departments are using reserves in greater numbers, and they are increasing the roles that reserves may perform. The fact that Texas, California, and other states are developing standards and training for reserves attests to the growing recognition of their importance and utilization. The task of policing is simply too great, and the demands on the peace officer are too many. With proper training and selection, reserve programs can and are becoming a vital part of American law enforcement. Second, crime prevention programs are being developed that enlist the eyes and ears of the public. The police cannot do the job alone, and they need information. For example, a good neighborhood antiburglary program not only marks valuables but trains neighbors to watch each other's homes, observe and record descriptions of people who are strange to the area, copy license numbers of suspicious vehicles, record make and model, and generally observe what goes on around them. By advising the public to observe and record significant information, the task of the police is greatly aided. Public involvement, either as a reserve or as being an observant neighbor, is likely to increase.

Alternative methods for the delivery of police services will continue to be developed and sought. Consolidation of agencies, contractual services and agency coordination will continue. The success of such consolidation as Jacksonville, Duval County and Miami, Dade County in Florida; Knoxville, Davidson County in Tennessee; and Indianapolis, Marion County in Indiana will be imitated where feasible. Contractual services, such as those in Los Angeles County, will be developed elsewhere. The joint task forces used to handle an area problem such as narcotics will probably be extended to other forms and functions as needs arise. Some jurisdictions like Spokane and Spokane County, are experimenting with joint usage of a public safety building. These are just a few of the interagency attempts to deliver better services. Within departments, new ways are also sought. In hardware, some police departments are experimenting with the use of small import cars, and the South San Francisco Police—located in a high smog area—use propane for cleaner emissions. Departments are using more cadets and civilian personnel in the stations in order to put more sworn personnel "on the streets." Community service officers in some areas are being employed to deliver services not requiring a uniformed officer. All of these are attempts to find new ways. This search will continue.

The years ahead will undoubtedly see a more militant stand by rank and-file police. For years police have been poorly paid, criticized, and generally held in low esteem. Today they are organizing into collective bargaining units. Whether the organizations representing policemen are desirable or not from a public service standpoint, and whether what they demand is right or not, one thing is certain—policemen have ceased to be quiet and will in the future make their desires known.[6]

During the twentieth century the role of the police has been changing

[6]See William J. Bopp, ed., *The Police Rebellion: A Quest for Blue Power* (Springfield, Ill.:Charles C Thomas, 1971).

seeking a definition acceptable to the expectations of the law, the community, and the police themselves. The likelihood is that the role assumed by community police will continue to vary from locality to locality as it always has. The direction is unquestionably toward professionalism, but community expectations will undoubtedly shape the form that this professionalism will take.

Certainly, professionalism is needed. The problems confronting police are complex and must be dealt with by well-educated, dedicated individuals. However, one of the unintended consequences of professionalism is that of developing the attitude that the professional is always right. Just as the police have isolated themselves in the past from the community by a negative attitude toward the public, they could also isolate themselves in the future by retreating into a narrow concept of "efficiency-oriented" professionalism.

This isolation must not be allowed to develop. A community–police partnership is essential if problems of crime and disorder are to be solved. To create this partnership, it will be necessary for the community to trust its police organization and police officers. This trust will come only after police officers begin making consistently equitable decisions in the treatment of citizens, and after police organizations balance their counselor and enforcer roles in the best interests of the community.

Summary

One of the major influences on policing is role concept: the role concept of the police organization, the role concept of the individual officer, and the role expectations of the community. If role expectations are not clearly communicated and, sometimes even if they are, role conflict may occur. Criminal law, substantive and procedural, may also cause role conflict. This role conflict requires that adjustments be made in role performance.

Generally speaking, police methods of reducing crime and maintaining order are directed at two broad causes of crime: opportunity and motive. The methods used are generally classified by the community as either positive (crime-solving) or negative (punishment). Typical methods employed by police agencies include: (1) education, (2) apprehension, (3) deterrence, (4) saturation, (5) mediation, and (6) referral/diversion. These methods are not inclusive, but they are the most common ones used at this time.

Depending on the degree of emphasis given to enforcer and counselor roles of police, several styles of community policing can be indentified. They are: (1) passive policing, (2) punitive policing, (3) personalized policing, and (4) integrated policing.

The individual police officer uses discretion in decision-making. Several forces effect his discretion: laws, opinions of other officers. personal orientation, and the facts of the case all play an important role.

1. Discuss the police role conflict and the causes.

2. Discuss the two broad causes of crime and the methods that police emplo against each cause.

3. Discuss community perceptions of police.

4. Discuss the integrated police style.

7

Police: current issues and future trends

The study of this chapter will enable you to:

1. **Understand the background of future issues for the police.**
2. **Comprehend the impact of police unions upon law enforcement.**
3. **Identify some current trends that may result in dramatic changes for police.**
4. **Realize some of the problems the police of the future may be confronted with.**

In Chapters 4, 5, and 6, we examined the past and the present; but what about the future? Can we expect major changes? Will the future produce issues for law enforcement that will have a profound effect on the American police system? If so, what are some of these issues?

Police unions

Police unionization, the trend that started a number of years ago, began with the organization of police groups called associations, which are evolving into full-fledged labor unions. In fact, in many areas police are now represented at the collective bargaining table by well-established labor unions, such as the Teamsters Union. This representation has created problems for the traditional police administrator who has typically managed his department with a great deal of autonomy. He is now confronted with the threat of strike, which may come in the form of "the blue flu," or mass "sick-ins," where the majority of his patrol force claim illness rather than report to work. An example was the Detroit Police Department during the early seventies: hundreds of the policemen refused to come to work. They would telephone in and claim that they had the flu. This was usually in response to failure to receive an adequate pay raise or as protest against any one of a number of working conditions that they wished changed. Although police have never had a tradition of the right to strike or to walk off the job, these tactics had the same effect as a labor strike. In California, when the Highway Patrol felt that they were being treated unfairly by their organization, they refused to issue traffic citations or, later, drastically increased the amount of citations issued. This, in turn, brought public pressure to resolve the issues of contention.

More and more, police administrators are concerned that they are losing their traditional control over their employees, and some feel they are losing control over the direction of their law enforcement efforts.

When a police agency is affiliated with a collective bargaining union, the public may ask, "Who is in control? Is it the union leadership, who may or may not have any responsibility toward us? Do elected officials who represent us still have the ability to decide the level of enforcement that we desire?"

When we examine the typical budget of a major law enforcement agency, we see that the majority of the taxpayer's dollar goes toward the payment of salaries. If the taxpayer cannot or will not exercise a voice in what the level of salary will be, what are the possible ramifications? If the public refuses to allocate sufficient money to support a law enforcement agency, and the police feel that their salaries are not adequate and that this is sufficient justification to go on strike, the effects are that the public is without police services. At that point the police administrator is called upon to resolve the question. The police administrator may feel as though he has been excluded from the decision-making process because of the collective bargaining, and he no longer has control over the major portion of his resources. However, police unionization is a reality; an issue of concern for both present and future police administrators.

Education

Another issue that some feel may be directly related to the concept of police unionization and collective bargaining is education. In the United States, advanced education has traditionally implied increased earning ability, increased salary. Higher education for police officers may be correlated with a demand for increased salaries. Police are moving rapidly toward minimum standards of a Bachelors Degree for entry-level positions. In those communities where these minimum standards of educational level have been met, the salaries paid to policemen are significantly higher than in those communities in which the educational standards are somewhat lower. In addition to the demand for higher salaries, higher education is generally accompanied by demands for more challenging and responsible positions.

There may be a need to reanalyze the typical duties assigned to a policeman; a police officer's job is frequently routine and may bore the more educationally advanced individual. Perhaps the police administrator will be confronted with providing a deeper and more challenging function. How will he do this? How will he address this demand? He cannot ignore the routine nature of law enforcement. Those basic tasks that his employees may now feel are not stimulating enough must continue to be performed.

Energy enforcement

Energy supply is one of the major issues confronting our society. We need not speculate that law enforcement will be caught up in the issue; it already has been. It began with the control of the automobile, when the nationwide speed limit was reduced to 55 miles per hour on all highways. It has been stated that that step was the first major change in the thrust of many of our law enforcement agencies. It was the first time, perhaps, that a law enforcement agency became an energy enforcement rather than a criminal enforcement agency. Our highway patrol departments and state police agencies throughout the nation are now in the business of enforcing energy-saving laws, which is a dramatic shift from previous concepts of their responsibilities. We now find vast amounts of resources allocated not toward the safety of the public, but toward conserving energy. When we consider that most of our nation's highways were built for speeds in excess of 70 miles an hour and that most automobiles are built to operate safely at those higher speeds, we must acknowledge that the major purpose of the 55 mile-an-hour speed limit law is to conserve energy. Many police officials find themselves uncomfortable in this new role of energy conservation regulators.

Nuclear control

Although the nuclear age has been with us for some time, law enforcement agencies have recently become specifically concerned with the control of nuclear substances. The prevention of nuclear theft may be the most critical issue in the future. A recent dramatic example occured when a nation was accused of committing a theft of plutonium, the substance necessary for nuclear development. The need for tight security exists, and much of the responsibility for this security will fall upon local law enforcement agencies. As uses of nuclear substances become more and more frequent, local law enforcement officials will be required to develop safeguards to transport and to prevent the theft and misuse of these substances. This will require a great deal more understanding of nuclear substances by the police official of the future.

International crimes

A conference entitled "Perspectives on Terrorism" was recently held at the International Institute of Higher Studies in Criminal Studies in Siracusa, Italy. Cherif Bassiouni, a law professor at De Paul University, who advises the State Department on international crime, suggested many dramatic actions that might be taken by terrorists. The targets might be water pump and filtration systems, fuel storage facilities, dams, off-shore drilling platforms, government headquarters, in addition to nuclear reactors.

Computerized crimes

Recent media crime coverage has made the public aware of the millions of dollars that are stolen annually through the use of computer technology. Most of the nation's banking and financial institutions have computers at the core of their transactions—computers that are interconnected. It has been discovered that criminals with expertise in computer technology have been able to intercept large amounts of money and transact illegal exchanges. The police cannot ignore these losses; they must develop strategies, train personnel, and allocate resources to the control of this sophisticated criminal activity. In addition, many industries, both governmental and private, utilize the computer to store data that are critical for their planning and growth. In the competitive, free market this information and data must be maintained under tight security to preserve the integrity of their future plans.

Political crimes

Throughout history, public officials have at various times been exposed for corruption and graft in office, but the level of public interest and the volume of public information have made discovery of this type of activity more prevalent in recent years. Since the Watergate era, it has become obvious that various acts committed by public officials, which may include the more traditional crimes of theft and of violence, may also include influence-buying. This is currently under investigation by the United States Department of Justice. The investigation of political crimes has been the responsibility of federal agencies, but in the future, local law enforcement agencies will probably become involved in the investigation and enforcement of legislation intended to protect the public from some of their public officials.

Rapid transit crime

To meet the needs of our increased population, our technology has improved the ability of people to travel across the nation, and more sophisticated methods of public transportation are being developed. The Bay Area Rapid Transit District (BART) in San Francisco is an example of a public transportation system that has its own police force. This force is separate from and responsible only to the BART officials, and yet it has the same police powers and responsibilities that any other traditionally recognized police force has. However, even though rapid transit districts will have their own police forces with the same traditional enforcement powers, they will not be able to survive using traditional techniques. They are dealing with a transient population, not a community where people have established homes or businesses. Providing police services to a constantly changing population will be a unique challenge for the police officer of the future.

Victimology

Our system of criminal justice has traditionally focused its energies and efforts toward the identification and apprehension, and prosecution and rehabilitation of *offenders*. Not enough attention has been paid to the needs of the *victims* of criminal acts; recently however, this has become an issue. Refer to Chapter 1, Figure 1-2: "The Criminal Injustice System." This figure clearly shows the current state of affairs; it contrasts our treatment of the offender with our treatment of the victim in any given criminal offense at each step of the process. More and more states are enacting legislation that provides various services to victims of crimes. In the mid-seventies, the state of California enacted legislation that makes indemnification of victims of serious crimes mandatory. When the police become aware that a victim of a serious crime has suffered either monetarily or physically, they must inform the victim how he or she can be reimbursed for their injuries by the state. A report must be filed demonstrating that this notification has been made. Under many circumstances the victims of a serious assault, for example, will have their medical bills and other expenses paid by the state.

In many courts restitution is becoming a condition of probation or parole or as part of the sentence of the offender. We can project that more demands will be made upon the police in the future to provide investigative services and support for victims of crimes, to insure that they are adequately reimbursed for their losses. It is entirely possible that at some point in the near future the state may be held liable for losses suffered by victims of crimes, since one of the fundamental purposes of tax-supported law enforcement agencies is to provide security and safety to citizens. The citizens may hold the police and other governmental agencies responsible if they fail in their duties.

As an example, the homeowner whose house is burglarized and whose television set has been stolen may take the position that he has been paying for protection against that type of intrusion. Since he did not receive the service, he may hold the public agency liable for the loss. This may not be a popular trend, especially among law enforcement officials. But it might provide a method of determining the effectiveness and efficiency of various law enforcement agencies.

One of the assumptions that has traditionally separated public agencies from private agencies is that public agencies do not operate on a profit-or-loss basis as does the private sector. A merchant is considered successful so long as he makes a profit. If police agencies were required to reimburse victims for property losses, they could be judged by the same criteria as are private businesses. This may prove to be unrealistic, but it is certainly a possibility if the trend of reimbursement, restitution, and indemnification continues.

At the very least, it is valid to suggest that the system as a whole, including the police, the courts, and corrections, be required to provide the same services to the victims as they do for the offenders. These may include medical benefits, legal advice, job retraining in the event of physical injury, and restitution for working time lost while testifying in court.

One study in 1976 in Multnomah County, Portland, Oregon, demonstrated that of $22 million spent in Law Enforcement Assistance Administration grants in that state during the period of 1970-76, only $287,900 was spent for victims during the same time period! Many people believe that it is time that law enforcement and criminal justice move toward justice for the victim as well as for the offender.

Civic liability

A final area that will produce issues which may have a profound effect upon trends of law enforcement in the future stems from an old statute in the federal law that permits public officials, namely police officers, to be held personally liable for official acts. Until the late sixties and early seventies police officers felt secure that if they did, in fact, violate the constitutional rights of an individual or in some other way injure a citizen, they would be protected by their employer, either by insurance or legal defense. Recently, however, more and more officers are being held responsible for their acts during the course of their duty. There have been a number of instances in which officers have been held responsible for settlements and awards over $100,000 for the excessive use of force which may or may not have resulted in injury. For example, as the result of a routine disturbance complaint in 1968, a suit was filed charging that a police officer in the Chicago Police Department had struck a pregnant woman who subsequently gave birth to a deformed child. As a result the Chicago police officer, the police superintendent, and several members of the Civil Service Commission were held liable for $131,000 in damages. This was a personal liability, not one assumed by the city of Chicago. Reference to that case is *Moon* v. *Winfield*, 368 F. Supp. 843 (N.D. Ill.).

Summary

In a textbook of this nature it is difficult to predict the future with a great deal of accuracy. Therefore, this brief chapter has demonstrated only those trends that seem to be most acute at this time.

Few experts in the field of law enforcement would deny that police unions will become a more complex issue during the next few years. The same belief exists for the other trends presented. They too will change the scope and nature of police services in the next decade. Serious students of criminal justice will certainly discover other patterns that also will change police service, but we have limited this chapter until the future provides more clarity and definition of those changes.

TOPICS FOR DISCUSSION

1. Discuss the issue of whether police unions should be permitted.
2. Discuss what may cause unions in police organizations.
3. Discuss whether police officers need higher education. Why or why not?
4. Discuss energy enforcement, nuclear control, and how a local police agency might be involved.
5. Discuss the relative merits of each trend presented. Should the police be responsible for their control?

PART 3
The Courts

8

The courts:
an historical
perspective

The study of this chapter will enable you to:

1. **Demonstrate the development of courts in America.**
2. **Explain the source of some inequities of the court system.**
3. **Present the different functions of various levels of courts throughout the United States.**
4. **Define the job responsibilities of paraprofessionals in the judicial function.**

No one can put his finger on a certain date in history and say, "This is when courts of law came into existence." Courts did not spring forth fully developed at any specific point in time, they evolved over a long period from primitive institutions and procedures. Courts could not have existed before there were written laws, although in the dim past the headman of a tribe dividing an animal (slain for food) among his people performed some of the functions of a judge. About 2000 B.C. the Code of Hammurabi (King of Babylon, 1947 B.C.–1905 B.C.), was engraved in 4000 lines of writing on a pillar of stone. This code of law covered crimes of adultery, personal violence, sorcery, and many others, and set forth the penalty for each violation. The Code had three essential features: individual responsibility for personal acts; belief in the sanctity of oaths sworn before God; and the necessity of producing written evidence in all charges made alleging violations of the Code. These features survive today in our court system.

Since the law was written and unquestionably enforced, some form of tribunals (courts) must have existed—perhaps in the form of a king or governor sitting as the sole judge and jury to decide guilt or innocence from the evidence presented.

Nineveh, the ancient capital of the Assyrian world, had tribunals that, according to ancient writings, meted out sentences to murderers, thieves, and adulterers. Egypt, one of the most ancient of civilizations, had a system of courts as early as 1500 B.C., punishing bribery and corruption. Enforcement of tax collection was one of the earliest forms of crimes referred to royal tribunals. Amenhotep, King of Egypt, in 1400 B.C., set up custom houses on his seacoast and punished tax evaders in special courts.

Since our original court systems in the United States were established under the influence of our British colonial heritage, the ancient origins of English courts are of interest to us. Courts in early Anglo-Saxon times, such as the courts of *pied poudre* ("dusty feet"), were set up in the county markets to handle minor matters with local officials appointed by the king sitting as judges. Certain practices that are in use today originated in these courts. The practice of suspending sentence, or withholding penalty on condition that the offender make restitution or reform his habits, developed in these courts as well as the practice of release on personal recognizance, whereby people who had sworn not to flee were given freedom until the date of their trial. Generally speaking, the sentences handed down by these courts were retaliatory—blinding, maiming, and execution were common forms of punishment.

Our system is based on the British common law that originated in decisions rendered by the English royal courts that were established by Henry II in the twelfth century. The basis of this law is legal precedent. In other words, the court looks backward to former court decisions in order to determine what the law is.

In the strict sense we do not have an American court system. We have 50 individual state court systems and one federal court system. These systems differ among themselves in some ways that may confuse the student, but they are similar in many other ways because they developed from a common British heritage and therefore show a strong family resemblance to each other. We shall concern ourselves mainly with criminal courts (as opposed to civil courts), which are the heart of justice administration in the United States. In general, we shall concentrate on the similarities of these courts, rather than on their dissimilarities, because it would be far beyond the scope of this book to attempt to describe each of the 50 systems in detail.

In the United States, courts originate from three sources; that is, they are created by three authorities: (1) the U.S. Constitution, (2) the state constitutions, and (3) legislative enactments. Therefore, there are two general types of courts in the United States, as far as their creation is concerned—constitutional courts and legislative courts. Remember that when we use the term constitutional court we mean a court created either by the U.S. Constitution or the constitution of a sovereign state. When we use the term legislative court, we mean one created by the U.S. Congress or the legislature of a sovereign state.

The United States has a highly complex dual court system. This complexity exists in part because our Founding Fathers decided upon a form of government that divided power between the states and the federal government. Because of their decision, each level has developed a distinct set of laws, which requires two unique court structures to administer each set of laws.

Another characteristic that produces complexity is the approach that each state has taken toward establishing a court structure; each state has developed its judicial system somewhat differently. Consequently, there are over 100 courts in the federal system and 50 state court systems that comprise the court system in the United States.

Generally, each state has some similarities and each has four levels as does the federal system. Table 8-1 demonstrates the hierarchical nature that exists in the state courts as well as in the federal courts. The lower case titles within the state structure indicate some of the more popular

Table 8-1

Court structure in the
United States.

Federal	State
Court of last resort U.S. Supreme Court	Court of last resort *Supreme, criminal *Appeals, court of appeals
Appellate courts U.S. Courts of Appeal	Appellate courts *Superior courts, District courts, etc.
Trial courts U.S. District Courts	Trial courts *Circuit court, state, county court, etc.
Lower courts U.S. Magistrates	Lower courts Municipal, justice, traffic, etc.

*Common names of state courts.

titles throughout the United States, but do not reflect all titles that may exist. For our purposes, the four general types of courts may be applied to every state. Recently, there have been several attempts by some states to reform the four-tier system.

For example, state court reform and reorganization appears to be taking a series of steps forward in California and elsewhere. First, there is an effort to simplify the structure by structuring it into a two-tier or three-tier level. The two-tier structure would consist of an appellate level and a unified trial court. In the three-tier system there would be an added court of limited jurisdiction below the unified trial court.

Strong state control by a supreme court is also a goal. Using this concept all budgets, personnel matters, and even physical facilities would come under this court. There would be a strong court administrator to manage this system. Alaska and Hawaii currently are organized in this manner.

Federal court structure has not changed significantly since 1958, but prior to that date several changes did occur. Article III of the Constitution provides for a Supreme Court and allows Congress to establish inferior courts as they deem necessary. The Constitutional Convention of 1787 could not agree upon a specific framework for the federal court system, thus Article III, by giving the power to Congress, represented a compromise. The first Congress, by passing the Judiciary Act of 1789, did establish an inferior court system that lasted, with some exceptions in its basic form, for over a century. The Judiciary Act of 1789 provided for a federal court district in each of the states. Congress also divided the country into three federal circuit court districts with two Supreme Court justices assigned to ride the circuit. Together with one district court judge, they would hold two sessions annually and hear appeals from district courts. Additionally, they had original jurisdiction to try some types of cases.

In 1801 the Federalists attempted to modify the system in two ways.

First, they eliminated the circuit riding of the judges; second, they enlarged the jurisdiction of the inferior courts. When the Jeffersonian Republicans took office in 1802, the Judiciary Act was repealed. Congress, at that time, divided the country into six circuits. They also reinstituted the circuit riding by the justices of the Supreme Court.

In 1869 the basic structure was modified. The Act of 1869 provided for one circuit court judge for each of the circuits. Supreme Court justices were required to sit with the circuit court only once every two years.

Congress made major modifications in the federal judicial system again in 1891 when they removed the appellate jurisdiction from the circuit courts and created a Circuit Court of Appeal from each circuit. The Act of 1891 itself was changed in 1911, when the circuit courts were abolished and their jurisdiction was assumed by the district courts. The name of the Circuit Court of Appeal was changed in 1958 to Courts of Appeal.

The structure of the judicial system at the local, state, and federal levels reflects the influence of social and political growth. An examination of the historical development of the courts reveals that social and economic forces have greatly influenced our laws and judicial operations. The court system, like other branches of our government, has, for better or worse, been molded by its environment.

As new social, economic, and political needs develop, modifications will be made in the court system to meet them. We cannot look into the future and say with any great accuracy what these modifications will be. We can say, judging from history, that the changes will not be made uniformly or without opposition.

State judicial systems

General characteristics

There are many kinds of state court systems presently operating in the United States. Although each of these systems may vary in terms of "jurisdiction," title, or function, all share three common attributes. These common attributes include (1) hearing appeals from lower courts (appellate jurisdiction); (2) conducting trials in cases arising from a broad array of crimes and civil matters (general jurisdiction); and (3) conducting trials in cases of specified or specialized crimes (limited jurisdiction). Furthermore, some of the state courts may perform combinations of these functions.

There is a level of hierarchy within the state court systems. If we look at these positions of hierarchy in a level of tiers, we can see that the first tier is occupied by inferior courts, which have limited jurisdiction. The second level of hierarchy, or second tier, is occupied by the trial courts, which have general jurisdiction. These trial courts are sometimes also referred to as county courts, circuit courts, superior courts, district courts, or state courts. The third tier is occupied by the state appellate courts. In some circumstances, if there is only one appeals court, the state supreme court will occupy this level. However, in some state systems there may be an intermediate appeals court at this third level, and the state supreme court will then occupy the fourth level.

The inferior courts

The inferior courts (also referred to as lower courts) are difficult to classify within many states. In contrast with courts of general jurisdiction, in which the matters that are heard are fairly uniform, the inferior courts in most states are completely fragmented. For example, prior to their 1972 constitutional change, Florida had ten different types of inferior court. Courts with the same names had different jurisdictions, depending upon the county in which they were located.

Early in our history each county, ward, city, town, village, or township had to have a court to hear cases involving violations of the law. Many were in remote, isolated areas. These small courts, completely out of contact with each other, developed in individual ways. They were given individual names that they maintained over the years. In Table 8-2 you may examine the titles of inferior courts throughout the country; the lack of uniformity will become apparent. If you were to compare a particular court in one state or area with one of the same name somewhere else, you would find yourself in a quandary. The name of an inferior court in one state may be the title of a court of general jurisdiction in another state!

In spite of their lack of uniformity, the inferior courts are often the most important courts in the criminal justice system. They often serve as the initial point of entry for those individuals being "adjudicated" through the criminal justice process. Since the lower courts are not courts of record, appeals originating from these courts must be tried in the next tier, the trial courts. Most of the cases within the jurisdiction of the lower courts are the minor infractions of the law, such as traffic violations, disorderly conduct, harrasment, and vagrancy.

Unfortunately, many individuals who initially come into contact with the judicial system see some of the inequities of the lower courts, which occupy the lowest level of hierarchy within the state system and hence are

Table 8-2
United States inferior court titles.

Courts of probate	Municipal courts
County courts	Courts of common pleas
Justice courts	Police courts
Recorders courts	Superior courts
Magistrate courts	Juvenile courts
City and town magistrates courts	Probate courts
Civil courts of record	Courts of ordinary
Courts of claims	Small claims courts
City courts	Mayor courts
Family courts	Traffic courts
Courts of criminal corrections	District courts
Surrogate courts	Land counts

the most visible to the public. The President's Commission on Law Enforcement and the Administration of Justice has noted some of the following inequities:

Initial presentment. *Following arrest, the defendant is initially presented in court, often after many hours and sometimes several days of detention. In theory, the judge's duty is to advise the defendant of the charges against him and of his rights to remain silent, to be admitted to bail, to retain counsel or to have counsel appointed, and to have a preliminary hearing. But in some cities, the defendant may not be advised of his right to remain silent or to have counsel assigned. In others, he may be one of a large group herded before the bench as a judge or clerk rushes through a ritualistic recitation of phrases, making little or no effort to ascertain whether the defendants understand their rights or the nature of the proceedings. In many jurisdictions counsel is not assigned in misdemeanor cases; even where lawyers are appointed, it may not be made clear to the defendant that if he is without funds he may have free representation. . . . The judges have little time to give detailed consideration to the question of bail. Little is known about the defendant other than the charge and his prior criminal record. The result is that bail is based on the charge instead of on the circumstances of each case; high money bonds are almost invariably set by established patterns, and large numbers of defendants are detained.*

Disposition. *The initial appearance is also the final appearance for most defendants charged with misdemeanors or petty offenses. While those who can afford to retain counsel are released on bond to prepare for trial at a later date or to negotiate a disposition, a majority of defendants plead guilty immediately, many without advice of counsel. Pleas are entered so rapidly that they cannot be well considered. The defendant is often made aware that if he seeks more time, his case will be adjourned for a week or two and he will be returned to jail.*

Trial. *An observer in the lower criminal courts ordinarily sees a trial bearing little resemblance to those carried out under traditional notions of due process. There is usually no court reporter unless the defendant can afford to pay one. One result is an informality in the proceedings which would not be tolerated in a felony trial. Rules of evidence are largely ignored. Speed is the watch-word. Trials in misdemeanor cases may be over in a matter of 5, 10, or 15 minutes; they rarely last an hour even in relatively complicated cases. Traditional safeguards honored in felony cases lose their meaning in such proceedings; yet there is still the possibility of lengthy imprisonment or heavy fine. . . . In some cities trials are conducted without counsel for either side; the case is prosecuted by a police officer and defended by the accused himself.*

Sentence. *Most defendants convicted in the lower criminal courts are sentenced promptly. Usually there are no probation services or presentence investigations. Unless the defendant has an attorney who has taken time to inquire into his background, little will be known about him. Sentence may be based on the charge, the defendant's appearance, and the defendant's response to such questions as the judge may put to him in the few moments allotted to sentencing. . . . Short jail sentences of one, two, or three months are commonly imposed on an assembly line basis. A defendant's situation can hardly be considered individually. When a defendant is fined but is unable to pay, he may be required to work the penalty off at the rate of $1 to $5 for each day spent in jail.*

Petty offenses. *The conditions described above are found in more aggravated form in lower courts which handle petty offenses. Each day in large cities hundreds of persons arrested for drunkenness or disorderly conduct, for vagrancy or petty gambling, or for prostitution are led before a judge. Among the defendants are slum dwellers who drink in public and young men who "loiter" on street corners or "fail to move on" when ordered to do so. Typically, they have no private place to go, no money to spend, and no family or lawyer to lend them support.*

Judges sometimes seem annoyed at being required to preside in these courts. Defendants are treated with contempt, berated, laughed at, embarrassed, and sentenced to serve their time or work off their fines. Observers have sometimes reported difficulty in determining what offense is being tried in a given case, and instances have come to light in which the disposition bears little relationship to the original charge.[1]

For the most part these inequities continue to exist because of overburdening of the courts, the lack of facilities, and insufficient numbers of personnel involved to ease the crowded conditions. Many of the staff members of the lower court are unqualified, and in many states there are no uniform qualifications for judges in the lower courts. In some areas judges serving as justices of the peace or presiding in other inferior courts are not required to be lawyers or to have formal legal training.

Trial courts   Trial courts, or courts of general jurisdiction, occupy the second tier in our level of hierarchy within the state court system. These courts have original jurisdiction in most of our serious or felony criminal cases. The trial court is also the lowest court of record. Cases originating from the trial courts are appealed to higher state courts (courts of appeals), but in some areas trial courts are also appellate courts in that they try cases de novo from courts of limited jurisdiction (lower courts).

Aside from having original jurisdiction in most serious criminal matters, the trial courts also have jurisdiction regarding civil actions, probate matters, and hearings on mental incompetency.

Civil actions are noncriminal actions, which constitute the majority of filings in superior courts. Filings for civil actions are for return of money, breach of contract, to determine title to personal or real property, to declare laws unconstitutional, and other actions. Civil actions are limited only by the imagination of the litigant.

Probate cases deal primarily with the estates of deceased persons: wills are administered and the assets are distributed. The California Superior Court has jurisdiction over probate hearings. However in Michigan and other states, probate jurisdiction is vested in independent courts.

Mental incompetency hearings are hearings conducted by the courts to establish the mental competency of the individual involved. At the conclusion of the hearing the judge, upon ruling the person incompetent, may commit him to a mental institution for safekeeping and treatment.

[1] President's Commission on Law Enforcement and the Administration of Justice, *Task Force Report: The Courts* (Washington D.C.: U.S. Government Printing Office, 1967), pp. 30–31.

The last tier in our level of hierarchy is the state appellate courts. All fifty states have provided a system of appeal from the decisions of trial courts. Most states call their court of last resort the supreme court. (In the state of New York, however, it is called the Court of Appeals; the New York Supreme Court is a court of general jurisdiction.) The supreme courts of most states hear both civil and criminal appeals. In Oklahoma and Texas there are two separate courts of last resort, one for civil and one for criminal cases. (For example, the Supreme Court of Texas handles only civil appeals, and the Court of Criminal Appeals does just what its name implies. Both are courts of last resort.)

"Court of last resort" is a misleading term. Its proper meaning is *the court that provides the last possible appeal of a judgment or finding within the state judicial structure.* If there are federal questions involved, the interested party may appeal for relief to the federal court system in either criminal or civil cases.

Originally, the state supreme courts could easily accommodate all cases that the system produced. Most state supreme courts had a chief justice and two associate justices. As the number of cases appealed increased, the state usually added additional justices to share the workload. This practice succeeded until it became apparent that there was a limit to the number of justices to be used in a single court.

In the 1960s New Mexico decided to create an intermediate appellate court to filter out some of the cases and thus limit the number of appeals reaching the docket of their supreme court. Other states have followed New Mexico's example. The intermediate appellate courts are organized on a regional basis. In large states they may be further subdivided into divisions. This regionalization creates a new problem—a lack of uniformity, since district court of appeal decisions may differ between districts.

In a court of appeals, whether it is a court of last resort such as a state supreme court or an intermediate appellate court, the appeal is heard by a panel of judges (3–9) and not by a jury. The court listens to oral arguments presented by both sides and makes a judgment regarding the issue of law or errors in the previous trial procedures. As in the United States Supreme Court, the state supreme court does have the discretionary power to decide which cases it will hear.

Juvenile courts

Juvenile proceedings differ markedly from adult legal proceedings in several aspects. The core of this difference lies in the philosophy of each setting. In the past the adult court has adhered to the concept of punishment and rehabilitation for criminal actions against the state or private individuals. Although this attitude has changed greatly in the past decades, it retains certain earmarks of that earlier trend. However, since the establishment of the first juvenile court in 1899 in Cook County, Illinois, the juvenile system has had the prevailing philosophy of treatment rather than that of punishment for the individual offender.

This concept of treatment stems from the doctrine of *parens patriae*, which was first initiated in England. The *parens patriae* doctrine allows the sovereign (state) to oversee the welfare of any child whose parents or guardian abuse or neglect it. In abiding by this belief the state would seek to protect children from either their parents' or their own wrongdoings by providing treatment and/or therapy. Juvenile courts were created to guide the child instead of "determining or placing emphasis on his or her guilt regarding a particular crime."[2]

The age of the child in regards to juvenile court jurisdiction is determined by each particular state. Those juveniles who come to the court's attention are, for the most part, below 18 years (in some states, 21) who have committed some particular criminal act, are suspected of "delinquent" behavior, have been neglected or abandoned by the parents or guardians, or fall under some other miscellaneous provisions of the law. The juvenile court differs from the adult court in that it is an informal private hearing. Note that the word hearing is used instead of the word trial. If the child is to come under the court's attention he is "summoned" rather than having been arrested. After the juvenile judge has studied the remarks, evidence, and matters brought forth in the hearing, the child is then "adjudicated." A disposition is made which attempts to consider the best interests of the child. It may range from having the child committed to a state training school, placing the child in a foster home, giving the child a mild reprimand, to dismissing the case entirely. The juvenile court does have the option however, if the case so warrants, to remand the child to another court to be tried as an adult. In an adult proceeding an individual would be sentenced rather than adjudicated.

Since the philosophy of the juvenile court was based on safeguarding the child from the stigma attached to adult criminal proceedings, many of the constitutional safeguards adhered to in an adult court were not granted to juveniles. Violations of due process were dramatized by the *Kent* (1966) and *Gault* (1967) decisions of the United States Supreme Court. In essence, these decisions guaranteed that juveniles had the right to counsel, had the right to cross-examine and confront witnesses, had the right to be notified of the charge, and the right to invoke the Fifth Amendment (self-incrimination). These cases further brought to light some of the prevailing inequities that were occuring in the juvenile courts regarding institutionalizing juveniles for status offenses. Status offenses are offenses that would not be considered criminal if they had been committed by an adult. Examples of status offenses would be running away from home, minor in possession of an alcoholic beverage, being beyond parental control, among others. In essence, the court was labeling a child delinquent

[2]Nicholas Kihrie, *The Right to be Different, Deviance and Enforced Therapy* (Baltimore, Md: Penguin Books, 1974), p.3.

for committing these status offenses and institutionalizing the child for several years. In the *Gault* decision, the defendant, Gerald Gault, was deemed to be a juvenile delinquent for having committed the crime of making a lewd telephone call to a neighbor. If he had been an adult, the offense he committed under the Arizona Statutory law would have carried with it a fine of $5–$50 and a term of imprisonment for not more than 2 months. Gerald Gault, age 15, was found to be a delinquent child and was sentenced to the state school until the age of 21.

However unjust the *Kent* and *Gault* decisions may seem before being overturned by the U.S. Supreme Court, they did help to establish certain rights guaranteed to juveniles under the Constitution. Since those decisions were made, reforms have been taking place in the juvenile court system.

Federal judicial system

Supreme Court

The U.S. Supreme Court is the highest court in the land. Currently, its membership consists of a chief justice and eight associate justices. The number of associate justices has varied from four to nine during the history of the country. The current membership size of the court was established in 1869.

Article III, Section 2 gives the Supreme Court both original and appellate jurisdiction. For practical purposes the majority of the Court's work is appellate in nature.

The appeal procedure is established by Congress. There are currently three principal ways in which a case reaches the Supreme Court. They are (1) by appeal, (2) by *writ of certiorari* (review), and (3) by certification (see Figure 8-1).

When considering appeals from state courts, the Supreme Court must accept cases that fall into two categories: (1) if the validity of a treaty or statute of the United States has been questioned and it has been held invoked by a state court; and (2) if a state law has been questioned on the grounds that it violates the Constitution, the laws of the United States, or treaties made by the United States with a foreign power, and the state court has upheld the law.

The Supreme Court also considers appeals from the courts of appeal. In certain instances the Court will also consider direct appeals from district courts. The right to appeal to the Court is extremely limited. since Congress has given the Court almost unlimited power to decide which cases it will hear.

The Court may approve a *writ of certiorari* to require a lower court to send the record of the case to it for review. This is done only when four justices believe the issues important enough to warrant consideration.

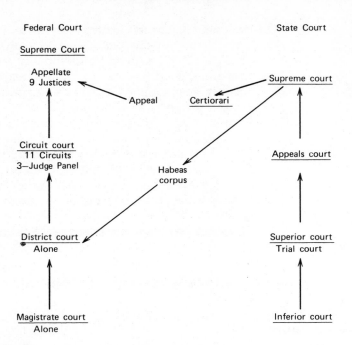

Figure 8-1
The appeals process.

The certification is a little-used device of the lower courts. In this process an appellate court asks the Supreme Court to answer a question of law. Currently, only courts of appeal and courts of claims may use this process.

Courts of appeal

The courts of appeal exist for much the same reason that the state district courts of appeal exist: to relieve the Supreme Court of some of its workload. They were created in 1891 as circuit courts of appeal and were given their current title in 1948. They hear appeals from U.S. district courts and independent regulatory agencies.

District courts

The district courts are courts of original jurisdiction. They hear, with some exceptions, all cases and controversies involving federal questions and consider both criminal and civil litigations. The district court is the only federal court that has jury trials.

Federal court-constitutionality

The foundation of the federal court, as well as that of most state courts, is contained in the Constitution. A brief overview of the constitutionality of the federal court system may assist in understanding the Supreme Court's functions.

The United States Supreme Court has three major functions; (1) it "umpires federalism," (2) it enforces the supremacy and uniformity of federal laws, and (3) it enforces limitations on government, both state and federal, concerning individual liberty. For the purposes of this discussion we will briefly define federalism as the "type of government in which the tasks of governing are constitutionally divided between a central or national government and the regional units or states."[3]

The constitutional provisions are; Article I Section 8, which empowers the federal government to collect taxes for the general welfare, to regulate commerce among the states, and other areas which are deemed to be necessary and proper. Amendments Thirteen, Fourteen and Fifteen give the Court the power to umpire the application of Article I, in the event of a controversy. It is interesting to note that the Tenth Amendment reserves all other powers for the state courts.

The Tenth Amendment is one provision of the United States Constitution that has created a great deal of criticism for the federal court. Many people seem to translate the Amendment to mean that the Court should not exercise any authority over state court decisions, beyond taxes and commerce issues. This issue is particularly acute over the death penalty question. However, when we examine the second and third major functions of the federal court we may understand more clearly why a major issue such as death penalty is addressed by the Court.

Article VI of the United States Constitution establishes the supremacy of federal law, which is, in essence, the Constitution. And when we examine further the third major task for the United States Court, we discover the area that has had the greatest impact upon criminal justice.

The United States Supreme Court becomes involved in the activity of state courts to limit the power of government to infringe upon personal liberty; freedom of speech; freedom of press; freedom of association and assembly, which are guaranteed in the First Amendment; the right to privacy (Fourth Amendment); cruel and unusual punishment, excessive bail (Eighth Amendment), and a complicated due process clause contained in the Fifth Amendment.

TOPICS FOR DISCUSSION

1. Discuss the early systems of justice.
2. Discuss the legal authority supporting the American courts.
3. Compare the federal and state appeals processes.

[3]Kenneth T. Palmer, *State Politics in the United States* (New York: St. Martins Press, 1972).

9

The judiciary and comparative systems

The study of this chapter will enable you to:

1. **Provide a fundamental explanation of the responsibilities of judical personnel.**

2. **Demonstrate how judges are selected..**

3. **Have an overview of the American court system in contrast to several foreign court systems.**

The role of the judge in a courtroom proceeding is not unlike that of a referee. Reid describes the function of the judge as follows:

> The defense attorney represents the defendant, and the prosecutor represents the state. They are therefore "advocates" in the adversary system, while the judge plays an impartial role. He is neither "for" nor "against" a particular position or issue, but, rather, is committed to the fair implementation of the rules of evidence and law. He is charged with the responsibility of making sure that the attorneys play by the rules of the game.
>
> He decides whether objections attorneys make to the questions asked of witnesses by other attorneys should be sustained or overruled. He decides whether evidence can be admitted or must be excluded. He decides whether there is sufficient evidence to let the case go to the jury for a decision on the factual question of guilt. He decides whether a mistrial must be declared as a result of some serious error that would prejudice the case. The judge must have the law, both statutory and case law, at his immediate disposal; he must, in most cases, make instant decisions on the issues under dispute.[1]

Although the judge is described as playing an impartial role in the "adversary" system, he can exert considerable influence over a jury by presenting them with a charge wherein he describes the laws applying to the particular case and the legal instructions that the jury must follow in reaching a verdict. The tone he uses in delivering those charges may characterize his attitude surrounding the case. The jury may also develop a certain preconceived idea about a defendant's innocence or guilt by the way the judge rules on objections, admissibility of evidence, or a witness' testimony in a trial proceeding. The ultimate power of the judge is in the sentencing of the defendant.

At the state level a justice or judge may be elected, appointed by the governor, or appointed from a list supplied by a nonpartisan commission composed of lawyers, judges, and laymen. There have been major criticisms of the elective and appointive processes for the judiciary. The major objection to these processes is that they fail to procure men qualified to become judges. Either system tempts candidates to "play politics" to obtain a judicial post.

[1]Sue Titus Reid, *Crime and Criminology* (Hinsdale, Ill.: Dryden Press, 1976) p. 394.

Missouri Plan   During the past century there has been an effort to avoid the defects of both the appointive and the elective system for the selection of judges. The Missouri Plan, which has been adopted either partially or totally by several states, provides for selection based upon merit. This plan calls for the following:

1. A nonpartisan nominating committee or commission composed of members of the bar association and laymen appointed by the governor, chaired by a judge.

2. A specified number of candidates nominated by the commission for each judicial vacancy.

3. The judicial vacancy will be filled by the governor from the list.

4. Judges will run for reelection solely on the question of whether they should be retained in office or not.

The Missouri Plan is based upon the concept that nonpolitical judges are more apt to be impartial than political judges. The plan attempts to eliminate the political process, elective or appointive, in the selection of judges by substituting the selection process, in the hope of procuring better qualified judges. The person appointed under this system theoretically will shed whatever political and social bias he might otherwise have when he assumes his role on the bench.

Retirement, discipline, and removal of judges   Until the 1960s the only methods of removal of judges were by impeachment by the legislature or defeat at the polls when they came up for election. Since both methods are inadequate for most situations, the feeling developed that traditional processes needed to be supplemented.

In 1960 California became the first state to pass a constitutional amendment providing for the retirement, discipline, and removal of judges. The amendment provides for the establishment of a Commission on Judicial Qualifications consisting of nine members: two judges of the courts of appeal, two judges of the superior court, one judge of the municipal court, two members of the bar, and two nonlawyers. The judge members are selected by the state supreme court, the two lawyers by the board of governors of the state bar association, and the two nonlawyers by the governor and approved by the state senate. The terms of office are for four years.

Any person may complain about a judge to the Commission, and any judge is subject to the action of the Commission. The procedure is that the staff conduct an informal, confidential investigation. If the facts warrant, the Commission may hold formal hearings or order hearings before three special masters appointed by the state supreme court.

The Commission can recommend to the state supreme court the removal, retirement, or censure of a judge. The supreme court will then review the matter and make the final decision. (See Chapter 16 for a fuller discussion of this subject.)

Marshal or bailiff   Ohio and Iowa use the title of bailiff, which is comparable to the title of marshal used in California. Both are charged with carrying out orders of the court; for example, serving warrants of arrest, writs, other civil processes, and maintaining order of the court while in session. They are also charged with taking custody of prisoners while awaiting court action and if necessary, transporting prisoners to other detention facilities after sentence.

During jury trials, they are sworn to closet the jurors, maintain seclusion, and tend to their requirements during deliberation. It is their duty to escort jurors to and from the courtroom during this time and be alert for any attempts to tamper with the jury.

Court administrators   The position of court administrator is a relatively new one. The first court administrator was appointed in 1950 for the Media, Pennsylvania, Court of Common Pleas. This concept did not flourish until the mid-sixties.

There are no uniform educational or experience standards established for this critical position. Several degree programs to train personnel in this field have been established; however, most job descriptions are similar to that of the court clerk.

Some of the more important duties of the court administrator are:

1. Personnel management services.
2. Financial management service including preparation of the budget.
3. Management of physical facilities.
4. Information services with law enforcement and public agencies.
5. Intergovernmental relations assistance.
6. Jury administrative services.
7. Statistical recordings.
8. Systems analysis.
9. Calendar management.
10. Training seminars, and providing of manuals for day-to-day operations for deputies.

Court clerk   Traditionally, most of the duties of the court administrator have been performed by the clerk of the court. In addition to these, the clerk is responsible for all ministerial duties of the court. All papers and processes except warrants of arrest are issued in the clerk's name.

Again, there have been no uniform educational or experience criteria developed for this position. It may be filled either by election, appointment, or through a competitive Civil Service examination.

As with other departments associated with the courts, the number of deputies depends upon the business of that particular jurisdiction. In large courts it is normally the practice to have three divisions, which specialize in civil (including small claim filings), criminal, and traffic matters. However, in smaller courts, these areas may be handled by one or two deputies, which requires that they be adept at all phases of the handling of the processes of the court.

Foreign judicial systems

We have already discussed the concept of law on which the Anglo-American judicial systems are based, with roots in the British common law. Common law, based on traditional customs and practices, was developed between the fifteenth and nineteenth centuries; the word "common" was used to denote its acceptance throughout England. In contrast, most of the Western European countries base their concept of law upon "civil law." Civil law is, in turn, based upon a blend of church (canon) law, medieval law, and Roman law. These laws were consolidated and written (codified) into the Code Napoleon from 1800–1810. During the period of Napoleonic domination of Western Europe the Code was imposed on all conquered territories. After Napoleon's defeat at Waterloo and his subsequent exile, most European countries retained his code of law.

A primary difference between the two concepts (common and civil law) is the guidance provided judges in adjudicating cases. In "code" countries, judges theoretically base their findings strictly on the written code and are not allowed to consider past court decisions. In contrast, the Anglo-American common law system theoretically requires the judges to rely upon past court decisions (*stare decisis*). The legislatures played a minor role in the development of common law, but have since written most common laws into the state codes.

The differences, either historical or philosophical, are less significant today than they were one hundred years ago. Modern society is gradually forcing the British and American lawmakers to pass laws with a far greater amount of detail than in the past. The Western European judge is finding that he must occasionally make some laws rather than rely solely on the codes.

The British system The British judicial system is generally considered to be more complex than our system. At the lower levels there are two separate court systems; one for criminal matters and the other for civil (noncriminal) matters. The states of Texas and Oklahoma have similar

structures except that the division extends to the courts of last resort (su
preme courts), although in England criminal and noncriminal use the
same appellate system.

The English criminal court system has three levels. In rural areas there
are justices of the peace; in cities magistrates try misdemeanor cases. A
the next higher level, the Quarter Session courts try less important felony
cases. At the top is the Assize Court, which hears the most important felony
cases.

The American judical system relies upon a grand jury to function as a
review body to pass judgment upon whether or not a crime has occurred
and whether there is reasonable belief that the defendant committed it
This process is based upon English common law practice. The English
discarded this practice in 1933 and have used the preliminary examination
exclusively in felony cases.

The French system The French judicial structure is more complicated
than either the English or American because the French provide more
specialized courts. Some of these are juvenile courts, labor relations
courts, farm problems courts, social security courts, and commercial law
courts.

This degree of specialization is followed in the United States to some
degree, with some specialized courts and administrative bodies that hear
judicial matters. Similar courts do not exist in England.

In France the lowest court is the Court of Instance, which hears misdemeanor cases. At the next higher level is the Court of Major Instance
with two divisions: the correctional tribunal and the civil section. This cour
hears low-grade felonies and civil litigation. They also hear appeals from
Courts of Instance. As in England, at the top of the trial court structure is the
Assize Court, which hears the serious felonies.

The highest French court is the Court of Cossation. Its rulings have
somewhat the same effect as those of the United States Supreme Court,
except that they rarely deal with public policy.

The U.S.S.R. system The legal system of the U.S.S.R. has had no
effect on the Western world, but it is interesting in its evolution. When the
Russian Revolution occurred in 1918, one of the first acts of the Soviet
authorities was to abolish all courts, retaining only those whose laws were
not specifically annulled by the new government.

The Soviet court system has been restructured several times, the last
occurring in 1960. The present organization is three-tiered: People's Court,
Regional Court, and Supreme Court. The People's Courts are the courts at
the lowest level, located in rural districts and towns. Their jurisdictions
cover all matters not specifically assigned to a higher court. The crime
categories they cover are not comparable to those in the Western countries, and include the following:

1. State crimes.
2. Crimes against state property.
3. Crimes against the political and working rights of citizens.
4. Crimes against private property of citizens.
5. Crimes against the administrative order.

Regional courts have jurisdiction over felony-type cases and crimes, such as anti-Soviet propaganda and disclosure of state secrets. The supreme court of each republic has broad jurisdiction over all cases of special interest.

Some significant differences

In philosophy and procedures, the judicial selection processes vary widely between different countries. In the United States popular control and political considerations are the dominant concerns. The British do not consider these factors important, but they do show some consideration for them.

The French consider neither popular control nor political considerations of importance; they are concerned with the level of training of judges. But judges in the U.S.S.R. must have the political support of the Communist party. Nominations of office are made by party organizations only.

The primary selection process is popular election in the United States. The Soviet judges—within the confines of the Communist party—are also chosen by an elective process, similar to any other election. It has been stated that in the 1965 Soviet elections, candidates for judge received 99.56 percent of the total votes cast.[2]

All British judges are appointed by the Lord Chancellor or by the Prime Minister. Although judges of the lowest criminal and civil courts are not required to have legal training, judges appointed to the high courts must have been barristers (trial lawyers) for a minimum of 10 years. This is similar to the rules of various states requiring that a lawyer should have practiced a specified number of years to qualify as a judge.

In France the practice used in judicial appointments is different in that the potential judge follows a curriculum in law school different than that prescribed for attorneys. After completion of law school, he must take a series of competitive examinations for admission to the National Center for Judicial Studies. Upon completion of a four-year course, the graduate is appointed to the Court of Instance.

There are no constitutional requirements for the candidate to have any legal training or experience in the U.S.S.R. It is estimated that in 1965 only 80.9 percent of the People's judges had received a higher education.

In the United States appointments or elections may be to any level of court in either the federal or state systems, if the candidate possesses the

[2]Robert Conquest, ed., *Justice and the Legal System in the U.S.S.R.* (New York: Praeger, 1968).

minimum requirements. A judge must run for election or obtain an appointment to advance to a higher court. Merit is not necessarily the basis for advancement.

The British judge is appointed initially to a higher level of court than his American counterpart, thus his chances for advancement occur more infrequently. When he is advanced to a higher court, it is through the same appointive process based upon merit.

The French jurist is promoted depending upon his performance evaluation. The actual advancement is supervised by the Supreme Judicial Council, composed of officials from the Ministry of Justice and senior judges.

Soviet judges, prior to the latest reorganization, had to rely for promotions upon evaluation by the Ministries of Justice. This practice has been abolished; today, promotions are based upon evaluation by other members of the judiciary.

Justice inequities

Certain social inequities were, of past necessity, built into the judicial system. These have led to contemporary demands for judicial reform. One of these is the bail-bond system, which will be discussed in Chapter 12.

Another systems defect is the matter of counsel for those accused of a crime. Historically, people charged with a crime have had to provide their own counsel or attempt to defend themselves as best they could. Congress specified early in our history that in federal capital cases counsel must be provided at no expense to the defendant if he had no money. Generally, this provision was not required in the states.

As the issue developed, more and more states adopted the federal concept of providing counsel for the indigent. In *Powell* v. *Alabama*, 287 U.S. 45 (1932), the Supreme Court held that the denial of effective counsel to an indigent defendant was a failure to provide due process of law. With this decision, the Court extended the right to counsel to those charged with state *capital* offenses. (Capital offenses are those punishable with death.)

In *Betts* v. *Brady*, 316 U.S. 455 (1942), the Supreme Court held that states were not required to furnish counsel at trial to every defendant unable to pay for counsel. From the decision one can infer that the Court was apprehensive of the logical lengths to which this extension would or could go.

However, in 1963, in *Gideon* v. *Wainwright*, 372 U.S. 335 (1963), the Court did extend the right to counsel to those charged with noncapital felony offenses in state courts. The Court ruled that the right to counsel at the time of trial was essential and further found that if a defendant is unable to employ counsel, one must be provided.

The question unanswered in this case was—did the right to counsel extend to misdemeanor cases? The "petty offense" standard was not ruled upon. Consideration was not given at that time as to what was expressed as "effective assistance." To a great degree these questions have been resolved by later decisions providing for counsel at all stages of the proceedings. The Court has also adopted a standard that has as its criteria the possible loss of liberty for the defendant.

The old axiom, "justice delayed is justice denied," was never more pertinent. The civil litigant and the criminal defendant are entitled to a speedy trial, yet this does not occur in most parts of the country. When a case is not heard promptly by a court, what are the resultant consequences? If the lawsuit is concerned with damages for personal injury, an indigent victim may be pressured by delay into accepting a reduced settlement. Undue delays cause problems with witnesses; they disappear or their memories fade.

In criminal cases, delays tend to be shorter, but the results may be more damaging. The indigent suspect may have to spend considerable time in custody or, to be released, he may be forced to engage in plea bargaining and perhaps even plead guilty to an offense he did not commit, in order to expedite release from custody.

What has been done to reduce court delay? The first approach has been normally to increase the number of judges available to try cases. This works, but with limitations, because of the high costs involved. It has been estimated that annual expenses run over $100,000, exclusive of salaries, to maintain one courtroom operational.

Plea bargaining is another activity used to reduce court congestion. The pros and cons of this procedure will be discussed in Chapter 12. Despite its conspicuous weaknesses, even an illustrious jurist (Chief Justice Warren Burger) has been quoted as stating that the judicial system can operate only because 90 percent of those charged with offenses plead guilty.

There are two solutions to the trial delay problem that have been used effectively. Some states have legally defined what constitutes a speedy trial. In California, for example, if the party charged is in custody on a misdemeanor charge, he must be brought to trial within 30 days. In instances where a misdemeanor citation has been issued, his trial must be held within 45 days. If the defendant does not waive his right to a speedy trial and his case is not heard within this period of time, it must be dismissed.

Another solution has been to utilize paraprofessionals to handle minor judicial functions so that the judges can concentrate on more important cases. In some states "referees" and "commissioners" are appointed to hear traffic violations and divorce matters.

The jury process itself has come under attack as creating court delay due to the time spent in jury selection and deliberation. To shorten selection and deliberation time, it has been suggested that the size of the jury be reduced from the traditional 12 members to 6, or that a majority only be necessary to reach a verdict of guilty or innocent, rather than a unanimous vote. Some states, such as Florida and Washington, have adopted the six-member jury to expedite the legal processes.

Sentencing

The judicial process ends with the completion of the trial if the defendant is found not guilty, and with sentencing if he is found guilty. The sentencing is the thorniest problem of the process.

For a defendant convicted of a criminal offense, sentencing becomes the most critical aspect of the court process. The options available to the sentencing authority vary substantially from leniency to application of the maximum penalty provided by law. For the defendant these alternatives may mean the difference between five and fifteen years in prison. For society, the sentencing decision often is evaluated in terms of how long it will keep an undesirable member out of circulation.[3]

The unanswered question confronting the justice systems—"Is the function of the courts penal or preventive?"—is today's dilemma in the sentencing processm The traditional answer has been that the courts must punish the wicked and not be concerned with matters of rehabilitation. These questions will be discussed in Chapter 12.

Summary

The court systems undergo periodic changes at the hands of state legislatures or the Congress of the United States. The present trend is toward consolidation of the lower court functions.

Historically, certain social inequities were built into the judicial system that have led to contemporary demands for judicial reform. One of these is the bail bond system, which tends to discriminate against the poor. The matter of counsel for the defendant is another defect in the system.

Unlike the British legal system, the legal system of the U.S.S.R. has had no effect on the Western world. Judges in the U.S.S.R. must have the political support of the Communist party, nor are there constitutional requirements that the judges have legal training or experience. In fact, only 80.9 percent of the People's judges received a higher education.

The judicial function ends with the completion of the trial if the defendant is found not guilty, and with sentencing if found guilty. The question confronting the justice system today is, "Is the function of the courts penal or preventive?" It is this unanswered question that is today's dilemma in the sentencing process.

[3]National Advisory Commission on Criminal Justice Standards and Goals, *Report on the Courts* (Washington, D.C.: U.S. Government Printing Office, 1973), p. 109.

1. Discuss the various means of judicial selection and the relative value of each selection process.
2. Discuss the concept of *stare decisis* as it applies to a criminal trial.
3. Compare and contrast American justice and systems with those of foreign countries.
4. Discuss the inequities of the American system of justice.

10

Rights of the accused

The study of this chapter will enable you to:

1. **Understand certain Supreme Court decisions.**
2. **Identify how the criminal justice process protects the individual rights of the accused.**
3. **Demonstrate the impact of some landmark Court decisions on the criminal justice system.**
4. **Be knowledgeable about some police practices that have been declared unconstitutional.**
5. **Have an overview of the constitutional rights contained in the Amendments of the Constitution.**

During the last decade perhaps the most profound effect upon the activities of our criminal justice system has come from the decisions of the United States Supreme Court. These decisions are generally based upon violations of the constitutional safeguards of all citizens. They have, in many cases, modified the activity of the participants of our criminal justice agencies, most specifically the police, who are the first contact a criminal offender may have with our system. Therefore, a chapter dedicated to the rights of the accused is an essential ingredient in a textbook. Perhaps nothing can be more important to a student studying criminal justice with hopes of becoming a practitioner in the field than to have a fundamental awareness of the constitutional safeguards afforded all citizens. The role of the police in the enforcement and apprehension of violators involves taking from the accused the fundamental ingredient of our democracy—his freedom. When an arrest is made, our system works exceedingly hard to insure that the subject of the arrest has not unnecessarily been deprived of any constitutional right to freedom, which is a basic ingredient of the American way of life.

Constitutional overview

Our original Constitution consisted of Articles 1 through VII and was adopted by the Constitutional Convention by 1787 by representatives from twelve states. Throughout our history there have been a number of weaknesses discovered in the first seven Articles of the Constitution, so since that time there have been Articles and Amendments to the Constitution, enacted pursuant to Article V of the original document which permitted this. This chapter will deal primarily with the Amendments rather than with the original Articles of the Constitution. We will deal specifically only with Amendments One, Four, Five, Six, Eight, Nine, and Fourteen, for it is within these Amendments that the Supreme Court has drawn upon to contrast the treatment of offenders with the intent of the Constitution. In the past, the first Ten Amendments applied only to defendants charged with federal crimes. It was not until the Fourteenth Amendment that these rights were granted to defendants charged with state crimes. (See Appendix A.)

The First Amendment
Congress shall make no law respecting an establishment of religion, or prohibiting the free exercise thereof; or abridging the freedom of speech or of the press; or the right of the people peaceably to assemble and to petition the government for redress of grievances.

The Fourth Amendment
The right of the people to be secure in their persons, houses, papers, and effects against unreasonable searches and seizure, shall not be violated and no warrants shall issue, but upon probable cause, supported by oath or affirmation and particularly describing the place to be searched and the persons or things to be seized.

The Fifth Amendment
No person shall be held to answer for a capital or otherwise infamous crime, unless on presentment or indictment of a grand jury, except in cases arising in the land or naval forces, or in the militia when in actual service in time of war or public danger; nor shall any person be subject for the same offense to be twice put in jeopardy of life or limb; nor shall be compelled in any criminal case to be a witness against himself, nor be deprived of life, liberty, or property without due process of law; nor shall private property be taken for public use without just compensation.

The Sixth Amendment
In all criminal prosecutions, the accused shall enjoy the right to a speedy and public trial, by an impartial jury of the state and district wherein the crime shall have been committed, which district shall have been previously ascertained by law, and to be informed of the nature and causes of the accusation: to be confronted with the witnesses against him, to have compulsory process for obtaining witnesses in his favor, and to have the assistance of counsel for his defense.

The Eighth Amendment
Excessive bail shall not be required nor excessive fines imposed, nor cruel and unusual punishment inflicted.

The Ninth Amendment
The ennumeration in the Constitution, of certain rights, shall not be construed to deny or disparage others retained by the people.

Section 1. All persons born or naturalized in the United States, and subject to the jurisdiction thereof, are citizens of the United States and of the state wherein they reside. No state shall make or enforce any law which shall abridge the privileges or immunities of citizens of the United States; nor shall any state deprive any person of life, liberty, or property without due process of law, nor deny to any person within its jurisdiction the equal protection of the laws.

Cases under discussion

We will examine each of the following cases under their major subject heading of the areas in which they had an impact upon the Court's decision. The illustrative cases will be in the areas of probable cause, detention, searches, confessions, informants, and the juvenile court systems. There are many other headings in which constitutional safeguards have been applied to criminal cases. However, this chapter is not intended to be an exhaustive presentation of consitutional law. We will therefore limit the discussion to some of the more notable cases that have had an effect upon the criminal justice system and, specifically, upon the police.

Probable cause

The first case we will present is *Beck* v. *Ohio*, of 379 U.S. 89 (1964). William Beck was driving his automobile in the city of Cleveland, Ohio. Police officers approached him and ordered him to pull over to the curb. The officers possessed neither an arrest warrant nor a search warrant. They placed him under arrest and searched his car; they found nothing of interest. They then took him to a nearby police station where they searched his person and found an envelope containing a number of clearinghouse slips beneath the sock of his leg. He was subsequently charged with possession of clearinghouse slips in violation of a state criminal statute. The defendant filed a motion to suppress as evidence the slips in question on the grounds that the police had obtained them by means of an unreasonable search and seizure in violation of the Fourth and Fourteenth Amendments. After a hearing, his motion was overruled, and he was subsequently convicted. The Supreme Court reviewed the case under the petitioner's claim that the slips were wrongly admitted in evidence against him because they had been seized by the Cleveland police in violation of the Fourth and Fourteenth Amendments. The Court acknowledged that in certain cases police officers are not required to obtain a warrant before arresting and searching a person. However, they did state that there are limits to the permissible scope of a warrantless search incident to a lawful arrest. Therefore, the constitutional validity of the search in this case had to depend upon the constitutional validity of the petitioner's arrest. Whether that arrest was consitutionally valid depended in turn upon whether at the moment the arrest was made, the officers had probable cause to make it; whether at that moment the facts and circumstances within their knowledge and of which they had reasonably trustworthy information were sufficient to warrant a prudent man to believe that the defendant had committed or was commiting an offense. The Court stated:

The rule of probable cause is a practical, nontechnical conception affording the best compromise that has been found for accommodating often opposing interests. Requiring more would unduly hamper law enforcement; to allow less would be to leave law-abiding citizens at the mercy of the officer's whim or caprice.

They cited *Brinegar* v. *United States*. The Supreme Court found that the trial court made no findings of fact in the case regarding the arrest: the judge simply made the conclusive statement that a lawful arrest had been made and that the search was incidental to a lawful arrest. And, in fact, none of the lower courts found anything different. They reached the conclusion that the arrest was lawful. In the Supreme Court's evaluation of the case, they overturned the conviction on the basis that the officers did not, in fact, have probable cause to make the arrest. Therefore, the subsequent search was found to be unconstitutional and in violation of the defendant's Fourth and Fourteenth rights of the Constitution.

This case was presented to demonstate what has commonly been referred to as "fruit of the poisonous tree." It clearly shows that police officers may not separate one activity from another; that if they begin with an unlawful arrest, any search or any other activity that may take place following that arrest may be invalidated. An illegal act to acquire evidence precludes its use in subsequent legal proceedings.

Searches and seizures

The next case we will examine is *Augilar* v. *Texas*, 378 U.S. 108 (1964). This case presents questions concerning the constitutional requirements for obtaining a search warrant. Two Houston police officers applied to a local justice of the peace for a warrant to search for narcotics in the defendant's home. In support of their application, the officers submitted an affidavit which in part stated:"Affiants have received reliable information from a credible person and do believe that heroin, marijuana, barbiturates, and other narcotics and narcotic paraphernalia are being kept in the above described premises for the purpose of sale and use contrary to the provisions of the law." The search warrant was subsequently issued and upon executing the warrant, local police and federal officers announced at the door that they were police with a warrant. Upon hearing a commotion within the house, the officers forced their way in and seized the defendant in the act of attempting to dispose of a packet of narcotics. At his trial in the state court, the defendant, through his attorney, objected to the introduction of evidence obtained as a result of the execution of the warrant. The objections were overruled and the evidence was admitted. The defendant was convicted of illegally possessing heroin and was sentenced to serve twenty years in the state penitentiary.

The Supreme Court agreed to review the case to consider the important constitutional questions involved. The Court cited *Ker v. California*, 374 U.S. 23 (1963). In that case the Court held that the Fourth Amendment's prescriptions are enforced against the state through the Fourteenth Amendment, and that the standard of reasonableness is the same under the Fourth and Fourteenth Amendments. Although *Ker* involved a search without a warrant, that case must be read as holding that the standard for obtaining a search warrant is "the same standard under the Fourth and Fourteenth Amendments."

An evaluation of the constitutionality of a search warrant should begin with the rule that the informed and deliberate determinations of magistrates empowered to issue warrants are to be preferred over the hurried actions of officers who may happen to make arrests. The reasons for this rule go to the foundations of the Fourth Amendment. A contrary rule—that evidence sufficient to support a magistrate's disinterested determination to issue a search warrant will justify the officers in making a search without a warrant—would reduce the Amendment to a nullity and leave the people's homes secure only in the discretion of the police officers. Thus, when a search is based upon a magistrate's rather than a police officer's determination of probable cause, the reviewing courts will accept evidence of a less judicially competent or persuasive character than would have justified an officer in acting on his own without a warrant, and will sustain the judicial determination so long as there was substantial basis for the magistrate to conclude that narcotics were probably present. The Court went on to point out:

The point of the Fourth Amendment which often is not grasped by zealous officers is not that it denies law enforcement the support of the usual inference which reasonable men draw from evidence; its protection consists in requiring that those inferences be drawn by a neutral and detached magistrate instead of being judged by the officer engaged in the often competitive enterprise of ferreting out crime. "It is clear that it does not pass muster because it does not provide any basis for the commissioner's determination that probable cause existed. The complaint contained no affirmative allegation that the affiants spoke with personal knowledge of the matters contained therein and does not indicate any source for the complainant's belief and it does not set forth any other sufficient basis upon which a finding of probable cause could be made. Although an affidavit may be based on hearsay information and need not reflect the direct personal observations of the affiant, the magistrate must be informed of some of the underlying circumstances from which the informant concluded that the narcotics were where he claimed they were, and some of the underlying circumstances from which the officer concluded that the informant, whose identity need not be disclosed, was credible or his information reliable, otherwise the inferences from the facts which lead to the complaint will be drawn not by a neutral and detached magistrate as the Constitution requires, but instead by a police officer engaged in the often competitive enterprise of ferreting out crime. The search warrant should not have been issued because the affidavit did not provide sufficient basis for finding of probable cause, and that the evidence obtained as a result of the search warrant was inadmissible in the petitioner's trial.

Under this heading we will examine *Terry* v. *Ohio*, 392 U.S. 1 (1968). This case concerns the role of the Fourth Amendment in the confrontation on the street between the citizen and the policeman investigating suspicious circumstances. The defendant was convicted of carrying a concealed weapon and was sentenced to the statutorily prescribed term of one to three years in the penitentiary. Following the denial of pretrial motion to suppress, the prosecution introduced in evidence two revolvers and a number of bullets seized from the defendant and the codefendant by the Cleveland Police Department. At the hearing on the motion to suppress this evidence, the officer testified that while he was patrolling in plainclothes in downtown Cleveland at approximately 2:30 P.M., his attention was attracted by two men standing on a street corner. He had never seen the men before and he was unable to say precisely what first drew his eye to them.

He testified that the had been a policeman for 39 years, a detective for 35 years, and had been assigned to patrol this vicinity of downtown Cleveland for shoplifters and pickpockets for 30 years. He had developed routine habits of observation over the years; he would stand and watch people or walk and watch people at many intervals of the day. In this case the defendants did not look "right" to him at the time. He subsequently took up a post of observation in the entrance of a store 300 to 400 feet away from the two men. He saw one of the men leave the other man and walk around the corner past some stores. The man paused for a moment and looked in the store window, then walked on a short distance, turned around and walked back toward the corner, pausing once again to look in the same store window. He rejoined his companion at the corner and the two conferred briefly, then the second man went through the same series of motions, strolling down the street, looking in the same window, walking on a short distance, turning back, peering in the store window again, and returning to confer with the first man at the corner. The two men repeated this ritual alternately between five and six times apiece—roughly a dozen trips. At one point, while the two men were standing together on the corner, a third man approached them and engaged them briefly in conversation. This man left the two others and walked away. The other two resumed their measured pacing, peering, and conferring. After this had gone on for ten or twelve minutes the two men walked off together, following the path taken earlier by the third man. By this time the officer had become thoroughly suspicious, and after observing their elaborately casual and oft-repeated reconnaissance of the store window, he suspected the two men of "casing a job, a stick-up." He testified that he considered it his duty as a police officer to investigate further. He also stated, "they may have a gun."

The officer followed the two men and saw them stop in front of a store to talk to the same man who had conferred with them earlier on the street corner. Deciding that the situation was ripe for direct action, the officer approached the three men. He identified himself as a police officer and asked for their names. At this point his knowledge was confined to what he had observed. He was not acquainted with any of the three men by name or by sight and he had received no information concerning them from any other source. When the men mumbled something in response to his inquiries, the officer grabbed the defendant, spun him around so that they were facing the other two with the defendant between the officer and the others, and patted down the outside of his clothing. In the left breast pocket of the defendant's overcoat the officer felt a pistol. He reached inside the overcoat pocket but was unable to remove the gun. At this point, keeping the defendant between himself and the others, the officer ordered all three men to enter the store. As they went in he removed the defendant's overcoat completely, retrieved a 38 caliber revolver from the pocket, and ordered all three men to face the wall with their hands raised. The officer proceeded to pat down the outer clothing of the other two men. He discovered another revolver in the outer pocket of one of the men, but no weapons were found on the third man. The officer testified that he only patted the men down to see whether they had weapons and that he did not put his hands beneath the outer garments of either defendant until he felt their guns. He subsequently arrested and took all three men to the police station where the two men carrying the guns were formally charged with carrying concealed weapons. The defendants subsequently appealed a conviction on the basis that their arrest and search and detention was in violation of the Constitution. They cited the Fourth Amendment, which provides "the right of the people to be secure in their persons, houses, papers, and effects against unreasonable search and seizure shall not be violated."

It was pointed out that there is no question that people are entitled to protection under the Fourth Amendment. The real question presented to the Court is whether all of the circumstances of this on-the-street encounter constituted an unreasonable search and seizure. The Court subsequently concluded that the revolver seized from the defendant was properly admitted in evidence against him. At the time that he seized the defendant and searched him for weapons, the officer had reasonable grounds to believe that the defendant was armed and dangerous, and it was necessary for the protection of himself and others to take swift measures to discover the true facts and neutralize the threat of harm if it materialized. The policeman carefully restricted his search to what was appropriate to the discovery of the particular items for which he sought.

Each case of this sort will, of course, have to be decided on its own facts. However, the Court held:

. . . that where a police officer observes unusual conduct which leads him to reasonably conclude in light of his experience that criminal activity may be afoot and that the persons with whom he is dealing may be armed and presently dangerous, where in the course of investigating this behavior he identifies himself as a policeman and makes reasonable inquiries, and where nothing in the initial stages of the encounter serves to dispel this reasonable fear for his own or others' safety, he is entitled for the protection of himself and others in the area to conduct a

carefully limited search of the outer clothing of such persons in an attempt to discover weapons which might be used to assault him. Such a search is a reasonable search under the Fourth Amendment, and any weapons seized may be properly introduced in evidence against the person from whom they were taken.

The defendant in this case was convicted, and the Supreme Court affirmed that conviction. This case should serve to point out the necessity for the police officer to be accurate in his observations and subsequent recall when he is called to testify at a later date.

Search of premises

The first case that we will examine will be *Spinelli* v. *United States*, 393 U.S. 410 (1969). In this case the defendant was convicted under a Federal Code violation of traveling across a state line with the intention of conducting gambling activities against state law. Throughout the court proceeding the defendant challenged the constitutionality of the warrant that authorized the FBI search and uncovered the evidence necessary for his conviction. The affidavit that served as the basis for the issuance of the warrant contained the following allegations:

1. The FBI had kept track of Spinelli's movements on five days during the month of August. On four of these occasions, the defendant was seen crossing one of two bridges leading from one state into another. On four of the five days the defendant was also seen parking his car in a lot used by residents of an apartment house. On one day the defendant was followed further and seen to enter a particular apartment in the building.

2. An FBI check with the telephone company revealed that the apartment contained two telephones listed under the same name.

3. The application stated that the defendant is known to the affiant and to federal law enforcement agencies and local law enforcement agents as a bookmaker, an associate of bookmakers, and a gambler and an associate of gamblers.

4. Finally it was stated that the FBI has been informed by a confidential, reliable informant that the defendant is operating a handbook and accepting wagers and disseminating wagering information by means of the telephones located in the apartment building.

The Court held that detailing the informant's tip has a fundamental place in the warrant application. Without it, probable cause could not be established. The first two items reflect only innocent-seeming activities and data. The defendant's travels to and from the apartment building and his entry into a particular apartment on one occasion could hardly be taken as bespeaking gambling activities, and there is nothing unusual about an apartment containing two separate telephones. Finally, the allegation that the defendant was known to the affiant and to other federal and local law enforcement officers as a gambler and an associate of gamblers is an unilluminating assertion of suspicion that is entitled to no weight in appraising the magistrate's decision. The Court concluded:

In this case the informant's tip, even when corroborated to the extent indicated, was not sufficient to provide the basis for a finding of probable cause. This is not to say that the tip was so insubstantial that it could not properly have been counted in the magistrate's determination. Rather, it needed some further support. When we look into the other parts of the application, however, we find nothing to allege that would permit the suspicions engendered by the informant's report to ripen into a judgment that a crime was probably being committed. As we have already seen, the allegations detailing the FBI's surveillance of the defendant and its investigation of telephone company records contain no suggestion of criminal conduct when taken by themselves, and they are not endowed with an aura of suspicion by virtue of the informant's tip. Nor do we find that the FBI's report takes on a sinister color when read in light of common knowledge that bookmaking is often carried on over the telephone and from premises ostensibly used by others for perfectly normal purposes. Such an argument would carry weight in a situation in which the premises contained an unusual number of telephones or abnormal activities are observed, but it does not fit this case, where neither of these factors is present. All that remains to be considered is the flat statement that the defendant was known to the FBI and others as a gambler. But just a simple assertion of police suspicion is not itself a sufficient basis for a magistrate's finding of probable cause. We do not believe it may be used to give additional weight to allegations that would otherwise be insufficient. The judgment of the Court of Appeals is reversed and the case is remanded to the Court for further proceedings consistent with this opinion.

It is interesting to point out that in this case the U.S. Supreme Court took the affidavit used to establish the basis for a search warrant and isolated each one of the points, in an effort to determine if they would, in and of themselves, lead one to believe that illegal activities were taking place.

Probable cause to search

One of the major cases that altered law enforcement procedures is *Chimel v. California*, 395 U.S. 752 (1969). In this case certain basic questions were raised concerning the permissible scope of a search incident to a lawful arrest under the Fourth Amendment. We have already established that police may search without a search warrant if it is incident to a lawful arrest. In this case the relevant facts are essentially undisputed. Late afternoon, September 13, 1965, three police officers arrived at the home of the defendant with a warrant authorizing his arrest for burglary. The officers identified themselves to the defendant's wife and asked if they might come inside. She ushered them into the home where they waited ten or fifteen minutes until the defendant returned home from work. When the defendant entered the house one of the officers handed him the warrant and asked for permission to look around. The defendant objected but was advised that "on the basis of a lawful arrest" the officers would nonetheless conduct a search. No search warrant had been issued. Accompanied by the wife, the officers then looked through the entire three-bedroom home, including the attic, the garage, and a small workshop. In some rooms the search was relatively cursory. In the master bedroom and sewing room, however, the officers directed the wife to open drawers and to physically move contents of the drawers from side to side so that they might view any items that would have come from the burglary. After completing the search they seized a number of items, primarily coins, but also several medals, tokens, and a few other objects. The entire search took between 45 minutes and an hour.

At the subsequent trial on two charges of burglary, the items taken from the house were admitted into evidence against him over his objections that they had been unconstitutionally seized. He was convicted and the judgments of convictions were affirmed by both the California District Court of Appeals and the California Supreme Court. Both courts accepted the petitioner's contention that the arrest warrant was invalid because the supporting affidavit was set out in conclusory terms, but held that since the arresting officers had procured the warrant "in good faith," and since in any event they had had sufficient information to constitute probable cause for the petitioner's arrest, that arrest had been unlawful. From this conclusion the appellate courts went on to hold that the search of the petitioner's home had been justified, despite the absence of a search warrant, on the ground that it had been incident to a valid arrest.

Without examining whether the arrest was sufficient, the Court held that they would assume that the arrest was valid under the Constitution. But they went on to examine the question whether the warrant to search the defendant's entire house can be constitutionally justified as incident to that arrest. After examining several principles that were discovered in other major cases, the Court had these comments:

The rule allowing contemporaneous searches is justified, for example, by the need to seize weapons and other things that might be used to assault an officer or effect an escape as well as by the need to prevent the destruction of evidence of the crime; things which might easily happen where the weapon or evidence is on the accused's person or under his control, but these justification are absent where a search is remote in time or place from the arrest. It is argued in the present case that it is reasonable to search a man's house when he is arrested in it, but that argument is founded on little more than a subjective view regarding the acceptability of certain sorts of police conduct and not on consideration relevant to Fourth Amendment interests. Under such unconfirmed analysis, Fourth Amendment protection in this area would approach the evaporation point. It is not easy to explain why, for instance, it is less subjectively reasonable to search a man's house when he is arrested on his front lawn or just down the street than it is when he happens to be in the house at the time of the arrest, or as Mr. Justice Frankfurter put it, to say that a search must be reasonable is to require some criteria of reason. It is no guide at all either for a jury or for a district judge or the police to say that an unreasonable search is forbidden. That search must be reasonable. What is the test of reason and what makes a search reasonable? The test is the reason underlying and expressed by the Fourth Amendment, the history and the experience which it embodies and the safeguards afforded by it against the evils to which it is a response. Thus, although the recurring question of the reasonableness of searches depends upon the facts and circumstances, the total atmosphere of the case, those facts and circumstances must be viewed in light of the established Fourth Amendment principle. . . . after arresting a man in his *home, to rummage at will among his papers in search of whatever will convict him appears to us to be indistinguishable from what might be done under a general warrant. Indeed, the warrant would give more protection for presumably it must be issued by a magistrate. True, by hypothesis, the power would not exist if the supposed offender were not found on the premises, but is small consolation to know that one's papers are safe only so long as no one is home.*

The Court concluded by stating that the application of sound Fourth Amendment principles to the facts of this case produces a clear result. The search here went far beyond the defendant's person and the area from which he might either have obtained a weapon or something that could have been used as evidence against him. There was no constitutional justification in the absence of a search warrant for extending the search beyond that area. The scope of the search was therefore unreasonable under the Fourth and Fourteenth Amendments and the defendant's conviction cannot stand.

It is interesting to note that the Court did not deny the police had a right to conduct a search incident to a lawful arrest, but they did define the parameters in which a search may be considered lawful following an arrest. And they severely restricted the scope of the search or the area that may be searched merely because the defendant had been arrested.

Confessions

The case that we will examine under this topic is one that has received considerable publicity and attention by the media and by the criminal justice community. It is *Miranda v. Arizona*, 384 U.S. 436 (1966). In this case Chief Justice Warren delivered the opinion of the Court. He stated:

The case before us raises questions which go to the roots of our concept of American criminal jurisprudence, the restraints that society must observe consistent with the federal Constitution in prosecuting individuals of crimes. More specifically, we deal with the admissibility of statements obtained from an individual who is subjected to custodial police interrogation and the necessity for procedures which assure that the individual is accorded his privilege under the Fifth Amendment to the Constitution, not to be compelled to incriminate himself. We encourage Congress and the states to continue their laudable search for increasingly effective ways of protecting the rights of individuals while promoting efficient enforcement of our criminal laws. However, we are shown other procedures which are at least as effective in apprising accused persons of their rights of silence and in offering a continuous opportunity to exercise it, the following safeguards must be observed. At the onset, if the person in custody is to be subjected to interrogation he must first be informed in a clear and unequivocal terms that he has the right to remain silent. For those unaware of the privilege the warning is needed simply to make them aware of it, the threshold requirement for an intelligent decision as to its exercise. More important, such a warning is an absolute prerequisite in overcoming the inherent pressures of the interrogation atmosphere. It is not just the subnormal or willfully ignorant who succumb to interrogators' imprecations, whether implied or expressly stated, that the interrogation will continue until a confession is obtained, or that silence in the face of accusations is itself damning and will bode ill when presented to a jury. Giving the warning will show the individual that his interrogators are prepared to recognize his privilege should he choose to exercise it. The Fifth Amendment privilege is so fundamental to our system of constitutional rule and the expedient of giving an adequate warning as to the availability of the privilege is so simple we will not pause to inquire in individual cases whether the defendant was aware of his rights without a warning being given. Assessment of this knowledge the defendant possessed based on information as to his age, education, intelligence, or prior contact with authorities can never be more than speculation. A warning is a clear-cut fact. More important, whatever the background of the person interrogated, a warning at the time of his interrogation is indispensable to overcome its pressures and to insure that the individual knows he is free to exercise the privilege at that point in time. The warning of the right to remain silent must be accompanied by the explanation that anything said can and will be used against him in court. This warning is needed in order to make him aware of not only the privilege but also the consequences of forgetting it. It is only through an awareness of these consequences that there can be an assurance of real understanding and an intelligent exercise of the privilege. Moreover, this warning may serve to make the individual more acutely aware that he is faced with a phase of the adversary system, that he is not in the presence of persons acting solely in his interest. Circumstances surrounding the in-custody interrogation can operate very quickly to overbear the will of one merely made aware of his privilege by his interrogators, therefore, the right to have counsel present at the interrogation is indispensible to the protection of the Fifth Amendment privilege under the system we delineate today. Our aim is to assure that the individual's right to choose between silence and speech remains unfettered throughout the interrogation process. A once-stated warning delivered by those who will conduct the interrogation cannot itself suffice to that end among those who most require knowledge of their rights. A mere warning given by the interrogator is not alone sufficient to accomplish that end. Prosecutors themselves claim that the admonishment of the right to remain silent without more will benefit only the recidivist and the professional. Even preliminary advice given to the accused by his attorney can be swiftly overcome by the secret interrogation process, thus the need for counsel to protect the Fifth Amendment privilege comprehense not merely a right to consult with counsel prior to questioning, but also to have that counsel present during any questioning if the defendant so desires. The presence of counsel at the interrogation may serve several significant subsidy functions as well. If the accused decides to talk to his interrogators the assistance of counsel can mitigate the dangers of untrustworthiness. With a lawyer present, the likelihood that the police will practice coercion is reduced and if coercion is nevertheless exercised, the lawyer can testify to it in court. The presence of a lawyer can also help to guarantee that the accused gives a fully accurate statement to the police and that the statement is rightly reported by the prosecution at trial. An individual need not make a pre-interrogation request for a lawyer. While such a request affirmatively secures his right to have one, his failure to ask for a lawyer does not constitute a waiver. No effective waiver of the right to counsel during interrogation can be recognized unless specifically made after the warning we here delineate has been given. The accused who does not know his rights and therefore does not make a request may be the person who most needs counsel. Accordingly, we hold that an individual held for interrogation must be clearly informed that he has the right to consult with *a lawyer and to have his lawyer present with him during interrogation under the system of protecting the privilege we delineate today. As with the warning of the right to remain silent and that anything stated can be used in evidence against him, this warning is an absolute prerequisite to interrogation. No amount of circumstantial evidence that the person may have been aware of his rights will suffice to stand on instead. Only through such a warning is there ascertainable assurance that the accused was aware of this right. If an individual indicates that he wishes the assistance of counsel before any interrogation occurs, the authorities cannot rationally ignore or deny his request on the basis that the individual does not have or cannot afford to retain an attorney. The financial ability of the individual has no relationship to the scope of the rights involved here. The privilege against self-incrimination secured by the Constitution applies to all individuals. The need for counsel in order to protect the privilege exists for the indigent as well as the affluent. In fact, were we to limit these constitutional rights to those who can retain an attorney, our decisions today would be of little significance. The case before us, as well as the vast majority of confessional cases with which we have dealt in the past, involve those unable to retain counsel. While authorities are not required to relieve the accused of his poverty, they have the obligation not to take advantage of indigents in the administration of justice. In order fully to appraise a person interrogated of the extent of his rights under this system, it is necessary to warn him not only of his right to counsel with an attorney, but also if he is indigent, a lawyer will be appointed to represent him. Without this additional warning, the admonition of the right to counsel would often be understood as meaning only that he can consult with a lawyer if he has one or has the funds to obtain one. As with the warning of the right to remain silent and of the general right to counsel, only by effective and expressed explanation to the individual of this right can there be an assurance that he was truly in a position to exercise it. Once the warnings have been given, the subsequent procedure is clear; if the individual indicates in any manner at any time prior to or during questioning that he wishes to remain silent the interrogation must cease. At this point he has shown that he intends to exercise his Fifth Amendment privileges. Any statement taken after the person invokes his privilege cannot be other than a product of compulsion, subtle or otherwise.*

The Court reversed the conviction. From the testimony of the officers and by the admission of the respondent, it was clear that Miranda was not appraised of his right to consult with an attorney and to have one present during the interrogation. Nor was his right not to be compelled to incriminate himself affectively protected in any other manner. Without these warnings the statements were inadmissible. The fact that he signed his statement which contained a typed-in clause stating that he had full knowledge of his legal rights did not approach the knowing and intelligent waiver required to relinquish constitutional rights.

Summary

The cases presented in this chapter were not intended to be conclusive, but merely to serve as a guide to some of the methods by which the Supreme Court applies constitutional rules and safeguards to criminal justice cases.

In some of the cases, the Court has applied several of the constitutional sections or Amendments or Articles. In others the Court restricted its review to a narrow constitutional issue. But nonetheless, we can appreciate how the constitutional safeguards against probable cause for arrest, unreasonable searches and seizures, detention, and confessions are applied to preserve the constitutional form of government and, in turn, law enforcement in the United States.

TOPICS FOR DISCUSSION

1. What applicable articles of the Constitution have had an effect upon law enforcement technique?

2. How does the Fourth Amendment right apply to protect a criminal defendant who has been charged with a crime?

3. Should the police be compelled to inform citizens of their constitutional rights or should they apply the old adage that ignorance of the law is no defense?

11

The role of the prosecution and the defense

The study of this chapter will enable you to:

1. **Present the function of the prosecutor and defense in a criminal trial.**
2. **Demonstrate the material differences between the defense and prosecuting attorneys.**
3. **Explain the adversary concept in criminal justice.**

The significant philosophy underlying the American system of criminal justice is the adversary process. This implies two competing sides struggling to overcome the opposing team's advantages and attacking their weaknesses. Nowhere throughout the system is the adversary role more pronounced than in the function of the prosecuting and defense attorneys in trial procedures. Other participants of the system are not expected to perform in an adversary manner: the police and the courts are generally expected to be fair and impartial in their approach and in meeting their responsibilities. But the two opposing attorneys are each expected to win a favorable decision for their client—even at the expense of fairness, if necessary. The prosecutor's client is the state, or the people. The defense attorney's client is the accused. This chapter will deal with the role of the prosecuting attorney and the defense attorney within the criminal justice system.

The prosecutor and the defense attorney

The prosecutor, also known as the district attorney or state's attorney, occupies a critical position in the criminal justice system. It is the prosecutor who must focus the power of the state upon those who defy the law. The majority of the nation's 2700 prosecutors serve in small offices with one or two assistants. Frequently, the prosecutor and his assistants are part-time officials who also engage in outside law practice. As Cole states:

The influence of the prosecutor flows directly from the legal duties, but it must be understood within the context of the administrative and political environment of the system. From the time of arrest to final disposition, the prosecution can make decisions that will determine to a great extent which cases are to be prosecuted, what charges are to be brought into the courtroom, and the kinds of bargains to be made with the defendant. The prosecutor has links with other actors throughout the system. For most states the prosecutor is an elected official, so he must be conscious of the public reaction.[1]

[1]George F. Cole, *The American System of Criminal Justice* (N. Scituate, Mass.: Duxbury Press, 1975).

Between the time of arrest and court appearances for trial on a serious charge, the accused usually asks for and is granted a preliminary hearing, or examining trial. The defendant requests this to find out in advance as much as he can about the evidence gathered against him, in an attempt to legally suppress or prohibit the use of as much of the evidence as possible. This is the first critical adversary encounter between the prosecutor and the defense counsel. This procedure often determines whether a trial will be held at all. If the defendant is successful in obtaining a judicial ruling suppressing most of the evidence against him, the charges may be dropped and the defendant freed, or the charges may be reduced. But even if this does not occur, the preliminary hearing tests the evidence and gives the defendant a better idea of the strengths of the case against him.

A trial can be compared to a boxing match between a professional and an amateur who is allowed to hire the services of a professional to fight for him. The prosecution has the district attorney or one of his assistants as its champion. The defendant, generally a nonattorney, must hire an attorney, have one appointed by the court, or seek the aid of a public defender. While the attorneys carry on their legal battle, the judge acts as an impartial referee, carefully watching, ready to intervene if he observes any illegalities or encroachments on the rights of the defendant.

The philosophy behind the adversary proceeding is that the contest between the two trained legal champions, fought in the presence of an impartial referee, will cause justice to prevail. The guilt or innocence of the defendant will be established beyond a reasonable doubt, and the jury will return a just verdict based upon this proven guilt or innocence. At the conclusion of the trial, if the jury does not find the defendant guilty, he is freed. If the jury cannot come to a unanimous verdict as to guilt or innocence and it deadlocks, the judge may declare a mistrial. Then the defendant will have to be tried again on the same charge before a different jury or a different prosecutor.

Major role differences

There are a few significant differences between the roles of prosecutor and defense attorney or public defender. One major difference is that in most jurisdictions the prosecutor is an elected public official who must therefore be sensitive to the political climate of his office. It is not enough that he strive to reach a successful prosecution in any given case; he must also satisfy public opinion in terms of which cases will be brought before the court for a potential trial. Defense attorneys, on the other hand, are private attorneys engaged in private practice, retained for a fee to defend a client in a criminal case. The defense attorney is rarely concerned with the political climate or any ramifications of public opinion for his efforts. In addition, the prosecutor's salary is an issue. When compared to that of many other public officials, it is fixed and low. Yet the criminal defense attorney often can command a rather large fee for defending an individual case. However, the majority of criminal defense attorneys are not in private practice and their fees are not high. When attorneys are appointed by the court to defend indigent clients, they receive a modest fee, somewhat below the salary of the prosecutor. In either event, the work of the attorneys in a criminal trial is usually on a part-time basis, whether it be as prosecutor (an elected public official), as a privately retained defense attorney, or from the public defender's office (appointed by the court). Because the attorneys are working on a part-time basis, they may not have the time to adequately prepare for their role, whether it be prosecution or defense. In the case of the public prosecutor, it is not uncommon that he have a number of cases pending at the same time; that he go into court unprepared to handle cases in which he has never met the client, never talked to the witnesses, never consulted with the arresting officer. Perhaps five or ten minutes before he is expected to go into court he may be told of the charges and read the complaint. This may also be true of the defense attorney, especially one who comes from the public defender's office or who has been appointed by the court. Frequently, the attorneys are able and thoroughly competent, but they just do not have the time to handle the large volume of cases with which they are confronted. Except in those rare cases where the client is wealthy or may have extensive public notoriety, few attorneys have the time to do the legal research, conduct the investigations into the backgrounds of the witnesses, or, under certain circumstances, develop a case against the judge for disqualification. And subsequent to the trial, in the event of a conviction, or even an acquittal, neither side may pursue all of the legal avenues that are open to them. In a conviction, except for a capital offense, there is no guarantee of appeal in many jurisdictions unless the defense attorney instigates it, which is an involved, lengthy process. This preparation of the legal documents and investigation into the valid reasons to request an appeal is so time-consuming that the attorneys may be forced to disregard it and instead handle the backlog of cases with which they are confronted. In an acquittal or perhaps a "hung" jury, where there is not an absolute verdict of guilt and the prosecution has the opportunity to request a new trial, they may choose not to, simply because of the time and effort involved and the lack of staff and resources to prepare the case adequately.

To clarify the issue of just how extensive the defense and prosecution team may work if the resources are available and if the participants have a sense of commitment, we shall examine the recent trial commonly referred to as the *San Quentin Six* trial. In that case, which occurred in San Quentin Prison in the San Francisco Bay area, six prisoners were charged with the murder of three prison guards. There were at least seven defense attorneys involved at one time in the defense of the accused. The trial, in total, lasted over seventeen months from the time the six men were originally charged with the crime. Thousands of individuals were brought in as potential jurors; it took five and a half months for the defense and prosecution to exhaust that process. The trial itself lasted an additional year and, in fact, it is not yet concluded, although a guilty verdict was returned on three of the defendants in late 1977. Appeals are currently pending. One of the chief defense attorneys, Mr. Charles Garry, has stated in a recent conversation that the appeal process may go on for an additional two to three years. The transcript of the trial itself, which will be used as a foundation for filing the legal documents for the appeal, consists of over 81,000 pages. This rather unusual circumstance serves to point out just how time-consuming a trial may be if the attorneys on both sides choose to utilize the legal avenues to pursue their cause.

When we contrast the *San Quentin Six* trial, which was the longest criminal trial in the history of the United States, with the vast number of criminal trials that occur throughout the United States daily, we can readily appreciate why the attorneys on both sides, either by choice or by imposition, are unable to offer the kind of legal prosecution or legal defense that may be available and, in fact, guaranteed, at least to the defendant, under the philosophy of our legal system. There are a number of steps that can be taken to improve the quality of service that attorneys may provide in a given criminal case. One major recommendation would be to insist upon full-time criminal attorneys to represent both prosecution and defense, adequately staffed with investigators and assistants, with resources sufficient to fulfill their obligations. In essence, create professional criminal attorneys; at the very least, eliminate the part-time, occasional, and slipshod activities we see daily.

There are a number of legislative changes that might help to achieve the goal of justice in our courtrooms. Some suggest the elimination of the "exclusionary rule"; others the elimination of plea bargaining; and still others the elimination of some of the laws that currently generate many of our criminal trials, such as the victimless crimes. These recommendations have been discussed more fully in other chapters. However, none of these recommendations nor all of them combined will provide a panacea, for our system is based upon conflict. This book cannot provide all of the solutions, but perhaps by describing reality we will take a major step toward developing solutions. And the reality of today is that seldom do we find justice in our courtrooms, and when it does occur, it often may be in spite of and not because of the attorneys involved in the criminal situation.

Recommendations for attorneys

1. Attorneys should be aware of the importance of the function of their offices for other agencies of the criminal justice system and for the public at large.

2. They should maintain relationships that encourage interchange of views and information and maximize coordination of the various agencies of the criminal justice system.

3. They should maintain regular liaison with the police departments in order to provide legal advice, to identify mutual problems, and to develop solutions to those problems.

4. They should participate in the training programs for the police and de-

velop and maintain a liaison with the police legal advisor in those areas relating to the police responsibilities.

5. The relationship between the prosecutor, the court, and the defense attorneys should be characterized by professionalism, mutual respect, and integrity. It should not be characterized by demonstrations of negative personal feelings or excessive familiarity. The officials should negate the appearance of impropriety and partiality by avoiding excessive camaraderie in their courthouse relations, remaining at all times aware of their public image.

6. They should establish regular communications with correctional agencies for the purposes of determining the effect of their practices upon correctional programs. They need to work toward maximizing the effectiveness of such programs.

7. They should regularly inform the public about the activities of their offices.

8. They should communicate their views to the public on important issues and problems affecting the criminal justice system.

This summary of recommendations may seem to conflict with the adversary nature of our court system. However, it is as advocates of justice, rather than as adversaries, that the courts must function.

TOPICS FOR DISCUSSION

1. Discuss the role of the prosecuting attorney.

2. Discuss the role of the defense attorney.

3. Discuss the resources available to the defense attorney as compared with those available to the prosecuting attorney.

4. Should the police provide the same support to each attorney?

12

Bail, plea bargaining, and sentencing

The study of this chapter will enable you to:

1. **Understand the meaning of the word "bail."**
2. **Understand the need for bail reform.**
3. **Be knowledgeable about the practice of plea-bargaining.**
4. **Understand the continuing arguments for the use of capital punishment.**

There have always been inequities in our ciminal justice system, but none are more apparent than in bail-setting procedures, plea bargaining, and sentencing practices. In this chapter we will examine these issues.

Bail

Before examining the bail system, we must define the term.

Bail is a sum of money put up by the defendant to secure his freedom until the date of his trial. If the defendant does not appear at the trial, this money is forfeited to the court. The amount is set by the judge, depending on the severity of the crime and the defendant's reputation.[1]

The practice of bail is a relatively old process, dating back as far as 1000 A.D., in England. At that time there were long delays in trials because judges spent considerable time traveling from one jurisdiction to another. Since prison conditions at the time were deplorable, instead of keeping a suspect accused of a crime in jail, a system of posting bail was instituted. The purpose was to assure the defendant's presence at his trial. It was then believed, and still is in many areas, that if an individual had to post money, he would be sure to appear in court at the appropriate time, instead of losing the bond that he had posted prior to his release.

The practice of posting money continued throughout this century, until several studies revealed that this system discriminated against the poor, who had to remain in jail because they did not have money to post the bond or pay a fee to a professional bondsman. As a result, the defendant suffered in several ways. First, he could not maintain his employment, which generally placed his family on some form of public support. Thus, the taxpayer had to pay not only for the maintenance of the prisoner while he was in custody, but also had to support the taxpayer's family. Second, since the defendant was confined to jail, he could not participate fully in the preparation of his defense. Counsel (if he had one) was hampered by not having easy access to his client in preparing his case for trial. Third, it

[1]Howard James, *Crisis in the Courts* (New York: David McKay, 1977), p. 118.

has been shown that those defendants who remain in jail because they cannot afford to post bail are more likely to be convicted than those who post bail or are released on their own recognizance. In 1953, a study based on 946 cases found that 58 percent of the defendants released on bail prior to their trial were not convicted, while only 18 percent of those who remained in jail prior to trial were not convicted.[2] Table 12–1 provides more recent figures on this phenomenon.

Finally, the system of justice suffered if the defendant was found not guilty. The injustice of confinement to jail for a long period of time and subsequent acquital could cause a bitter and extreme reaction against the system. The President's Commission on Law Enforcement and the Administration of Justice cited several examples of this problem. In one case a man was jailed on a serious charge brought on a Christmas Eve: he could not afford bail and spent 101 days in jail until a hearing. Then the complainant admitted the charge was false. In another case a man spent two months in jail before being acquitted. During that period he lost his job and his car, and his family was split up. He did not find another job for four months.

These are not the only documented cases of gross injustice caused by the economic factors of a person's inability to post bond. In 1973, a CBS documentary entitled, "Justice Delayed, Justice Denied," cited several disparities in our bail system. It reported that in Marion County, Indiana, at that time, approximately 75 to 80 percent of all the people in jail were awaiting trial. When asked how long an individual would have to wait before going to trial, a jailer replied that it was any time from one day to four years. One defendant awaiting trial in that facility was interviewed by CBS. They found that he had been waiting approximately 13 months for his case to come to trial. The state-appointed attorney wanted him to plead guilty and the defendant refused. It is ironic to note that if the defendant had pleaded guilty, he probably would have faced a parole board and been freed long before the 13-month interim.

Although bail is used to ensure that an individual be present at his trial, bail is sometimes used to ensure that a defendant be detained because he presents a dangerous threat to society if he were released. (Although this practice is sometimes used for such cases it is not legally prescribed.) Bail in this case is used as a preventative measure.

Despite the lack of statutory authority to impose bail for preventative detention, many judges do so, especially in connection with people who are considered dangerous or who have been involved in riots or demonstrations. The irony of this system is that even bail for preventative detention does not serve the claimed purpose of protecting society. Dangerous offenders who have adequate financial resources may be set free, while persons who are not dangerous to themselves or to society may languish in jail.[3]

[2]C. Foote, et al., "Compelling Appearance in Court: Administration of Bail in Philadelphia," *University of Pennsylvania Law Review*, June 1954, pp. 1031–1079.

[3]Sue Titus Reed, *Crime and Criminology* (New York: Holt, Rinehart & Winston, 1976), p. 346.

Table 12-1
Summary of relationship
between pretrial status
and outcome with each of
six characteristics held
constant.

Control	Pretrial status	Outcome				
		Not convicted	Convicted, No jail	Convicted, Short sentence	Convicted, Long sentence	(N)[1]
Severity of Charge						
Felony	Detained	24%	21%	29%	28%	(300)
	Released	59	27	10	4	(115)
Misdemeanor	Detained	16	12	65	7	(161)
	Released	45	36	19	0	(108)
Evidence Found						
Found	Detained	19	15	43	22	(367)
	Released	50	32	15	3	(168)
None found	Detained	23	28	36	14	(124)
	Released	54	34	12	0	(74)
Prior Record						
Recent felony	Detained	21	16	40	23	(274)
	Released	55	17	21	6	(47)
Other arrest	Detained	18	18	46	18	(153)
	Released	39	44	15	2	(66)
No record	Detained	18	32	37	13	(54)
	Released	55	32	11	2	(130)
Family Ties						
Weak	Detained	19	16	45	20	(188)
	Released	43	30	12	6	(51)
Some	Detained	22	17	30	22	(198)
	Released	50	31	17	2	(101)
Strong	Detained	20	22	30	18	(104)
	Released	56	30	13	1	(93)
Employment Status						
Employed	Detained	17	23	43	17	(163)
	Released	54	27	17	1	(139)
Unemployed	Detained	21	16	42	22	(209)
	Released	47	40	10	3	(94)
Amount of Bail						
$500 or less[2]	Detained	23	11	58	7	(187)
	Released	37	43	20	0	(54)
$1000 or more	Detained	19	22	30	29	(299)
	Released	33	33	19	14	(21)

[1]Row percentages may total 99% or 101% due to rounding.
[2]Excludes cases of those released on their own recognizance. The figures would show an even greater disparity if the "$500 or less" category included these cases.

Source: Eric W. Single, "The Consequences of Pretrial Detention," paper presented at the 1972 annual meeting of the American Sociological Association, New Orleans.

If this practice is not prescribed by law, why does it happen? In some cases it may be that the setting of extremely high bail for preventative practice serves to disperse the responsibility of releasing the accused. When bail is set and it is set extremely low, or if the defendant is released on his own recognizance, the judge bears a responsibility if the defendant commits another crime while on release.[4] This would be particularly dramatic if the crime were an heinous act. However, if the bail is set extremely high, the judge, prosecutor, and detention agents can say that they did all they could within the limits of the law, thereby dispersing the responsibility.

We must not overlook the fact that bail can be legitimately used to prevent the defendant from fleeing in order to avoid prosecution. High bail would prevent the defendant from posting bail and skipping his trial in many cases. Again we see that we are accomplishing the legality of the assurance of the defendant's presence at trial.

During the 1960s several programs of bail reform were started because of the growing dissatisfaction with the bail bond system. Los Angeles started an O.R. (Own Recognizance) program in 1963. Every defendant was given an application to fill out. A staff of five investigators and a clerical assistant then evaluated a person's character based on his past record. Interviews with neighbors and employers, and checks with schools attended were conducted. Based on the subsequent findings, a person might be released without having to post bond if the report was favorable. If the report was unfavorable, an individual could still post bail and be released.

One of the most formidable bail reform projects was started in 1961 at New York University under assistance from the Vera Foundation. Law students from this institution participated in an experiment to see if more individuals could be released on bail if certain information about them concerning their character and residency in the area could be documented. The students interviewed defendants, seeking information that would help them in evaluating the possibility of release. The following criteria were used: (1) no previous convictions; (2) current employment (six months or more in length); (3) present address and length of residence at the same address; (4) relatives in New York with whom the defendant had current contact; and (5) residence in New York for at least ten years.

The defendants were randomly assigned to experimental and control groups. On the basis of the information received, the staff decided which defendants might be eligible for parole. A copy of the information concerning those deemed eligible was then sent to the court where the arraignments would be heard. However, the staff sent copies of the recommendations only for the experimental group. The study revealed that the judges recommended 60 percent of those defendants recommended by the staff to be released on parole, while only 14 percent of those who were not recommended by the staff were released.

This study had a tremendous effect in reforming bail-setting practices and release procedures in other cities. Criteria similar to those used in the Vera Project were used in San Francisco. Other states, such as Illinois and

[4]Frederick Suffet, "Bail Setting: A Study of Courtroom Interaction," *Crime and Delinquency*, October 12, 1966, p. 329.

Oregon, require the defendant to post 10 percent of the amount of bail. In addition to the 10 percent plan, Oregon also releases defendants on their own recognizance (R.O.R.). Those who fail to make R.O.R. are released if they can post 10 percent of the bail allotted for the crime they committed.

How successful are these bail reform programs? Aside from saving the city and taxpayers millions of dollars by releasing subjects instead of keeping them in jail at the cost of $15 to $20 per day, the failure rates of those placed on R.O. R. is exceedingly low. It is estimated that only 2 percent of those released on the R.O.R. program in San Francisco failed to show for trial, while Los Angeles had a slightly higher rate of failure in 2.9 percent. An individual connected with the R.O.R. program in San Francisco estimated that bail bondsmen in that city had a 6 percent failure rate.[5]

The President's Commission on Law Enforcement and the Administration of Justice also made further recommendations concerning pretrial releases. They stated that bail projects should be undertaken at the state, county, and local levels to furnish judicial officers with sufficient information to permit the pretrial release, without financial condition, of all but that small portion of defendants who present a high risk of flight or dangerous acts prior to trial. They recommended that each state should enact comprehensive bail reform legislation after the pattern set by the Federal Bail Reform Act of 1966. They believe that each community should establish procedures to enable and encourage police departments to release, in appropriate cases, as many arrested persons as possible promptly after arrest, upon issuance of a citation or summons requiring their subsequent appearance.

Plea bargaining

The other pretrial issue that has caused considerable debate among courtroom officials, law enforcement personnel, and defense attorneys is the practice of plea bargaining. Plea bargaining is the process by which a defendant pleads guilty in exchange for prosecutorial concessions, such as reduced charges or reduced sentences. This process requires the defendant to waive an entire array of constitutional rights, including the right to remain silent, the right to confront witnesses against him, the right to a jury trial, and the right to be proven guilty beyond a reasonable doubt. In addition to requiring the accused to waive fundamental rights, the plea bargaining process affects other parties involved in the criminal justice system—the victim who has suffered, the police who have gathered the evidence, and the public at large.[6]

[5]Howard James, *Crisis in the Courts*, p. 123.

[6]National Institute of Law Enforcement and Criminal Justice, Law Enforcement Assistance Administration, *Plea Bargaining, A Selected Bibliography* (Washington, D.C.: U.S. government Printing Office, February 1976).

In spite of the many people who are adversely affected by the plea bargaining process, it remains a common practice in our courts when dealing with the criminal offender. Numerous individuals involved in the process of plea bargaining deplore its use but continue to utilize the practice. They claim that it is essential to continue its use as long as our courts are jammed and backlogged with cases.

It was estimated that in 1970 it took 2½ months for a defendant just to enter a plea of guilty or not guilty in the city of Chicago. In New York it may take up to 16 months for a criminal case to come to trial. The backlog is even more staggering for civil cases. In Los Angeles it may take 2 years for an auto accident claim to be heard in a court of law. The same type of case may take up to 6 years in in New York or Chicago.

This logjam is due to several factors. First, we have had a continual increase in population with the result that more people are forced to compete for space in a given geographical area. Overcrowding may induce stress and tension between neighbors, landlords, and tenants. This increase in human contact then results in human conflict, which is often settled in court.

The second cause of our overburdened court system may be explained in terms of our changing times. More individuals, corporations, and private industries are using the courts to settle contract disagreements or violations. We have added hundreds of new regulations in the past few decades. When these regulations are violated, the parties concerned seek court intervention. We have seen hundreds of cases such as those involving professional sports and player contracts, zoning regulations in cities or counties, population controls, acts of environmental control, violations of civil rights, and more recently, the Equal Rights Amendment. In addition, many drug or narcotic arrests are being contested in court on the grounds of illegal searches or seizures. These issues often involve second hearings and additional time delays to decide the legality of the search or seizure. If the removal of a drug from a suspect or suspect's property is found to be illegal, then another hearing may result in order to suppress the evidence (narcotic or drug) found. All this creates additional time lags in the court's scheduling.

Last, crime has increased at the rate of 10 times that of the number of judges able to hear such cases. As a result of this tremendous burden, the courts, prosecutors, judges, defense attorneys, and defendants are participating in plea bargaining to alleviate the logjam. The defendant is encouraged to plead guilty, thereby saving the court time in picking the jury, hearing the case, and waiting for the jury to deliberate in deciding the innocence or guilt of the defendant. For his willingness to participate in such a practice, the defendant is allowed to plead guilty to a lesser crime (e.g., murder reduced to manslaughter), or he is encouraged to plead guilty in order to receive a shorter sentence than he would if he went to trial.

The plea bargaining process is further encouraged when the court seemingly punishes the defendant for demanding his right to a jury trial. The prosecution may promise a lenient sentence if the subject pleads guilty. However, if the defendant demands that his case go to trial, the sentence is often overwhelmingly harsh and several times longer than it would have been if the defendant has pleaded guilty originally.

Although plea bargaining may be a common solution to reducing the court's load, it is also a practice that is frequently abused. One defense attorney practicing criminal law was frequently quoted as saying, "One of the reasons that plea bargaining is so prevalent in this county is that the district attorney overcharges crimes so that he has bargaining power and can offer such good deals." Another common occurrence in the bargaining process is that of obtaining multiple indictments for one person from the grand jury. With numerous charges against him, the defendant is coerced into pleading guilty to one charge so that the other charges against him will be dropped.

Additional pressure to participate in plea bargaining is brought about by the economics of the court appointment system. An attorney may receive $1000 to $5000 from a private client for a circuit court trial, but a court-appointed attorney receives $50 for a guilty plea and $100 a day for an indigent client whose case goes to trial. Since a negotiated guilty plea may take only minutes or hours and can be accomplished over the telephone, it far outweighs the fee ($100 per day) for going to trial, which may take weeks of preparation plus the additional expenses of a secretary's wages and office overhead. It is because of these economic realities that some defense attorneys may suggest to their clients that they plead guilty and accept the prosecutor's offer.

Perhaps the greatest disparity in the plea bargaining process is that of the innocent defendant waiting weeks and months in jail to go to trial, who agrees to plead guilty to get out of jail and back to his family or job. Waiting in detention facilities is hard on any person, but it may seem a lifetime to an innocent person who cannot afford to post bail and be released. After sleepless nights listening to inmates snoring, crying, vomiting, or perhaps even being a victim of a jailhouse assault, it is not unrealis-

The unpredictability of verdicts

Recently one defendant in a criminal trial in Oregon was promised a one to three year sentence if he pled guilty to the charge of auto theft and burglary. The defendant refused and demanded a jury trial. He is currently serving a *nineteen* year sentence for the crimes in the Oregon State Penitentiary.

The prevalence of "the deal"

Everytime I have prepared for trial—and I have done that numerous times—they (the D.A.'s office) offer such incredible deals that my clients can't pass them up. Or they will give in and drop the case.

Source: An attorney who has been practicing in a western state for a number of years and who has never gone to trial on a criminal case in circuit court.

tic to expect to find many innocent clients pleading guilty to a crime they did not commit.

What effect does this process have on the values of society? Consider the victim who observes the offender charged with armed robbery pleading guilty to a lesser charge. Does he understand the caseload pressures exerted on the district attorney and the courts that force them to channel as many cases as possible through this sytem in the shortest time? He probably does not—and he loses his respect for the system. Sometimes defendants plead guilty to lesser offenses even if they have reasonable defenses. Their attorneys stress the uncertainties of a jury trial to obtain consent to a quick guilty plea in exchange for a fine or short sentence. Here, the defendant will lose his respect for the system.

It is not only victims and defendants who may lose respect for the system, but law enforcement officers who serve the public and the criminal justice system as well. If you were a police officer who continually worked hard to make a good arrest; gathering evidence, talking to witnesses, and safeguarding the suspect's rights, only to watch the defendant receive probation for a serious crime, you might become disheartened at the system you are serving to protect.

Needless to say, the public at large questions our sense of justice and wonders whether the criminal justice system is serving to protect his family when serious offenders are being released with little or no penalty.

Sentencing

Sentencing is one of the most difficult and complicated decisions in the criminal justice process.

A sentence prescribes punishment, but it also should be the foundation of an attempt to rehabilitate the offender, to insure that he does not endanger the

Plea bargaining banned in Alaska

Alaska recently concluded a three-year study on the effects of banning the practice of plea bargaining for all defenses in that state. The practice was abolished by State Attorney General Avrum Gross on Aug 15, 1975.

Contrary to court officials' predictions that the judical system would bog down without the benefit of plea bargaining, the study indicated that the time it takes to process a case has decreased significantly while sentencing has increased. Prior to this change in policy, the average felony case in Anchorage took approximately 192 days to process and reach a deposition, but after one year when the practice of plea bargaining was prohibited, it took the average felony case 90 days to be processed. Fairbanks and Juneau also reported similar reductions in the length of time to dispose of felony cases.

The number of sentences also rose significantly. There was a 300 percent increase in felony drug offenses, a 50 percent raise for violent crime sentences, and a 200 percent raise for white-collar crimes.

In the past many of the officials in the criminal justice system have advocated the process of plea bargaining because of the tremendous overburdening of the court. To reduce or ban this policy would create havoc and excessive backlog in the courts. However, the director of the Alaska Judicial Council, Mike Rubstein, was recently quoted by the Associated Press in referring to Alaska's ban on the practice, as saying, "There has been a collateral effect of causing judges to be more efficient."

Source: *Statesman Journal*, Salem, Oregon, May 14, 1978.

community, and to deter others from similar crimes in the future. Often these objectives are mutually inconsistent, and the sentencing judge must choose one at the expense of others. The difficulty of making such important choices is compounded by the fact that a sentence is in large part a prediction. It tries to predict how an offender will behave under certain circumstances and how other potential offenders will behave. But judges do not have much predictive data to guide them.[7]

As a result of the lack of adequate information and ability to predict, judges may often, in error, impose an ineffective disposition on a case by making an erroneous decision in sentencing an individual.

One instrument used by judges to assist in reaching a decision about imposing a sentence on a defendant following the determination of guilt in a court, is a presentence report. This report, usually done by a probation

[7]The President's Commission on Law Enforcement and the Administration of Justice, *The Challenge of Crime in a Free Society* (Washington, D.C.: U.S. Government Printing Office, 1967) p. 141.

officer, provides the judge with current information and a background history of the defendant. (See Chapter 13 for a further discussion of presentence investigations.)

Probation Probation is the conditional release of the offender into the community; the imposition or execution of sentence is withheld on the condition that the offender show good behavior. All who have been convicted of a crime are theoretically entitled to probation in some form; although in practice we find, ironically, that probation is more frequent in cases involving serious crimes (felonies) than in cases involving minor offenses (misdemeanors). Although this appears patently unfair, it is necessary to note that judges in minor courts can easily use variations of probation—for example, simple suspension of sentence without investigation or the use of fines. The convicted felon has by law the right of consideration for probation in most states. Some exceptions are stated in the laws, usually for certain crimes, primarily murder, and a range of other offenses that vary from state to state. Noteworthy here is that persons convicted of more than one felony in many states are not eligible for probation.

There is no state that does not use probation. Its effectiveness is constantly being questioned; attacks on probation are frequent. Some of the criticism is justifiable—much is not. As a method of dealing with the offender, it is at least as effective as other methods and, unlike imprisonment, it is considerably cheaper.

Indeterminate sentences Indeterminate sentences are those affixed by a judge in which the sentence specifies a range of years. For example, at the conclusion of a trial where the defendant has been found guilty, or pleaded guilty to a crime, the judge may impose a sentence of from one to five years. The authority of the judge to set the range of years may be limited by state law. Under some state laws, he may fix the maximum; under others, the minimum; under still others, the minimum and maximum. Where a minimum and maximum sentence is levied, a considerable amount of discretion is within the prerogative of the parole board although the board may not keep a man beyond his maximum. Sometimes a judge may fix the minimum and maximum so close together that little discretion is left to the parole board.

There is a school of thought that would like to see the entire sentencing function moved out of the court and the responsibility for sentencing placed with sentencing boards. Numerous studies show wide disparity in sentencing practices. The effect on the system in terms of commitment levels and on the offender in terms of injustices is a serious issue.

Parole Parole differs from probation in that a portion of the sentence is served in a correctional institution, and release into the community before the completion of the sentence is provided for with conditions similar to probation—

namely, good behavior. In both probation and parole, if the behavior of the individual violates any of the conditions, the person may be committed or recommitted to prison.

In practice, the statutes of the 50 states governing both probation and parole make for a wide variety of operational conditions. It is because of this that injustices within the system are so widespread. In urban areas passing of a bad check is usually treated as a probation case, whereas in small towns this offense may be considered more harshly. Similarly, use of drugs is dealt with in different ways in different sections of the country.

Parole, too, is subject to many variations—the type of offense, the nature of the paroling organization, the confidence in parole practices, and (a factor not to be overlooked) how a community feels about an individual returning to that community. A good deal of community pressure against release, for example, would develop in the case of a rapist/murderer returning to a small town, the scene of the offense.

In the past 50 years, parole has become an indispensable part of the justice system. Parole as we know it today is closely identified with the American reformatory movement. The development of institutional classification emphasized the importance of individualizing the treatment of the offender in terms of the causes of his criminal behavior and his potentials for treatment and training. Some time later the indeterminate sentence laws and the appointment of parole boards to administer parole statutes were instituted.

There is not yet a standardized method for releasing an offender on parole, but one board can and will make much more consistent decisions in individual cases than the courts and their many judges could ever accomplish. Boards seek to selectively release a prisoner at the psychologically opportune time when, in the board's estimation, he has received the maximum benefit from his institutional experience.

In recent years, there has been a sharp movement to bring to the parole hearing, especially the revocation hearing, all of the procedural safeguards of a court of law.

Death penalty

Of all the sentencing practices, the one that has been argued most vehemently is the use of capital punishment. Disagreement about applications of the death penalty have not been confined to the past few decades; the debate has raged throughout the last two centuries.

Until the late seventeenth century the death penalty had been imposed repeatedly on offenders for offenses that are now considered to be relatively petty. During the fifteenth century in England alone, there were approximately 17 capital offenses (type of crime in which the punishment is death). Capital crimes increased in England until about 1780 when over 200 capital offenses existed. In 1814 three boys aged 8 and 9 were sentenced to death for stealing a pair of shoes. By 1839 England had repealed the death penalty on all but 17 offenses.

In the United States we have seen periodic trends to abolish the death penalty. However, these trends are usually followed by a period of restoration of the penalty. Since 1967 there has only been one execution in the United States, that of Gary Gilmore, who was executed by a firing squad in Utah (1977) for murder. Prior to Gilmore's death and following his execution, groups identifying themselves either as abolitionists or favoring the death penalty picketed the streets campaigning for their beliefs concerning the death penalty. As a result of the Gilmore case, heated debates ensued and continue over an issue which has been constantly challenged by both the public and the courts.

Several arguments have been repeatedly used by advocates of the death penalty as well as by those who are in favor of the abolition of the death penalty. These arguments have centered around the issues of public opinion, revenge, deterrence, cruel and unusual punishment, cost, and the irreversibility of the penalty.

Public opinion At periodic intervals, surveys have polled the American public about their views on capital punishment. If we look at Table 12-2 we find variations in preference concerning the death penalty during the past 25 years. These variations and fluctuations will probably continue on into the future.

Although there is no overall agreement in society on using capital punishment, public opinion on the issue is used by courts and legislatures in deciding to abolish or restore the penalty in individual states and at the judicial level. Most laws and existing statutes are reviewed in regard to contemporary behavior and governing philosophy. (The reduction in penalty against possession of small amounts of marajuana and relaxation of laws governing sexual preference are examples of legislative changes due to society's changing mores.) In referring to Table 12-2 you note there was a decline in favoring the use of capital punishment in the mid-sixties. Perhaps reflecting this view, use of the death sentence literally came to a standstill in 1967, and various states that had previously used capital

Table 12-2

1. Gallup Poll—"Are you in favor of the death penalty for persons convicted of murder?"

1953—68% yes
1960—52% yes
1965—45% yes
1966—42% yes
1969—climbed to 51% yes
1972—(December) climbed to 57% yes

2. 1958 Roper poll (nationwide poll).

42% favored execution over life imprisonment
50% against death penalty
 8% no opinion
low income—53% against
highest income—42% against
blacks interviewed—78% opposed

punishment repealed the law. In the seventies polls indicated public opin
ion was again in favor of the death penalty, and many states who had
once abolished the death penalty sought to restore it. California was one of
the states that restored the death penalty in 1977. Criminologists largely
believe that the rapid momentum in reestablishing the death penalty is
due to the public's frustration over the continued rise in violent crime.

The Gilmore incident

On Monday, January seventeenth, a convicted murderer was duly executed in Utah. It was the first legal execution in America since July 2, 1967.

Long before the five-man firing squad took aim at the multiple murderer I was sick and tired of hearing and seeing in the newspapers and on radio and television about the legal fights being made to save his life—to block the execution.

Although the National Sheriffs' Association formally passed a resolution supporting capital punishment at its Annual Informative Conference at Memphis, Tennessee, in 1975, this page is not intended to discuss the death penalty per se. It is, rather, meant to criticize that portion of the populace that attempted to make a folk hero out of a cold-blooded murderer while virtually ignoring the two men who were murdered and their families.

Gary Gilmore had been found guilty last October of the murder of Provo, Utah, motel clerk, Bennie Bushnell, who had taken the job to support his pregant wife and infant son. He was studying accounting and planned to return to college in one year. The robbery netted Gilmore $130.00

His widow, Debbie Bushnell, now in Pasadena, California, commented after the execution that she was "happy to get it over with, to get it off the air, and out of the news."

The convicted slayer had also admitted to the murder of Max Jensen, a twenty-four-year-old law student, who was working as a part-time gas station attendant. He was found in the rest room of the service station with two bullet holes in his head. That robbery netted Gilmore $130.00 and was committed the night before Bushnell was killed. In both cases, the killer coldly placed a pistol behind their ears and murdered them.

No songs about victims.
Colleen Jensen, now a high school art teacher in Clearfield, Utah, said: "I get upset when they glorify the man who killed my husband. It hurts very much and I have to wonder if justice is being done." We agree with her comments wholeheartedly.

What about the song written to glamorize him? The murderer could listen to it being played over the radio. There was no song written about his victims, and if there had been they couldn't hear it.

What about the national news magazine that put his picture on the cover and gave an extensive article on his life? There was no one there to photograph the two young men whose lives he snuffed out.

What about the wheeler-dealer who paid Gilmore $125,000 for the rights to a book and a movie to be shown on television? All but $40,000 of this goes to Gilmore's relatives and to his much-publicized girlfriend who is confined to a Utah State mental hospital.

What about the $50,000 paid by a national magazine for an interview with the killer? No one has offered Debbie Bushnell nor Colleen Jensen money for interviews?

He wouldn't have stopped.
The killer received some seven thousand "fan" letters. Judges were awakened in the middle of the night and asked for a stay of execution. Prayer vigils were organized. There were those who urged compassion for the killer. What kind of compassion did he show? He was asked: "If you hadn't been caught, do you think there would have been a third and a fourth (murder)?"

He replied: "There might have been more than that, that night . . . I was going to just continue . . . until I got caught or shot to death by the police or something like that."

A well-known Greek historian wrote: "Compassion is due to those who can reciprocate the feeling, not to those who never pity us in return." I agree completely.

The killer callously forced Jensen into a rest room of the gas station and fired two bullets into his head.

The following night he ordered Bushnell to lie on the floor back of the counter then cooly blew his head apart.

Jensen left his widow and infant daughter Monica who had to move in with Mrs. Jensen's mother and go to work.

Bushnell left his pregnant widow and infant son Bennie, Jr., who had to move in with her mother. Because of the expense of shipping her husband's remains back to California, she's still paying for expenses incurred because of his death.

Their killer was first sentenced as a juvenile delinquent when he was fourteen. During his life of crime he had been arrested many times for armed robbery, assault, rape, and other charges. He had spent twenty-three years of his life in trouble and eighteen years of it in prison.

Source: Ferris E. Lucas, National Sheriffs' Association, February-March 1977.

Retribution One of the most heated arguments surrounding the death penalty is retribution. Those in favor of capital punishment often use the proverb of "an eye for an eye" or like punishment. These statements are a reflection of our past modes of punishment. The ideology of revenge was found in the Code of Hammurabi in 1900 B.C. and in numerous places in the Old Testament of the Bible.

Analyzing this argument of revenge leads to the ultimate collapse of this philosophy. It might be argued that in seeking revenge by equal punishment we would be justified in stealing from someone who stole from us or assaulting an individual and causing equal torment to those who inflicted pain upon their victims. Such actions would crumble society into a chaotic state. The criminal justice system was instituted to prevent such actions.

The use of retribution as a justification for punishment has been challenged by several Supreme Court justices in commenting about the use o retribution as a reason for the use of capital punishment. Justice Brennan argued that since most people who are convicted of capital crimes are no given that sentence but rather are sent to prison, that the use of capita punishment cannot be justified by the philosophy of retribution, "The as serted public belief that murders and rapists deserve to die is flatly incon sistent with the execution of a random few."[8]

Table 12-2 indicates how inconsistent our beliefs are about imposing the death penalty on all of these convicted prisoners of a capital crime who were sentenced to die.

Justice Brennen also reflected about the issue of capital punishment: "I would be reading a great deal into the Eighth Amendment to hold that the punishments authorized by legislatures cannot constitutionally reflect o retributive purpose." (The Eighth Amendment deals with the issue of crue. and unusual punishment.)

The death penalty is irreversible One of the most devastating arguments against the death penalty is the finality of the punishment itself and the inability to revoke the error after execution of the sentence. Although advocates of the death penalty believe this to be a rare occurrence, mistakes do happen. Some mistakes are averted by our judicial system (appeal) and by executive clemency, but others occur. The reasons most often cited for errors include mistaken identification, inadequate circumstantial evidence, perjury, unreliable expert testimony, overlooking supporting evidence, and extreme zeal on the part of investigators and prosecutors.

Several studies examined the problem of sentencing errors. One such study was done over a 40-year period. The study found that 12.3% of the 406 persons sent to Sing Sing for execution were found, upon reconsideration, to have been sentenced in error.[9] Another study in Michigan, which was an abolitionist state at the time of the research, found that judges and juries erred in 10.9% of 759 life imprisonment convictions for first degree murder. This study was conducted from 1942–1951.[10]

**TOPICS FOR
DISCUSSION**

1. How does bail discriminate against the poor?

2. What factors should be included in an R.O.R. report?

3. Is preventative detention a legal concept of bail?

4. What factors contribute to the practice of plea bargaining?

5. Name several of the disparaties associated with plea bargaining.

[8]Furman v. Georgia US (1972).

[9]Lewis E. Lawes, *Twenty Thousand Years in Sing Sing* (New York: R. Long and R. R. Smith, 1932), pp. 146–147, 156.

[10]Otto Pollak, "The Errors of Justice," *Annals of the American Academy of Political and Social Science,* 284:115–123, November, 1952; and Jerome Frank and Barbara Frank, *Not Guilty* (New York: Doubleday, 1957).

PART 4
Corrections

13

Corrections

The study of this chapter will enable you to:

1. **Understand the historical development of the prison system.**
2. **Understand the impact that prison design and architecture have on prison treatment and rehabilitation programs.**
3. **Understand the dilemma of the policies of treatment or punishment for prison officials.**
4. **Realize the conditions of institutional life.**
5. **Identify the various treatment programs operating in our prisons.**

W*e lock them away very often before anything has been proved against them. We deprive them of their human rights and dignity. We give them little if anything, to do all day. Then we wonder why they aren't reformed.*
Source: Jessica Mitford, "Women in Cages," *McCalls,* September 1972.

Corrections is the least visible and least understood segment of the criminal justice system in America. Its prisons, jails, juvenile training schools, and probation and parole machinery deal with the most troubling and troublesome members of society—the unrespectable and irresponsible. The institutions in which about one-third of the "corrections" population lives are out of view of most citizens, often in rural areas remote from the population centers. The two-thirds of the population on probation and parole are dispersed in the community and nearly invisible to all. Society seldom looks at corrections, except when there is a riot, jailbreak, or sensational scandal. Society has been content to keep corrections out of sight.

The invisibility of corrections belies its size, complexity, and importance in the control of crime. Corrections consists of scores of different kinds of institutions and programs of the utmost diversity in approach, facilities, and qualities. On any given day it is responsible for approximately 1.5 million offenders; in the course of a year it will handle 2.5 million "new" cases at a cost of over a billion dollars a year, with costs rising each year.[1]

Historical background

The ways in which society has dealt with lawbreakers have evolved from primitive peoples' simple revenge or retaliation to today's concepts of rehabilitation and return to society. As governments developed, they took

[1]The President's Commission on Law Enforcement and the Administration of Justice, *The Challenge of Crime in a Free Society* (Washington, D.C.: U.S. Government Printing Office, 1967).

over the protection of persons and property and the punishment of offenders in the name of peace and order. But the basis of the government's intervention remained retribution. In England alone, toward the end of the sixteenth century, there were 600 executions in one year—a high rate for a comparatively small population. The death penalty was the most common response to common crime. In Europe during the sixteenth and seventeenth centuries, there were some 30 ways of administering death penalties, from drawing and quartering to burning at the stake or breaking on the rack. Public floggings were administered for relatively minor offenses. Imprisonment was looked upon not as a means of punishment but rather as a form of safekeeping to insure the presence of the offender at his trial. Imprisonment as a form of corrections is an idea of rather recent origin.

The Pilgrim Fathers in 1620 brought the stern criminal codes from Europe nearly intact. It was not until well into the eighteenth century that William Penn and the Quakers introduced a more humane element: the substitution of imprisonment for capital and corporal punishment.

In 1794 Pennsylvania adopted a new code that reduced the list of capital crimes to first degree murder and prescribed fines or imprisonment for other crimes.

The Walnut Street jail, the first American penitentiary (1790) located in Philadelphia, stressed two features: (1) solitary confinement without labor for more serious offenders, and (2) labor together in small groups at approximately the prevailing wage for less serious offenders.

Incarceration for felons had been initiated in England by the reformer, John Howard (1726–1790), as a worthy substitute for the death penalty, the most frequently used penalty at the time. It was Howard who coined the word *penitentiary*, and the philosophy of penitence or expiation gradually became the prevailing hope. But it was Pennsylvania and later New York that were destined to implement and develop Howard's ideas, first in the Walnut Street Jail in Philadelphia and later in the Western Penitentiary in Pittsburgh, Cherry Hill (Eastern Penitentiary), and Auburn, New York.

The degree of optimism about the effectiveness of the penitentiary approach is seen in the following report:

From the experiments already made, we have reason to congratulate our fellow citizens on the happy reformation of the penal system. The prison is no longer a scene of debauchery, idleness, and profanity; an epitome of human wretchedness; a seminary of crimes destructive to society; but a school of reformation and a place of public labor.[2]

The Quakers in this period campaigned for moral regeneration through solitary confinement without labor. By 1827, the Western Penitentiary in Pittsburgh was in operation; it had tiny solitary cells—cells that were miniature prisons too small for labor. It was thought that isolation would prevent criminal contagion, and that solitary reflection would be a means of achieving moral regeneration.

[2]Francis C. Gray, *Prison Discipline in America* (London: John Murray, 1848), p. 22.

In this period there was much controversy about types and kinds of facilities and, eventually, a variety of architectural types and approaches were developed. Naturally, architecture alone solved no problem except, perhaps, that of "security," because in this period all approaches sought to break the spirit by using isolation coupled with work. Prison discipline was as unique as its architecture. For example, where prisoners worked together, silence was maintained. Other harsh punitive measures prevailed. Prisoners were treated as less than human. The failure to rehabilitate was inevitable because of the very same problems that beset us today: idleness, monotony, crowding, and poor custodial personnel.

Cherry Hill, the notoriously famous model of the system of separate confinement, still stands today in Philadelphia. This Bastille-like structure of stone and iron cell block warrens is considered by some to be the most famous prison in the world—certainly not for its enlightened approach, but as a monument to social futility. In its 141 years of existence (1829–1970), 75,000 men and 1900 females were entombed for many years of their lives. Negley K. Teeters, sociologist and chronicler of this special prison and penology generally, provides the opportunity to live in its history by a moving account of that institution.

Actually, this old structure has been not so much a prison as it has been the epitome of one of the most unique concepts of penal treatment ever conceived. Its founders, citizens primarily of the city of Philadelphia, created it on the principle of separate, but not solitary, confinement (however, this subtle distinction might be regarded by some as merely a bit of casuistry), by which a prisoner could be separated from all others. This was accomplished by providing an individual cell for each inmate in which he worked, slept, and ate alone. He was provided an exercise yard attached to his cell where he was permitted to enjoy the outside for a few short intervals each day. His only contacts were his keepers, the chaplain, and a few interested citizens, members of the Philadelphia Prison Society, who by law were not only permitted to visit him, but admonished to do so. When it became necessary for a prisoner to leave his cell he was obliged to wear a mask or hood drawn over his face in order to prevent recognition. He carried a number and was known by name only to the warden and keepers.

The first prisoner to enter Cherry Hill was an eighteen-year-old black youth from Delaware County, named Charles Williams. He was sentenced on October 22, 1829 to serve two years for larceny of "one silver watch, value $20; one gold seal, value $3; one gold key, value $2" from the home of Nathan Lukens, known as Dowling House in Upper Darby. He entered the prison three days after sentence was passed and as there were no cells yet completed, he was temporarily housed in a room fitted up as an apothecary shop in the massive central tower. He was removed to his individual cell on the following November 10th. [3]

Like the optimism that prevailed at the time of the Walnut Street Jail reflected in Francis Gray's report, the eminent Frenchman, De Tocqueville (statesman and author) in 1831 similarly was to be deceived. He wrote:

[3]Negley K. Teeters, "The Passing of Cherry Hill," *The Prison Journal.* L, No. 1, The Pennsylvania Prison Society (Spring-Summer, 1970).

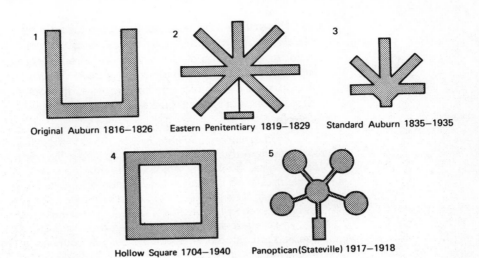

Figure 13-1

Types of prison structure.

Original Auburn 1816–1826 Eastern Penitentiary 1819–1829 Standard Auburn 1835–1935

Hollow Square 1704–1940 Panoptican(Stateville) 1917–1918

The man works with ardor. His mind seems tranquil; his disposition excellent. He considers his being brought to the Penitentiary as a signal benefit of Providence. His thoughts are in general religious. He read to us in the Gospel the parable of the Good Shepherd, the meaning of which touched him deeply; one who was born of a degraded and depressed race, and had never experienced anything but indifference and harshness. The young man was set to making shoes and the French visitors reported that he made as many as ten pair per week. While all prisons are the receptables of heartache, despair, rascality, gloom, and vitriolic hostility mixed with a slight modicum of hope and compassion, Cherry Hill, at least in its inception, was dedicated in the name of reform and rehabilitation. It was believed that this worthy objective could be consummated by means of expiation. [4]

In this period, the Auburn System, a bold new experiment, was begun. While subscribing to the essential elements indicated above, the Auburn prison in New York began to look seriously at the prisoner as an individual.

Auburn incorporated the one important principle that was excluded from other experiments—the classification of prisoners. A three-grade system was used:

1. Solitary cells for incorrigibles without labor.

2. Tractable persons in solitary cells with labor as recreation. Not incredibly, labor was accepted readily and considered a privilege.

3. The best candidates for reformation were offered group work during the day and held in isolation during the night. [5]

[4]Gustave de Beaumont and Alexis De Tocqueville, *On the Penitentiary System in the United States and its Application to France,* trans. Francis Lieber (Philadelphia: Carey, Lea and Blanchard, 1933).

[5]Orlando F. Lewis, *The Development of American Prisons and Prison Customs, 1776-1845* (Albany Prison Association of New York, 1922), pp. 11-12.

Nevertheless, the Auburn system failed also, especially with the incorrigibles held in solitary idleness. Many went insane; some attempted suicide. The health of many was impaired and the experiment did not lead to moral regeneration. Auburn was a failure in these terms, but it did provide an economic advantage over the other systems because of the cheap contract labor it offered.

It is a paradox that practically every prison system abroad adopted the system, but it was rather universally shunned by the several states. This is largely due to the fact that the Auburn System appealed more to the capitalist economy because of its use of power machinery which was beginning to be utilized at the time and hence made possible a maximum exploitation of convict labor. Reformers persisted in taking the policy of redemption or reformation of prisoners seriously. Handcraft labor pursued in the prisoners' cells, it was believed, would hasten reformation.

The cornerstone of penology, reformation in isolation, had many critics. Keeping men locked up in solitary cells 24 hours each day with few human contacts is hardly a respectable criterion of reformation. As the late Harry Elmer Barnes, noted authority of corrections, put it some years ago: "No system can be successfully tested by its ability to turn out Robinson Crusoes or broken down unoffending hermits." Thomas Mott Osborne wrote that the system "showed a touching faith in human nature although a precious little knowledge of it." These remarks are reminiscent of the classic statement made by the British prison expert, Alexander Paterson, when he likened a prison to a "monastery inhabited by men who do not choose to be monks."[6]

In the nineteenth century, a heavy religious influence was felt. In fact, most prison administrators considered their Christianity, common sense, and practical experience sufficient qualification for their task. The strongly religious Zebulon Brockway, for example, surpassed the average reformer of the time. He incorporated some important measures in the reformatory at Elmira, New York, in 1877. Included was the grading of prisoners (the forerunner of modern classification), work for wages, and the mark system with the indeterminate sentence providing an opportunity for a prisoner to make his way out.

Probably the first steps toward the indeterminate sentence were taken by Maconchie, who in 1840 used the mark system to allow a man to work his way out of prison. . . . This system utilized the prisoner's desire for freedom as an incentive for reformation. Maconchie said of the mark system, "When a man keeps the key of his own prison he is soon persuaded to fit it into the lock."[7]

The reformatory idea ripened in the early 1900s, but declined in a decade or so. The reformatories had basic characteristics that made them junior prisons; their punitive philosophy overcame their major improvements. Nevertheless, a modern penal philosophy was emerging. In 1916, when Thomas Mott Osborne at Elmira insisted on inmate participation in

[6]The Pennsylvania Prison Society, *The Prison Journal*, L, No. 1 (Spring-Summer, 1970), pp. 6-9.

[7]Barner and Teeters, *New Horizons in Criminology*, 2nd ed. (Englewood Cliffs, N.J.: Prentice-Hall, 1951), p. 520.

the operation of a prison, a major breakthrough was made in viewing the prisoner as a person. The old idea that all prisoners should be treated alike now gave way to classification of individuals to be treated as individuals.

Contemporary concepts Administrators and employees of the correctional system are becoming more aware of the impact that architectural design has on the inmate climate and subculture. In our historical look at prison architecture and the philosophies advocated by the Auburn and Pennsylvania systems, we saw that the design of the prisons facilitated the implementation of silence, isolation, and prison labor. Today's institutions are incorporating designs that will enhance rehabilitation.

If our stated philosophy surrounding corrections is to return the offenders to the community as useful, law-abiding citizens, we need not only the manpower to enable this to happen, but also the physical means to help reintegrate inmates with normal patterns of socialization. In the past our prison systems were designed to impede the socialization that is necessary to prepare the individual to compete and function in society. Having inmates in cells for long periods of time decreases the prisoner's opportunity to communicate with other inmates, guards, or visitors. Limiting their outside contacts puts an added strain on their difficulties in becoming an accepted member in the community upon their release.

Some of the newer designs for detention centers and penal institutions would alter the previous telephone-pole-like structure of our prisons. The telephone-pole structure is a building designed with tiers of cells of identical design. The cells are usually aligned down long corridors; all floors are exactly alike. New designs are using more courtyard space and more individualized buildings. The additional buildings contain libraries, classrooms, chapels, and vocational trade and industry shops. By placing these facilities in other buildings, it allows the inmates to move outside and around courtyards, which alleviates overcrowding and the consistent interaction with other inmates. Inmates placed in this type of correctional setting indicate that they felt there were fewer cases of aggressive behavior because of the increased amount of movement.

Many juvenile institutions are using a campus-like design. Instead of the one or two main buildings found in traditional penal institutions, the campus design uses many individual buildings. Eating may be done in each separate dormitory or cottage or in a large dining hall, at separate tables and chairs rather than at the rows of tables and benches found in most institutions. This less rigid atmosphere increases the opportunity for greater communication among the inmates. In addition, the campus-like design allows the prisoners to move more freely with less regimentation.

Perhaps the greatest drawback to these newly designed prisons is that they cost more than the traditional telephone-type structures. In 1965 it was estimated that the traditional dormitory-type facility cost $5,400 per inmate while the campus-like facility would cost between $12,000 and $25,000 per inmate to construct. With the recent enormous increases in construction costs, these estimates could easily double at today's inflation rate. In addition to the problem of rising costs is the ten-year moratorium on building new prisons suggested in 1973 by the National Advisory Committee on Criminal Justice Standards and Goals. This recommendation is forcing communities and states to find other resources and facilities to handle law violators.

The offender in the system

There is a selection process that takes place in the criminal justice system, one which results in a disproportionately small number of offenders officially handled, who "represent" crime in the United States. Those who come into the correctional system are a small percentage of the offenders in the society. The fallout is greatest between the point where an offense is committed and the point where charges are filed. Arrests reflect one-fourth of known serious crimes. Charges filed will be reduced as much as one-third and, of those charged, there can be another one-third fallout. Again, we can expect the screening out of a large number, as much as 20 percent who are not found guilty. Figure 13–2 depicts this fallout for one jurisdiction.

The data shown are not unusual. They are similar for most jurisdictions. It is important, therefore, to realize that the numbers in prison do not truly represent the numbers of criminals in the United States.

Corrections follows last in the sequence of activities after police arrest, prosecution, and court disposition. It is the court disposition that sets corrections in motion. Corrections follows two broad paths: institutionalization or community treatment (most commonly, probation or parole).

Commitment or punishment

Throughout history there has been a continual debate surrounding the philosophy of our penal institutions. Aside from the obvious obligation of protecting society, the question remains whether our prisons serve as instruments of punishment and deterrence or as institutions of rehabilitation and help. There are good arguments both for and against these prevailing attitudes.

There are not many people who do not believe that society must be protected from *some* individuals. Most people realize that in spite of treatment or therapy, there are individuals who will not derive benefit from treatment and who remain a constant threat to the safety of others. We have no alternative but to incapacitate that person. However, there are others who have committed relatively petty crimes and as a result, are

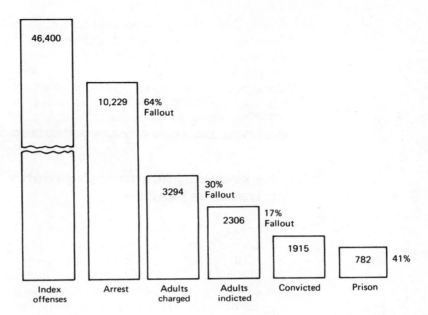

Figure 13-2

Criminal justice fallout, 1971. *Source:* Dallas Police, 1972.

incarcerated in prison as punishment for their crimes. If these individuals are functioning members of society, would not rehabilitation be more meritorious than punishment? The question here arises as to the worth of the individual and what he might contribute on his return to society. If an individual can contribute something to society, rehabilitation and re-integration into society would be more functional than sentencing to an institution for the pure merit of punishment for committing a relatively small crime.

No one should be condoned for committing a criminal act that is harmful to society. (The public has despaired numerous times with individuals who are acquitted of crime because of a violation of their constitutional

What are our goals?

Rehabilitation is a splendid goal; everyone favors it; but it is not the only goal: punishment, deterrence, retribution, and simple incapacitation are also splendid goals.

Source: Gary McCuen, *American Prisons: Correctional Institutions or Universities of Crime* (Minneapolis, Minn.: Greenhaven Press, 1971).

rights.) But we must remember that of all those individuals who receive prison sentences as a result of committing a criminal act, there are very few who will not in time return to society. Therefore, the protection of society depends largely upon the correction of the criminal. Punishment alone will not correct him. We need other methods of treatment to rehabilitate the offender and make him a law-abiding citizen. Unfortunately, we are still groping for solutions.

The presentence investigation and institutionalization

Following a determination of guilt in court, all offenders are generally subject to a presentence investigation. The Standard Probation and Parole Act of 1955 states: "No defendant convicted of a crime, the punishment for which may include imprisonment for more than one year, shall be sentenced or otherwise disposed of before a written report of investigation by a probation officer is presented to and considered by the court." This is a written report to the court setting forth a systematic, thorough inquiry into the offender's life and background, the details of the immediate offense, and any prior criminal history. This report is used to analyze and interpret the offender's personality for the purposes of determining if he or she should be sentenced to prison and for how long, or if he or she can be released into society on probation and with what degree of risk to the community. The personal history of the defendant set forth in the report includes developmental data, health, education, employment habits, character, behavioral patterns, associates, marital history, and mental and physical condition. This basic information assists the court in making its determination. Although presentence investigations have been kept confidential in the past, the present trend has been against this. Many judges share the information at least with the defense attorneys at the time of sentencing. Sentencing takes place at a special hearing set at a date in the future by the judge at the time the defendant is found guilty. This usually entails a two-week to four-week waiting period.

It is estimated that in the United States about one-half of the convicted offenders in the criminal courts are imprisoned and the other half are released to the community under supervision. Statutory limitations in many states preclude anything but imprisonment for certain offenses. In fact, some states quite narrowly limit the use of probation as an alternative. The presentence investigation is used for more than merely an aid to the judge in passing sentence. It is also used as a basis upon which a program of individual treatment and classification is begun in prison. If the person is granted probation and remains in the community, the report is used by the probation department in its treatment program.

Reform?

Prison conditions

There is a wide range and variety in the more than 400 institutions for adult offenders in this country. Some are grossly deficient; conditions are such that racial, ethnic, and religious tensions build up to the breaking point.

Prisons designed of stone, steel, and concrete for custody purposes are not humanizing atmospheres. Sixty-one prisons opened before 1900 are still in use. The American Correctional Association (ACA), the professional organization of wardens and other allied correctional groups, reports an average population of over 2000 inmates in each of the 21 larger prisons. Four have over 4000 inmates each. The ACA studies indicate that the prison system itself causes the riots and demonstrations; they recommend strongly that a prison house fewer than 500 inmates and that it be located near the urban center from which the majority of inmates come.

A correctional institution, whether maximum security prison, reformatory, or minimum security farm or ranch, is an inmate community; a society with its own culture, its own set of values and attitudes. This inmate "culture" is the all-important focus of the individual offender, and often it is in strong opposition to the objectives of prison programs. Prisonization, which means the adopting of the values of prisoners and prison life as normal by the inmates, is an important way of enabling the inmate to avoid devastating psychological effects.

The welfare of the individual inmate, to say nothing of his psychological well-being and dignity, does not importantly depend on how much education, recreation, and consultation he receives but rather depends on how he manages to live and relate with other inmates who constitute his crucial and only meaningful world.[8]

The social gap between the staff and the inmates is such that it reinforces the need of inmates to conform to the inmate subculture. The mass handling of prisoners contributes mightily to maintaining this social distance. Furthermore, security concerns dominate all staff activity. High walls, fences, and gun towers seek to insure security and custody. Censorship of mail, monitoring of visits, lack of privacy, and identification by number all lead to insuring an increasing social distance between staff and inmates.

In spite of the philosophy of reform, many penal institutions remain frontiers of human degradation. Repeatedly, incidents of inhumane treatment, stabbings, suicides, and questionable deaths have surfaced from various correctional institutions across the nation. As a result of these bizarre, but all too common, occurrences, committees, investigation units, and gubernatorial edicts have been established to reform prison conditions. But many institutions have failed to produce any major reforms in prison conditions in the last few decades.

A prisoner's view of prisons

I'm afraid the men who run the prisons as I have seen them do not share this view with respect to converting prisoners. They do not want to progress and reform the system. They want to keep the inmates back in their archaic, brutal and inhumane situation because they do not know any better or are afraid of progress.

Source: Testimony of Dr. Sam Sheppard before the United States Senate Subcommittee to Investigate Juvenile Delinquency, Washington, D.C., July 8, 1969, p. 7.

For the most part, many of our prisons are vastly overcrowded and poorly understaffed; the structures are old and antiquated. It is estimated that nearly one-quarter of the prisons in this country are over 100 years old. Since the federal government and many states have moratoria on building new correctional institutions, it seems unlikely that these figures will change drastically in the next decade.

Life in many institutions is at best barren and futile, at worst unspeakably brutal and degrading. Although the offenders in such institutions cannot commit further crimes against society while serving their sentences, the conditions in which they live are the poorest possible prepara-

[8]Lloyd W. McCorckle, "Social Structure in a Prison," *The Welfare Reporter*, 8 (December 1956), p. 6.

tion for a successful reentry into society and often merely reinforce patterns of manipulation or destructiveness. These conditions are, to a great extent, the result of a drastic shortage of resources together with widespread ignorance of how to use the resources available.

Corrections, by its very nature, is at the end of the line of our criminal justice system. In the other two major sections of our criminal justice system, both the police and the courts have several alternatives in dealing with clientele with whom they come into contact. The police, for instance, may or may not make an arrest based on an individual officer's discretion. Similarly, a prosecuting attorney may or may not choose to prosecute a case once the individual has been arrested by the police. The judge also has some discretion and choice in sentencing individuals when they have been found guilty by a court of law. The corrections facilities have no choice; they must accept all clientele sentenced to serve time in their institutions.

In spite of the tremendous burden and lack of resources correctional institutions have to deal with, there are signs that some administrators can make far-reaching changes under the present conditions. But there are still conditions that remain unsolved in prison and are likely to remain so for some time. One of these problems is the threat to new inmates of homosexual rape. It is not uncommon that an inmate can buy another prisoner for a carton of cigarettes and have him at his disposal for the duration of that inmate's sentence.

In brief, we found that sexual assaults in the Philadelphia prison system are epidemic. As Superintendent Henrick and three other wardens admitted, virtually every slightly built young man committed by the courts is sexually approached within a day or two after his admission to the prison. Many of these men are repeatedly raped by gangs of inmates. Others, because of the threat of gang rape, seek protection by entering into a homosexual relationship with an individual tormentor. Only the tougher and more hardened young men, and those few so obviously frail that they are immediately locked up for their own protection, escape homosexual rape.[9]

Unfortunately, this condition exists in many of our prisons despite the efforts of many administrators and guards to curtail it. In the hope of reducing this problem, some administrators in some correctional institutions are advocating conjugal visits and periodic home leaves.

Classification and treatment in prison

Classification of the prisoner is an extension of the presentence investigation. Classification, a basic tool of modern penology, serves two purposes. Its first and most basic purpose is to determine security or custody consid-

[9]Alan J. Davis, "Sexual Assaults in the Philadelphia Prison," *Trans-Action*, December 1968.

erations for each inmate, where he is to be housed, and what his (or her) assignment will be while serving the sentence. Its second basic purpose is to determine the type of treatment to be afforded the inmate.

During the initial period of confinement, the offender is studied and diagnosed by the various specialists who make up the classification committee. Psychiatric, medical, and psychological studies are made, and written reports providing information on the inmate's background and conduct are given to the classification committee, whose judgments and analyses will be the basis of the inmate's assignment and treatment plan. The inmate is interviewed and the information obtained becomes a part of the classification committee's data bank. Within the institution's scope of resources for employment and treatment, the inmate is given an assignment. Table 13–1 provides an idea of the variety of classification schemes.

Treatment

Today's correctional institutions have as their stated purpose the rehabilitation of the offender. In reality, however, correctional institutions are sorely lacking in trained personnel with the treatment skills needed for rehabilitation. In the 24-hour-a-day total institution, "treatment" as a separate facet of a person's life is not possible—every detail of living is ultimately intertwined with all others. Therapy, with its permissiveness or its exposure of hidden emotions, carries over to the inmate's life beyond therapy sessions. Emotions loosed in therapy spill over into the life of the prison community. Often this means fights with inmates, attacks on guards, or anger turned inward toward the self.

Individual treatment The traditional institutional approach to rehabilitation has been the individual treatment approach; that is, the "sick person" model. The offender is regarded as one suffering from a defect of personality that has led to crime. The medical approach of organizing treatment based on diagnosis, prescription, and application of therapy is the fundamental current approach to treatment in corrections. Psychotherapy (or variations of psychotherapy) coupled with casework have been the basic treatment approach. It is practiced by psychologists, psychiatrists, and social workers. Others at lesser levels of training practice unique innovations upon this treatment—these include institutional parole officers, institution counselors, and even correctional guards. The psychological form of treatment relies on the healer's ability to mobilize healing forces within the sufferer by psychological means.[10] "Talking" is the basic tool of the therapist. There are three ingredients in this treatment mode—a trained healer accepted by the sufferer; a sufferer seeking relief; and a circumscribed, somewhat formal series of conversations between healer and sufferer intended to help the sufferer solve his problems.

This approach to the offender was held out hopefully as an important

[10]James D. Frank, *Persuasion and Healing* (Baltimore: Johns Hopkins Press, 1961).

rehabilitation method. Its practice has dominated the field since World War II. Yet there are many indications that it has not achieved the degree of success expected, so it has been supplemented with a group approach.

Group treatment In addition to the offender's own personality structure, his or her group affiliations are often cited as causes for the persistence of criminality. Human personality is acquired and shaped through social relationships. Therefore, groups are employed in rehabilitation programs, as both the instrument of change and the targets of change.

This approach sprang from attempts to restore delinquent soldiers to duty at army rehabilitation centers through group methods. The use of group therapy reached a peak of popularity in American corrections by the mid-1950s and early 1960s.

Guided group interaction is one term used to describe the approach in which offenders freely discuss their problems in a supportive group atmosphere under a leader. The object is to create a group climate without threat. A marked give-and-take discussion is encouraged, in which members are free and equal and the leader adopts a permissive but noncondoning role. Successful interaction is heavily dependent on the leader's skill in developing a pattern of meaning for the participants. The leader's primary technique is to turn questions and issues back to the group for discussion rather than addressing them directly.

Group therapy is intended to have several benefits—participants should gain new insights into their problems and themselves, attitudes should change, and a reevaluation of the participants' place in the environment should begin.

Other programs of rehabilitation in prison Both individual and group therapies have been supported in prisons by a series of other programs that were aimed at the goal of rehabilitation.

Since the establishment of the Elmira Reformatory in 1876, correctional education has been a standard rehabilitation program in prison. The great value that we Americans place on education, in terms of its potential for providing the good things in life—position, money, and social acceptance, is reflected in the expenditure it represents in our personal lives. Our faith in education to do as much for the offender is based on our own experience with it. However, we cannot expect education alone to achieve correction and rehabilitation goals, but it can offer a greater likelihood of this achievement. As many studies have shown, prison populations are considerably behind the norms in academic achievement. Providing basic education to inmates may return them to society with social and vocational assets that they lacked before. It also aids in their treatment programs. In both individual and group therapy programs, the enhanced ability to use language in communication makes for a more effective patient-therapist relationship.

The importance of education in prison has been stressed in the past

Table 13-1

Cross-classification of offender typologies.

Subtypes	Jesness	Hunt	Hurwitz	MacGregor	Makkay	Quay	Reiss	Warren
1. Asocial		Sub I	Type II	Schizo-phrenic	Antisocial character disorder-primitive	Unsocialized-psychopath		I_2
Aggressive	Immature, aggressive				Aggressive			Asocial, aggressive
Passive	Immature, passive				Passive-aggressive			Asocial, passive
2. Conformist		Stage I			Antisocial character disorder-organized			I_3
Nondelinquently oriented	Immature, passive				Passive-aggressive	Inadequate-immature		Conformist, immature
Delinquently oriented	Socialized conformist					?Subcultural/	?Relatively integrated/	Conformist, cultural
3. Antisocial-manipulator	Manipulator			Autocrat	Antisocial character disorder-organized aggressive		Defective superego	I_3 Manipulator
4. Neurotic		Stage II	Type III		Neurotic		Relatively weak ego	I_4 Neurotic
Acting-out	Neurotic, acting-out			Intimidated				Neurotic, acting-out
Anxious	Neurotic, anxious Neurotic, depressed					Neurotic-disturbed		Neurotic, anxious
5. Subcultural-identifier	Cultural delinquent	Stage II	Type I	Rebel	Subcultural	Subcultural	Relatively integrated	I_4 Cultural identifier
6. Situational		Stage II						I_4 Situational, emotional reaction
Types not cross-classified					Mental retardate psychotic			

Table 13-1 (continued)

Subtypes	APA	Argyle	Gibbons	Jenkins and Hewitt	McCord	Reckless	Schrag	Studt
1. Asocial	Passive-aggressive personality	Lack of sympathy					Asocial	Isolate
Aggressive	Aggressive		Overly aggressive	Unsocialized aggressive				
Passive	Passive-aggressive							
2. Conformist	Passive-aggressive personality	Inadequate superego			Conformist			
Nondelinquently oriented	Passive-dependent							
Delinquently oriented			Gang offenders	/?Social-ized/			Antisocial	Receiver
3. Antisocial-manipulator	Antisocial personality	Inadequate superego			Aggressive (psycho-pathic)	Psychopath	Pseudo-social	Manipulator
4. Neurotic	Sociopathic personality disturbance	Weak ego control				Neurotic personality	Prosocial	
Acting-out		Joyrider	Behavior problems					
Anxious				Overinhibited	Neurotic-withdrawn		Loveseeker	
5. Subcultural-identifier	Dyssocial reaction	Deviant identification	Gang offenders	Socialized			Antisocial	Learner
6. Situational	Adjustment reaction of adolescence		Casual delinquent			Offenders of the moment		
Types not cross-classified			Heroin user Delinquent			Eruptive behavior		

Source: Northwestern University School of Law, *The Journal of Criminal Law, Criminology, and Police Science,* 62, No. 2 (June 1971).

decade, and more resources are now placed at the disposal of educational efforts than ever before. Correspondence courses, adult basic education, and programmed learning are quite common today in most institutions. The recent increase in college-level course work is a great step toward the education of offenders in correctional institutions.

The important role of academic education in career vocations is the main reason for the flourishing of academic education within institutions. This factor, more than any other, has provided the impetus to develop the widespread upper-level education programs.

Career training Career preparation in prison to better fit the inmate for employment upon release has long been part of the prison rehabilitation concept. Almost all institutions have fairly sophisticated vocational training programs. These are usually tied into the institution's maintenance and industrial program where possible. In the more sophisticated programs, academic courses and vocational training are closely linked together. In the United States today, about 3.5 percent of all institutional staff are teachers. Although this is not an optimum figure, it is a significant increase over the past decade and points to a heavier involvement in the future.

Other programs Religious and psychiatric counseling and recreational programs are fairly standard in nearly all institutions. All are geared toward encouraging the inmate to adopt a life of responsibility after release.

Today, the use of prisons, whatever their programs, is being seriously questioned. Of the $1.5 billion spent annually for corrections, three-fourths goes to maintain institutions that hold only one-fourth of the total number of convicted offenders. The remaining three-fourths of the offenders remain in the communities at a fraction of the total cost. The data available show that treatment of offenders in the community is at least as successful as institutional treatment. In fact, it is generally agreed that institutional experience is more damaging.

Personnel in corrections

Correctional personnel work today takes place in widely differing settings and under a variety of auspices. The American public has never quite made up its mind which is more important: to punish offenders, to protect society by locking them up or keeping them under close supervision; or to try to change them into useful citizens. There is little argument against keeping the dangerous offender under control, both as an immediate protection to society and as a deterrent to future crime. But since almost all offenders must legally be released to the community someday, the public is coming to see the need for rehabilitating and equipping them to become productive members of the community. Otherwise (as is far too often the case today) they are likely to return to crime and eventually into the correctional system. Reintegration of the offender into society, therefore, is seen by correctional personnel as one of the major objectives.

Correctional programs are carried on in institutions and in the community through probation and parole. Although states have the major responsibility for corrections, local jurisdictions are involved (primarily in providing probation services), and the federal government is heavily involved in a parallel system of courts, probation, institutions, and parole. There is wide variation among the public agencies that have responsibility for corrections at any given level and, often, several agencies at the same level of government may operate different facets of corrections. This illustrates the complexity of the corrections system today—and how seriously it is fragmented. This has contributed to inadequate funding, scattershot programming, and a lack of public support.

Staff training programs in corrections were literally nonexistent until the early 1970s. An impetus to provide staff development programs was provided in the creation of the Law Enforcement Assistance Administration by Congress in 1968. LEAA has created a remarkable surge of staff programs in the nation's agencies and institutions of corrections. Furthermore, it has provided funds to 80,000 students in 962 schools to attend college courses for either preservice training or continuing education.

Nevertheless, there are far too many employees in corrections who are there not because they are educated and trained for their jobs, but because they are political appointees. There are also too many trained corrections workers who leave the field and seek employment elsewhere because they cannot earn a decent living in corrections.

Educational preparation

The educational level of correctional employees ranges from high school dropouts to Ph.Ds. Generally, those working with juveniles have a higher level of education than those working with adults.

Field personnel (people in probation and parole) are better educated on the average than are employees in institutions. Most institutional guard personnel have only a high school education. Nowhere is the published preferred standard for probation and parole officers—a master's degree from an accredited school of social work or comparable study in psychology, sociology, or a related field of social science—being met. Over three-fourths of correctional employees, *excluding line workers*, are college graduates. However, only 13 percent of those in adult institutions, 21 percent in adult probation and parole, 27 percent in juvenile institutions, and 30 percent in juvenile probation and parole have graduate degrees.

There is no consistent education pattern. College graduates working in corrections represent an extremely broad array of major areas of study.

Although just over half have B.A. degrees in sociology, education, or psychology, the remainder have degrees in a wide range of other subjects. Undergraduates in social work and criminology or corrections programs represent a very small minority of college graduates in the field.

In the past, there was little connection between educational background and the performance of particular functions. Corrections had no well-defined link to any level or discipline of the educational system. A college graduate with a B.A. in history who somehow had managed to get into correctional work was as likely to be an institutional counselor as was a person holding a master's degree in social work. But the emphases have shifted. Many state legislatures are encouraging individuals currently employed in corrections to acquire additional education. In the near future, promotions for correctional guards will include educational requirements for each level of rank. In effect, more correctional personnel will be forced to return to school before they are eligible for an increase in rank, or a raise in merit pay. Furthermore, some legislatures have suggested that correctional guards be certified by state licensing agencies. The certification would be contingent upon employees' satisfactory completion of training classes. The certification process would be similar to the process currently being used by many states for their various police agencies.

Summary

This chapter gives a brief historical view of corrections. The Pilgrims brought the stern European penal code with them that provided the base for our penal code today. The Quakers sought confinement without labor to replace harsh criminal penalties. This action brought about the Western Penitentiary in Pittsburgh.

The Auburn system, developed in New York, began to consider the prisoner as an individual; classification of prisoners began here. Auburn failed because many of the inmates became insane or attempted suicide, although it did succeed in providing cheap contract labor.

Religious influence was strong in the nineteenth century. This brought about many reforms in prisons, particularly at Elmira, New York.

Recently, architectural structures of prisons have been analyzed. It has been found that designs of prisons have an impact on the prison community.

The chapter also addressed the question of whether the prevailing philosophy of the prison should be punishment or rehabilitation. Corrections consists of scores of institutions and programs of the utmost diversity in approach, facilities, and qualities. Some of these institutions are grossly deficient with conditions that produce racial, ethnic, and religion tensions that build up to breaking points.

A correctional institution, whether maximum or minimum security, is an inmate community; a society with its own culture, its own set of values and attitudes. The social gap between the staff and the inmates frequently reinforces the need for inmates to conform to the inmate subculture.

Correctional institutions have as their stated purpose the rehabilitation of the offender. However, most institutions lack trained personnel needed for rehabilitation. The traditional approach has been the "individual treatment"; that is, the "sick person" model. Psychotherapy coupled with casework has been the basic treatment approach. The group therapy approach has been used to supplement individual treatment. Group therapy is intended to help participants gain new insights into their problems and themselves, so that negative attitudes can be changed, and a reevaluation of the participant's place in the environment can emerge. Both individual and group therapies have been supported in prisons by a series of other programs.

In the past the educational level of correctional employees ranged from high school dropouts to Ph.Ds. There has been little connection in current practice between educational background and the performance of particular functions. However, the trend toward greater education for corrections personnel is gaining momentum.

TOPICS FOR DISCUSSION

1. What are the causes of some of our poor prison conditions in the United States?

2. Outline the various types of prison structures and discuss their respective strengths and weaknesses.

3. How were criminals dealt with by society during the seventeenth and eighteenth centuries?

4. What are two of the main reasons for classification in prison?

5. What are some of the general characteristics of personnel in corrections?

14

Community-based corrections

The study of this chapter will enable you to:

1. **Outline and question the effectiveness of our prisons.**
2. **Cite the differences between probation and parole.**
3. **Understand some of the community alternatives to treatment.**

Community-based corrections may be one solution to our prisons' crowded conditions and a way to provide a new method of rehabilitation. But how will community-based corrections survive if individuals in the community themselves will not support the system?

Correctional effectiveness

Despite increased staffing in correctional institutions, newly designed correctional facilities, treatment programs, vocational programs, career awareness, educational leaves, and work-release centers, national statistics accumulated in the Uniform Crime Reports consistently show that our correctional institutions are failing to rehabilitate the offender.

If corrections could return all or most of the people in its charge to a law-abiding life in the community, America's crime rate would drop significantly. Today, however, a substantial percentage of the correctional population become repeaters—they go on to commit more crimes. Estimates vary, but rates of recidivism (falling back into previous criminal habits, especially after punishment) range between 65 and 68 percent.

Of the over 2 million prisoners each year in prisons, juvenile institutions, and jails, 99 percent are released within a year. As for the 250,000 serious offenders in our prisons, the following information constitutes a serious indictment of the ineffectiveness of the system of corrections: 90 percent have a juvenile delinquency record or other criminal record; and 50 percent have served at least one previous prison sentence. Of the approximately 115,000 serious offenders released from prison each year, most are released on parole. The only sound way to find out how many of those are imprisoned again is to follow all the people released in a given period for a number of years and determine what percentage commit new crimes and are returned to prison (see Figure 14-1).

There is a substantial foundation for the belief that prison and parole (and probation) do not begin to satisfy the cost benefits expected from our investments in these systems. There is equal doubt about the effectiveness of the many new approaches in corrections. The latest of these approaches, group counseling, has been devastated by one of the truly hon-

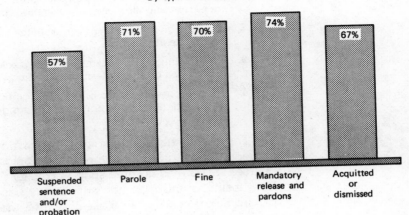

By type of release in 1972

57% — Suspended sentence and/or probation
71% — Parole
70% — Fine
74% — Mandatory release and pardons
67% — Acquitted or dismissed

Figure 14-1

Percentage of persons rearrested within four years. *Source: Crime in the United States, 1975, Uniform Crime Reports,* p. 46.

est efforts to assess effectiveness in corrections. This is the Kassebaum, Ward, and Wilner study, which found group counseling to be as unrelated to prisoner success as were most of the other enlightened approaches.[1]

Parole, which was seen to be a vital tool in offender rehabilitation, has not achieved its promise. As an intermediate step between the institution and the free community, it was meant to be instrumental in helping to reestablish the offender in the community while protecting society by means of a surveillance of the released offender. Today, most prisoners are released on parole. Their release is usually to a parole plan, which, at a minimum, includes a place to live and employment. Certain conditions are imposed, many of which if strictly enforced, would ensnare most free citizens, let alone former offenders. When it is realized that violations of these conditions is cause for revocation of parole and return to prison, some idea may be had of the pressure that the parolee experiences. The parolee must obtain approval before leaving the town or country or changing residences, must submit regular reports, and must not drink to excess. The parolee must not associate with "disreputable persons," must obtain approval to drive, and must get permission to marry. If any condition is violated, that is theoretically the basis for return to prison. In practice, return depends on the judgment of the parole officer.

It has been determined that survival on parole following prison treatment is not significantly different than from the rate of those who received no treatment.[2] This startling conclusion is reported on in the aforementioned Kassebaum, Ward, and Wilner study, in which the following conclusions are also cited:

[1]Gene Kassebaum, David A. Ward, and Daniel M. Wilner, *Prison Treatment and Parole Survival* (New York: Wiley, 1971).

[2]As long ago as 1940, Lewis Diana of the University of Pittsburgh made a follow-up study of 280 delinquents in 1959–51, in which one group received treatment and another group received no treatment. There was no difference in success rates.

1. There is no evidence to support claims that one correctional program has more rehabilitation effectiveness than another.

2. Statistics on recidivism exaggerate the extent to which convicted offenders return to serious crime.

3. The likelihood of a citizen being subjected to personal injury or property loss can be only infinitesimally lessened by the field of corrections.

4. The increase in public protection gained by imprisonment of large numbers of offenders, of whom few are dangerous, is outweighed by the public cost involved.

The study makes a strong case that various correctional treatments are ineffective and that imprisonment is the most ineffective and uneconomic course. This provides some sound basis for the trend to divert the offender from institutionalization into community-based programs. Whether these programs are more or less effective then those of the institutions and corrections in general is not yet known; but they are surely more economical. If only for economic reasons, the trend to community treatment is on the rise.

The Oregon statistics

We must interpret national figures with some caution, for they do not allow for individual success rates. We shall see from the statistics in the Oregon study that there are various penal institutions that can accomplish the feat of returning the offender back into society as a productive, law-abiding citizen.

Figure 14-1 indicates the percentage of individuals rearrested within a four-year period following their release from prison or jail. Seventy-four percent of the offenders released after serving their prison time are rearrested within four years. Of those persons released on parole, 71 percent repeated, as did 57 percent of those placed on probation. Of those persons acquitted or who had their cases dismissed in 1972, 67 percent were rearrested for new offenses within four years. When criminal repeating is examined by the type of crime for those released in 1972, rearrests range from 28 percent for embezzlers to 81 percent for burglars. Largest repeater rates of the same crime were for narcotic offenders, with 31 percent being rearrested for the same crime; and gambling law violators, with 23 percent being rearrested on gambling violations within four years. Of the 3855 offenders being released in 1972 from weapons violations, 12 percent were rearrested for a violent crime within four years. Sixty-eight of these offenders were rearrested for murder, 355 for weapons violations, and 337 for narcotics violations.

In contrast to the national statistics used in Figures 14–1 and 14–2, which indicate correctional failure, Oregon Corrections Division shows some surprising success rates. In a three-year study done from July 1, 1971 to June 30, 1974, on return of Oregon felony institution releasees, fewer than 11.7 percent of all offenders released from Oregon felony penal institutions committed a new crime within a three-year period following their

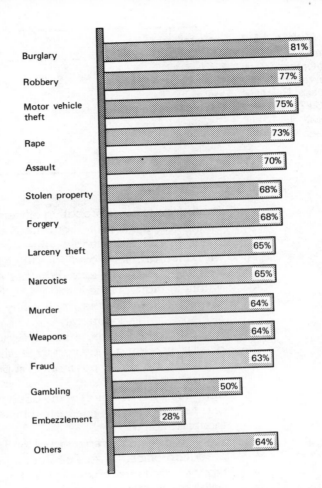

Figure 14-2

Percentage of repeaters
by type of crime in 1972:
persons released in 1972
and rearrested within four
years. *Source: Crime in
the United States, 1975,
Uniform Crime Reports,*
p. 45.

Chart data:

- Burglary 81%
- Robbery 77%
- Motor vehicle theft 75%
- Rape 73%
- Assault 70%
- Stolen property 68%
- Forgery 68%
- Larceny theft 65%
- Narcotics 65%
- Murder 64%
- Weapons 64%
- Fraud 63%
- Gambling 50%
- Embezzlement 28%
- Others 64%

release (see Table 14–1). Following a parole violation 10.6 percent were returned to the institution, and only 6.7 percent of those who were released on probation after a court judgment were returned to the Oregon Corrections/Probation Department.

Probation

The most frequently used community-based alternative to incarceration is probation, which started in 1841 when a Boston shoemaker, John Augustus, urged the court to release certain offenders to his custody rather than send them to prison. The use of probation is widespread in America and abroad, especially in the United Kingdom. After a finding of guilt, the court decides to place the defendant on probation with the understanding that he will live up to certain conditions and submit to the supervision and

Table 14-1

Three-year returns. Trends in returns of Oregon felony institution releasees, by type of release. Releases 7/1/71—6/30/74, followed 36 months each, from date of release.

Total for all cases	N=3486
Rtd. to Ore. Div. Prob.—New Crime	6.7 percent
Rtd. to Ore. Corr. Div. Inst.—Rules PV	10.6 percent
Rtd. to Ore. Corr. Div. Inst.—New Crime	11.7 percent
Not Rtd. to Ore. Corr. Div. Control	71.0 percent
Total	100.0 Percent

assistance of court probation officers. If the probationer violates any of the conditions of his probation, the court may impose sentence to imprisonment. In some situations, sentence is *imposed* at the time of granting of probation and its *execution* withheld on the condition that the individual live up to the conditions. Whether it is the imposition or execution that is withheld matters little to the probationer. If he abides by the conditions of probation, he has the opportunity to remain out of prison, serving his sentence in the community.

In addition to requiring acceptable modes of personal conduct, the court may order a wide variety of other conditions, such as restitution to the victims of the crime, payment of support to dependents, or fines to be paid on the installment plan. In most jurisdictions in which probation is used, approximately one-half of the adult offenders and considerably more than one-half of the juveniles are placed on probation as an alternative to incarceration.

The essential weakness of probation has been the lack of qualified probation officers. Caseloads that vary widely in terms of numbers and types of offenders make supervision difficult. Probation officers are essentially caseworkers who also have peace-keeping functions. These two roles frequently conflict. Interest in "helping" versus "keeping the peace" is a continuing dilemma.

As the use of probation has grown, it has been recognized that the task of the probation officer has become more specialized, requiring highly developed skills and special training. For a time, the preferred training was social work. Since three-fourths of those on probation are male, it was generally accepted that they should be supervised by male officers. But most trained social workers are women. Recruitment of a sufficient number of trained men to work in probation was not successful, resulting in the recruitment of many persons with considerably less than the needed skills.

Today, people with a startling mix of educational backgrounds work in the field. Disciplines from anthropology to zoology are represented. A large number of teachers, especially those with religious backgrounds, work in juvenile probation. In the adult field, many workers have military and law enforcement backgrounds. Training in social work as a

Table 14-2 Myths about criminal justice: (what "everybody knows"—falsely).	**Belief**	**Fact**
	Felony crime is increasing in Oregon and throughout the nation.	In Oregon there were 152,855 Index Crimes during 1975; but only 147,919 in 1976. The national trend is similar.
	Most felonies are crimes against persons.	Crimes against persons constituted only 7.2% of all FBI Index Crimes in Oregon during 1976.
	Most criminals are identified and arrested by the police.	Oregon's police are 14% more efficient in arresting felons than national average. Nevertheless, in 1976 100 Index Crimes known to Oregon police resulted in 20 arrests.
	District attorneys prosecute all arrested felons.	20 Index Crime arrests result in 10 Circuit Court case filings.
	Most people prosecuted for felonies go to prison.	10 Circuit Court case filings result in 2 people going to probation, and 1 going to prison.
	Most felonies are committed by repeat offenders.	53% of those arrested are under age 18; too young to have been handled by the adult courts. 66% of the adults received in prison are people never before known to the Corrections Division, either as inmates or as probationers.
	The Corrections Division controls when and how release occurs.	Once a person is placed under Corrections Division control, the only ways release can occur are: by court order; by parole board order; by expiration of time set by the court; or by Governor's action.
	Long terms of imprisonment can reduce the amount of crime.	Since 100 felonies result in less than one commitment: if 100% success was guaranteed with every prisoner, it would reduce crime less than 1%. If every released prisoner committed a new crime, it would increase crime less than 1%.
	If prisoners were required to serve out their full sentence without parole, they would be less likely to commit new crimes.	3-year follow-up studies show that 26% of those who serve their full terms return to control for new crimes; 14% of those granted parole return for new crimes.
	Work release is dangerous to the neighbors.	Of over 5000 who were on work release during the first 10 years of the program, only 43 have been convicted of new crimes committed while in program . . . none of these were committed in the neighborhood of the center where the releasee lived. Work releasees are significantly less likely to return to control for new crime than are those released directly from institutions.
	Most people sent to prison are murderers, rapists, or robbers.	Only 1/3 (34%) of those received in our prisons are sent there because of any offense against persons.

Source: Neil Chambers, Department of Corrections, state of Oregon, May 1977.

requirement is giving way to the broader behavioral science requirements (college work in sociology, anthropology, and psychology) in recruiting specifications.

The probation officer's task falls into three roles: the punitive officer who is the guardian of middle-class morality and who protects society through the exercise of controls; the "protective agent" who vacillates between helping the offender and protecting the community; and the welfare worker whose primary goal is the offender's well-being.[3] But the probation officer has many other roles—employment agent, vocational counselor, marital counselor, school counselor, junior-grade psychoanalyst, father confessor, and law enforcement officer. He is the one who helps the offender comply with the order of the court; he has the option of playing many roles.

As the use of probation increased, studies of its effectiveness were made. An early one was the Saginaw Project, conducted in Michigan between 1957 and 1962. The study demonstrated that most of those placed on probation succeeded, that no appreciable risk to the community was incurred, and that it was an economical venture saving money by reducing construction and maintenance costs of institutional facilities. Many other studies supported these findings.

Probation is the prerogative of various branches of government: the executive and judicial branches in some states, and welfare authorities in others. The different formats have produced confusion for those studying the process and its effectiveness. The question of where jurisdiction over probation should lie becomes critical as its use and staff size are expanded. A primary question now is whether probation should be granted and administered by the judiciary or by the executive branch.

The best argument against court-based probation is that courts, particularly criminal courts, are adjudicatory and regulatory rather than service-oriented. As long as probation remains a part of the judicial branch, it will remain an extension of the courts and have no identity of its own.

A strong argument for having probation within the purview of the executive branch is that most service-oriented agencies are already located there. It would increase the interaction between corrections and other allied human services and increase the prospects for using the full resources of the community.

Probation takes place in the community. Probation officers are responsible for assisting the convicted offender to adjust to the community. The probation process has overwhelmingly been one closely identified with casework; that is, the probation officer diagnoses the client's problem and develops a treatment plan, in a one-to-one relationship. Probation officers have been concerned with developing interviewing skills, creating

[3]Lloyd E. Ohlin, Herman Piven, and Donnel M. Pappenfort, "Major Dilemmas of the Social Worker in Probation and Parole," *National Probation and Parole Association Journal* (July 1956), p. 215.

therapeutic relationships with their clients, counseling, providing insight, and modifying behavior. The typical caseload is heavy, often totaling more than 100 clients.

Some authorities believe that probation is beginning to move away from this medical model, which relies heavily on the therapist-client relationship. They see probation officers taking on the advocacy role, assisting their clients in overcoming the social, legal, educational, and political barriers to their full and responsible participation in the community.

Probation means surveillance for many. Requirements or conditions are imposed by the court for the probationer to follow, and the probation officer is responsible for seeing that they are followed. In many cases, this regulatory function becomes the sole or overriding concern of the officer, demanding extensive surveillance and supervision. This function often conflicts with treatment. Probationers often must obtain permission to buy a car, change jobs, get married, change residence, and so on. These restrictions interfere mightily with the individual probationer's freedom of choice. Technical violations of probation conditions can result in revocation and commitment to an institution. Probation officers have great authority, and the way they use it determines, in large part, the nature of their relationship with the probationer.

Often probationers are assumed to be similar to one another. This assumption is wrong. Adults differ from juveniles; girls and women differ from boys and men and, as individuals, they all differ from each other. The range of individuality demands a like range of individual treatment.

Casework is the most frequently used model, but probation staffs also utilize several others. These include specialized supervision programs, guided group interaction, delinquent peer-group programs, and out-of-home placement, as well as residential treatment. These are essentially treatment-oriented programs. Increasingly, correctional staffs urge a move away from concentration on "changing" the offender to changing the conditions in society that cause crime and produce offenders.

The National Advisory Commission on Standards and Goals for the Criminal Justice System in 1973 proposed a new direction for the delivery of probation service. To implement an effective system for delivering services to all probationers, it will be necessary to:

1. Develop a goal-oriented service delivery system.

2. Identify service needs of probationers systematically and periodically, and specify measurable objectives based on priorities and needs assessment.

3. Differentiate between those services that the probation system should provide and the services that should be provided by other resources.

4. Organize the system to deliver services, including the purchase of services for probationers, and organize the staff around workloads.

5. Move probation staff from courthouses to residential areas and develop service centers for probationers.

6. Redefine the role of the probation officer from caseworker to community resource manager.

7. Provide services to misdemeanants (those charged with lesser offenses than felonies).

The most important goal must be to maintain in the community all offenders who can function acceptably with probation support and to select for confinement only those who, on the basis of evidence, are a danger to themselves or to others and cannot complete probation status successfully, even with optimal probation support.

Parole

Parole is the second most frequently used form of corrections in the community. Over 95 percent of the offenders committed to a correctional institution will eventually be released, and most of these will be under some form of parole. Parole has been defined as the release of an offender from a penal or correctional institution, after he has served a portion of his sentence, under continued custody of the state, and under conditions that permit his reincarceration in the event of misbehavior.

Parole is similar to probation in many ways. Data about offenders are gathered and presented to an authority with power to release the person to community supervision under specific conditions. If the person violates the conditions, he is usually sent to prison. Probation and parole differ in one major way: probation is granted by a jduge as an alternative to incarceration; parole is a release from incarceration after a period of time in a penal institution. Probation is a court function; parole is almost always an administrative decision.

Parole in this country began at the Elmira Reformatory in New York, which opened in 1876. Under the Elmira system, sentences were indeterminate, dependent on "marks" earned by good behavior. Release was for a six-month parole term, during which the parolee reported to a volunteer. This practice spread and, by 1945, parole laws had been passed in all the states.

Parole and the sentencing structure

All parole systems are part of a larger process involving trial courts and legislative mandates. Sources of sentencing authority and limits on sentencing alternatives affect the parole systems of the different states. Uniform sentencing does not exist in this country in spite of the long-standing efforts of professional organizations such as the National Council on Crime and Delinquency, the American Correctional Association, and the American Bar Association.

The National Advisory Commission on Standards and Goals for the Criminal Justice System states that the sentencing system that seems most consistent with parole objectives has the following characteristics:(1) sentencing limits set legislatively with the sentencing judge having discretion to fix the maximum sentence up to legislative limits; (2) no minimum sentences, either by mandate or by judicial sentencing authority; (3) comparatively short sentences for ordinary offenses with a legislation maximum not to exceed five years for most offenders; (4) a system of mandatory release with supervision for offenders ineligible for parole, yet not held in an institution until their absolute discharge date; (5) all parole conditions set by the paroling authority, but with the opportunity for a sentencing judge to suggest special conditions if he so desires; (6) legislative prohibition against the accommodation of consecutive sentences if it interferes with minimum parole eligibility; (7) legislative provisions for alternatives to reimprisonment upon parole revocation; and (8) no offense for which parole is denied by legislation.

Parole board decisions

Parole board members decide on parole primarily on the basis of risk to the community and the offender's potential for further crime. Other factors are also important: fairness and procedural regularity; supporting appropriate and equitable sanctions (equalizing penalties); and the need to support other criminal justice operations, such as aiding in the solution of institutional problems of population control or the like within the facility.

The parole function has gone through three periods in which it has been directed by an overriding philosophy. Originally it was assumed that its purpose was to reform the offender—to make him a contributing member of the society in every way. In the 1930s, parole came under the influence of the medical model, with its diagnostic methods and stress on individual treatment as the means of rehabilitating the offender. Today, the emphasis appears to be on reintegration, changing the conditions causing crime, and creating realistic alternatives through which the offender can find a satisfying life style that is tolerable to the larger community.

Parole board personnel have long been in the center of controversy because of several conditions—their means of appointment, the range of their responsibilities, and the part-time status of some members. Most experts agree that parole board members should have knowledge in three basic fields: law, the behavioral sciences, and corrections. They should have full-time positions with appropriate training. Most appointments of board members today are subject to criticism. Ideal standards for appointment that would eliminate the most common criticisms would include:

1. Full-time status.
2. Appointment for six-year terms by an advisory group that is broadly representative of the community.
3. Understanding of legal issues and behavioral and decision-making processes.
4. Opportunity to receive training periodically.
5. Maximum number set at five members on each board.

Representation at the hearings

No other issue has unsettled the parole process more than that of the offender's right to have legal representation at parole-granting hearings and revocations. The trend is clearly toward provision of legal representation at hearings on parole or revocation. In addition, the parolee must be able to be present at the hearing and also have access to a review of the information on the basis of which the decisions are made. Parole effectiveness and fairness depend upon these two rights.

The rights of the prisoner to representation, to access and disclosure of information, to witnesses, and cross-examination are being granted more and more in a continuing reversal of the procedures existing before the late 1960s. This increased emphasis and insistence on prisoner rights has been achieved as the result of numerous court decisions.

The community as site and source of corrections

Community-based corrections—probation and parole—have three aspects: humanitarian, restorative, and managerial. Custodial coercion places the offender in personal physical jeopardy, reduces access to sources of personal satisfaction, and reduces self-esteem. To the extent that an offender can be relieved of the burden of custody, a humanitarian objective is realized. The restorative aspect involves taking measures expected to achieve for the offender a position in the community in which he or she does not violate the laws. Efforts are made to reintegrate the offender into the community. Finally, the managerial aspect involves keeping the offender in the community at reduced fiscal costs while providing protection to the public. The emphasis must be on insuring public safety as programs are developed to bring about effective rehabilitation.

The greatest significance of the move toward community corrections is the implication that communities must assume responsibility for the problems they generate. Problems and people, crime and the criminal, are imbedded in community life and must be dealt with there.

Community programs have two operating objectives: to use and coordinate existing community service agencies offering resources in areas such as family planning, counseling, general social services, medical treatment, legal representation, and employment; and to involve public-spirited volunteers in the mission of corrections.

Community alternatives to corrections

Nonresidential treatment Structured correctional programs that supervise a substantial part of an offender's day but do not include "live-in" requirements are one form of community corrections. The clients need more intensive services than probation usually offers, and yet they are not in need of 24-hour-a-day confinement. School and counseling programs, day treatment centers with vocational training, and guided group interaction are among the strategies used, along with many related services to families.

Foster and group homes are used. The group homes appear to have the greater success because they are detached from the family while still providing a supportive environment and rewarding experiences.

Work and training release began to be used extensively in the 1950s. The practice permits selected inmates to work for pay outside the institution, returning at night. Variations include weekend sentences, furloughs, and release for vocational and academic training. Each helps reestablish links to the community.

The federal prison system pioneered in the development of prerelease programs in the early 1960s. In several cities it organized small living units, usually in rented quarters, to which inmates could be transferred for the final months of a sentence as part of a preparation for release. Halfway houses, both halfway in and halfway out, have been used by corrections in the continuing move to use the community as the site and source of rehabilitation.

Treatment strategies

Throughout correctional history several strategies of treatment have been created and applied. They can be grouped under four major headings:

1. Clinical models.
2. Group interaction models.
3. Therapeutic community models.
4. Social action models.

The assumptions underlying each strategy should be discussed.

Clinical models The basic assumption underlying the clinical model is that the clients are disturbed in their emotional and mental development and are in need of assistance to work out their problems. Correcting disorders comes through a one-to-one relationship in which a skilled therapist works with the client, helping him to gain insight and emotional support to solve the troubling emotional and mental disorders. The clinical model has been referred to as a medical model because it is built on the doctor–patient role in medicine.

The clinical process usually takes place in an office, is a verbal exchange that is heavily dependent upon an understanding of emotional reactions, is intensely interpersonal, intellectual in nature, and is clearly a dominant-submissive relationship between the helper and the one to be helped.

This model has been widely applied to the probation, parole, and institutional treatment function because of its adaptability to a casework approach.

Group interaction models The assumptions underlying this model are similar in many ways to those of the clinical model. The major difference is that the treatment mode changes from the one-to-one to the one-to-many. Intellectual and emotional experiences are shared by members of the group as well as the therapist. The concentration is mainly upon correcting faulty thought processes, disorders of the mind, and behavior that hurts or offends the self or others. The clinical dimension is expanded by adding more to the relationship and by increasing the size of the group. Troubled persons can test out their thoughts, feelings, and behavior on other troubled persons in a therapeutic setting.

Therapeutic community model This model is deeply influenced by the assumptions underlying the clinical and group interaction models. But it differs in the belief that a concentration on the person's total social and personal environment will help the treatment process. Departing from the narrow confines of the office and the therapeutic hour, this model rests on the belief that the total life experience is therapeutic and, if all the actors in the setting are guided by this belief, the individual will be able to overcome the troubling malady and emerge as a well person. The programs following this model are residential in nature, with strong controls applying to almost all behavior. Successful treatment is usually measured by movement from a totally controlled environment toward freedom. An assumption is made that the person has intense trouble in personal and social relations and can only overcome these in a 24-hour-a-day, residential, treatment-controlled environment. Some adult and juvenile correctional programs have adopted similar programs in halfway houses, residential treatment facilities, and specialized institutions.

Social action models This model differs considerably from the others. Its basic assumption is that the problems lie in the structure and function of the social order and, to reduce crime and assist the offender, the conditions responsible for the trouble within society must be changed. The focus is away from treating the offender and toward changing the social world wherever it operates to the detriment of many. Some people see corrections moving toward this role, particularly as advocacy replaces therapy and community-based corrections become less like correctional centers placed in the community, and more like a link to social action.

The proponents of this model emerged in the 1960s and are associated with the civil-rights and poverty-workers' movements; they have been joined by student activists and reform-minded political and legal activists. The major goals of this group are the elimination of racism, removal of ghettolike conditions in urban areas, establishment of justice and equity throughout the criminal justice system, eradication of poverty, provision for access to equal opportunity for all citizens, renewal of social institutions to make them responsive to needs of the citizenry, and the provision for relevance in education, employment, and government. The people who foster this model are often at odds with the proponents of the three other models. The emerging debate and conflict will have an impact on the criminal justice system as well as on society in general.

Two treatment techniques that gained currency in the early 1970s and are being used quite widely are behavior modification and transactional analysis.

Behavior modification Behavior may be defined as anything a person does, says, or thinks that can be observed directly or indirectly. Shaping or changing of behavior by contingent reinforcement (giving approval or disapproval) is a simple and direct manner of influencing behavior. It is useful in learning and can be used for control. The latter purpose, control, may be one reason why this approach has been heartily endorsed by many people in corrections, especially in institutions, where control of groups is basic. Behavior modification in prison has also been applied to learning through *programmed* instruction. Courses are programmed in such a way that the learner is reinforced (rewarded) by getting the right answer at each step. Much progress has been made in education through this method, especially in basic arithmetic, English, and other related coursework.

Transactional analysis Psychiatrist Eric Berne's experience in therapy led him to believe that there are three ego states, popularly called parent, adult, and child. These states are present in everyone, and one or another of them is operative at any one time. In various situations a person may act as a child, an adult, or a parent. This may be reflected in facial expressions, positions, gestures, vocabulary, and the like. A parent may stiffen when being defied by his or her child, may turn pale and tremble on hearing the police siren, or may exclaim with childlike excitement when hitting the jackpot. Changes from adult to child or parent to child, for example, can be observed in the same person. Thomas Horns, a disciple of Berne, depicts transactions as units of social intercourse in which two persons are involved. One speaks or gestures, and this transactional stimulus leads to a transactional response. Transactional analysis is the determination of what part of the parent, adult, or child is providing the stimulus or giving the response. And it systematizes these transactions in words that mean the same thing to each person that uses them. This agreement on the meanings of the words is an important element of the therapy's effectiveness.

The concepts of transactional analysis have been used in a range of institutions, generally in group sessions. A therapist leader participates and in the first stages uses a blackboard for diagramming explanations and studying transaction. Although transactional analysis does not have all the answers, remarkable improvements in offenders have taken place. The process seeks to inspire each individual to improve and to become responsible for his or her behavior and, in the terminology of the transactional analysis school, to "feel O.K."

There are many specific techniques used in corrections to help the offender. Most have some degree of effectiveness and can assist the individual. That some persons are not helped does not mean the treatment is bad; it is simply ineffective for that person. There is a growing mandate to match the treatment to the person to be treated. Soon now, we might expect a person to take some sort of standardized test that will determine the type of treatment needed. Some progress has also been made in matching the person to be treated with the treater. For example, the offender and parole officer can be assigned to each other on the basis of certain personality characteristics that are found in both, which might be useful in the development of their relationship.

Toward a consistent system of corrections

The American system of criminal justice is complex, and the interrelationships among its components are so varied that few people understand it. Some call it a nonsystem.

The National Advisory Commission reports that this nonsystem includes:

1. Thousands of probation departments, some adult, some juvenile, some large, and some small.

2. Competing state agencies that are attempting to establish and supervise probation and parole standards, frequently without power of enforcement.

3. Thousands of county jails and hundreds of prisons ranging in size up to an average daily population of more than 3000.

4. Departments or bureaus of corrections operating many institutions, ranging from small halfway houses and facilities for juveniles to large maximum-security penitentiaries.

5. Hundreds of unrelated and unsupervised juvenile detention centers servicing some parts of states while the majority of youngsters in other parts are left to the uncertain mercies of the county jails.

6. Departments of social services and public welfare operating hundreds of youth development centers and forestry camps.

7. State planning agencies attempting to use the power of the federal dollar to bring order and change, and working against political pressures to maintain the status quo.

The result is confusion. To overcome this, effective systems planning must be instituted from top to bottom. Uniform state planning is an attainable goal that must be pursued.

Finally, the thrust is toward increased public involvement—a move long overdue. The correctional system is one of the few public services left today that is characterized by almost total isolation from the public. This condition must be reversed; meaningful roles must be given to an involved and concerned citizenry.

The future of corrections

The field of corrections has many plans, procedures, policies, and laws that have failed to achieve their purposes, but which have survived regardless of their limited usefulness or obsolescence. Corrections has emphasized the banishment of offenders to isolated, large-scale, dehumanizing institutions.

The present shift in emphasis is clearly toward using the community as the site and source for rehabilitation rather than relying on the institution. Because most recognize the failures of institutions, solutions are being sought that are closer to the seat of the problem—the offender's community. Where confinement is needed, it should be within a community rather than in a remote and isolated cage, detached from the vital resources of the environment to which the ex-offender will return. The trend toward community-based corrections is one of the most promising developments in corrections today, being based on the recognition that much delinquency and crime is a symptom of failure of the community, as well as of the offender, and that a successful reduction of crime requires changes in both.

Institutionalization costs are soaring. Because of their limited effectiveness, they are being criticized because of these expenditures. Community-based corrections are more economically advantageous, because they use all of the existing community resources and human service agencies that are, or can be, related to crime prevention and control.

Summary

At the beginning of the chapter we looked at the effectiveness of our penal institutions. We noted that the national statistics have shown that we have a remarkable recidivism rate based on a four-year follow-up study of releasees from various types of institutions.

The most frequently used community-based alternative to incarceration is probation. After a finding of guilt, the court may place a defendant on probation. It does so with the understanding that the probationer will live up to certain standards and submit to the supervision and assistance of a court probation officer. The essential weakness of probation has been the lack of qualified probation officers. The most important goal of probation must be to maintain in the community all offenders who can function acceptably with probation support and to select for confinement only those who are a danger to themselves or others, and who cannot complete probation status successfully even with optimal probation support.

Parole is the second most frequently used form of corrections in the community. Parole is defined as the release of an offender from a penal or correctional institution, after he has served a portion of his sentence, under continued custody of the state and under conditions that permit his reincarceration in the event of misbehavior. Parole is granted by parole boards. They have been criticized because of their means of appointment, range of responsibilities, and the part-time status of some members. At the present the trend is toward allowing the parolee to attend hearings with legal representation on granting and revocation of parole.

Throughout correctional history four major treatments have been used: (1) clinical models; (2) group interaction models; (3) therapeutic community models; and (4) social action models. In the 1970s, two treatment techniques being used were behavior modification and transactional analysis.

TOPICS FOR DISCUSSION

1. How effective are penal institutions today?

2. What are two examples for justifying the presentence investigation report?

3. Cite at least two objectives for probation.

4. What are the various treatment strategies used in penal institutions?

5. What is the future of corrections, and what is the best hope for the future for the protection of society?

PART 5
Profession-
alism

15

Profession-
alism within
the justice
system

The study of this chapter will enable you to:

1. **Define the general characteristics found in a professional occupation.**
2. **Understand the essential elements of a profession for the student.**
3. **Know the codes of conduct for each of the major criminal justice components.**
4. **Identify examples of critical issues.**
5. **Identity subject areas for additional study.**

The general characteristics and descriptions found in a professional occupation are described in this chapter. The essential elements that tradition has ascribed to a profession will be demonstrated. It is anticipated that the reader will compare and contrast the general characteristics and the elements of a profession with those found in the major components of our criminal justice system—police, courts, and corrections. Where applicable, the codes of conduct or codes of ethics are included.

Members of the police, courts, corrections, and the subsystems are today being freely referred to as professionals. When we examine the definition of a profession, and the requisites (essential elements) attached, we find that some people employed in the criminal justice system have reached professional status and some have not.

The dictionary definition of a profession is: "A calling requiring specialized knowledge and often long and intensive academic preparation: a principal calling, vocation, or employment." A more detailed and in-depth definition might be:

A vocation whose practice is founded upon an understanding of the theoretical structure of some department of learning or science, and upon the abilities accompanying such understanding. This understanding and these abilities are applied to the vital affairs of man. The practices of the profession are modified by knowledge of a generalized nature and by the accumulated wisdom and experience of mankind, which serve to correct the errors of specialism. The profession, serving the vital needs of man, considers its first ethical imperative to be altruistic (unselfish) service to the client.[1]

Professionalism throughout the system

There is an increasingly wisespread belief that all members of the other criminal justice subsystems—the police, probation, corrections, and parole—should attain a professional status equal to that of the members of

[1]Morris L. Cogan, "Toward a Definition of a Profession," *Harvard Educational Review, XXIII* (Winter 1953), pp. 33–50.

the courts. In weighing this belief, the individual citizen should consider some questions. Would any person want an amateur to deliver his wife of a baby or tend a seriously ill member of his family? Faced with a serious lawsuit, either criminal or civil, how many would want to enter court and be represented by someone not thoroughly trained in the law? Who, among knowledgeable citizens, would permit their children to be tutored by an illiterate? Each of these instances calls for a professional: a physician, an attorney, and a teacher. Why then should the people trust their personal safety, the protection of their property, and the safeguarding of their constitutional rights and civil liberties to other than professionals?

It has been previously stated that all components of the criminal justice system had not reached the status of a true profession. However, if we apply Cogan's definition of a profession to each subsystem of the criminal justice system, it is our contention that the practitioners in the subsystems; the police, courts, probation, parole, and corrections are professionals. They do fall within the definition in the following ways: their practices are founded upon an understanding of law and the social sciences; these understandings and abilities are daily applied to the most vital affairs of man, modified by generalized knowledge and accumulated experience; and for the most part, the practitioners have an altruistic dedication to the service they render to their communities and to their fellow man.

The education and training requirements in police, probation, parole, and corrections are steadily increasing, and the bulk of relevant case law that must be absorbed by judges, defense attorneys, and prosecuting attorneys is growing at a tremendous rate.

In view of this, the professional must reconcile two things: the ideal for which he enters a profession and the remuneration or fee that he receives. Although a professional should not render service for the fee alone, ideals do not provide for physical sustenance. There must be adequate remuneration so that financial worries do not plague the professional, distract him from his work, and even tempt him to take bribes to support his family and educate his children. The members of the criminal justice system should be recognized as professionals and be assured of an income commensurate with the services performed and the risks taken.

The elements of a profession

The many views expressed concerning the essential elements or requisites of a profession are all contained within the following paragraphs.

1. A basis of systematic theory or a discrete (individually distinct) body of knowledge. It has often been stated that the basic difference between professional and nonprofessional vocations lies in the element of greater skill. But great skill at a complicated task is not, by any means, restricted to recognized professions. Vocations such as engraving or cabinetmaking require a greater degree of skill and intricacy than do many recognized

professions. The real distinction lies not in the lengthy training to perfec an intricate skill, but in gaining the knowledge of the basic theory suppor ing the profession, and by applying this theory to concrete situations. Thi requires long, sometimes arduous academic training, lengthened b periods of internship, or on-the-job training, wherein the candidate gain experience in concrete application of his academic training.

2. Authority recognized by the clientele of the professional group. Customer seeking ordinary goods and services can comparison shop for the bes price and quality, presumably knowing what is best for them. But, in the case of professional service, the assumption is that the professional knows what is best for the client because of his specialized knowledge and ability to apply this in judging what is good or bad for his client.

3. Broader community sanction and approval of this authority. The profes sion has persuaded the community to confer certain powers on it. Some o those powers are the right to say who can enter the profession, who can use the titles pertaining to the profession, and what the training and academic course content will be.

4. A code of eithics regulating relations of professional people with clients and with colleagues. Without a code of ethics, the professional could charge exorbitant fees, restrict entry into the profession to such a degree as to create a shortage of practitioners, and cause all sorts of other abuses against the public interest. Without binding codes of ethics, biased or prejudicial practices within the profession could become rampant due to a lack of control. Maximum quality professional service would be endangered, since the codes generally insure the sharing of new knowledge within the profession, thereby assuring the clientele of the benefit of up-to-date service.

5. A professional culture sustained by formal professional association. Besides establishing norms and values, these associations have the informal power to ostracize these members who may display undesirable qualities, such as a lack of dedication to the profession and their clientele.

6. A formal licensing authority or agency. This implies that the profession has persuaded the community to grant it the legal power to say who may practice the profession and who may be excluded. This may include administering a standard examination approved by a board, and the enforcement of criminal penalities against those who practice the profession without obtaining licenses.[2]

In most countries of the world the practice of law is a recognized profession. When one of the prerequisites to becoming a member of the judiciary is that the candidate be an attorney, the judiciary, too, becomes a recognized profession. This condition exists in all but the lowest courts in the United States. Therefore, we have professionals conducting our courts (the judges) and acting as officers of the court (the attorneys).

Shortcomings   When we begin to apply the requisites of a profession to each of the components of our criminal justice system, some shortcomings can be perceived. Certainly, the members of the judiciary system; the judges,

[2]Ernest Greenwood, "Attributes of a Profession," *Social Work*, 2, No. 3 (July 1957), pp. 44–45.

Keeping pace with the legalities

Since the careers of today's senior administrators began, police work has become more difficult, more complicated, more professional. A large part of that change is a result of rapidly expanding legal developments including new statutes, court decisions, and reform in courtroom procedures. The most publicized aspect of these developments is the creation of a system of strict safeguards of the constitutional rights of the accused:

❑ The Miranda Warning which must precede custodial questioning.
❑ Strict scrutiny of probable cause for arrest, search, or seizure of evidence.
❑ Tough testing of the sufficiency of warrants.
❑ Restrictions on the use of tape recordings and wiretaps.

This developing body of constitutional requirements is only part of the picture of legal change. Improved (indeed, required) legal representation of defendants has led to vigorous testing of police conduct in case after case. Defendants and community members are increasingly aware of their rights and opportunities for protest. Legislation comes from Congress and state legislatures every year, changing previously acceptable acts into crimes and vice versa. Statutes on the books are ruled unconstitutional, limited, explained, or broadened—while their words remain unchanged.

In the midst of these legal requirements—and facing a generally rising incidence of reported crime—stands the police officer. If he fails to keep pace with legal changes, if his judgment is in error, both the rate of crime and police image may suffer as a result.

An Exemplary Report, "Legal Liaison Division of the Dallas Police Department," National Institute of Law Enforcement and Criminal Justice, U.S. Department of Justice, March 1976,

prosecutors, and defense attorneys belong to an established, universally recognized profession. It is in the police, probation, parole, and corrections that shortcomings are noted. The bodies of knowledge within these subsystems have not all been completely systematized, and there are areas of disagreement as to what should be taught, and how it should be taught.

The recognition of professional authority by the clientele has not been thoroughly gained; nor do police, probation, parole, and corrections yet have complete community sanction and approval as professionals.

Formal professional associations in police, probation, parole, and corrections are to be found in abundance. In fact, in some areas, these associations are so numerous that their numbers dilute their effectiveness. An answer might be a nationwide association for the members of each group (similar to the American Bar Association) with state and local chapters.

Formal licensing agencies or authorities for police, probation, parole, and corrections are becoming more common but are not universal. This requisite needs to be met.

The case for professionalism has been briefly stated and leaves the student wide latitude for more research on the subject. We have, however, left one requirement of a profession to be discussed more in depth: a code of ethics.

Codes of ethics

The mere existence of a code of ethics does not satisfy the requisite. Unless the professional and his clientele apply the meaning and the intent of the words contained within the code, it has no value. This application must become routine in the day-to-day relationship between professional and client.

In 1957 the International Association of Chiefs of Police adopted a Law Enforcement Code of Ethics. This had been developed the previous year by the Peace Officers Research Association of California and the California Peace Officers Association. Many law enforcement accrediting agencies have since adopted this code.

Law Enforcement Code of Ethics

As a law enforcement officer, my fundamental duty is to serve mankind; to safeguard lives and property; to protect the innocent against deception, the weak against oppression or intimidation, and the peaceful against violence or disorder; and to respect the consitutional rights of all men to liberty, equality, and justice.

I will keep my private life unsullied as an example to all; maintain courageous calm in the face of danger, scorn, or ridicule; develop self-restraint; and be constantly mindful of the welfare of others. Honest in thought and deed in both my personal and offical life, I will be exemplary in obeying the laws of the land and the regulations of my department. Whatever I see or hear of a confidential nature or that is confided to me in my official capacity will be kept ever secret unless revelation is necessary in the performance of my duty.

I will never act officiously or permit personal feelings, prejudices, animosities, or friendships to influence my decisions. With no compromise for crime and with relentless prosecution of criminals, I will enforce the law courteously and appropriately without fear or favor, malice or ill will, never employing unnecessary force or violence, and never accepting gratuities.

I recognize the badge of my office as a symbol of public faith, and I accept it as a public trust to be held so long as I am true to the ethics of the police service. I will constantly strive to achieve these objectives and ideals, dedicating myself before God to my chosen profession—law enforcement.

Parole Officers Code of Ethics

The Board of Pardons and Paroles of the state of Texas adopted the Parole Officers' Code of Ethics in 1961. Other states have similar codes. The Texas code of ethics is typical of the majority.

As a parole officer I shall:

Abide by and uphold the laws of my community, state, and nation, remembering always my duty to protect the community which I serve; and, share, within the limits of my office, in a general responsibility for making my community a better place in which to live;

Regard as my professional obligation, consistent with the public welfare, the interests of those assigned to my supervision; and respect both their legal and moral rights at all times;

Assure that professional responsibility and objectivity take precedence over my personal convenience or biases; and, when not inconsistent with my obligation to my agency or the welfare of society, to maintain in strict confidences any personal revelations which are given to me; support the policies of my agency; work to improve its standards and performance; and dedicate myself to improve my knowledge and understanding in order to better serve my community and those from whom I have responsibility;

Treat the accomplishments of my colleagues with respect and express critical judgment of them only through established agency channels; support them always in fulfilling their responsibilities; respect differences of opinion between myself and my colleagues and take positive steps to resolve them;

Work cooperatively with other agencies in matters affecting the welfare and protection of the community; protect the confidentiality of shared information; and respect the functions and limitations of other agencies;

Conduct myself, both privately and publicly, in such a manner as to enhance public confidence in my agency and its objectives; neither grant nor receive favors in the performance of the duties of my office; and treat all persons with whom I have contact with courtesy and respect;

Always recognize my office as a sacred trust which has been given to me to guard and sustain.

Probation and parole are closely linked in the criminal justice system. Since they perform similar functions, it is only natural that organizations of both probation and parole officers have adopted codes of ethics similar to the one set forth above.

The Legal Code of Ethics

The American Bar Association, in writing the Code of Professional Responsibility for lawyers, divided it in three separate, interrelated parts: canons, ethical considerations, and disciplinary rules. The canons express, in general terms, the standards of professional conduct for lawyers in their dealings with the public, the legal system, and the profession. They are as follows:

A lawyer should assist in maintaining the integrity and competence of the legal profession.

A lawyer should assist the legal profession in fulfilling its duty to make legal counsel available.

Personal grooming versus uniformity

Reversing the U.S. Court of Appeals for the Second Circuit, the U.S. Supreme Court gave wide latitude to states and local governments in promulgating grooming regulations for their uniformed personnel. The rule challenged had regulated the style and length of hair, sideburns and mustaches; it banned beards and goatees except for medical reasons; it limited the use of wigs to those which conformed with the regulation and were worn for cosmetic purposes. The regulation was adopted by the Suffolk County, New York, Police Department. It was struck down by the appellate court as violative of an officer's choice of personal appearance and liberty and purportedly did not have a rational relationship to a legitimate governmental interest. The Supreme Court, in a 6 to 2 decision, reversed that rationale and holding.

First, the high Court distinguished the "liberty" interest here from those cases involving personal choice in matters of marriage, family life and procreation. But the regulation could not be viewed in isolation, the court said, but must be weighed "in the context of the county's chosen mode or organization for its police force." "Choice of organization, dress and equipment for law enforcement personnel," the Court said, "is a decision entitled to the same sort of presumption of legislative validity as are state choices designed to promote other aims within the cognizance of the state's police power." The Court continued:

The overwhelming majority of state and local police of the present day are uniformed. This fact itself testifies to the recognition by those who direct those operations, and by the people of the states and localities who directly or indirectly choose such persons that similarity in appearance of police officers is desirable. This choice may be based on a desire to make police officers readily recognizable to the members of the public, or a desire for the esprit de corps which such similarity is felt to inculcate within the police force itself. Either one is a sufficiently rational justification for regulations so as to defeat respondent's claim based on the liberty guarantee of the Fourteenth Amendment.

Inasmuch as either uniformity of appearance or esprit de corps are justification for hairstyle regulations, such rules would be consitutionally applicable to both uniformed and nonuniformed personnel in a primarily uniformed department. (*Kelley v. Johnson*, 96 S. Ct. 1440 [April 5, 1976]).

Source: Americans for Effective Law Enforcement, *Litigation Digest*, January 1976, p. 7.

A lawyer should assist in preventing the unauthorized practice of law.

A lawyer should preserve the confidences and secrets of a client.

A lawyer should exercise independent professional judgment on behalf of a client.

A lawyer should represent a client competently.

A lawyer should represent a client zealously within the bounds of the law.

State judgeships——political plums?

These men are given judgeships as a reward for long and faithful service to a political party, or to some political leader. While many make excellent judges, dozens of others do not belong on the bench.

"The most important thing, if you want to become a judge, is to have good political contacts," says one bitter New York trial lawyer. "You don't get to be a judge by practicing law. You've got to sit in the clubhouse and build your contacts."

"Almost all state judges are picked because of their experience in public life—in politics," says Geoffrey C. Hazard Jr., executive director of the American Bar Foundation.

Source: Howard James, *Crisis in the Courts* (New York: David McKay, 1967), p. 6

A lawyer should assist in improving the legal system.

A lawyer should avoid even the appearance of professional impropriety.[3]

It should be remembered by all, especially by those working within the criminal justice system, that the term lawyer as used in the canons of the American Bar Association is intended to include lawyers who are engaged in the prosecution of cases as well as the lawyers in private practice who represent their clients as lawyers for the defense.

In February 1978, the American Bar Association approved a new plan for the disciplining, removal, and retiring of state and federal judges who are unfit for duty or disabled. Many of these judges had been previously untouchable, except by impeachment. For over 40 years, no federal judge has been impeached.

This code of judicial discipline will have to be adopted by Congress and state legislatures to become effective. The code would authorize the disciplining of judges for the following reasons: conviction of a felony; willful misconduct that would bring the bar into disrepute; willful misconduct in office; conduct prejudicial to the administration of justice or unbecoming a judicial officer; and conduct violating existing codes of legal or judicial ethics.

The Judicial Code of Ethics

In addition to the canons for professional conduct of lawyers which it has formulated and adopted, the American Bar Association, mindful that the character and conduct of a judge should never be objects of indifference, and that declared ethical standards tend to become habits of life, deems it desirable to set forth its

[3]Henry Campbell Black, *Black's Law Dictionary*, 4th rev. ed. (St. Paul: West Publishing Company, 1968).

views respecting those principles which should govern the personal practice of members of the judiciary in the administration of their office. The Association accordingly adopts the following canons, the spirit of which it suggests as a proper guide and reminder for judges, and as indicating what the people have a right to expect from them.[4]

The Canons of Judicial Ethics, including the amendments of January 1, 1968, are summarized below. Students who want to read the complete version are directed to *Black's Law Dictionary*, 4th rev. ed., pp. 59–73, or to the American Bar Association.

Relations of the judiciary with the people whom he serves, the practitioners of law in his court, the witnesses, etc. should be duties recognized as incumbent on him when he assumes the office.

The judges should conduct their courts in the best interests of the public, assuring speedy and careful administration.

The judges are duty-bound to support the U.S. Constitution and that of the state whose laws they administer.

A judge's official conduct should be free from impropriety and the appearance of impropriety.

A judge should be temperate, attentive, patient, impartial.

A judge should exhibit an industry and application commensurate with the duties imposed upon him.

A judge should be prompt in the performance of his judicial duties.

A judge should be courteous and considerate of all in attendance upon the court.

The remainder of the canons deal with the specific areas of responsibility that are unique with the judiciary, such as appointments made by judges, interference in conduct of trials, ex-parte (one-sided) communications, continuances, review, private law practice, and others. Canon 34 best summarizes the obligations of a member of the judiciary:

In every particular his conduct should be above reproach. He should be conscientious, studious, thorough, courteous, patient, punctual, just, impartial, fearless of public clamor, regardless of public praise and indifferent to private political or partisan influences; he should administer justice according to law, and deal with his appointments as a public trust; he should not allow other affairs or his private interests to interfere with the prompt and proper performance of his judicial duties, nor should he administer the office for the purpose of advancing his personal ambitions or increasing his popularity.

The Correctional Code of Ethics

The American Correctional Association has issued a Declaration of Principles for its members. Although this document does not address itself directly to what is and what is not ethical conduct for the correctional

[4]Preamble to the Canons of Judicial Ethics, American Bar Association, adopted at its 47th annual meeting on July 9, 1924.

JUDICIAL EDUCATION AND SELECTION

Education

Every state should create and maintain a comprehensive program of continuing judicial education. Planning for this program should recognize the extensive commitment of judge time, both as faculty and as participants for such programs, that will be necessary. Funds necessary to prepare, administer, and conduct the programs, and funds to permit judges to attend appropriate national and regional educational programs, should be provided.

Each state program should have the following features:

1. All new trial judges, within 3 years of assuming judicial office, should attend both local and national orientation programs as well as one of the national judicial educational programs. The local orientation program should come immediately before or after the judge first takes office. It should include visits to all institutions and facilities to which criminal offenders may be sentenced.

2. Each state should develop its own state judicial college, which should be responsible for the orientation program for new judges and which should make available to all state judges the graduate and refresher programs of the national judicial educational organizations. Each state also should plan specialized subject matter programs as well as 2- or 3-day annual state seminars for trial and appellate judges.

3. The failure of any judge, without good cause, to pursue educational programs as prescribed in this standard should be considered by the judicial conduct commission as grounds for discipline or removal.

4. Each state should prepare a bench manual on procedural laws, with forms, samples, rule requirements and other information that a judge should have readily available. This should include sentencing alternatives and information concerning correctional programs and institutions.

5. Each state should publish periodically—and not less than quarterly—a newsletter with information from the chief justice, the court administrator, correctional authorities, and others. This should include articles of interest to judges, references to new literature in the judicial and correctional fields, and citations of important appellate and trial court decisions.

6. Each state should adopt a program of sabbatical leave for the purpose of enabling judges to pursue studies and research relevant to their judicial duties.

Selection

The selection of judges should be based on merit qualifications for judicial office. A selection process should aggressively seek out the best potential judicial candidates through the participation of the bench, the organized bar, law schools, and the lay public.

Judges should be selected by a judicial nominating commission. Representatives from the judiciary, the general public, and the legal profession should organize into a seven-member judicial nominating commission for the sole purpose of nominating a slate of qualified candidates eligible to fill judicial vacancies. The governor should fill judicial vacancies from this list.

With the exception of the judicial member, the members of the commission should be selected by procedures designed to assure that they reflect the wishes of the groups they represent. The senior judge of the highest court, other than the chief justice, should represent the judiciary and serve as the commission's presiding officer. The governor should appoint three public members, none of whom should be judges or lawyers. No more than two should be of the same political affiliation or be from the same geographic vicinity. Three members from the legal profession should be appointed or elected by the membership of the unified bar association or appointed by the governor when no such organization exists. A lawyer member of the commission should not be eligible for consideration for judicial vacancies until the expiration of his term and those of the other two lawyer members and three lay members serving with him. Commission members representing the public and the legal profession should serve staggered terms of three years.

For the appointment procedure to function efficiently, the commission staff should maintain an updated list of qualified potential nominees from which the commission should draw names to submit to the governor. The commission should select a minimum of three persons to fill a judicial vacancy on the court, unless the commission is convinced there are not three qualified nominees. This list should be sent to the governor within 30 days of a judicial vacancy, and, if the governor does not appoint a candidate within 30 days, the power of appointment should shift to the commission.

Source: The National Advisory Commission on Criminal Justice Standards and Goals, 1973.

community, the principles formally state the beliefs of this subsystem of the criminal justice system. In summary, 36 principles cover the attitudes of the Association toward the following:

1. The application of the growing body of knowledge in the behavioral sciences against the problem of crime.

2. The strengthening and expansion of correctional methods.

3. The preparation and dissemination of objective information needed for public policy decisions at all jurisdictional levels.

4. The need for a direct relationship between the length or severity of the punitive sentence assessed and the seriousness of the offense perpetrated.

5. The need to assure that no law, procedure, or system of correction should deprive any offender of his ultimate return to full, responsible membership in society.

6. The aim of the correctional process to reintegrate the offender into society as a law-abiding citizen.

7. The integration of institutional- and community-based programs into a system that is responsible for guiding, controlling, unifying, and vitalizing the correctional process.

8. The release of all offenders under parole supervision with parole being granted at the earliest date consistent with public safety and the needs of the individual.

9. The use of work and study furlough programs to provide a smoother transition for the offender from institutional life to community life.

10. The assurance of the preservation of an offender's human dignity.

Although each of the principles espoused by the American Correctional Association is not paraphrased in the sampling above, some of the more obvious points have been noted. These Declarations of Principles may be found in their entirety in the *Manual of Correctional Standards*, 3rd ed., issued by the American Correctional Association.

Characteristics of a professional group

In addition to accepted codes of conduct, there are several characteristics that must be met so that an occupational group may be considered professional.

Although the succeeding pages will not attempt to present a conclusive discussion on professional criteria, we will provide comment on those characteristics commonly referred to when a group is evaluated as a profession. The fundamental purpose of the selected discussion topics is to demonstrate the difficulties in describing a professional *group*, as differentiated from individuals who conduct themselves as professionals.

We began this chapter by suggesting that law enforcement and corrections personnel are, in fact, professionals. Perhaps the discussions presented will enhance that contention. In any event, the student will find fertile ground for additional study.

Licensing/ certification

The American Bar Association is widely recognized as the professional body of the legal and judicial units of criminal justice. It serves as a licensing body on a national basis for its members. Although there are a multitude of national organizations for law enforcement and corrections, none of them issue professional licenses.

Some states have certification for police and correctional personnel, which is considered by many as meeting the licensing characteristic of a profession. A key question would be whether or not the issuing authority may revoke the certificate. If, for example, the certificate is not revocable, then one may question whether or not it will meet the criteria of a professional license.

Certification and/or licensing have been treated as fixed criteria for a profession. It may be appropriate to examine the purpose and method of issuing these documents. If, for example, a license or certificate is nothing more than a testimonial for successful completion of a specific course of study or a one-time examination, the document may mean one thing. But if the recipient of a license must undergo periodic review to ensure compliance with the professional precepts, the certification process has a different significance. The distinction may lie in whether or not the issuing authority is legitimate and if the document is subject to revocation.

Legitimacy may be determined by asking: Can an individual serve in or hold a position without the license or certificate? If a person is required by law to hold the license to perform the duties, then we could consider the document as legitimate. But even a legitimate certificate may not be valid unless it is current. In other words, the issuing authority must have the right of revocation; and a reexamination of the recipient's qualifications must occur periodically before the license is considered legitimate and valid. It may be interesting to examine the criminal justice field to determine whether or not the licensing/certification process is valid. Particular attention should be given to the comparison between the units of the system (legal and judicial) that are accepted as professional groups and those units that are not yet accepted as being professional (law enforcement and corrections). Refer to Table 15-1 for data concerning law enforcement and correctional certification in the United States.

See Appendix B for A Model Rule for Certifying Police and Corrections Officers, including provisions for revocation, developed by the National Association of State Directors of Law Enforcement Training, January 1976.

Education/training

It is frequently suggested that true professionals require a specific body of knowledge, such as in law or medicine. Law enforcement does not meet the general professional status because the educational characteristics of

State	Certifies	Does not certify	Authority to revoke certification	
			Yes	No
1. Alabama[3]				
2. Alaska	X		X	
3. Arizona[3]				
4. Arkansas		X[1]		
5. California	X		X	
6. Colorado	X		X	
7. Connecticut	X			X
8. Delaware	X			X
9. Florida	X		X	
10. Georgia	X		X	
11. Hawaii[4]				
12. Idaho	X		X	
13. Illinois		X[1]		
14. Indiana	X		X	
15. Iowa	X			X
16. Kansas	X			X
17. Kentucky		X[1]		
18. Louisiana[4]				
19. Maine	X		X[2]	
20. Maryland		X[1]		
21. Massachusetts	X			X
22. Michigan		X[1]		
23. Minnesota	X		X	
24. Mississippi[4]				
25. Missouri[4]				
26. Montana	X		X	
27. Nebraska	X			X
28. Nevada	X			X
29. New Hampshire	X			X
30. New Jersey	X			X
31. New Mexico[3]				
32. New York	X			X
33. North Carolina	X		X	
34. North Dakota	X			X
35. Ohio	X			X
36. Oklahoma	X			X
37. Oregon	X		X	
38. Pennsylvania[4]				
39. Rhode Island	X			X
40. South Carolina	X			X
41. South Dakota	X			X
42. Tennessee		X[1]		
43. Texas	X		X	
44. Utah	X		X	
45. Vermont[3]				
46. Virginia		X[1]		
47. Washington	X			X
48. West Virginia[4]				
49. Wisconsin	X			X
50. Wyoming	X		X	

[1]Issues certificate for completion of training.
[2]Revokes authority to enforce criminal law.
[3]Failed to answer questionnaire after second mailing.
[4]Information not available.

most curricula are considered "technical training." In other words, it is suggested that in order that the police be accepted as professional, their education must be broad and intellectual rather than skill-oriented. Let us examine that suggestion.

The study of law or medicine, occupations readily accepted as professional, certainly involves a great deal of technical or skill training. We might easily assume that much of the training a surgeon must undergo is highly technical. And during the study of law, the student is expected to develop technical knowledge regarding procedural techniques.

To summarize the issue of education and training as the criteria for an occupational group to be considered professional, perhaps we should determine the purpose rather than the nature of the acquired knowledge. Most of us tend to equate the word professional with the word expertise and we are also willing to refer to an expert as a professional. Therefore, it may be appropriate to accept any learning process as professional preparation as long as the knowledge improves the individual's ability to fulfill the occupational demands. Table 15-2 reflects a national survey of training requirements for police officers.

Employment standards

It is interesting to note that employment standards for police officers are generally more rigorous than are the standards for other criminal justice members. Although specific standards for police employment vary greatly throughout the nation, individuals who want a police position are more thoroughly examined and evaluated than are applicants for any other criminal justice occupation.

Police officers are subject to preemployment evaluation in the following areas: citizenship, criminal record, oral interviews, written examinations, physical and psychological testing, and an investigation of personal history. In several states, the individual police officer is required to meet additional standards throughout his or her career. As an example, the Peace Officers Standards and Training Commission (POST) in California has additional requirements for police officers as they are promoted to supervisory, management, and executive positions.

One could only wonder what the reaction would be if judges and attorneys in the criminal justice field were required to undergo periodic psychological and physical examinations to determine their fitness for public service.

Perhaps it is presumptuous to suggest that the only criteria an occupational group must meet in order to be considered professional are specific training, licensing, and employment standards. William Bopp suggests that the following characteristics are also found in professional groups:

1. A higher loyalty. A true professional, in addition to being loyal to the employing agency, is primarily loyal to the professional goals of the occu-

Table 15-2
National survey of
training requirements for
police officers.

State	Mandatory training		Hours
	Basic	Advanced	
Alabama	X	[1]	240
Alaska²			
Arizona	X	[1]	280
Arkansas	[1]		220
California	X	X	200
Colorado	X	[1]	260
Connecticut	X	[1]	400
Delaware	X	[1]	350
Florida	X	X	320
Georgia	X	[1]	240
Hawaii²			
Idaho	X	X	300
Illinois	X	[1]	240
Indiana	X	[1]	400
Iowa	X	[1]	400
Kansas	X	[1]	200
Kentucky	[1]	X	400
Louisiana	X		240
Maine	X	[1]	480
Maryland	X	X	350
Massachusetts	X	X	480
Michigan	X	[1]	280
Minnesota	X	X	280
Mississippi²			
Missouri²			
Montana	X	X	280
Nebraska	X	X	300
Nevada	[1]		120
New Hampshire	X	[1]	280
New Jersey	X	[1]	280
New Mexico	X	[1]	240
New York	X	X	285
North Carolina	X	[1]	160
North Dakota	[1]		200
Ohio	X	[1]	280
Oklahoma	X	[1]	160
Oregon	X	X	280
Pennsylvania²			
Rhode Island	X	[1]	400
South Carolina	X	[1]	320
South Dakota	X	[1]	200
Tennessee	[1]		240
Texas	X	[1]	240
Utah	X	X	320
Vermont	X	X	240
Virginia	X	X	249
Washington	[1]		440
West Virginia²			
Wisconsin	X	[1]	240
Wyoming	X	[1]	150

[1]Training available but not mandatory.
²Questionnaire not returned April 1977.

pational group. An example would be that of a physician whose primary dedication is to the patient, with dedication to the hospital being secondary.

2. Teamwork. Most professional groups emphasize utilizing individual skills and strengths without the restriction of organizational jurisdiction. We could exemplify this concept by visualizing a police officer serving in the capacity of a parole officer and vice versa, in an effort to reduce recidivism.

3. Paraprofessionals. This concept suggests that professional groups clearly recognize different levels of expertise and that the most highly trained and competent persons should be assigned to the most demanding positions.[5]

Summary

The system of justice of our land has developed through the years with service to people as the main objective. Throughout this development, the members of the legal profession have been the only group belonging to one of the classic professions (military, medicine, law, and the ministry). The police, corrections, probation, and parole groups are attaining professionalism or are on the threshold of that status. They have specialized training and skills derived from a discrete body of knowledge which are, in many cases, systematically passed on to new members through both formal and informal training and education; they have professional organizations and codes of ethics; members of some of the groups must be licensed or certified after having met certain minimum requirements; and all demonstrate a spirit of public service.

Precisely what a professional is, or what he may not be, depends entirely upon one's perception. A judge of a trial court is readily accepted as being a member of a profession, primarily because he is a lawyer. But can we be certain that the individual conducts his office as a professional? On the other hand, we can identify individual police and correctional officers who conduct themselves as professionals who have not met the established criteria of education or licensing.

This chapter has demonstrated some of the more salient characteristics of accepted professional bodies. Those characteristics are but one measure of the individuals who may have positions in the occupational group. To assume any individual is a professional merely because of membership in any group may be erroneous and should be avoided.

Cogan, whose definition of a professional was mentioned at the beginning of the chapter, draws the one thread from all of the codes of conduct that can best tie the American criminal justice system together: altruistic service to the client. No other profession deals more consistently

[5]Donald T. Shanahan, *The Administration of Justice System* (Boston: Holbrook Press, 1977), p. 93.

with the problems of people's interactions with people than does the system of justice. People and their problems are the ingredients that justify the existence of the system of justice. Yet, in dealing with these problems, criminal justice practitioners must maintain their altruistic approach if they are to truly serve the justice needs of their clients.

1. Discuss why certain components of the criminal justice system are generally accepted as professionals and other components are not considered professionals.

2. Discuss whether or not attorneys and judges should meet the same employment standards as the police.

3. Compare and contrast the legitimacy and validity of licensing and/or certification processes.

4. Discuss the relative merit of national licensing of criminal justice practitioners.

16

Future trends in criminal justice

The study of this chapter will enable you to:

1. **Identify the areas of needed reform in corrections and the courts.**
2. **Examine the trends and innovations in the criminal justice field.**
3. **Be informed about the expanding role of women in criminal justice.**
4. **Discuss the impetus for change in preexisting standards in the criminal justice field.**
5. **Study further recommendations for change in criminal justice.**

Beginning in the mid-sixties attention to the criminal justice system became intensified. Prior to this, there was a reluctance on the part of many to openly criticize the criminal justice process, whose problems were evident and growing. Once the criticism started, it appeared as though the floodgates were opened. Problems were pointed out rapidly by society; some were real, some were imaginary. Nothing remained sacred. Efforts were made by some to radicalize the system, to abandon all that went on before.

During this turbulent era in the sixties, these inadequacies that had previously gone undetected were closely scrutinized by the Supreme Court, whose decisions brought to light many questionable practices being used by these agencies of the criminal justice system. For instance, certain police procedures that had not attracted much of the public's interest were reviewed by the Supreme Court in such cases as *Mapp v. Ohio, Terry v. Ohio, Escobeda v. Illinois, Gideon v. Wainright,* and *Miranda v. Arizona.* Out of these cases came significant court decisions, which set in motion new trends in police procedure, further protecting the constitutional rights of individuals.

Not only were the police closely scrutinized by the Supreme Court, but the lower courts themselves underwent some radical changes as far as juvenile proceedings were concerned. This was brought about by the *Gault* and *Kent* decisions, which indicated that individual rights guaranteed in the Constitution were not being adhered to in matters regarding youthful offenders in juvenile court proceedings.

The correctional element of the criminal justice system also came under scrutiny, for it was during the sixties that many violent prison riots occurred throughout the United States. Riots took place not only behind prison walls but also on the streets, as the government underwent critical analysis by the public. It was here that many students, individuals, and private concerns began to rebel against certain governmental actions such as the war in Vietnam. Legislative statutes and state laws were being severely tested by demonstrators expressing their concern over discrimination, fair housing, free speech, and the death penalty debate.

Problems and public attention continued to plague the criminal justice system through the seventies. Watergate illustrated the fact that many individuals who held positions in the criminal justice system (even the United States Attorney General), with backgrounds in law and memberships in the American Bar Association or other law enforcement agencies could be involved in a scandal that rocked the nation. It is unfortunate to say that it was not until some of these tragic events occurred that the consciences of the American public and governmental officials were forced into taking some action. This action taken by the legislators eventually acted as a catalyst that helped to bring about a change in the criminal justice system.

Part of this concern was channeled into committees that had been established in 1965, during the heat of national concern about law and order. These committees led to the formation of the President's Commission on Law enforcement and the Administration of Justice. Another program that was established during this same period was the Law Enforcement Assistance Administration (LEAA). These two developments provided fiscal backing by the government and produced teams of professionals who had expertise in the various fields of criminal justice, which enabled the Commission to formulate standards, goals, and recommendations for state, local, and national agencies of criminal justice.

Much of the material developed through the studies done by the President's Commission on Law Enforcement and the Administration of Justice has been of great value for further development by the criminal justice participants. Other suggestions and recommendations have not received the attention they warranted. As a result of the varieties of the studies and the multiplicity of books released, many important recommendations were overlooked. There appeared to be a need to gather an additional group of experts in the field of criminal justice to discuss the wealth of material available and, in addition, to expand upon ideas or develop new ones so that they could make some firm recommendations to improve the process. Another commission was formed to do this work, which was entitled The National Advisory Commission on Criminal Justice Standards and Goals. Their first release of information was made early in 1973. Since that time more work has been done by the Commission, and recommendations are being released as the work continues.

National Advisory Commission on Criminal Justice Standards and Goals

The ultimate goal of the Commission's work is to reduce crime through the combined effort of all in the criminal justice process, including federal, state, and local governments. The Commission did not undertake new research, rather it developed standards that take a fresh look at the

process, unhampered by traditional practices that no longer apply. It fur
ther took the view that wherever policy, program, procedures, and law ar
in need of improvement or should be eliminated, the legislatures shoul
make the necessary changes, and the agencies in the process shoul
implement the changes.

As with any study where recommendations are made, the recom
mendations are subject to attack. And those who oppose several recom
mendations might try to discredit the entire work because of some opposi
tion. The work of this Commission may be subject to this pitfall. There ar
many ideas put forth that should receive serious attention to upgrade the
criminal justice process. Some of these recommendations will be enumer
ated as they relate to police courts, corrections, and crime prevention
These recommendations may also be viewed as an impetus toward initia
ing new trends in the related fields of the criminal justice system.

Recommendations for the police

Seven objectives were indentified by those studying the police. They di
not give priorities for their objectives nor for those specific items that can b
developed as programs to tackle the objectives. The Commission called fo
immediate action to: fully develop the offender-apprehension potential c
the criminal justice system; stimulate the police and the citizens to worl
together as a team; motivate those in the criminal justice system to work ir
unison; clearly determine and act on local crime problems; make the mos
of human resources; use technological advances to their fullest capacities
and fully develop the police response to special community needs. The
Commission made numerous recommendations for implementation c
each objective.

Offender-apprehension potential To fully develop the offender
apprehension potential of the criminal justice systems, programs of crime
prevention need to be implemented by police agencies. Voluntee
neighborhood security can be developed where citizens mark persona
property with identification numbers or call in suspicious acts taking place
in their community, for example. Crime prevention through physical plan
ning can be undertaken for citizens or businesses by using design idea:
calculated to reduce the opportunity to commit crime. Security standard:
can be enhanced by the enactment of necessary laws and ordinances.

Police and citizen teamwork The objective to get the police and the
people working together as a team could be met with programs that make
the people aware of written police policy that deals with authority, law
misconduct of the police, and every aspect where the police and the public
must work together. It would follow that the public would also be made
aware of the police role in society.

Criminal justice system teamwork Where the need exists to get the criminal justice system working together as a team, the police and all others in the process must communicate with one another. They must execute their roles to keep adults and juveniles from being enmeshed in the criminal justice process. Alcohol and drug abuse centers are examples of areas that require a tremendous team effort.

Other recommendations Some of the about 50 program recommendations are: the deployment of officers; use of communication equipment; command and control; developing specialists; resources development; combination of services; developing intelligence information; use of civilian personnel; personnel development; and the administration of promotions.

Current trends within police work

Many of these recommendations are already into effect in various law enforcement agencies throughout the country. Police are becoming more and more aware that they cannot fight crime alone and are enlisting community support. Volunteer neighborhood security programs of the type suggested by the Commission are known by a variety of names, such as theft guard, crime stop, and crime watch. Many cities with the aid of their police departments have set up neighborhood security programs known as block house programs. A block house is a home situation in a residential area where children walking to and from school or en route to some other location may seek refuge if a suspicious person follows them. They may also use the block house to report suspicious incidents or emergencies. Residents of the block houses are screened by the police. After a screening process, a poster is placed on the door or window of the house so a child may clearly identify its location. Ideally, a block house should be located in each residential block.

Crime prevention through environmental design is another suggestion made by the Commission, which has been implemented in Portland, Oregon. Federal funding provided financial backing and police, urban planners, architects, and sociologists worked together to create a safer city core area. Other cities are beginning to realize the impact that police might have on urban planning in an effort to reduce crime and vandalism throughout their communities.

Further citizen involvement with the police has taken place with the establishment of citizen advisory boards. These advisory boards are not to be confused with citizen review boards, which review complaints against police officers and procedures. Citizen advisory boards work with members of the police departments to discuss community needs and areas of public concern. Through these discussions the police are able to determine the needs and feelings of the community and to respond to those needs as they are identified. If the board and police department members are effective in working together, this channel also provides an opportunity for citizens to understand police practices and limitations. In establishing this two-way communication and accessibility, police can reduce some of the potential problem areas that often arise through misunderstanding. It is essential that the advisory board members represent all segments of the community.

Some police departments have attempted to use citizens in a review board capacity. Various opinions have been expressed about the advantages and disadvantages of citizens serving in this capacity. Perhaps the largest concern is expressed by the police officers themselves. Most officers feel that citizens would not understand the circumstances that can arise out of the police officers' position, that citizens might unduly criticise or overreact to certain situations. Citizens, on the other hand, feel that this gives the people of the community a better way to control and regulate the policies of the police department in their community.

In addition to the increasing trend of utilizing citizens in advisory and review boards, police are also using civilian personnel in many capacities within the police department, in tasks that were previously handled by uniformed personnel. More police officers are thus allowed to return to the occupations for which they were specifically trained and hired, while allowing civilians trained in computer operation, bookeeping, laboratory analysis, personnel and management skills to fill these positions within the police department.

Innovative professional police departments are also beginning to break away from the paramilitary organizational structure and rank hierarchy that has existed for many years in law enforcement agencies. This is partly being accomplished by a trend in participatory management. In essence, participatory management is the involvement of more officers and personnel in the departmental decision-making process. Although this process has traditionally been performed by the top management in police departments, the trend has been to involve civilian employees, sergeants, and patrol officers in decision-making. The initial thrust toward this involvement may have been brought about by the increasing power of organized police unions and bargaining agents.

The power of these unions has become more apparent in recent years, as many agencies with union backing have begun flexing their muscles for more pay and increasing fringe benefits (see Figure 16-1). Police departments seem to want a tough union.[1]

Some cities are fearful of these unions, and as a result have incorporated provisions into their city charters making it illegal for police or public safety officers to strike. In August 1977 firemen in Dayton, Ohio, decided to strike in order to achieve a 6.9 percent pay raise and a reduction in

[1]"As Teamsters Step Up the Drive to Unionize the Police," *U.S. News and World Report*, Oct. 4, 1976, pp. 85–88.

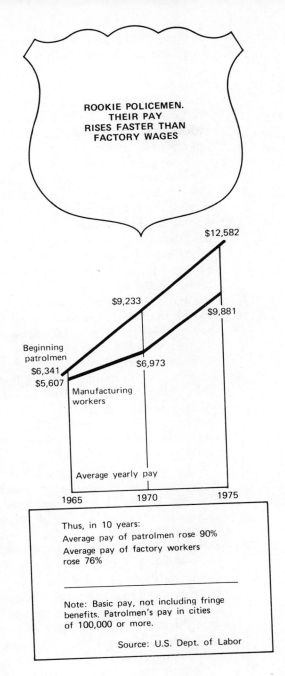

ROOKIE POLICEMEN.
THEIR PAY
RISES FASTER THAN
FACTORY WAGES

$12,582

$9,233

$9,881

Beginning
patrolmen
$6,341

$6,973

$5,607

Manufacturing
workers

Average yearly pay

1965   1970   1975

Thus, in 10 years:
Average pay of patrolmen rose 90%
Average pay of factory workers
rose 76%

Note: Basic pay, not including fringe
benefits. Patrolmen's pay in cities
of 100,000 or more.

Source: U.S. Dept. of Labor

Figure 16-1

Source: *U.S. News and World Report*, October 4, 1976.

working hours from 52 hours to 48 hours. During the three-day strike 1 fires burned, destroying homes and other buildings. One hundred police officers in the same city called in sick, apparently in support of the fire fighters' strike. The question of unions becomes a two-sided coin for public safety officers when we realize the impact that a strike can have on the welfare of the civilian population. Yet we realize that if police are unable to strike as do other public employees, they might not be able to achieve the strength required to negotiate their demands.

The demands that police are negotiating, however, may not be keeping abreast of the demands for their services throughout the community. The continuously rising crime rate has pitted police officers against an advancing tide of lawbreakers. In an effort to control the rapid growth of crime, police agencies are employing the use of sophisticated equipment and technology to help stem the tide. For example, large metropolitan areas are finding the use of helicopters useful in detection and apprehension of crimes and criminals. More and more computerized technology is being used more intelligently by police departments. Computers are becoming an essential element in data-gathering and information services used by police agencies. Computerized communications systems are also being used by many departments nationwide. In an effort to increase efficiency in the field, police are beginning to have some of this computerized technology available to them at a moment's notice. Units of computerized equipment are being installed in patrol cars, which enables the police officer in the field to retrieve information from the National Crime Information Center (NCIC) without having to go through police headquarters or the communications center. This saves radio transmittal time and also prevents persons who monitor police calls from being able to intercept some transmitted information.

Perhaps the most significant trend in police work, however, is the enormous shift in emphases toward crime prevention rather than crime fighting. Statistical analyses have repeatedly shown that police are not extremely effective in solving crime or apprehending criminals. It is hoped that by spending more money and man hours on crime prevention, a reduction in crime will occur, which would create a more successful image for the police. Crime prevention is an inclusive term for any number of programs that aid in deterring criminals from committing crimes. We have already mentioned some of these programs; crime stop, theft guard, block houses. In addition, police officers specializing in crime prevention meet with businessmen and private citizens to discuss securing their property with solid locks and the installation of alarms that are monitored at the police department.

Prevention may also come in the form of specialized units being used as spearheads against specific crimes, such as mugging, burglary, vice, and narcotics. Law enforcement agencies are also organizing other units to work directly in the public schools. These school-liasion units work primarily as resource units rather than as enforcement agents, although this may vary from department to department. Officers attached to these units are assigned to a number of specific schools, and in some cases assigned to one school if it is a high school. Police officers at the school become involved in many of the school functions, and some are teaching classes in criminal justice to the students as part of the curriculum.

Recommendations for judicial reform

Largely because of a rapid population expansion and the development of a legalistic society, the workload of our judicial system has increased tremendously over the past few years. Unfortunately, developments and improvements in the day-to-day administrative functions of the courts have not kept pace with the rapid increase in workload. In concise terms, most courts need study, structural overhaul, and reform.

Because the court system has evolved over a period of many years, the methods employed to deal with its problems have largely been piecemeal. There has been little systematic planning and development. In many jurisdictions, problems have not been dealt with effectively and, in some cases, they have not even been identified.

Attempts to improve the quality of criminal justice that ignore the courts, prosecutors, and defenders will fall short of their objectives. There is a need for future developments that will aid the entire process. The following items discussed briefly are only a few of many suggestions for judicial reform.

Reduction of delay The reduction of congestion and undesirable delay has a high priority, since it involves all levels of the judicial process. Also, because the courts must hear both civil and criminal cases, problems of civil delay are related to problems of criminal delay. Furthermore, the guarantees of a fair and speedy trial are more than a constitutional mandate; they are essential to effective criminal justice.

The effective management of existing resources is essential to the reduction of delay. Calendar management experts and supporting staff could be established to provide the necessary expertise for dealing with complex calendar problems. Present calendaring practices should be examined to develop more effective procedures. A program to conduct a training conference on calendar management for court administrators and presiding judges would be a useful tool.

The courts should develop rules or laws regarding continuances, which will promote speedier trials. Stern enforcement of these requirements should reduce the number of continuances granted for frivolous or insubstantial reasons.

Training of judges and court executives The training of judges in the conduct of trials and administration of the courts should be enhanced. Continuing education of the judiciary is of critical importance to the improvement of courts, prosecution, and law reform. Training programs and conferences should be developed for court executives also, to aid in the development of a comprehensive body of court management theory, and of the standards, qualifications, and functions of court executives.

Using technology Judicial participants have been slow in adopting technological advances. Significant time is wasted in processing large amounts of paper through traditional methods: computerized case scheduling and calendaring systems could provide a speedier system for the court. This system would make it possible for the judge or administrator in charge of the calendar to monitor the flow of cases, measure cases against fixed standards or timetables for disposition, and assign priorities among cases. The system could allow identification of those cases that have not met time standards at various stages of the trial process, and thus facilitate the flow of cases.

A videotape examination of witnesses could be experimented with. This might reduce the court time spent examining witnesses; allow witnesses to testify at their convenience; and would eliminate the possiblity of the jury hearing inadmissible testimony.

Electronic data-processing techniques could be developed for the operation of the courts. A study may produce a modular integrated court information system adaptable to use in small, medium, and large courts.

Other recommendations Additional items that may be developed are: court administrators for larger courts would become involved with general management, personnel management, and data management; alternatives to grand jury and preliminary hearings that would be aimed at reducing the present unnecessary consumption of time; crime-charging standards to develop uniform police reporting and prosecutor charging, uniform citations, and pleading and practice forms; increased use of citation to district attorneys with informal, voluntary probation by the police; judicial workload studies and the development of standards; and not last in any regard—the legislative changes in existing law.

Two areas that are receiving great attention today that must be dealt with, both legislatively and judicially, are pretrial release programs and preventive detention. Pretrial release programs have done much to alleviate inequities in the bail system. These programs have conclusively proven their success, effectiveness, and value: they result in substantial human and monetary savings to the public and to local agencies. Preventive detention is a complex issue which must be considered realistically. The major problem is to codify the categories of persons to be detained by the court. These and other programs that have been described can be developed in the future to the benefit of the entire process and society.

In addition to these suggestions for judicial reform, the National Advisory Committee also made several recommendations for the courts which are discussed on the following pages.

The subcommittee set forth the major components of the court procedure to include judiciary, prosecution, defense, and court administration. It viewed each component in terms of changes that could be implemented to reduce crime on a national scale. The committee developed programs for: screening; diversion; negotiated plea; the litigated case; sentencing; review of the trial court proceedings; the judiciary; the lower courts; court administration; the prosecutor; and the defense. Within these major items are 50 programs for the improvement of the total court's effort.

Screening Screening is the action taken before formal entry into the process; diversion, after some of the formal action of the process has started. The subcommittee indicated that an accused should be screened out of the criminal justice process when the benefits gained from prosecution or diversion would be outweighed by the costs of such action. Screening standards should be developed so that they can identify the cases when a person would not be taken into custody.

Diversion Diversion programs can be developed that would state the categories to be selected. No program should impair the impact that criminal punishment may have. The person subject to diversion must offer some hope of rehabilitation as a protection against the commission of further crimes.

Negotiated pleas A strong position was taken against plea bargaining, yet there is a need to develop some form of negotiated plea with uniform policies and practices. These standards or guidelines must take into consideration the impact of the plea on society, the offender, and his rehabilitation.

Sentencing Sentencing of offenders is an important aspect of the process, crucial both to society and the defendant. The reaction of the defendant to a sentence can materially affect the outcome of a rehabilitation program. The feeling was expressed that juries should be removed from the sentencing procedure and that courts should be required to impose the sentences provided by statute.

Review of proceedings The committee sees the need for improvement for: unified proceedings in review; dispositional time in reviewing court decisions; further review at all levels in prior adjudication; and prior factual determination.

Judicial selection Judicial selection should be based on merit. Although this may seem obvious, the committee stated that selection procedures must be aggressive in seeking out the best qualified individuals to sit on the bench. In addition, after the selections are made, judges should be subject to discipline or removal from office for reasons that would interfere with the performance of their duties.

Other recommendations The subcommittee has made recommendations for: the unification of state court systems; state court administrators; local and regional trial court administrators; case flow management; professional standards for prosecuting attorneys; public presentation of convicted offenders; and workload and salaries for public defenders. All of these are worthy of study, development, and implementation for the benefit of the courts and society.

Trends in the courts

One current trend might aid in the streamlining process; that is, the reduction of required jurors from 12 to 6 in limited jurisdictions. Other jurisdictions are implementing the concept that jurors may reach a decision without a unanimous vote. Six states are currently operating under this plan. The state of Oregon requires that 10 out of 12 jurors reach the same decision in all felony cases with the exception of murder, which requires a unanimous vote. Other states that are using this variation in unanimous decisions require no less than 10 of the 12 members to reach the same conclusion about the defendant's innocence or guilt. A few of these states allow only one juror out of the 12 to differ in his opinion about the verdict.

Some communities are also requiring police officers to serve as their own lawyers in presenting cases in court concerning minor violations. This frees county and city prosecutors to spend more of their time on major criminal cases and to help clear the court backlog. Along with police acting as their own attorneys, private citizens who are unable to afford attorneys are not getting the benefit of free counsel in traffic cases and minor misdemeanors. They must also present their own cases in court.

In an effort to reduce the mounting population in federal and state penitentiaries and local jails, the courts are increasingly using restitution as an alternative means to incarceration. Not only is restitution helping to reduce the tremendous overcrowding in our institutions, but it is also beginning to repay the victim who has long been overlooked by our criminal justice system.

Trends within correctional procedures

Corrections has received much publicity in recent years. The discovery of improper treatment, lack of facilities, riots, and formation of prisoner and citizen groups have done much to spotlight the correctional situation. The attention noted here refers to those in custody, who are only one-third of those to be affected. Probation and parole have also attracted considerable criticism.

Treatment programs in correctional institutions are being expanded. Some are experimental and quite controversial; others, although experimental, are more acceptable to society. In the general field of probation and parole there are diversion programs in which, rather than admit the guilty individual into an institutional program, he may be diverted before trial into remedial programs to convert his behavior patterns. A probation subsidy program in California, which has been under fire since 1970, provides a payment to a jurisdiction to keep a person on probation rather than send him to a state prison. The controversy centers around the fact that payment is taken and the individual is kept in the community, and both are considered detrimental to society.

Halfway houses are being used in many areas to reintroduce an inmate to society. The inmate is released several weeks or months before his expected discharge from an institution to a "house" on the outside. The inmate gets employment, but is supervised in the house—halfway between custody and final release. Other treatment programs include weekend release and work furlough. The weekend program entails releasing an inmate into his community for a period of 48 to 72 hours when he is close to his final release date. Work furlough is employed in many areas, and has been extended to selected inmates where the risk is minimal. When an inmate meets given criteria, he maintains a job during the week, but he spends the remainder of his time in a custodial situation receiving further education and therapy. His wages are handled by the institution.

One of the major points of change in the field of corrections concerns its physical facilities. Most state and federal prisons built in the past have been large brick and mortar units housing many hundreds of inmates. These units have been described in many accounts over the past few years as breeding places for crime. Violence has broken out in numerous prisons because of overcrowded and dehumanizing conditions.

Overcrowding is so crucial in Louisiana and Maryland that they have been forced to convert old naval ships into temporary facilities to house prisoners. The Law Enforcement Assistance Administration loaned 475 trailers to the states of Arizona, Arkansas, Louisiana, Michigan, Missouri, New Jersey, New York, Oklahoma, Pennsylvania, and Virginia in September of 1975 to help ease the crowded conditions in those states' institutions. The federal prison population was reported in 1976 to be operating at 21 percent over its capacity. In the same year Texas reported it had beds for only 19,500 convicts and expected 21,000 inmates by the next year. Two hundred inmates in Florida are forced to live in tents to alleviate the overpopulation there, and in Maine 400 prisoners are living on an area built for 250.

A concerted effort is now being made to reduce the size of the units or institutions and to deploy the units into the community. Some of the goals are that a unit should not house more than 200 persons, and that the housing be a vastly different configuration of buildings than the existing ones. Furthermore, the need for family and community involvement suggests that the units be located in the area in which the inmates normally reside. The contention is that the family and friends can help in the rehabilitative process, if the smaller units are in the community.

Rather than the traditional cell-block concept, more recent designs provide for fewer persons to be placed in the same close proximity to one another. The design also includes more space for varied programs, such as education, training, and counseling activities. The American Institute of Architects has taken an active role in the development of new designs after discussing the needs with progressive institutional administrators.

Conjugal visits (married inmates meeting in private with their spouses) is a program that has received wide attention outside of the United States and is now being promoted in this country. And programs in which either corrections personnel or volunteers transport families to institutions for visits are also in the experimental stage. These programs require more facilities, equipment, and personnel, but they will probably be more widely used in the future.

Educational programs—remedial, formal, or vocational—will receive more attention. Each of these can be of benefit to those who are willing to accept and participate in the programs. The expectation is that they will reduce recidivism in violations of the law.

Aside from these upcoming changes which are slowly taking place in the correctional field that we have already mentioned, the National Advisory Committee made additional recommendations with regard to this segment of the criminal justice system.

Recommendations for corrections

Sixty-three recommendations covered all aspects of corrections. The emphasis was on developing standards for the following: the right of the offender; diversion; pretrial release and detention; sentencing; offender classification; corrections and the community; juvenile intake and detention; local adult institutions; probation; major institutions; parole; manpower; research and development, information and statistics; and statutory framework. Although some of the standards may seem minor, when the corrections procedure is viewed nationally, it becomes apparent that many rather simple or minor items have not been dealt with in a great many institutions or by correctional personnel.

One standard suggests that each correctional unit develop and implement policies and procedures that fulfill the right of persons under supervision to have free access to the court. People under supervision have the right to access to the following: challenge the legality of conviction or confinement; seek redress for illegal conditions or treatment while under control; seek remedies in connection with civil problems; and seek all remedies against any one individual or group that violates the person's constitutional or statutory rights. The access is also to be extended for the person to receive all legal services.

A number of standards are recommended that relate to the person in custody, for health, welfare, and the protection of his rights. They can be described in a few words and are self-explanatory: healthful surroundings, searches, rules of conduct, discipline, grievance procedures, exercise of religious beliefs, and access to the public.

This subcommittee also had suggestions for standards on the subjects of diversion, pretrial release, pretrial detention, and alternatives to arrest. Again, this points up the need for active communication between police, courts, and corrections, each of whom has attitudes based on different perspectives. All recognize the twofold responsibility of the rehabilitation of the offender and the protection of society, with a common interest in sentencing.

Classification teams or committees should be established to provide the offender with meaningful programs: often the program that an offender is placed in does more harm than good. There is a need to develop the criteria to be used by classification committees composed of both professionals and the community.

Since the community becomes involved in many areas, a plan for community-based alternatives to confinement could prove helpful. This plan could specify the services to be provided directly by the correctional unit and those provided through community resources. This requires that the correctional process establish a good working relationship with major social institutions and agencies in the community.

Other areas of recommendation The committee also considered problems of juveniles, and it suggested standards for the police, juvenile intake, and diversion programs. It also suggested the need for legislation in this general area to enable the court to establish organized intake services. Juvenile detention, another field of attention, became involved because of the need to renovate facilities to accommodate intake.

Other standards thought to be helpful were in areas such as: total correctional systems planning; state operation and control of local institutions; service of probation; planning new institutions; parole grant hearings; community services for parolees; recruitment of personnel; evaluation of corrections; and corrections legislation.

A subcommittee of the Commission dealt with community crime prevention. The suggestions covered the need to organize, implement, and manage everyone's effort to reduce crime, delinquency, and recidivism. Although this same theme ran through the recommendations on police, courts, and correction, the Commission felt that this area had sufficient impact to develop a special public committee to emphasize its importance.

In spite of the concerted efforts of the National Advisory Committee to cite the needed improvements in corrections, plus federal moneys in support of the programs, the programs fall short of their stated goals. A few prison administrators realize that because of the limited manpower and resources actually available to them, they are unable to do anything more than to serve as a storehouse. An interesting survey done by Schnur in the 1950s documents the lack of means that institutions had to formulate a major rehabilitative thrust. Although this study was done in the middle fifties, follow-up surveys completed 10 years later concluded that little change had taken place. The picture for the seventies may not show much improvement. Schnur's report studied the number of personnel hired to keep and care for inmates in state and federal prisons and reformatories. The survey reports showed that there was a total number of 17,280 prison personnel and 161,587 inmates. Of the personnel, only 7.7 percent were classified as people who were "there to get them ready to go out and stay out," and many of these were clerical. There were 23 full-time psychiatrists, 67 psychologists and psychometrists, 96 institutional parole officers, 155 chaplains, and 257 caseworkers. They could provide an average of 82 seconds of psychiatric help each month, about 4 minutes of psychological attention, about 6 minutes of parole counseling, about 10 minutes of religious counseling, and 16 minutes of casework per month. There were 739 academic, vocational, and trade school teachers who averaged about 45 minutes per month for each inmate.[2]

With the tremendous push toward reducing prison populations and finding further diversion programs in order to keep one-time offenders out of the criminal justice system, we may see an improvement in this picture yet to come. With these improvements, we hope to see a more productive effort on the part of the community and criminal justice agencies to reintegrate inmates back into society as productive citizens.

Although the United States and many other countries are striving toward this goal, we see differences in opinion expressed by the actions of other countries toward their crime problems. For example, in Pakistan, the government has taken severe counter-measures against crime, including the orthodox Moslem punishment of amputating the hands of thieves. The chief of police was quoted as saying, "People are really terrified. We haven't even had any cases of disorderly conduct."

This situation illustrates the wide swing of the pendulum in the field of corrections. Today, in some areas of the world we see a trend toward rehabilitation; in other areas we see a return to punitive action. Although most states in our country are implementing community-based corrections and other new programs, we have seen a vast increase in the number of states reinstating the death penalty. The state of California was the latest state to reestablish the death penalty, in August 1977.

At the beginning of this chapter we discussed the impetus that the LEAA had on improving several aspects of the criminal justice process. However, many have challenged the LEAA program and its forerunner, the Office of Law Enforcement Assistance program, as being a waste of

[2]Alfred Schnur, "The New Penology: Fact or Fiction?" *The Journal of Criminal Law, Criminology, and Police Science*, Vol. 49., November-December 1958.

taxpayer funds. But there have been benefits from both programs. There has been the development of a planning capability for people involved in the entire system—a planned effort rather than one of response to crisis. If the federal dollars spent have achieved nothing more than getting the participants together, it is a tremendous plus for the entire process. It has been the Office of Law Enforcement Assistance and Law Enforcement Assistance Administration dollar programs that have produced some valuable studies. Some, such as project STAR, are still not complete.

Project STAR

Project STAR (Systems and Training Analysis of Requirements for Criminal Justice Systems Participants) was undertaken through a contract between the California Commission on Peace Officer Standards and Training (POST) and the American Justice Institute. The project includes California, Michigan, New Jersey, and Texas criminal justice personnel. It is based on the assumption that better identification of job requirements and improvement in the performance of operational criminal justice personnel will increase the effectiveness of the criminal justice system.

The project involves a comprehensive research effort to define roles, functions, and objectives, as well as knowledge and skill requirements for operational criminal justice personnel. In addition, the project will involve the development of recruitment and selection criteria and the design and demonstration of education and training modules predicated upon the findings of the research.

Objectives The project's objectives are to do the following: identify and describe the various roles of operational criminal justice personnel, identify major functions and formulate performance objectives for appropriate tasks; determine knowledge and skill requirements for operational criminal justice personnel, including police officers, probation or parole officers, custodial officers, prosecutors, defenders, and judges; formulate education and training recommendations related to these criminal justice personnel and the public; develop education and training modules that address those performance objectives not satisfied by existing education and training programs; demonstrate new or improved training modules in cooperation with local criminal justice agencies; and set forth implementation plans and procedures for a continuous assessment of knowledge and skill requirements, as well as changing job responsibilities for operational criminal justice personnel.

Personnel selection and training can be materially changed in the entire process with the exception of judicial selection. One small example can be shown in the police field. Presently, most police departments recruit all male sworn personnel from a single set of standards. This project could prove the feasibility as well as the advantages of various standards for selection of peace officer personnel, thereby drastically changing present selection procedures.

The training modules being developed in this project are based on empirical studies. Up until this time, most of the training in the criminal justice system has been based on "what we think we need to know." These new modules will not only make the participants more aware of what they need to know, but they will give them a real grasp of what they have learned. In addition, the modules can be used interchangeably by various elements of the system, easily adapted to the varying sophistication of the students.

Another benefit of STAR is that the criminal justice process will have its roles identified and clearly stated; something that many have talked about, some have undertaken, but none have accomplished. Once the roles are spelled out, selection of personnel can be made according to new criteria. This will have a profound impact on each subsection of the system. If duplication in roles can be eliminated and tasks assigned differently, the selection procedure will be of enormous significance. And when a person is employed in the system, there will be the need to provide a training package that not only prepares him for the direct assignment, but also provides cross-training in the entire system.

As STAR has developed, other activities have also been moving forward. Two programs that are receiving much attention are the employment of more females in the criminal justice system and the manner in which training and education are being delivered.

Affirmative action

The Equal Employment Opportunities Act became law in 1965. Until March 1972, the provisions of the EEOA applied principally to private industry employers but, after that date, it became applicable to all agencies within the United States. The federal agency responsible for the administration and enforcement of the Act is the Equal Employment Opportunity Commission.

Its purpose is to reinforce and secure the accepted personnel policy that all employment be made without regard to a person's race, color, religion, sex, or national origin. The EEOA specifies those actions that are discriminatory and unlawful, and it states procedures to insure compliance with the Act.

In the latter part of 1971, the Office of Federal Contract Compliance, the Equal Employment Opportunity Commission, and the Department of Labor adopted new regulations to develop and evaluate the good-faith effort required to transform programs from paper committments to equal employment opportunity. The new regulations were to be known as Revised Order No. 4 or Affirmative Action Programs, and they were made applicable to any agency contracting with the federal government with an employee population of 50 or more.

An affirmative action program does not function in a social, economic, or political vacuum. It must, in order to be truly effective, have complete support from all segments of the government and community. In addition, such a program must reaffirm the EEOA policies and goals. In concert with the EEOA, an effective affirmative action program is intended to accomplish the following objectives: to maximize the participation of persons who continue to suffer the effects of discrimination—because of race, color, religion, sex, or national origin—in the employment process through an active affirmative action program; to have, as an ultimate goal, an employee population that fairly and objectively represents the labor market population with regard to race, color, religion, sex, and national origin; to reaffirm the commitment that the agencies' decisions regarding employment and promotion shall be made on the basis of merit and valid job-related factors; to eliminate all artificial and arbitrary barriers to employment and promotion; to demonstrate that the employment actions of the agency are made without regard to a person's race, color, religion, sex, or national origin; and to provide a systematic ongoing procedure to evaluate the agencies' effectiveness in accomplishing the above.

There are several major elements in any of the programs in a jurisdiction. The activities start with total commitment by the policy-makers (legislators) and department heads of any jurisdiction. Classification is another element. This is the process of organizing jobs in a systematic manner to reflect similarities and differences in job title, duties, responsibilities, and employment qualifications in the form of class specifications. An accurate classification plan is used to establish internal salary relationships, establish recruitment and selection criteria, analyze and develop training programs, establish career ladders, and assist in general administrative and budget processes. This is usually the responsibility of the personnel department.

Recruitment and selection are the major goals of the program. Recruitment includes those procedures used to attract applicants for employment: selection involves those procedures used to evaluate and select applicants for referral to the appointing department head. The personnel department, with assistance from the respective justice system agency, is normally responsible for the implementation of the recruitmen and selection elements. After a person has been recruited, there is a need to appoint. The appointment process includes the offering of a position to an applicant and taking the necessary action for final processing. Department heads should accept the responsibility for the effective implementation of the affirmative action program for their agency. In the larger agencies the department head may select a responsible member of the management team to implement the program. The training process develops skills for improved performance through education and selected learning experiences. A personnel department can be responsible for the implementation of the training elements. Personnel rules and procedures should be developed for the jurisdiction; all personnel must be informed of their existence and meaning. There are normally two sets of rules and regulations one for the entire jurisdiction, the other for the separate agencies. Each program should be evaluated to make sure that the objectives and goals are being met and that the program is viable.

Women in criminal justice

Another effect that affirmative action may have had in criminal justice is the expansion of opportunities in employment for women and minority members. Since women have been employed in police work there has been controversy concerning their ability to be competent officers in the field or on patrol duty. Most police administrators and patrol officers agree that women are capable of handling most police functions. In fact, some say that the female officers often excel in detective work, in violent crimes against the person (assault, rape), and working with juveniles. However, if women are truly to be involved in police work, they must be accepted into all functions of police work, and that includes patrol duty. Most departments have realized this, and have employed hundreds of women in this capacity across the nation. Many studies have reported on the success of this innovation. One particularly noteworthy study, done in Washington, D.C. concluded that male and female officers on patrol had no significant differences in job performance and that it was appropriate to assign women to patrol duty on the same terms as men. The study further indicated that felony arrest rates were the same for newly hired police, both women and men. Women who had previously been employed in the department and who were later reassigned to patrol made fewer citations for moving traffic violations, but made felony and misdemeanor arrests at about the same rate as did their male counterparts.

Many departments will not employ women on patrol duty. The most consistent reason given by these departments is that they believe that women lack strength in violent confrontations. Women respond to this allegation by pointing out that most calls (90–95%) on patrol are not hazardous, and that when a female officer is present, people frequently react differently so that there is no need for physical prowess.

Recent studies compiled in California on the training of female athletes might provide a greater insight into this question. In starting their study, the researchers summarized that many females entering into athletic competition had not had the consistent training and coaching that their male counterparts had. They pointed out that women often did not have access to the training facilities men had, and during their earlier years had not participated in the strength-building activities that boys their age had. The women in this study were placed in rigid training schedules, including activities such as weight-building. At the termination of the study, researchers concluded that female athletes were competitive with male athletes in similar events. In events such as swimming and running, females were able to cut seconds off their time and close the gap between them and male swimmers and runners. Theoretically, the application of this study might apply to prospective female patrol officers and the necessary job-related skills that needed to be improved. This could be the end then of the continuing debate on whether women have the strength to deal effectively with violent situations when circumstances prove it necessary to do so.

Women are slowly becoming established in other segments of the criminal justice system. For instance, in the courts, women have consistently objected to the lack of female appointments to the bench. The National Organization for Women (NOW) has urged President Carter to appoint a woman to the Supreme Court during the next vacancy. Other states, feeling the pressure from women's groups and recognizing the lack of their membership in the judiciary, are appointing and recommending women for significant posts in the courts. However, these positions become available slowly, and it may take many years for woman to become firmly established in the courts.

In corrections, some experimentation concerning increased job opportunities for women is taking place. For example, the Department of Corrections in California is employing females to work as correctional officers in male institutions—in those areas that do not invade the privacy of the males.

One midwestern institution for men hired women to work in the same capacity as do male guards. This resulted in a great deal of controversy and a court injunction regarding the propriety of female guards strip-searching male inmates. It is not certain that the trend of women in this capacity will continue. However, it is certain that more women will be employed in the correctional field as probation and parole officers and as prison guards in some limited areas.

Education techniques

A revolution is taking place in educational techniques. These are gradually being applied to the training of criminal justice personnel. Multimedia is the catchphrase used to describe methods being used for the presentation of educational materials. Some of the multimedia programs have been in existence for years in business and industry and should be adapted to criminal justice. Videotape, 16mm film, 35mm film, tape recording, computers, and others should all be used for training in criminal justice. The future will bring to the participant individually tailored training modules by the use of these methods.

In spite of the innovations taking place in criminal justice, whether it be the police, courts, or corrections, we will not know for several years whether the innovations and recommendations are trends or merely fads being used as stop-gap measures to deal with crime. One thing for certain is that crime is not a trend or fad, but a phenomenon of our society.

Summary and prospects for the future

The 1960s brought the attention of the public to the criminal justice system. This public attention brought with it federal and state money for the system. This money allowed many different programs to be initiated. One such program is STAR.

Project STAR was undertaken through a contract between the California Council on Criminal Justice, the California Commission on Peace Officer Standards and Training, and the American Justice Institute. Project STAR is based on the assumption that a better identification of job requirements and an improvement in the performance of operational criminal justice personnel will increase the effectiveness of the criminal justice system. The project involves a comprehensive research effort to define roles, functions and objectives, as well as knowledge and skill requirements for operational criminal justice personnel. One program that is receiving attention in STAR is the employment of women in the entire criminal justice system.

Corrections has also received a great deal of publicity in recent years. A great many programs are now underway in the field of corrections. Work release, halfway houses, and other programs are constantly being viewed.

There is also a concerted effort being made to equalize employment opportunities. In concert with the EEOA, an effective affirmative action program has been started to provide for equal opportunity for employment for all.

The judiciary has been plagued by the same problems as the other branches of the criminal justice system. They suffer from a lack of training, insufficient manpower, and a lack of funds. However, programs are underway to correct some of these problems.

The National Advisory Commission on Criminal Justice Standards and Goals had as its objective the reduction of crime through a combined effort of all in the criminal justice process. The Commission did not effect new research, but viewed data already collected. They have released several recommendations with more to follow. These recommendations cover all phases of the criminal justice system.

This book in its entirety sets forth the tone of what needs to be done in the future. Each of the chapters makes suggestions for those in the criminal justice process. One recurrent theme throughout is the need within each subsection of the process to turn the process into a real system. This is probably the greatest single challenge. If each of the suggestions or recommendations of this book are viewed objectively, it should be obvious that a systems approach is needed, if many of the problems of the process are to be solved and eliminated. The future must develop personnel that are working together to make a system and personnel that are working with society to make it a system.

In an effort to deal with the challenge of crime in modern society, the process must develop and make use, as fully as possible, of modern scientific and technological advances. Of extreme importance is the need to develop data-gathering coordination. A criminal justice information system that can provide comprehensive, up-to-date information on which policy, programs, procedures, and management decisions can be made for the entire process is an absolute necessity.

Everyone must realize their responsibility. The process can gear up, reduce delay, and perform hundreds of other activities, but society must reassert its emphasis on the individual's responsibility for his conduct and the conduct of others. If there is a refusal to obey, there should be a certainty of punishment. Besides protecting the rights of the accused, we must remember the rights of the rest of society. Each person in our society has the right to expect to be able to live and work in safety without the threat against his person or property.

It is often said that the final goal of criminal justice is to reduce crime, delinquency, and recidivism. To ascertain the truth is the constitutional role of the courts, and they should be restored to this activity. Future participants in the system can arrest those practices that contribute to delay in the courts, that abuse technicalities of the law, and that encourage lawlessness. These must be replaced by a method to assure equal, fair, speedy, and certain justice.

All of the suggestions mentioned in this book can be achieved: better law enforcement, efficient corrections, and certain justice can all be accomplished. Crime, delinquency, and recidivism can be greatly reduced without the system developing a "police state." Effective criminal justice guarantees individual freedom, and it will also provide domestic tranquility.

TOPICS FOR DISCUSSION

1. Discuss the aspects and benefits of project STAR.

2. Discuss the impact of the results of the National Advisory Commissions' recommendations.

3. Discuss the hypocrisy of rehabilitation in corrections in conjunction with the return of the death penalty.

4. In your opinion, what is the single greatest area of reform related to the criminal justice system?

5. Discuss the future role of women in the criminal justice system.

Appendix A

THE CONSTITUTION OF THE UNITED STATES OF AMERICA

We the People of the United States, in Order to form a more perfect Union, establish Justice, insure domestic Tranquility, provide for the common defence, promote the general Welfare, and secure the Blessings of Liberty to ourselves and our Posterity, do ordain and establish this Constitution for the United States of America.

ARTICLE I

Section 1. All legislative Powers herein granted shall be vested in a Congress of the United States, which shall consist of a Senate and House of Representatives.

Section 2. The House of Representatives shall be composed of Members chosen every second Year by the People of the several States, and the Electors in each State shall have the Qualifications requisite for Electors of the most numerous Branch of the State Legislature.

No Person shall be a Representative who shall not have attained to the age of twenty five Years, and been seven Years a Citizen of the United States, and who shall not, when elected, be an Inhabitant of that state in which he shall be chosen.

Representatives and direct Taxes shall be apportioned among the several States which may be included within this Union, according to their respective Numbers, which shall be determined by adding to the whole Number of free Persons, including those bound to Service for a Term of Years, and excluding Indians not taxed, *three fifths of all other persons.*[1] The actual Enumeration shall be made within three Years after the first Meeting of the Congress of the United States, and within every subsequent Term of ten Years, in such Manner as they shall by Law direct. The Number of Representatives shall not exceed one for every thirty Thousand, but each State shall have at Least one Representative; and until such enumeration shall be made, the State of New Hampshire shall be entitled to choose three, Massachusetts eight, Rhode-Island and Providence Plantations one, Connecticut five, New-York six, New Jersey four, Pennsylvania eight, Delaware one, Maryland six, Virginia ten, North Carolina five, South Carolina five, and Georgia three.

When vacancies happen in the Representation from any State, the Executive Authority thereof shall issue Writs of Election to fill such Vacancies.

The House of Representatives shall choose their Speaker and other Officers; and shall have the sole Power of Impeachment.

Section 3. The Senate of the United States shall be composed of two Senators from each State, *chosen by the Legislature thereof,*[2] for six Years; and each Senator shall have one Vote.

Immediately after they shall be assembled in Consequence of the first Election, they shall be divided as equally as may be into three Classes. The Seats of the Senators of the first Class shall be vacated at the Expiration of the second Year, of the Second Class at the Expiration of the fourth Year, and of the third Class at the Expiration of the sixth Year, so that one third may be chosen every second Year; *and if Vacancies happen by Resignation, or otherwise, during the Recess of the Legislature of any State, the Executive thereof may make temporary Appointments until the next Meeting of the Legislature, which shall then fill such Vacancies.*[3]

No Person shall be a Senator who shall not have attained to the Age of thirty Years, and been nine Years a Citizen of the United States, and who shall not, when elected, be an Inhabitant of the State for which he shall be chosen.

The Vice President of the United States shall be President of the Senate, but shall have no Vote, unless they be equally divided.

The Senate shall choose their other Officers, and also a President pro tempore, in the Absence of the Vice President, or when he shall exercise the Office of President of the United States.

The Senate shall have the sole Power to try all Impeachments. When sitting for that Purpose, they shall be on Oath or Affirmation. When the President of the

---

[1]Italics indicate passages altered by subsequent Amendments. This was revised by the Sixeenth (apportionment of taxes) and Fourteenth (determination of persons) Amendments.

[2]Revised by Seventeenth Amendment.

[3]Revised by Seventeenth Amendment.

United States is tried, the Chief Justice shall preside: And no Person shall be convicted without the Concurrence of two thirds of the Members present.

Judgment in Cases of Impeachment shall not extend further than to removal from Office, and disqualification to hold and enjoy any Office of honor, Trust or Profit under the United States: but the Party convicted shall nevertheless be liable and subject to Indictment, Trial, Judgment and Punishment, according to Law.

Section 4. The Times, Places and Manner of holding Elections for Senators and Representatives, shall be prescribed in each State by the Legislature thereof; but the Congress may at any time by Law make or alter such Regulations, except as to the Places of choosing Senators.

The Congress shall assemble at least once in every Year, and such Meeting shall be *on the first Monday in December,*[4] unless they shall by Law appoint a different Day.

Section 5. Each House shall be the Judge of the Elections, Returns and Qualifications of its own Members, and a Majority of each shall constitute a Quorum to do Business; but a smaller Number may adjourn from day to day, and may be authorized to compel the Attendance of absent Members, in such Manner, and under such Penalties as each House may provide.

Each House may determine the Rules of its Proceedings, punish its Members for disorderly Behavior, and, with the Concurrence of two thirds, expel a Member.

Each House shall keep a Journal of its Proceedings, and from time to time publish the same, excepting such Parts as may in their Judgment require Secrecy; and the Yeas and Nays of the Members of either House on any question shall, at the Desire of one fifth of those Present, be entered on the Journal.

Neither House, during the Session of Congress, shall, without the Consent of the other, adjourn for more than three days, nor to any other Place than that in which the two Houses shall be sitting.

Section 6. The Senators and Representatives shall receive a Compensation for their Services, to be ascertained by Law, and paid out of the Treasury of the United States. They shall in all Cases, except Treason, Felony and Breach of the Peace, be privileged from Arrest during their Attendance at the Session of their respective Houses, and in going to and returning from the same; and for any Speech or Debate in either House, they shall not be questioned in any other Place.

No Senator or Representative shall, during the Time for which he was elected, be appointed to any civil Office under the Authority of the United States, which shall have been created, or the Emoluments whereof shall have been increased during such time; and no Person holding any Office under the United States, shall be a Member of either House during his Continuance in Office.

Section 7. All Bills for raising Revenue shall originate in the house of Representatives; but the Senate may propose or concur with Amendments as on other Bills.

Every Bill which shall have passed the House of Representatives and the Senate, shall, before it become a Law, be presented to the President of the United States; if he approve he shall sign it, but if not he shall return it, with his Objections to that House in which it shall have originated, who shall enter the Objections at large on their Journal, and proceed to reconsider it. If after such Reconsideration two thirds of that House shall agree to pass the Bill, it shall be sent, together with the Objections, to the other House, by which it shall likewise be reconsidered, and if approved by two thirds of that House, it shall become a Law. But in all such Cases the Votes of both Houses shall be determined by Yeas and Nays, and the Names of the Persons voting for and against the Bill shall be entered on the Journal of each House respectively. If any Bill shall not be returned by the President within ten Days (Sundays excepted) after it shall have been presented to him, the Same shall be a Law, in like Manner as if he had signed it, unless the Congress by their Adjournment prevent its Return, in which Case it shall not be a Law.

Every Order, Resolution, or Vote to which the Concurrence of the Senate and House of Representatives may be necessary (except on a question of Adjournment) shall be presented to the President of the United States; and before the Same shall take Effect, shall be approved by him, or being disapproved by him, shall be repassed by two thirds of the Senate and House of Representatives, according to the Rules and Limitations prescribed in the Case of a Bill.

Section 8. The Congress shall have Power To lay and collect Taxes, Duties, Imposts and Excises, to pay the Debts and provide for the common Defence and general Welfare of the United States; but All Duties, Imposts and Excises shall be uniform throughout the United States;

To borrow Money on the credit of the United States;

To regulate Commerce with foreign Nations, and among the several States, and with the Indian Tribes;

[4]Revised by Twentieth Amendment.

To establish a uniform Rule of Naturalization, and uniform Laws on the subject of Bankruptcies throughout the United States;

To coin Money, regulate the Value thereof, and of foreign Coin, and fix the Standard of Weights and Measures;

To provide for the Punishment of counterfeiting the Securities and current Coin of the United States;

To establish Post Offices and post Roads;

To promote the Progress of Science and useful Arts, by securing for limited Times to Authors and Inventors the exclusive Right to their respective Writings and Discoveries;

To constitute Tribunals inferior to the Supreme Court;

To define and punish piracies and Felonies committed on the high Seas, and Offences against the Law of Nations;

To declare War, grant Letters of Marque and Reprisal, and make Rules concerning Captures on Land and Water;

To raise and support Armies, but no Appropriation of Money to that Use shall be for a longer Term than two Years;

To provide and maintain a Navy;

To make Rules for the Government and Regulations of the land and naval Forces;

To provide for calling forth the Militia to execute the Laws of the Union, suppress Insurrections and repel Invasions;

To provide for organizing, arming, and disciplining, the Militia, and for governing such Part of them as may be employed in the Service of the United States, reserving to the States respectively, the Appointment of the Officers, and the Authority of training the Militia according to the discipline prescribed by Congress;

To exercise exclusive Legislation in all Cases whatsoever, over such District (not exceeding ten Miles square) as may, be Cession of particular States, and the Acceptance of Congress, become the Seat of the Government of the United States, and to exercise like Authority over all Places purchased by the Consent of the Legislature of the State in which the Same shall be, for the Erection of Forts, magazines, Arsenals, dock-Yards, and other needful Buildings;—And

To make all Laws which shall be necessary and proper for carrying into Execution the foregoing Powers, and all other Powers vested by this Constitution in the Government of the United States, or in any Department or Officer thereof.

Section 9. The Migration or Importation of such Persons as any of the States now existing shall think proper to admit, shall not be prohibited by the Congress prior to the Year one thousand eight hundred and eight, but a Tax or duty may be imposed on such Importation, not exceeding ten dollars for each Person.

The Privilege of the Writ of Habeas Corpus shall not be suspended, unless when in Cases of Rebellion or Invasion the public Safety may require it.

No bill of Attainder or ex post facto Law shall be passed.

No Capitation, or other direct, Tax shall be laid, unless in Proportion to the Census or Enumeration herein before directed to be taken. [5]

No Tax or Duty shall be laid on Articles exported from any State.

No Preference shall be given by any Regulation of Commerce or Revenue to the Ports of one State over those of another: nor shall Vessels bound to, or from, one State, be obliged to enter, clear, or pay Duties in another.

No Money shall be drawn from the Treasury, but in Consequence of Appropriations made by Law; and a regular Statement and Account of the Receipts and Expenditures of all public Money shall be published from time to time.

No title of Nobility shall be granted by the United States: And no Person holding any Office of Profit or Trust under them, shall, without the Consent of the Congress, accept of any present, Emolument, Office, or Title, of any kind whatever, from any King, Prince, or foreign State.

Section 10. No State shall enter into any Treaty, Alliance, or Confederation; grant Letters of Marque and Reprisal; coin Money; emit Bills of Credit; make any Thing but gold and silver Coin a Tender in Payment of Debts; pass any Bill of Attainder, ex post facto Law, or Law impairing the Obligation of Contracts, or Grant any Title of Nobility.

No State shall, without the Consent of the Congress, lay any Imposts or Duties on Imports or Exports, except what may be absolutely necessary for executing its inspection Laws: and the net Produce of all Duties and Imposts, laid by any State on Imports or Exports, shall be for the Use of the Treasury of the United States; and all such Laws shall be subject to the Revision and Control of the Congress.

No State shall, without the Consent of Congress, lay any Duty of Tonnage, keep Troops, or Ships of War in time of Peace, enter into any Agreement or Compact

---

[5] Revised by Sixteenth Amendment.

with another State, or with a foreign Power, or engage in War, unless actually invaded, or in such imminent Danger as will not admit of delay.

ARTICLE II

Section 1. The executive Power shall be vested in a President of the United States of America. *He shall hold his Office during the Term of four Years,*[6] and, together with the Vice President, chosen for the same Term be elected as follows:

Each State shall appoint, in such Manner as the Legislature thereof may direct, a Number of Electors, equally to the whole Number of Senators and Representatives to which the State may be entitled in the Congress but no Senator or Representative, or Person holding an Office of Trust or Profit under the United States, shall be apointed an Elector.

The Electors shall meet in their respective States, and vote by Ballot for two Persons, of whom one at least shall not be an Inhabitant of the same State with themselves. And they shall make a List of all the Persons voted for, and of the Number of Votes for each; which List they shall sign and certify, and transmit sealed to the Seat of the Government of the United States, directed to the President of the Senate. The President of the Senate shall, in the Presence of the Senate and House of Representatives, open all the Certificates, and the Votes shall then be counted. The Person having the greatest Number of Votes shall be the President, if such Number be a Majority of the whole Number of Electors appointed; and if there be more than one who have such Majority, and have an equal Number of Votes, then the House of Representatives shall immediately choose by Ballot one of them for President; and if no Person have a Majority, then from the five highest on the List the said House shall in like Manner choose the President. But in choosing the President, the Votes shall be taken by States, the Representation from each State having one Vote; A quorum for this purpose shall consist of a Member or Members from two thirds of the States, and a Majority of all the States shall be necessary to a Choice. In every Case, after the Choice of the President, the Person having the greatest Number of Votes of the Electors shall be the Vice President. But if there should remain two or more who have equal Votes, the Senate shall choose from them by Ballot the Vice President.[7]

The Congress may determine the Time of choosing the Electors, and the Day on which they shall give their Votes; which Day shall be the same throughout the United States.

No Person except a natural born Citizen, or a Citizen of the United States, at the time of the Adoption of this Constitution, shall be eligible to the Office of President; neither shall any Person be eligible to that Office who shall not have attained to the Age of thirty five Years, and been fourteen Years a Resident within the United States.

In case of the Removal of the President from Office, or of his Death, Resignation, or Inability to discharge the Powers and Duties of the said Office, the Same shall devolve on the Vice President, and the Congress may by Law provide for the Case of Removal, Death, Resignation or Inability, both of the President and Vice President, declaring what Officer shall then act as President, and such Officer shall act accordingly, until the Disability be removed, or a President shall be elected.[8]

The President shall, at stated Times, receive for his Services, a Compensation which shall neither be increased nor diminished during the Period for which he shall have been elected, and he shall not receive within that Period any other Emolument from the United States, or any of them.

Before he enter on the Execution of his Office, he shall take the following Oath or Affirmation:—"I do solemnly swear (or affirm) that I will faithfully execute the Office of President of the United States, and will to the best of my Ability, preserve, protect and defend the Constitution of the United States."

Section 2. The President shall be Commander in Chief of the Army and Navy of the United States, and of the Militia of the several States, when called into the actual service of the United States; he may require the Opinion, in writing, of the principal Officer in each of the executive Departments, upon any Subject relating to the Duties of their respective Offices, and he shall have Power to grant Reprieves and Pardon for Offences against the United States, except in Cases of Impeachment.

He shall have Power, by and with the Advice and Consent of the Senate, to make Treaties, provided two thirds of the Senators present concur; and he shall nominate, and by and with the Advice and Consent of the Senate, shall appoint Ambassadors, and other public Ministers and Consuls, Judges of the supreme Court, and all other Officers of the United States, whose Ap-

[6]See Twenty-second Amendment.

[7]Superseded by Twelfth Amendment.

[8]Revised by Twenty-fifth Amendment.

pointments are not herein otherwise provided for, and which shall be established by Law: but the Congress may by Law vest the Appointment of such inferior Officers, as they think proper, in the President alone, in the Courts of Law, or in the Heads of Departments.

The President shall have Power to fill up all Vacancies that may happen during the Recess of the Senate, by granting Commissions which shall expire at the End of their next Session.

Section 3. He shall from time to time give to the Congress Information of the State of the Union, and recommend to their Consideration such Measures as he shall judge necessary and expedient; he may, on extraordinary Occasions, convene both Houses, or either of them, and in Case of Disagreement between them, with Respect to the Time of Adjournment, he may adjourn them to such Time as he shall think proper; he shall receive Ambassadors and other public Ministers, he shall take Care that the Laws be faithfully executed, and shall Commission all the Officers of the United States.

Section 4. The President, Vice President, and all civil Officers of the United States, shall be removed from Office on Impeachment for, and Conviction of Treason, Bribery, or other high Crimes and Misdemeanors.

ARTICLE III

Section 1. The judicial Power of the United States, shall be vested in one supreme Court and in such inferior Courts as the Congress may from time to time ordain and establish. The Judges, both of the supreme and inferior Courts, shall hold their Offices during good Behavior, and shall, at stated Times, receive for their Services, a Compensation, which shall not be diminished during their Continuance in Office.

Section 2. The judicial Power shall extend to all Cases, in Law and Equity, arising under this Constitution, the Laws of the United States, and Treaties made, or which shall be made, under their Authority:—to all Cases affecting Ambassadors, other public Ministers and Consuls: to all Cases of admiralty and maritime Jurisdiction:—to Controversies to which the United States shall be a Party;—to Controversies between two or more States;—*between a State and Citizens of another State:*—between Citizens of different States;— between Citizens of the same State claiming Lands under Grants of different States, *and between a State or the Citizens thereof, and foreign States, Citizens, or Subjects.*[9]

In all cases affecting Ambassadors, other public Ministers and Consuls, and those in which a State shall be Party, the supreme Court shall have original Jurisdiction. In all the other Cases before mentioned, the supreme Court shall have appellate Jurisdiction, both as to Law and Fact, with such Exceptions, and under such Regulations as the Congress shall make.

The Trial of all Crimes, except in Cases of Impeachment, shall be by Jury; and such trial shall be held in the State where the said Crimes shall have been committed; but when not committed within any State, the Trial shall be at such Place or Places as the Congress may be Law have directed.

Section 3. Treason against the United States, shall consist only in levying War against them, or in adhering to their Enemies, giving them Aid and Comfort. No Person shall be convicted of Treason unless on the Testimony of two Witnesses to the same overt Act, or on Confession in open Court.

The Congress shall have Power to declare the Punishment of Treason, but no Attainder of Treason shall work Corruption of Blood, or Forfeiture except during the Life of the Person attainted.

ARTICLE IV

Section 1. Full Faith and Credit shall be given in each State to the public Acts, Records, and judicial Proceedings of every other State. And the Congress may by general Laws prescribe the Manner in which such Acts, Records, and Proceedings shall be proved, and the Effect thereof.

Section 2. The Citizens of each State shall be entitled to all Privileges and Immunities of Citizens in the several States.

A Person charged in any State with Treason, Felony, or other Crime, who shall flee from Justice, and be found in another State, shall on Demand of the executive Authority of the State from which he fled, be delivered up, to be removed to the State having Jurisdiction of the Crime.

No person held to Service or Labour in one State, under the Laws thereof, escaping into another, shall, in Consequence of any Law or Regulation therein, be discharged from such Service or Labour, but shall be delivered up on Claim of the Party to whom such Service or Labour may be due.[10]

Section 3. New States may be admitted by the Congress into this Union; but no new State shall be

[9]Revised by Eleventh Amendment.

[10]Superseded by Thirteenth Amendment.

ormed or erected within the Jurisdiction of any other State; nor any State be formed by the Junction of two or more States, or Parts of States, without the Consent of the Legislatures of the States concerned as well as of the Congress.

The Congress shall have Power to dispose of and make all needful Rules and Regulations respecting the Territory, or other Property belonging to the United States; and nothing in this Constitution shall be so construed as to Prejudice any claims of the United States, or of any particular State.

Section 4. The United States shall guarantee to every State in this Union a Republican Form of Government, and shall protect each of them against Invasion: and on Application of the Legislature, or of the Executive (when the Legislature cannot be convened) against Domestic Violence.

ARTICLE V

The Congress, whenever two thirds of both Houses shall deem it necessary, shall propose Amendments to this Constitution, or, on the Application of the Legislatures of two thirds of the several States, shall call a Convention for proposing Amendments, which, in either Case, shall be valid to all Intents and Purposes, as Part of this Constitution, when ratified by the Legislatures of three fourths of the several States, or by Conventions in three fourths thereof, as the one or the other Mode of Ratification may be proposed by the Congress; Provided that no Amendment which may be made prior to the Year One thousand eight hundred and eight shall in any Manner affect the first and fourth Clauses in the Ninth Section of the first Article; and that no State, without its Consent, shall be deprived of its equal Suffrage in the Senate.

ARTICLE VI

All Debts contracted and Engagements entered into, before the Adoption of this Constitution, shall be as valid against the United States under this Constitution, as under the Confederation.[11]

This Constitution, and the Laws of the United States which shall be made in Pursuance thereof; and all Treaties made, or which shall be made, under the Authority of the United States, shall be the supreme Law of the Land; and the Judges in every State shall be bound thereby, any Thing in the Constitution or Laws of any State to the Contrary notwithstanding.

[11]See Fourteenth Amendment, Section 4.

The Senators and Representatives before mentioned, and the Members of the several State Legislatures, and all executive and judicial Officers, both of the United States and of the several States, shall be bound by Oath or Affirmation, to support this Constitution; but no religious Test shall ever be required as a Qualification to any Office or public Trust under the United States.

ARTICLE VII

The Ratification of the Conventions of nine States, shall be sufficient for the Establishment of this Constitution between the States so ratifying the Same.

Done in Convention by the Unanimous Consent of the States present the Seventeenth Day of September in the Year of our Lord one thousand seven hundred and eighty seven and of the Independence of the United States of America the twelfth. In witness whereof We have hereunto subscribed our Names.

. . .

ARTICLES IN ADDITION TO, AND AMENDMENT OF, THE CONSTITUTION OF THE UNITED STATES OF AMERICA, PROPOSED BY CONGRESS, AND RATIFIED BY THE SEVERAL STATES, PURSUANT TO THE FIFTH ARTICLE OF THE ORIGINAL CONSTITUTION. (Ratification of the first ten Amendments was completed December 15, 1791.)

AMENDMENT I

Congress shall make no law respecting an establishment of religion, or prohibiting the free exercise thereof; or abridging the freedom of speech, or of the press; or the right of the people peaceably to assemble, and to petition the Government for a redress of grievances.

AMENDMENT II

A well regulated Militia, being necessary to the security of a free State, the right of the people to keep and bear Arms, shall not be infringed.

AMENDMENT III

No Soldier shall, in time of peace be quartered in any house, without the consent of the Owner, nor in time of war, but in a manner to be prescribed by law.

AMENDMENT IV

The right of the people to be secure in their persons, houses, papers, and effects, against unreasonable searches and seizures, shall not be violated, and no Warrants shall issue, but upon probable cause, supported by Oath or affirmation, and particularly describing the place to be searched, and the persons or things to be seized.

AMENDMENT V

No person shall be held to answer for a capital, or other infamous crime, unless on a presentment or indictment of a Grand Jury, except in cases arising in the land or naval forces, or in the Militia, when in actual service in time of War or public danger; nor shall any person be subject for the same offence to be twice put in jeopardy of life or limb; nor shall be compelled in any criminal case to be a witness against himself, nor be deprived of life, liberty, or property, without due process of law; nor shall private property be taken for public use, without just compensation.

AMENDMENT VI

In all criminal prosecutions, the accused shall enjoy the right to a speedy and public trial, by an impartial jury of the State and district wherein the crime shall have been committed, which district shall have been previously ascertained by law, and to be informed of the nature and cause of the accusation; to be confronted with the witnesses against him; to have compulsory process for obtaining witnesses in his favor, and to have the Assistance of Counsel for his defence.

AMENDMENT VII

In Suits at common law, where the value in controversy shall exceed twenty dollars, the right of trial by jury shall be preserved, and no fact tried by a jury, shall be otherwise reexamined in any Court of the United States, than according to the rules of the common law.

AMENDMENT VIII

Excessive bail shall not be required, nor excessive fines imposed, nor cruel and unusual punishments inflicted.

AMENDMENT IX

The enumeration in the Constitution, of certain rights, shall not be construed to deny or disparage others retained by the people.

AMENDMENT X

The powers not delegated to the United States b the Constitution, nor prohibited by it to the States, ar reserved to the States respectively, or to the people.

AMENDMENT XI (JANUARY 8, 1798)

The Judicial power of the United States shall not b construed to extend to any suit in law or equity, com menced or prosecuted against one of the United State by Citizens of another State, or by Citizens or Subjects c any Foreign State.

AMENDMENT XII (SEPTEMBER 25, 1804)

The Electors shall meet in their respective state and vote by ballot for President and Vice President, on of whom, at least, shall not be an inhabitant of the sam state with themselves; they shall name in their ballots th person voted for as President, and in distinct ballots th person voted for as Vice President, and they shall mak distinct lists of all persons voted for as President and o all persons voted for as Vice President, and of th number of votes for each, which lists they shall sign an certify, and transmit sealed to the seat of the governmen of the United States, directed to the President of th Senate;—The President of the Senate shall, in the pres ence of Senate and House of Representatives, open al the certificates and the votes shall then be counted;— The person having the greatest number of votes fo President, shall be the President, if such number be a majority of the whole number of Electors appointed; and if no person have such majority, then from the persons having the highest numbers not exceeding three on the list of those voted for as President, the House of Representatives shall choose immediately, by ballot, the President. But in choosing the President, the votes shal be taken by states, the representation from each state having one vote; a quorum for this purpose shall consist of a member or members from two-thirds of the states, and a majority of all the states shall be necessary to a choice. And if the House of Representatives shall not choose a President whenever the right of choice shal devolve upon them, *before the fourth day of March next following,*[12] then the Vice President shall act as President, as in the case of the death or other constitutional disability of the President.—The person having the greatest number of votes as Vice President shall be the Vice President, if such number be a majority of the whole

[12]Revised by the Twentieth Amendment.

umber of Electors appointed, and if no person have a
majority, then from the two highest numbers on the list,
he Senate shall choose the Vice President; a quorum
or the purpose shall consist of two-thirds of the whole
number of Senators, and a majority of the whole number
hall be necessary to a choice. But no person constitu-
onally ineligible to the office of President shall be eligi-
le to that of Vice President of the United States.

AMENDMENT XIII (DECEMBER 18, 1865)

Section 1. Neither slavery nor involuntary ser-
itude, except as a punishment for crime whereof the
arty shall have been duly convicted, shall exist within
he United States, or any place subject to their jurisdic-
on.

Section 2. Congress shall have the power to en-
orce this article by appropriate legislation.

AMENDMENT XIV (JULY 28, 1869)

Section 1. All persons born or naturalized in the
United States, and subject to the jurisdiction thereof, are
citizens of the United States and of the State wherein
hey reside. No State shall make or enforce any law
which shall abridge the privileges or immunities of citizens of the United States, nor shall any State deprive
any person of life, liberty, or property, without due process of law; nor deny to any person within its jurisdiction
he equal protection of the laws.

Section 2. Representatives shall be apportioned
among the several States according to their respective
numbers, counting the whole number of persons in each
State, excluding Indians not taxed. But when the right to
vote at any election for the choice of electors for President and Vice President of the United States, Represen-
atives in Congress, the Executive and Judicial officers
of a State, or the members of the Legislature thereof, is
denied to any of the male inhabitants of such State,
being twenty-one years of age, and citizens of the United
States, or in any way abridged, except for participation in
rebellion, or other crime, the basis of representation
therein shall be reduced in the proportion which the
number of such male citizens shall bear to the whole
number of male citizens twenty-one years of age in such
State.

Section 3. No person shall be a Senator or Representative in Congress, or elector of President and Vice
President, or hold any office, civil or military, under the
United States, or under any State, who, having previously taken an oath, as a member of Congress, or as an
officer of the United States, or as a member of any State
legislature, or as an executive or judicial officer of any
State, to support the Constitution of the United States,
shall have engaged in insurrection or rebellion against
the same, or given aid or comfort to the enemies thereof.
But Congress may by a vote of two thirds of each House,
remove such disability.

Section 4. The validity of the public debt of the
United States, authorized by law, including debts incurred for payment of pensions and bounties for services in
suppressing insurrection or rebellion, shall not be questioned. But neither the United States nor any State shall
assume or pay any debt or obligation incurred in aid of
insurrection or rebellion against the United States, or any
claim for the loss or emancipation of any slave; but all
such debts, obligations, and claims shall be held illegal
and void.

Section 5. The Congress shall have power to enforce by appropriate legislation, the provisions of this
article.

AMENDMENT XV (MARCH 30, 1870)

Section 1. The right of citizens of the United
States to vote shall not be denied or abridged by the
United States or by any State on account of race, color,
or previous conditions of servitude.

Section 2. The Congress shall have power to enforce this article by appropriate legislation.

AMENDMENT XVI (FEBRUARY 25, 1913)

The Congress shall have power to lay and collect
taxes on incomes, from whatever source derived, without apportionment among the several States, and without regard to any census or enumeration.

AMENDMENT XVII (MAY 31, 1913)

The Senate of the United States shall be composed
of two Senators from each State, elected by the people
thereof, for six years; and each Senator shall have one
vote. The electors in each State shall have the qualifications requisite for electors of the most numerous branch
of the State legislatures.

When vacancies happen in the representation of
any State in the Senate, the executive authority of such
State shall issue writs of election to fill such vacancies:
Provided, That the legislature of any State may em-
power the executive thereof to make temporary appointments until the people fill the vacancies by election
as the legislature may direct.

This amendment shall not be so construed as to affect the election or term of any Senator chosen before it becomes valid as part of the Constitution.

AMENDMENT XVIII (JANUARY 29, 1919)

Section 1. After one year from the ratification of this article the manufacture, sale, or transportation of intoxicating liquors within, the importation thereof into, or the exportation thereof from the United States and all territory subject to the jurisdiction thereof for beverage purposes is hereby prohibited.

Section 2. The Congress and the several States shall have concurrent power to enforce this article by appropriate legislation.

Section 3. This article shall be inoperative unless it shall have been ratified as an amendment to the Constitution by the legislatures of the several States, as provided in the Constitution within seven years from the date of the submission hereof to the States by the Congress.[13]

AMENDMENT XIX (AUGUST 26, 1920)

The right of citizens of the United States to vote shall not be denied or abridged by the United States or by any State on account of sex.

Congress shall have power to enforce this article by appropriate legislation.

AMENDMENT XX (FEBRUARY 6, 1933)

Section 1. The terms of the President and Vice President shall end at noon on the 20th day of January, and the terms of Senators and Representatives at noon on the 3rd day of January, of the years in which such terms would have ended if this article had not been ratified; and the terms of their successors shall then begin.

Section 2. The Congress shall assemble at least once in every year, and such meeting shall begin at noon on the 3rd day of January, unless they shall by law appoint a different day.

Section 3. If, at the time fixed for the beginning of the term of the President, the President elect shall have died, the Vice President elect shall become President. If a President shall not have been chosen before the time fixed for the beginning of his term, or if the President elect shall have failed to qualify, then the Vice President elect shall act as President until a President shall have

qualified; and the Congress may by law provide for the case wherein neither a President elect nor a Vice President elect shall have qualified, declaring who shall then act as President, or the manner in which one who is to act shall be selected, and such person shall act accordingly until a President or Vice President shall have qualified.

Section 4. The Congress may by law provide for the case of the death of any of the persons from whom the House of Representatives may choose a President whenever the right of choice shall have devolved upon them, and for the case of the death of any of the persons from whom the Senate may choose a Vice President whenever the right of choice shall have devolved upon them.

Section 5. Sections 1 and 2 shall take effect on the 15th day of October following the ratification of this article.

Section 6. This article shall be inoperative unless it shall have been ratified as an amendment to the Constitution by the legislatures of three-fourths of the several States within seven years from the date of its submission.

AMENDMENT XXI (DECEMBER 5, 1933)

Section 1. The eighteenth article of amendment to the Constitution of the United States is hereby repealed.

Section 2. The transportation or importation into any State, Territory, or possession of the United States for delivery or use therein of intoxicating liquors, in violation of the laws thereof, is hereby prohibited.

Section 3. This article shall be inoperative unless it shall have been ratified as an amendment to the Constitution by conventions in the several States, as provided in the Constitution, within seven years from the date of submission hereof to the States by the Congress.

AMENDMENT XXII (FEBRUARY 26, 1951)

Section 1. No person shall be elected to the office of the President more than twice, and no person who has held the office of President, or acted as President, for more than two years of a term to which some other person was elected President shall be elected to the office of President more than once. But this Article shall not apply to any person holding the office of President when this Article was proposed by the Congress, and shall not prevent any person who may be holding the office of President, or acting as President, during the term within which this Article becomes operative from holding the

---

[13]Repealed by the Twenty-first Amendment.

office of President or acting as President during the re-mainder of such term.

Section 2. This article shall be inoperative unless it shall have been ratified as an amendment to the Constitution by the legislatures of three-fourths of the several States within seven years from the date of its submission to the States by the Congress.

AMENDMENT XXIII (MARCH 29, 1961)

Section 1. The District constituting the seat of Government of the United States shall appoint in such manner as the Congress may direct:

A number of electors of President and Vice President equal to the whole number of Senators and Representatives in Congress to which the District would be entitled if it were a State, but in no event more than the least populous State; they shall be in addition to those appointed by the States, but they shall be considered, for the purposes of the election of President and Vice President, to be electors appointed by a State; and they shall meet in the District and perform such duties as provided by the twelfth article of amendment.

Section 2. The Congress shall have the power to enforce this article by appropriate legislation.

AMENDMENT XXIV (JANUARY 23, 1964)

Section 1. The right of citizens of the United States to vote in any primary or other election for President or Vice President, for electors for President or Vice President, or for Senator or Representative in Congress, shall not be denied or abridged by the President or any state by reason of failure to pay any poll tax or other tax.

Section 2. The Congress shall have the power to enforce this article by appropriate legislation.

AMENDMENT XXV (FEBRUARY 10, 1967)

Section 1. In the case of the removal of the President from office or of his death or resignation, the Vice President shall become President.

Section 2. Whenever there is a vacancy in the office of the Vice President, the President shall nominate a Vice President who shall take office upon confirmation by a majority vote of both Houses of Congress.

Section 3. Whenever the President transmits to the President pro tempore of the Senate and the Speaker of the House of Representatives his written declaration that he is unable to discharge the powers and duties of his office, and until he transmits to them a written declaration to the contrary, such powers and duties shall be discharged by the Vice President as Acting President.

Section 4. Whenever the Vice President and a majority of either the principal officers of the executive departments or of such other body as Congress may by law provide, transmit to the President pro tempore of the Senate and the Speaker of the House of Representatives their written declaration that the President is unable to discharge the powers and duties of his office, the Vice President shall immediately assume the powers and duties of the office as Acting President.

Thereafter, when the President transmits to the President pro tempore of the Senate and the Speaker of the House of Representatives his written declaration that no inability exists, he shall resume the powers and duties of his office unless the Vice President and a majority of either the principal officers of the executive departments or of such other body as Congress may by law provide, transmit within four days to the President pro tempore of the Senate and the Speaker of the House of Representatives their written declaration that the President is unable to discharge the powers and duties of his office. Thereupon Congress shall decide the issue, assembling within forty-eight hours for that purpose if not in session. If the Congress, within twenty-one days after receipt of the latter written declaration or, if Congress is not in session, within twenty-one days after Congress is required to assemble, determines by two-thirds vote of both Houses that the President is unable to discharge the powers and duties of his office, the Vice President shall continue to discharge the same as Acting President; otherwise, the President shall resume the powers and duties of his office.

AMENDMENT XXVI (JUNE 30, 1971)

Section 1. The right of citizens of the United States, who are eighteen years of age or older, to vote shall not be denied or abridged by the United States or any state on account of age.

Section 2. The Congress shall have the power to enforce this article by appropriate legislation.

Appendix B

A MODEL RULE FOR CERTIFYING POLICE AND CORRECTIONS OFFICERS, INCLUDING PROVISIONS FOR LAPSING OR REVOKING CERTIFICATION GRANTED

DEFINITIONS

a. "Council" means the Police Standards Council appointed pursuant to statute.

b. "Executive Director" means the Executive Director of the Council.

c. "Law Enforcement Unit" means a police force or organization of a city, county, port, or state whose primary duty, as prescribed by law or ordinance, is detecting crime and enforcing the criminal laws of this state or laws or ordinances relating to airport security; or the custody, control, or supervision of individuals convicted of or arrested for a criminal offense and confined to a place of incarceration or detention other than a place used exclusively for incarceration or detention of juveniles.

d. "Police Officer" means an officer or member of a law enforcement unit who is employed full time as a peace officer commissioned by a city, county, port, school district, mass transit district, or state; and who is responsible for enforcing the criminal laws of this state or laws or ordinances relating to airport security.

e. "Corrections Officer" means an officer or member of a law enforcement unit who is employed full time thereby and is charged with and actually performs the duty of custody, control, or supervision of individuals convicted of or arrested for a criminal offense and confined in a place of incarceration or detention other than a place used exclusively for incarceration or detention of juveniles.

f. "Certification" means the issuing of a certificate to a police or corrections officer upon documentation that the officer has been employed and trained in compliance with the established minimum standards.

g. "Certificate" means the document issued to a police or corrections officer when documentation has established compliance with the minimum entrance and training requirement and has completed the required probation period.

Source: National Association of State Directors of Law Enforcement Training, April 1976.

h. "Lapsing of Certificate" means the process of automatically cancelling a certificate when certificate holder is no longer employed as a police or corrections officer for three consecutive months.

i. "Revoking of Certificate" means the process of removing a certificate when certificate holder has committed a criminal offense that calls for revocation, is discharged for cause, or resigns employment as a police or corrections officer when disciplinary action is pending that could result in the officer being disciplined for cause.

MINIMUM STANDARDS AND TRAINING ESTABLISHED FOR CERTIFICATION

(1) In accordance with any applicable provisions of _____(statute)_____, to promote enforcement of law by improving the competence of police and corrections officers the Council shall:

a. Establish for police and corrections officers, respectively, reasonable minimum standards of physical, emotional, intellectual, and moral fitness.

b. Establish for police and corrections officers, respectively, reasonable minimum training, including but not limited to courses or subjects for instruction, facilities for instruction, qualification of instructors, and methods of instruction.

c. Establish a procedure or procedures to be used by law enforcement units to determine whether a police or corrections officer meets minimum standards or has minimum training.

d. Subject to such terms and conditions as the Council may impose, certify police and corrections officers as being qualified, and revoke such certification in the manner provided in _____(statute)_____.

(2) The Council shall cause inspection of police standards and training and corrections standards and training to be made.

(3) The Council may:

a. Contract or otherwise cooperate with any person or

agency of government for the procurement of services or property.

b. Accept gifts or grants of services or property.

c. Maintain and furnish to law enforcement units information on applicants for appointment as police or corrections officers in any part of the state.

d. Provide optional training programs for persons who operate lockups. The term "lockup" has the meaning given it in _____ *(statute)* _____.

(4) Pursuant to _____ *(statute)* _____ the Council shall adopt rules necessary to carry out its duties and powers.

MINIMUM STANDARDS FOR EMPLOYMENT

(1) Every officer employed by a department shall:

a. Be a citizen of the United States.

b. Be at least 21 years of age.

c. Be fingerprinted and a search made of state and national fingerprint files to disclose any criminal record. Procedure as prescribed in Specification _____, Fingerprint Record Check.

d. Not have been convicted by any state or by the federal government of a crime, the punishment for which could have been imprisonment in a federal penitentiary or a state prison.

e. Be of good moral character as determined by a thorough background investigation as prescribed in Specification _____, the Personal History Investigation.

f. Be a high school graduate or have passed the General Educational Development Test indicating high school graduation level, or have attained the equivalent to a high school education as determined by criteria established by the Council and prescribed in Specification _____, High School Graduation.

g. Be examined by a licensed physician and surgeon and meet the physical requirements prescribed in Specification _____, Physical Examination.

h. Be interviewed personally prior to employment by the department head or his authorized representative or representatives.

(2) It is emphasized that these are minimum standards for employment. Higher standards are recommended whenever the availability of qualified applicants meet the demand. It is also recommended that the applicant be examined by a licensed psychiatrist or clinical psychologist who, after examination, concludes that the application is suitable for police or corrections work.

Probation period

(1) Every officer employed by a department below the level of department head shall satisfactorily complete a probation period of not less than nine months. This requirement shall apply also to officers who transfer laterally into a department.

(2) Every officer who is promoted or appointed to a supervisory, middle management or assistant department head position shall satisfactorily complete a probationary period of not less than six months.

(3) No police or corrections officer who lacks the training qualifications required by the Council may have his temporary or probationary employment extended beyond one year by renewal of appointment or otherwise.

Extension of Time Limit for Course Completion

The Council may grant an extension of the time limit for completion of any course required by Section _____ of the Regulations upon presentation of evidence by a department that an officer was unable to complete the required course within the time limit prescribed due to illness, injury, military service, or special duty assignment required and made in the public interest of the concerned jurisdiction.

Examinations

Written examinations are recommended and may be required of each trainee in each course certified by the Council.

Waiver for Equivalent Training—Reciprocity

(1) The Council may waive the completion of any course required by Section _____ of the Regulations upon presentation of documentary evidence by a department that an officer has satisfactorily completed equivalent training.

(2) Training received in a state with laws governing or regulating police or corrections training must, if subject to such review, have been approved or certified in the state in which the training was received.

(3) The Council may elect to prescribe as a condition of certification supplementary or remedial training necessary to equate previous training with current standards.

(4) The Council is authorized to enter into standing reciprocity compacts or agreements with those states which by law regulate and supervise the quality of police or corrections training and which require a minimum number of hours of classroom training in the basic or recruit course equivalent to standards established by the Council.

Personnel Action Reports

(1) All law enforcement units shall furnish to the Police Standards Council on Council Form _____ the name, address, and other pertinent information concerning each newly appointed police or corrections officer within 30 days after employment.

(2) Whenever an officer is promoted or demoted, it shall be reported to the Police Standards Council on Personnel Action Form _____ within 30 days of the action.

(3) Whenever an officer is discharged from a department for cause or resigns, retires, or terminates employment, the department shall forward to the Council within 30 days appropriate information on the Council Form _____.

Certificates and Awards

(1) Certificates and awards may be presented by the Council for the purpose of raising the level of competence of law enforcement and to foster cooperation among the Council, agencies, groups, organizations, jurisdictions, and individuals.

(2) Certificates and awards remain the property of the Council and the Council shall have the power to revoke or recall any certificate or award as provided in the Act.

a. The Council may revoke the certification of any police or corrections officer after written notice and hearing, based upon a finding that the officer falsified any information required to obtain certification, has been discharged for cause from employment as a police or corrections officer, or resigns employment as a police or corrections officer when disciplinary action is pending which could result in the officer being disciplined for cause.

b. The revocation by the Council of an individual's police or corrections officer certification pursuant to this Section shall concurrently revoke all other certificates of any nature issued by the Council.

c. The certification of any police or corrections officer shall be considered lapsed if the officer does not serve as a police or corrections officer for three consecutive months.

CERTIFICATION OF POLICE OFFICERS

No person shall be employed as a police officer by any law enforcement unit for a period to exceed one year unless he has been certified as being qualified as a police officer under the provisions of ___(statute)___ and the certification has neither lapsed nor been revoked pursuant to ___(statute)___, and not been reissued under ___(statute)___.

The certification of any police officer who does not serve as a police officer for any period of time in excess of three consecutive months, unless he is on leave from a law enforcement unit, shall be considered lapsed. Upon reemployment as a police officer, the person whose certification has lapsed may apply for certification in the manner provided in ___(statute)___.

CERTIFICATION OF CORRECTIONS OFFICERS

No person shall be employed as a corrections officer by any law enforcement unit for a period to exceed one year unless he has been certified as being qualified as a corrections officer under the provisions of ___(statute)___ and the certification has neither lapsed nor been revoked pursuant to ___(statute)___, and not been reissued under ___(statute)___, or he is exempted from the certification requirement under ___(statute)___.

The certification of any corrections officer who does not serve as a corrections officer for any period of time in excess of three consecutive months, unless he is on leave from a law enforcement unit, shall be considered lapsed. Upon reemployment as a corrections officer, the lapsed certification may be restored as provided in ___(statute)___.

Application of Minimum Standards and Training to Certain Officers and Police Officers: Certification Based on Experience

(1) The minimum standards and minimum training requirements established pursuant to ___(statute)___ do not apply to:

a. Any individual who is a constable of the district or justice court.

b. Any sheriff's deputy appointed with authority only to receive and serve summons and civil process.

c. Any municipal parole officer.

d. Any animal control officer commissioned by a city or county.

   (2) The Council may, upon application of an individual police officer or corrections officer, at its discretion, certify an officer as provided in ___(section and statute)___ upon a finding that the officer's professional experience is equal in professional value to the training required for certification.

Procedures Prior to Revocation of Certification

When the Council believes there is a reasonable basis for revoking the certification of a police or corrections officer, notice and opportunity for a hearing shall be provided in accordance with ___(statute)___ prior to such revocation.

Grounds for Revocation of Certification of Officer

The Council may revoke the certification of any police or corrections officer after written notice and hearing, based upon a finding that:

a. The officer falsified any information required to obtain certification.

b. The officer has been convicted of a felony or any crime involving moral turpitude.

c. With respect to a police officer, he has been discharged for cause from employment as a police officer.

d. With respect to a corrections officer, he has been discharged for cause from employment as a corrections officer.

e. He resigns employment as a police or corrections officer when disciplinary action is pending which could result in the officer being disciplined for cause.

VIOLATION OF REGULATIONS

It is the intent of the Council that the requirements set forth in the Regulations be administered in a cooperative manner for the benefit of the criminal justice system. Toward that end, the Council and its representatives shall make a concerted effort to insure that where a violation of the Regulations appears to exist, the individual involved shall be apprised of the requirements and the methods of compliance. Where a cooperative resolution is legally possible, the policy of the Council shall be to vigorously seek that resolution. Where such a resolution is not legally possible or where the efforts of the Council are unsuccessful, the provisions of this section shall apply.

   (1) When any person certified by the Council is found to have knowingly and willfully violated any provisions or requirements of the Regulations, the Council may take the action deemed necessary to correct the violation and to insure to the extent possible that the violation does not reoccur. Such corrective and preventive action may include:

a. Oral warning and request for compliance.

b. Written warning and request for compliance.

c. Issuance of official reprimand.

d. Suspension of certificate.

e. Revocation of certificate.

   (2) When any person is found to have knowingly and willfully by deceit, fraud, or misrepresentation attempted to obtain or obtained certification, or when any person is found to have aided another in attempting to obtain or obtaining certification by means of deceit, fraud, or misrepresentation, the Council shall for both the principal and the aidor:

a. For the first violation, suspend or deny certification for not less than six months.

b. For any subsequent violation, revoke or deny certification permanently.

   (3) No person who has had his certification suspended or revoked may remain employed or appointed as a police or corrections officer. No person may exercise the authority of a police officer during a period of suspension or revocation.

   (4) No person who has been denied certification may be employed or appointed as a police or corrections officer or exercise the authority of a police or corrections officer.

Hearings on Council Action

   (1) Authority of the Council. The Council, having considered granting or having granted certification pursuant to the provisions of ___(statute)___, is empowered to:

a. Deny,

b. Withhold renewal of,

c. Suspend, or

d. Revoke

any such certification.

(2) Hearing privilege. Any person subjected to any action specified in this Section shall be entitled to a hearing to show cause why such action should not be taken by the Council.

(3) Notification and hearing request.

a. Upon denial of any certification by the Council, the applicant shall be notified in writing of that action. The notice shall contain a statement of the reasons for denial and shall be sent by registered or certified mail to the last known address of the applicant. This shall be considered an adequate notice under this Section. Upon receipt of the notice, the applicant may request a hearing in order to show cause why the application should be honored and certification should be granted. A request by the applicant for hearing shall be made within ten (10) days after his receipt of notice of denial, and if no request is made within that period for a hearing, the denial shall be final.

b. Before the Council may withhold renewal of, suspend, or revoke any certification the person to be affected shall be notified in writing at least ten (10) days prior to such contemplated action. The notice shall contain a statement of the reasons for the proposed Council action and shall be sent by registered or certified mail to the last known address of the person involved. Upon receipt of the notice, the person may request a hearing to show cause why the contemplated action should not be taken. A request by a person for hearing shall be made within ten (10) days after receipt of notice, and if no request is made within that period for a hearing, the Council may carry out the contemplated action and its decision shall be final.

(4) Hearing process

a. Upon request for a hearing, the Council shall notify the affected party of a time and place to appear. That hearing shall be conducted not less than ten (10) days nor more than forty-five (45) days after receipt of request by the Council.

b. The Director of the Council may act as a Hearing Officer or designate another to do so. The Hearing Officer shall have full authority to hold hearings and make findings of fact and conclusions of law.

c. The Hearing Officer shall have the authority to call witnesses, to require the production of pertinent records, to administer oaths or affirmations to witnesses called to testify, to take testimony, to examine witnesses, and to grant continuances in any case.

d. A person entitled to be heard pursuant to this Section shall have the right to counsel, to present evidence, and to examine all witnesses on any matter relevant to the issues.

e. If the person requesting the hearing fails to appear and no continuance has been granted, the Hearing Officer may hear the evidence of such witnesses as appear and may proceed to consider the matter based upon the evidence before him.

f. In proceedings held pursuant to this Section, rules of evidence shall be applicable as prescribed in _(statute)_ .

g. After hearing the evidence in the case, the Hearing Officer shall render a decision in writing as soon as practicable, but in no case later than ninety (90) days after the close of the hearing. The decision shall contain findings of fact, conclusions of law, and an order or orders based upon those findings and conclusions.

h. The Council shall review the findings and orders of the Hearing Officer at its next regularly scheduled meeting held at least ten (10) days after the Hearing Officer's decision is rendered. Upon approval by the Council, the findings and orders of the Hearing Officer shall become the findings and orders of the Council, provided that the Council may amend the orders as it deems advisable based upon the findings of the Hearing Officer.

i. Within five (5) days after action by the Council, a written notice of the findings and orders of the Council shall be sent by registered mail to the person affected directly by the decision.

j. Any person aggrieved by an adverse decision of the Council shall be entitled to appeal for judicial review as prescribed in _(statute)_ .

Glossary

Perhaps the fastest way to gain a general knowledge of a particular profession is to acquire an understanding of the terminology used. The criminal justice system uses many unique words and phrases in carrying out its duties. Many of the most frequently used terms will be defined in this terminology guide. It must be emphasized that the definitions presented here are not intended to be complete interpretations of the words. For a complete explanation, consult a law dictionary or a textbook on criminal justice terminology.

Abet   To encourage or advise another to commit a crime. To aid by approval.

Accessory   One who aids or conceals a criminal so that he may avoid arrest or punishment.

Acquit   To find a person not guilty of the crime charged.

Addict   Usually a person who is addicted to the taking of narcotics in some form.

Admission   A statement by a defendant tending to prove his guilt. Not a complete confession.

Adultery   Sexual intercourse by a married person with one who is not a wife or husband.

Affidavit   A written statement made under oath.

Alias   A false or assumed name.

Alibi   The defense that the accused was in some place other than that where the crime was committed.

Alien   A subject of another government.

Alienist   A person who specializes in the study of mental diseases.

Ante Mortem   Before death.

Appeal   The transfer of a case to a higher court, in which it is asked that the decision of the lower court be altered or reversed.

Appellant   One who makes an appeal or who takes an appeal from one court to another.

Appellate Court   A court that has jurisdiction of review and appeal.

Arraignment   A court proceeding in which the defendant is informed of the charge against him, advised of his constitutional rights, and at which he may enter a plea or deposit bail.

Arrest   Detaining a person in a manner authorized by law, so that he may be brought before a court to answer charges of having committed a crime. Both peace officers and private persons may make the arrest.

Arson   Willfully burning property.

Assault   An unlawful attempt to physically hurt another person. If the person is actually struck, the act is called "battery."

Bail Security, in the form of cash or bond, deposited with a court as a guarantee that the defendant, if released, will return to court at the time designated to stand trial.

Ballistics The science of the study of bullets and firearms.

Barratry The unlawful practice of initiating lawsuits or police complaints without just cause.

Battery The unlawful use of force or violence against a person without his consent.

Bertillon System A method of identifying criminals by body measurements and description. See **Portrait Parle.**

Bigamy The crime of being married to two persons at the same time.

Blackmail The extortion of money from a person through threats of accusation or exposure of an unfavorable nature.

Blue Laws Rigid laws regulating activities on the Sabbath.

Bribery The offering or accepting of any undue reward to or by a public official in order to influence his official actions.

Brief A summary of the law pertaining to a case, which is prepared by the attorneys for submission to the judge. Useful in police work for case law reference.

Brothel A house used for the purpose of prostitution.

Bunco A type of theft perpetrated by the use of false or misleading representations.

Burglary The crime of entering a building with the intent to steal or commit some felony. Not to be confused with robbery, which is a theft from the immediate presence of the victim through force or fear. In burglary, the victim is seldom present at the time.

Capital Crime A crime punishable by death.

Caption and Asportation Generally, to prosecute for theft, it is necessary that both taking (*caption*) and carrying away (*asportation*) be proved.

Certiorari *(writ of certiorari)* An order issued by a higher court to a lower court directing that a case be transferred to the higher court for review or trial.

Change of Venue A change of the place of trial in a criminal or civil proceeding.

Circumstantial Evidence Evidence tending to prove a fact through a logical association of other facts, but without an actual witness to the act to be proven.

Citation An official summons issued by a court or peace officer directing a person to appear before the court for some official action. Frequently referred to as a ticket.

Civil Action A law suit to recover damages or correct some wrong between two parties. Does not usually involve a crime and is apart from a criminal action. A person may be convicted in a criminal court and also sued in a civil court for the same act. *Example:* A drunk driver may be sentenced to jail in a criminal proceeding and then sued in civil action by the owner of a car damaged by the drunk driver.

Commitment An official court order directing that a person be taken to a jail, prison, hospital, or other location (usually a place of confinement).

Common Law The basic, unwritten concepts of English and American law. In many states, there are no "common law crimes." For an act to be a crime, there must be a specific, written statute so declaring it.

Complaint The formal accusation of crime presented to the court and which acts as the formal commencement of a criminal prosecution.

Compounding a Crime The unlawful act of accepting money or other reward for agreeing to refrain from prosecuting a crime—concealing it from the authorities or withholding evidence.

Compromising a Crime (misdemeanors only) The proceeding by a court whereby a person charged with a misdemeanor may be discharged without prosecution upon payment of damages to the party injured.

Conspiracy A secret combination or agreement between two or more persons to commit a criminal act.

Confession A voluntary declaration admitting the commission of a crime.

Confidential Communication Communications between a person and his attorney or clergyman, or between husband and wife, which may be legally concealed in court testimony.

Contempt of Court Disobedience to the court by acting in opposition to the authority, justice, or dignity thereof. Punishable as a crime.

Conviction The finding of a person guilty of a criminal charge.

Coroner A county official whose principle duty is to determine the manner of death of any person.

Corpus Delicti The complete set of elements necessary to constitute a particular crime.

Crime An act committed or omitted in violation of a law forbidding or commanding it, for which a punishment is provided.

Criminal Action A court proceeding instituted and prosecuted by the state for the punishment of crime. Not to be confused with civil action.

Criminal Procedure The method prescribed by law for the apprehension, prosecution, and determination of punishment for persons who have committed crimes.

Criminology The science that deals with crimes, their causes, and their prevention and punishment.

Defendant The person sued or charged in a court action, whether criminal or civil.

Demurrer A plea made to the court that the actions alleged in the complaint, even if true, do not constitute a crime.

Deposition The written testimony of a person, who, for some reason, cannot be present at the trial.

District Attorney A county official whose duties require him to act as attorney for the state in prosecution of criminal cases.

Double Jeopardy The act of placing a person on trial a second time for a crime for which he has already been tried once (forbidden by criminal procedure).

Duces Tecum A subpoena whereby a person is summoned to appear in court as a witness and to bring with him some piece of evidence (usually a written document).

Dying Declaration A statement made by a dying person regarding the cause of his injuries. Acceptable evidence in a homicide prosecution. Based on the theory that a person about to die will be inclined to be truthful in any statements he makes.

Embezzlement The crime of stealing property or money that has been entrusted to one's care.

Et Al. And others. For example: "*People v. Jones*, et al." indicates that Jones and others are the defendants in a criminal case. This form is used to prevent repeating the names of all persons involved every time the case is referred to.

Evidence Testimony, physical objects, documents, or any other means used to prove the truth of a fact at issue in a court proceeding.

Ex Post Facto After the facts. Usually refers to a law that attempts to punish acts that were committed before it was passed.

Extortion Similar to blackmail.

Extradition The surrender by one state or nation to another, on its demand, of a person charged with a crime by the requesting state.

Felony A major crime punishable by death or imprisonment in a state or federal prison. All other crimes are called misdemeanors.

Fence A person who makes a business of purchasing or receiving stolen goods from criminals.

Fingerprints A reproduction of the ridge formation on the outer joint of the fingers. Although a definite identification can be made using only one finger, it is usually necessary that the prints of all ten fingers be available for a successful search of fingerprint files.

Fine The financial punishment levied against a lawbreaker that is paid to the government funds.

Forgery Any of several crimes pertaining to the false making or alteration of any document with intent to defraud.

Former Jeopardy Same as double jeopardy.

Fugitive One who has fled from punishment or prosecution.

Grand Jury A group of men and women whose duty it is to make inquiries and return recommendations regarding the operation of local government. They also receive and hear complaints in criminal cases, and if they find them sustained by evidence, present an indictment against the person charged. It is called a grand jury because it is composed of a greater number of jurors than a regular trial jury.

Habeas Corpus (writ of) A court order directing that a person who is in custody be brought before a court in order that an examination may be conducted to determine the legality of the confinement.

Habitual Criminal Many states have statutes providing that a person convicted a certain number of times may be declared an habitual criminal and, therefore, unsuited for attempts for rehabilitation. A person so declared may then be sentenced to life imprisonment for the protection of society.

Hearsay Evidence Evidence that deals with what another person has been heard to say. This evidence is usually excluded in a trial.

Heroin An opium derivative drug. It is a coarse white or gray powder that is taken hypodermically, orally, or by sniffing. It is completely outlawed for any purpose in the United States.

Homicide The killing of a human being by another human being.
Fratricide—killing of one's own brother
Matricide—killing of one's own mother
Infanticide—killing of a child
Patricide—killing of one's own father
Uxoricide—killing one's own wife

Impeachment The process whereby a public official may be removed from office through judicial proceedings. Also, the discrediting of a witness in order to show that his testimony is probably false.

Indeterminate Sentence A court- or board-imposed sentence with neither minimum nor maximum limits.

Indictment An accusation in writing, which is presented by the grand jury, charging a person with a crime.

Information An accusation in writing, presented by a prosecuting official; i.e., district attorney or city attorney, charging a person with a crime.

Informant One who supplies information leading to the apprehension of a criminal.

Injunction A court order whereby a person is ordered to do, or restrained from doing, a particular thing. Not enforced by the police without an additional court order to that effect.

Inquest An inquiry with a jury conducted by the coroner to establish the cause of death.

Intent In general, there must be a concurrence between a person's acts and his intentions in order to constitute a crime. A person cannot be convicted of a crime if he committed the act involuntarily, without intending injury. If a person acts negligently, however, without regard for the rights of other people, this is sufficient in itself to establish criminal intent. Thus, the drag racer who kills an innocent party may be convicted of manslaughter even though he did not intend the death or injury of anyone.

Interrogation The art of questioning or interviewing, particularly as applied to obtaining information from someone who is reluctant to cooperate. May apply to the questioning of witnesses, victims, suspects, or others. Requires the use of psychology, salesmanship, good judgment, and a knowledge of human nature. The use of physical force to obtain information has no legitimate place in modern law enforcement.

Jail A place of confinement maintained by a local authority, usually for persons convicted of misdemeanors. The terms prison or penitentiary apply to such institutions operated by the state or federal government, usually for more serious offenses.

Judiciary That branch of the government concerned with the administration of civil and criminal law.

Jurisprudence The science of laws.

Jury A group of men and women whose duty it is to determine the guilt or innocence of persons charged with a crime.

Juvenile Court Generally, a special court or department of another court that hears cases involving juveniles. Proceedings are less formal, and the primary objectives are rehabilitation and protection, rather than punishment.

Kleptomania An abnormal desire to steal.

Larceny Same as theft. The unlawful taking of the property of another. Divided into grand theft and petty theft. Grand theft includes the taking of money or goods in excess of $200; the theft of any item from the immediate possession of another; theft of an automobile of any value; the theft of certain domestic animals; and the theft of certain fruits, vegetables, and fowl over the value of $50. All other theft is petty theft.

Libel The circulation of written matter that tends to discredit or injure the character of another. It is not necessary that the material be false. The prime consideration is the motives under which it was issued. Slander is of the same nature except it is verbal rather than written. *Note:* There are few criminal prosecutions for libel or slander. It has become largely a civil matter.

Limitations, Statute of The statutory time limit within which a criminal prosecution must be begun. For felonies, this is usually three years from the date the crime was committed. For misdemeanors it is one year. There are some crimes that have a longer time limit and a few, such as murder, that have no time limit.

Lynching In popular usage, the killing of an accused criminal by a mob that has taken him from the authorities by force. Technically, it is the act of a group unlawfully taking a person from the custody of a peace officer for any purpose.

Magistrate A judicial officer having authority to conduct trials and hearings in criminal and civil matters and to issue writs, orders, warrants of arrest, and other legal documents.

Maim The crime of willfully disfiguring another.

Mala in Se and Mala Prohibita A basic grouping of crimes according to the nature of the act. *Mala in se* means "bad in itself" and refers to those crimes, such as murder, robbery, and rape, which are deemed to be wrong in almost all civilized societies. *Mala prohibita* means "bad by prohibition" and refers to those offenses, such as building and safety regulations and certain traffic violations, established by statute for the public convenience, which are not immoral or bad in themselves.

Mandamus, Writ of An order issued by a court, directed to a government agency or to a lower court, commanding the performance of a particular act.

Mann Act The federal statute relating to the interstate transportation of females for immoral purposes.

Manslaughter The unlawful killing of a human being without premeditation or intent to take life.

Marijuana A narcotic produced from the East Indian Hemp plant (*cannibis sativa*). The leaves and flowering tops are ground into a form resembling tobacco, but which is drier and coarser. It is then rolled into cigarettes and smoked.

Misdemeanor A crime punishable by other than imprisonment in the state prison.

Modus Operandi Literally, method of operation. Refers to the habit of criminals to continue to pursue a particular method of committing their crimes. Through a study of a criminal's habits (or *modus operandi*), it is possible to link several crimes committed by the same person and even to determine where he can be expected to commit his next crime.

Murder The unlawful, deliberate, or premeditated killing of a human being. It is not required that the premeditation be of any specific length of time. The instant of time necessary to form a specific intent to kill is sufficient.

Nolle Prosequi A motion by the prosecuting attorney in which he declares that he will not prosecute a case. Used when extenuating circumstances in a case indicate that, although a crime has been committed, it is in the best interests of justice to forego prosecution.

Notary Public A public officer authorized to administer oaths, witness signatures, and acknowledge the genuineness of documents.

Oath Any form of attestation by which a person signifies that he is bound to perform a certain act truthfully and honestly. A person making a false statement while under oath to tell the truth may be prosecuted for perjury.

Opium A narcotic substance prepared from the juice of the original poppy. It is further refined to produce morphine, heroin, and other narcotics. Opium is normally found as a dark, sticky mass that is smoked in special pipes. Opium smoking is decreasing in the United States in favor of the much stronger derivative, heroin.

Ordinance Term used to designate any law enacted by a local governmental legislative body.

Panel A group of men and women summoned for jury duty. A panel of approximately 25 prospective jurors is examined by attorneys for both sides prior to the start of the case. Through this examination, 12 are selected to hear and decide the case.

Pardon An act of grace, proceeding from the power entrusted with the execution of the laws, that exempts the individual on whom it is bestowed from the punishment the law inflicts for a crime he has committed.

Parole The conditional release of a prisoner from jail prior to the completion of his sentence, usually on the condition that he remain under the supervision of a parole officer.

Peace Officer General term used to designate a member of any of the several agencies engaged in law enforcement.

Penal Code A collection of statutes relating to crimes, punishment, and criminal procedures. This is the portion of the law most frequently used by police officers.

Perjury The crime of knowingly giving false testimony in a judicial proceeding while under oath to tell the truth. Subornation of perjury is the crime of procuring or influencing someone else to commit perjury.

Plaintiff In a civil action, the party initiating the suit. One who signs a complaint or causes a complaint to be signed. Other party to the suit is the defendant.

Plea The answer that the defendant makes to the charges brought against him.

Pleadings Written statements reciting the facts that show the plaintiff's cause for bringing the action and the defendant's grounds for defense to the charges. These are prepared by the attorneys for each party and are presented to the judge.

Policy In gambling, a game in which bets are made on numbers to be drawn in a lottery.

Portrait Parle (word picture) Method of identification established by Alphonse Bertillon wherein a description of physical characteristics is used to identify a person. This is one of the identification methods used in America today.

Posse Comitatus The authority of the sheriff to assemble all able-bodied male inhabitants of the county to assist in capturing a criminal, keeping the peace, or otherwise defending the county. Refusal to obey the summons is a criminal offense.

Post Mortem After death. Refers to the examination of a body after death. Also called an autopsy.

Precedent A parallel case in the past that may be used as an example to follow in deciding a present case.

Preliminary Hearing An examination before a judge of a person accused of a crime in order to determine if there is sufficient evidence to warrant holding the person for trial.

Prima Facie "On its face" or "at first view." Refers to evidence that, at first appearance, seems to establish a particular fact, but that may be later contradicted by other evidence.

Principal A person concerned in the commission of a crime, whether he directly commits the offense or aids in its commission. All principals to a crime are equally guilty; therefore, the driver who waits in the getaway car during a robbery is as equally guilty of murder as the accomplice inside the building who fires the fatal shot.

Private Person's Arrest The authority granted to a private party to make an arrest under certain conditions. Sometimes referred to as a "citizen's arrest," although it is not limited only to citizens.

Privileged Communication See **Confidential Communication.**

Probate Court A court that establishes the legality of wills and administers the distribution of the estate of a deceased.

Probation Allowing a person convicted of a criminal offense to go at large under the supervision of a probation officer rather than confining him to prison or jail. The probationer must comply with certain conditions set forth by the court and must be on good behavior. Failure to comply with these conditions will cause the probationer to be placed in jail to serve his sentence.

Proof The establishment of a fact by evidence.

Prosecutor or Prosecuting Attorney A public officer whose primary duty is to conduct criminal prosecutions as attorney in behalf of the state or people. The district attorney and city attorney are examples.

Prostitute A woman who engages in sexual relations for hire.

Pyromania An unnatural, overpowering attraction to fire.

Rape Unlawful sexual intercourse with a woman against her will, usually accomplished by physical violence, but it may be committed when the woman is drunk, unconscious, feeble-minded, or otherwise unable to resist. Statutory rape is where the female is under the age of eighteen, even though giving her consent to the act.

Recidivist An habitual criminal.

Recognizance Official recognition of some fact by a court. In criminal procedure, it applies to a person accused of an offense being released on his own recognizance without being required to post bail, on his promise to appear for trial. Employed where the accused is well known to be reputable or is charged with a minor offense.

Res Gestae Things done. Facts and circumstances surrounding a particular act. Refers particularly to acts or exclamations overheard by a third party, which would be inadmissible in court under normal rules of evidence but which, because they occurred at the moment of the particular act in question, are admissible under the rules of *res gestae* evidence.

Resisting an Officer Any person resisting, delaying, or obstructing a public officer in the discharge of his duties is guilty of a misdemeanor.

Return A short account in writing made by an officer in respect to the manner in which he has executed a writ or a process.

Reversal The setting aside or annulment of the decision of a lower court made by a higher court. See **Appeal.**

Rigor Mortis The stiffening or rigidity of the muscles and joints of the body which sets in within a few hours after death.

Robbery The unlawful taking of personal property in the possession of another, from his person or immediate presence, against his will, and accomplished by use of force or fear.

Search Warrant An order to a peace officer, issued by a court, directing that a certain location be searched and that certain specifically described property, if found, be seized and delivered to the judge. A search warrant can be executed only by a peace officer and is valid for ten days from issue.

Seduction The offense of inducing a woman to engage in sexual relations under a false promise of marriage.

Statute Law A written law enacted and established by the legislative department of a government.

Stay of Execution An order of a court postponing the carrying out of the penalty or other judgment of the court.

Stipulation An agreement between opposing attorneys relating to certain portions of a case. Usually refers to minor points in a case that are accepted without demanding proof in order to shorten the time of trial.

Subpoena An order issued by a court commanding the attendance of witnesses in a case. See **Duces Tecum.**

Summons In a civil case, an order directed to the defendant giving notification that an action has been filed against him and giving instructions as to how and when he may answer the charges. Failure to answer the summons will result in the case being awarded to the plaintiff by default.

Supreme Court Highest court of appeal, either state or federal.

Suspended Sentence and Judgment Suspended sentence is where no sentence is pronounced by the court, and the offender is released after being found guilty on condition that he abide by certain rules laid down by the court, such as making restitution to the victim. Suspended judgment is where the offender is released as above after sentence has been pronounced. In either case, the offender may be returned to court at any time to be sentenced or, in the case of suspended judgment, have the sentence carried out.

Testimony Oral evidence given by a witness under oath.

Theft See **Larceny.**

Tort A civil wrong. An invasion of the civil rights of an individual.

Transcript A printed copy of a court record, including the verbatim testimony of witnesses.

Trauma An injury to the body caused by external violence.

Trial That step in the course of a judicial proceeding that determines the fact. A judicial examination in a court of justice. May be held before a judge and jury, or a judge alone.

Versus (against). Abbreviated "vs." or "v."

Valid Having full legal force and authority.

Waive To surrender or renounce some privilege or right.

Warrant A written order from a court or other competent authority, directed to a peace officer or other official, ordering the civil protection of the person executing the order. Examples are a warrant of arrest and a search warrant.

Witness A person who has factual knowledge of a matter. One who testifies under oath.

Index

Drug Enforcement Administration, 91, 92
Drugs, *see* Narcotics and dangerous drugs
Drunkenness, 27, 160
Due process of the law, 159, 165, 174, 181, 254
  in juvenile courts, 162, 163
  in parole hearings, 213-214
Duress, 27

Economic determinism of crime, 58-61
  see also Crime, causation
Educational programs:
  for community, 132
  for offenders, 235, 238, 258-259, 296
Education and training of justice personnel,
    275-279
  concepts of, 275-277, 303-304
  for corrections personnel, 234, 238-240,
    241, 296-298
    educational programs for, 239-240, 241
    juvenile institutions, 239, 248
  for court personnel, 14, 170, 266
    basic training standards for lawyers,
      275-277
    judges, 14, 160, 173, 174, 272, 291
      training of, 291-292
    judicial education, 273
  future trends in training, 291, 303-304
  higher education and training require-
    ments, 265
  for police personnel, 78, 81, 275-277
    California Commission on Peace Officer
      Standards and Training (POST),
      277, 299
    education of, 78, 79, 81, 119, 137, 275-278
    educational requirements, controversy
      over, 145
    postemployment and continuing,
    recommendations by President's
      Commission on Law Enforcement
      and Administration of Justice, 81
    training of, 275-278
      in-service training, 79
      lack of, 119
  regional criminal justice training and
    resource system, 299-300, 304
  state standards councils, creation and
    expansion of, 299-300
  techniques of education and training,
    303-304
  see also Professionalism; Reform and
    trends

Eighteenth Amendment to the Constitution,
    78, 79, 314
  Prohibition, 78, 79
Eighth Amendment to the Constitution, 165,
    181, 312
Electrical devices, use of, 33, 267, 292
Embezzlement, 246
Energy enforcement, 145-146
Entrapment, 27, 33
Environmental influences, and crime, 62-64
Equal Employment Opportunity Commission,
    300-301
Employment standards in criminal justice
    system, 277-279
Ervin Committee Senate Hearings, 106
Escobeda v. *Illinois*, 284
Ethical conduct, canons of, 269-271, 272
Evidence:
  admissibility of, 168, 183
  examination of, 184
  illegally seized, 185, 186
  rules of, 159, 168
  suppressing of, 10
Extenuating circumstances, 27

Family:
  counseling, *see* Counseling
  disputes, police handling of, 83, 126, 133
    see also Counseling; Referral
  as source of criminal behavior, 63, 64, 65
    see also Crime, causation
Father image, lack of, and crime, 64
Federal Aviation Administration, 93
Federal Bail Reform Act, 208
Federal Bureau of Investigation (FBI), 29, 34
  contributions to police system, 79
  crime statistics of, 34-42
    see also Federal crime statistics
  fingerprints, 8, 112
  formation of, 91
  jurisdiction of, 29, 92
Federal Communications Commissions, 94
Federal court system, 9, 156
  see also Court system
Federal crime statistics, 32-42, 43, 58
  Crime Clock, 37, 39
  Crime Index, 32-42, 43
  crime rate, 35, 36, 62
    versus arrest rate, 36, 38, 39, 40
    national, 37, 44
    policing styles and, 134